Learn Objective-C
for Java Developers

James Bu

Apress®

Learn Objective-C for Java Developers

Copyright © 2009 by James Bucanek

ISBN-13 (pbk): 978-1-4302-2369-6

ISBN-13 (electronic): 978-1-4302-2370-2

Printed and bound in the United States of America 9 8 7 6 5 4 3 2 1

Trademarked names may appear in this book. Rather than use a trademark symbol with every occurrence of a trademarked name, we use the names only in an editorial fashion and to the benefit of the trademark owner, with no intention of infringement of the trademark.

Lead Editors: Clay Andres, Douglas Pundick
Technical Reviewer: Evan DiBiase
Editorial Board: Clay Andres, Steve Anglin, Mark Beckner, Ewan Buckingham,
    Tony Campbell, Gary Cornell, Jonathan Gennick, Jonathan Hassell, Michelle Lowman,
    Matthew Moodie, Jeffrey Pepper, Frank Pohlmann, Douglas Pundick,
    Ben Renow-Clarke, Dominic Shakeshaft, Matt Wade, Tom Welsh
Project Manager: Kylie Johnston
Copy Editor: Elizabeth Berry
Compositor: Lynn L'Heureux
Indexer: Ann Rogers/Ron Strauss
Artist: April Milne
Cover Designer: Anna Ishchenko
Manufacturing Director: Michael Short

Distributed to the book trade worldwide by Springer-Verlag New York, Inc., 233 Spring Street, 6th Floor, New York, NY 10013. Phone 1-800-SPRINGER, fax 201-348-4505, e-mail orders-ny@springer-sbm.com, or visit http://www.springeronline.com.

For information on translations, please e-mail info@apress.com, or visit http://www.apress.com.

Apress and friends of ED books may be purchased in bulk for academic, corporate, or promotional use. eBook versions and licenses are also available for most titles. For more information, reference our Special Bulk Sales–eBook Licensing web page at http://www.apress.com/info/bulksales.

The information in this book is distributed on an "as is" basis, without warranty. Although every precaution has been taken in the preparation of this work, neither the author(s) nor Apress shall have any liability to any person or entity with respect to any loss or damage caused or alleged to be caused directly or indirectly by the information contained in this work.

The source code for this book is available to readers at http://www.apress.com.

To the memories of my brother, John, and my father, "Dr. B."

Contents at a Glance

PART 3 ■■■ Programming Patterns

PART 4 ■■■ Advanced Objective-C

Contents

PART 1 ▪▪▪ Language

PART 2 ■■■ Translating Technologies

PART 3 ■■■ Programming Patterns

PART 4 ■■■ Advanced Objective-C

About the Author

James Bucanek has spent the past 30 years programming and developing microprocessor systems. He has experience with a broad range of computer hardware and software, from embedded consumer products to industrial robotics. His development projects include the first local area network for the Apple II, distributed air conditioning control systems, a piano teaching system, digital oscilloscopes, silicon wafer deposition furnaces, and collaborative writing tools for K-12 education. James holds a Java Developer Certification from Sun Microsystems and was awarded a patent for optimizing local area networks. James is currently focused on Macintosh and iPhone software development, where he can combine his deep knowledge of UNIX and object-oriented languages with his passion for elegant design. James holds an Associates degree in classical ballet from the Royal Academy of Dance.

About the Technical Reviewer

 **Evan DiBiase** lives in Pittsburgh, Pennsylvania with his fiancée, Ellen, and their cat, Millie. After graduating from high school, he spent several years working at a software startup developing machine learning applications in Java before enrolling in the School of Computer Science at Carnegie Mellon University, where he will graduate in May 2010. Evan also hosted the Pittsburgh chapter of Cocoaheads from 2007 to 2009, has interned at Apple in the Objective-C group, and enjoys programming in Cocoa for Mac OS X and iPhone in his spare time.

Acknowledgments

This book would not have been possible without the tireless efforts of the Apress editors. I am eternally indebted to my technical editor, Evan DiBiase, who painstakingly checked every symbol, method, and line of code for accuracy. I thank Douglas Pundick for his astute structural changes, and I would have been completely lost without the talented red pen of my copy editor, Elizabeth Berry. The unflagging Kylie Johnson held the entire project on course and, amazingly, on schedule. Finally, I'd like to chastise Clay Andres who once plucked me out of a WWDC conference and told me I could write books.

Introduction

Objective-C is a wonderful language that has received far less attention than it deserves. It has suddenly become (more) popular with the success of Apple's Mac OS X and iPhone, where it is the supreme development language. If you're going to learn a language to write applications for Mac OS X or the iPhone, Objective-C is *the* language to learn.

The Objective-C language does not feel like it was developed by a committee or a computer science major. It's a language for minimalists and anarchists. Yet it retains many of the features that make Java one of the great programming languages of our time. Objective-C lets you write applications that are every bit as structured and formal as anything you can write in Java. But at the same time, if you want to bore a hole through the language and head off in a direction where no one has gone before, it won't stand in your way.

After programming in Objective-C for a few years, I was struck at how "Java-like" my programs were. If I'd known then just how many of my Java techniques and concepts were directly transferable to Objective-C, it would have saved me months of study and experimentation. I wrote this book so that you can avoid the same fate.

Who This Book Is For

This book is for any Java developer interested in learning and exploring Objective-C as quickly as possible.

How This Book Is Structured

This book is organized into four parts: the Objective-C language, translating technologies, design patterns, and advanced Objective-C.

The first part describes the basics of the Objective-C language itself. It explains how Objective-C is like, and unlike, Java. It details the language syntax, class declarations, inheritance, and so on.

The second part examines specific technologies, like garbage collection, the file system, and introspection. Each chapter presents side-by-side examples of Java code and the equivalent code in Objective-C. Tables list the Java classes that you're familiar with along with the Cocoa classes that perform the same role. Each chapter then goes on to advanced topics, often exploring techniques unique to Objective-C.

The third part is organized by design pattern. Java developers use many important design patterns, such as the factory and Model-View-Controller patterns. These chapters show how each pattern is implemented in Objective-C—often in ways that may surprise you.

The final section of the book explores advanced Objective-C topics: memory management, integrating Objective-C with C, and the Objective-C runtime environment.

I strongly encourage you to read the first part in its entirety. The second and third parts can be read straight through, or you can skim them and refer back to them later for solutions. The advanced topics in the final section address specific situations, like working with the iPhone's memory manager, which can be explored as needed. Many chapters start out with the basics and then progress to more esoteric features, so feel free to skip to the next chapter once you've learned what you want.

Prerequisites

This book assumes that you have some experience programming in Java. You should be familiar with the basics of the language, the concepts of classes, objects, inheritance, and interfaces, and have a working knowledge of the core Java classes. It will help if you have some functional knowledge of individual Java technologies, like introspection and exceptions, but these aren't absolutely necessary to learn the Objective-C equivalents. While I would hope that you are already familiar with design patterns, they aren't a prerequisite.

Downloading the Code

The source code for this book is available to readers at `http://www.apress.com` in the Downloads section of this book's home page. Please feel free to visit the Apress web site and download all the code there. You can also check for errata and find related titles from Apress.

Contacting the Author

You can reach me at `james@objectivec4java.com`.

PART 1

■■■

Language

CHAPTER 1

■■■

Introduction

Welcome to *Learn Objective-C for Java Developers*. This book will help you transition from programming in Java to programming in Objective-C, the primary language used to develop applications for Apple's line of Mac OS X–based computers and consumer products. You will learn to write effectively in a dynamic and flexible language that powers many of today's cutting-edge applications and mobile devices. More important, this book will show you how to leverage the coding practices, design patterns, and problem-solving skills you've learned in Java and apply them to Objective-C.

What is Objective-C?

So what, exactly, is Objective-C and what's so great about it? Objective-C adds the concept of objects to the standard C language. It elevates C by overlaying it with a smattering of new keywords and a SmallTalk-esque method calling syntax. The result is an object-oriented programming language with remarkable properties:

- Modern object-oriented design paradigms
- State of the art compiler
- Exceptional performance
- Direct access to C and C APIs
- Dynamic behavior

Unlike most other object-oriented languages, Objective-C does not create a completely new language—it is a strict superset of C. The Objective-C keywords and syntax are quite distinct from regular C. Listing 1-1 shows a brief snippet of Objective-C, along with equivalent Java code for comparison. The basic control statements are plain C. The statements between brackets invoke Objective-C methods.

Listing 1-1. Sample of Java and Objective-C Syntax

```
Java
public void setSize( Dimension size )
    {
    if (size.height!=0 && size.width!=0) {
        if (!this.size.equals(size)) {
            super.setSize(size);
            for ( MapItem i: mapItems )
                i.resize();
            }
```

```
        }
    }
Objective-C
- (void)setFrameSize:(NSSize)size
{
    if (size.height!=0.0 && size.width!=0.0) {
        if (!NSEqualSizes(self.size,size)) {
            [super setFrameSize:size];
            [mapItems makeObjectsPerformSelector:@selector(resize)];
        }
    }
}
```

How Objective-C came to be and what makes it special is an interesting story.

History

Brad Cox and Tim Love were the principal forces behind Objective-C. It began life as "Object-Oriented Programming in C" or OOPC. The goal was to add the capabilities of SmallTalk—which required an interpreter—to C, without designing an entirely new language. Cox published the first formal description of what had by then become Objective-C in 1986. In 1988, NeXT Computer adopted Objective-C as its primary development language. NeXT enriched Objective-C, creating a broad collection of classes that became the foundation for new applications, development tools (most notably Interface Builder), and a significant portion of their operating system. The NEXTSTEP operating system eventually led to the OpenStep API, which defined a consistent set of objects and interfaces that could be ported to multiple platforms. Ports of OpenStep, beginning with OPENSTEP, ran on Sun's Solaris and Microsoft's Windows NT, among others. The GNU (GNU's Not Unix) project eventually created an open-source implementation called GNUstep.

Together, Objective-C and NEXTSTEP were lauded as an innovative development environment, one of the few to truly deliver on the promise of object-oriented design. Application design and creation was rapid and flexible. But for a variety of reasons—most notably the industry inertia behind C++—NeXT and Objective-C remained little more than a curiosity, a shining example of what could be accomplished, if only they had been embraced by a major segment of the industry.

That threshold was finally crossed in 1996, the year Apple bought NeXT Computer, the NEXTSTEP operating system, and their entire suite of Objective-C based development tools. Apple made NEXTSTEP a cornerstone of their new Mac OS X operating system. The object frameworks were re-branded as "Cocoa" and have since grown and matured into a rich and powerful toolset—not just for personal computer applications, but also for innovative consumer devices like the iPhone.

A Modern Object-Oriented Language

Objective-C accomplishes a rather remarkable feat. The actual language is spare, almost to the point of being barren, yet it manages to implement a rich object paradigm that rivals far more complex languages. The language is simple to learn and simple to implement. Many features can be added or enhanced simply by creating new classes, rather than requiring changes to the language itself. For example, using Objective-C you could wake up one morning and decide to instantiate objects in a new way. Objective-C does not define how objects are created or destroyed—that's provided by the runtime framework via class methods. It's unlikely you'd want to redefine object instantiation, but the example underscores the flexibility of the language.

State of the Art Compiler

Because Objective-C is a thin layer on top of C, it follows the tide of C language changes. As new features, optimizations, target processors, and other technologies are added to C, Objective-C comes along for the ride. This allows Objective-C to remain current with modern technology and techniques.

The state of compiler technology today also means that Objective-C code is remarkably portable. Not too long ago, it was highly unlikely that C written for one platform would compile and run on a different system or architecture. This was one of the joys of Java's "write once, run anywhere" design. Today, a single C compiler can target scores of different processors and hardware with the flick of a (command-line) switch. Case in point: Apple decided not too long ago to convert their entire line of personal computer systems from Motorola/IBM to Intel processors. Tens of millions of lines of Objective-C were ported to an entirely new architecture with little or no disruption in development. Apple did it again when they ported their Cocoa framework to the embedded processor used in the iPhone, and might port their entire software library to yet another processor should the opportunity arise. Today, Apple maintains a single repository of Objective-C source code that is regularly recompiled to run on no less than five different processor architectures. Objective-C is "write once, run anywhere" in practice, if not principle.

Performance

Language performance and benchmark wars are infamous, but few would argue that C is the fastest high-level computer language available today. There are many that claim to be nearly as fast, but it's almost impossible to exceed C's performance without resorting to hand-coded optimizations or just trickery. It's no wonder that almost all interpreters are written in C or C++—and that includes Java's own virtual machine.

Because Objective-C is also C, you can optimize your application right to the limits of the hardware. It's easy to start with a simple object-based design. If performance analysis shows that the solution isn't fast enough, it can be optimized with snippets of C. Or the code can be rewritten entirely in C. If that's not fast enough, the C compiler gives you direct access to the operating system kernel, graphics coprocessors, vector unit instructions, and even raw machine code. If your goal is to create the fastest possible application, Objective-C will not get in the way.

Programming in Objective-C also means you have direct access to the vast library of C APIs. The POSIX C functions available today represent some of the most mature, stable, and secure code in the industry.

Dynamism

Objective-C is often described as a *dynamic* language. That's a difficult term to define. After all, every program is dynamic in some form. The term does describe some aspects of the Objective-C language itself, but most often refers to the design patterns embraced by Objective-C developers.

The Objective-C language is more dynamic than languages like Java and C++. In Java, the variables and methods you define for a class are exactly those at runtime. In Objective-C, class definitions are more malleable. Other objects and frameworks, which you may or may not have developed, can augment your classes and objects with new capabilities. Conversely, you can augment other classes—even system classes—with new functionality.

Another intriguing feature of Objective-C is the ability of the runtime system to modify the behavior of an object on the fly. A particularly dramatic example of this is in the observer pattern. In Java, an observable object is responsible for maintaining a set of listener objects and notifying them of changes to its properties. In Objective-C when an object wants to observe the property of another object, it makes a request to the Key-Value Observing framework. This framework *spontaneously subclasses* the target object, wrapping its setter method with code to notify interested observers of changes. This remarkable ability means that *every* object is observable without writing a single line of code or requiring you to do any design work ahead of time. The contrast between Java and Objective-C—in broad strokes—is shown in Listing 1-2. The Key-Value Observing framework does all the work of maintaining the set of observers for each object and sending the requested notifications. All you have to do is declare the property and request to be notified of changes to it.

Listing 1-2. *Observer Pattern in Java and Objective-C*

```
public interface SecurityGateListener
{
    void gateStateChanged( SecurityGate gate );
}

public class SecurityGate
{
    private HashSet listeners;
    private boolean open;

    public void addListener( SecurityGateListener listener )
        {
        listeners.add(listener);
        }

    public void removeListener( SecurityGateListener listener )
        {
        listeners.remove(listener);
        }

    private void fireStateChange( )
        {
        for ( SecurityGateListener listener: listeners )
            listener.gateStateChanged(this);
        }

    public boolean getOpen( )
        {
        return open;
        }

    public void setOpen( boolean open )
        {
        if (this.open!=open) {
            this.open = open;
            fireStateChange();
            }
        }

}
```

```
class SecurityManager implements SecurityGateListener
{
    SecurityGate gate;

    SecurityManager( )
        {
        gate = …
        gate.addListener(this);
        }

    public void gateStateChanged( SecurityGate gate )
        {
        // security gate changed ...
        }

}


@interface SecurityGate : NSObject {
    BOOL open;
}
@property BOOL open;

@end

…

@implementation SecurityManager

- (id)init
{
    if ( (self=[super init])!=nil ) {
        gate = …
        [gate addObserver:self forKeyPath:@"open" options:0 context:NULL];
    }
    return self;
}
- (void)observeValueForKeyPath:(NSString*)keyPath
                      ofObject:(id)object
                        change:(NSDictionary*)change
                       context:(void*)context
{
    if (object==gate) {
        // security gate changed...
    }
}

@end
```

The dynamic nature of Objective-C applications often stems more from the design patterns embraced by developers than anything inherent in the language—although Objective-C does make those patterns easier to adopt. Take the simple example of implementing copy and paste methods for a custom view object. The Cocoa framework defines something called the *responder chain*. It starts with the view object that currently has the user's focus, say some selected text or graphic displayed by your custom view object. The chain consists of that object, the view object that contains it, the window that contains that, and eventually the single application object that contains all of the windows. When the user selects the Paste command from the menu, Cocoa examines the objects in the chain to find the first one that implements a `-paste:` method. Similarly, the menu item itself is enabled and disabled automatically, based on the presence or absence of an object in the responder chain that implements `-paste:`. This arrangement does not require any object to "look" for a Paste command event or register itself with the menu item. The Paste command comes to life simply because an object implemented a `-paste:` method.

But, you might ask, what if the Paste command needs to be enabled conditionally? That's simple: your custom view object should implement the `-validateMenuItem:` method. Objects in the responder chain that implement *that* method are queried to determine what commands should be enabled for the user. Otherwise, the Cocoa framework makes up its own mind.

The emphasis here is not on what an object *is* but what it *does*. The capabilities or roles of an object are determined by examining what methods it implements, rather than what class it is or requiring it to register itself with other objects. This philosophy has its roots in aspect-oriented programming. Objective-C developers call these methods *informal protocols*.

The end result is a fluid application that adjusts itself and responds to users based largely on what functions the objects in the program do, or don't do. The knowledge required by one object about another is minimal, as are its relationships to other view objects. In Objective-C, object implementations are simpler, more encapsulated, make fewer assumptions, and are generally more reusable.

Developer Productivity

For all of the reasons just mentioned, Apple considers Objective-C its "secret weapon." Apple regularly produces high performance, cutting-edge applications faster, and with fewer developers, than other major software companies. They publicly attribute Objective-C as a key component in their success. After you begin to work with Objective-C, especially when building GUI applications, you'll discover just how productive and efficient you can be.

Learning a New Language

Computer systems and software change continually, and computer languages change along with them. You will probably change computer-programming languages several times. I've changed my principal programming language at least eight times during my career, with side excursions into a dozen or more other languages along the way.

Becoming proficient in a new language requires a significant investment, so there's a natural resistance to migrate away from a language with which you are already comfortable and productive. Yet, the reward for learning a new language is often access to new opportunities, technologies, and markets. Objective-C is the preferred programming language for Apple's Mac OS X operating system, and (as of this writing) the only language for developing native applications for Apple's iPhone and iPod touch products. Given that change is inevitable, anything that will minimize the transition to a new programming language is welcome. That is the reason I wrote this book.

It took me years to become proficient in Java. It took me years to become proficient in Objective-C. Only afterward did I begin to see the striking similarities between the two. The similarities are not found in the languages themselves—Java and Objective-C are as different as the Moon and Manhattan. The similarities are in the solutions; that is, how the architects of Java and Objective-C solve problems.

Effective software development is less a matter of knowing the syntactical details of a language (although that's clearly important), than the ability to create solutions. As an experienced Java programmer, you've accumulated a toolkit of solutions to address all kinds of common programming problems. When you start a new language, you abandon those skills for a completely new set of tools and techniques—which is ironic, since you're often solving the same set of problems you were before.

This book aims to reduce that agony by providing a kind of translation service between the solutions you already understand in Java and equivalent solutions in Objective-C. The problems are the same and you'll discover that the philosophies of the solutions are remarkably similar. What's often radically different is the technique.

To give you an example, consider the method to draw a string of characters on a graphics display. In most object-oriented languages, the logical place to implement this method is in the drawing object class—the class responsible for drawing primitive shapes in a graphic context. In Java, the class is `java.awt.Graphics` and the method for drawing a string is `drawString(String,int,int)`. In Cocoa, the base graphics context class is `NSGraphicsContext`. But in it you won't find any drawing primitives. The method to draw a string is found in the `NSString` class itself. The methods are `-drawAtPoint:withAttributes:` and `-drawInRect:withAttributes:`.

Being used to working in Java, you probably have a question or two. You might be wondering how the system's primitive string class was subclassed to include a `-drawAtPoint:withAttributes:` method. Or, you might want to know what idiot system architect decided it was a good idea to include something as domain specific as a graphic drawing primitive in the base string class. The answer is neither. Objective-C allows arbitrary methods to be attached to *other* classes. In this case, the AppKitFramework (the core framework for all GUI applications) attaches a `-drawAtPoint:withAttributes:` method to the base string class. It's called a category, and it stands the normal rule of class method organization on its head. If you went looking for a `-drawString:AtPoint:withAttributes:` method in the various `NSGraphics` classes you would—as I did—waste hours of time. Eventually finding them in the `NString` class was my first introduction to Objective-C categories and forever changed my approach to class method organization. It also changed my habits for searching the documentation.

But the really valuable lesson I learned was that Java and Objective-C are still more similar than they are different. Both embrace the Model-View-Controller design pattern. Both organize window contents using a hierarchy of visual container objects. Each container has a `-draw` (`paint()`) method that is called when its contents should be rendered. The `-draw` method uses a graphics context object to perform the actual drawing of lines, polygons, strings, and images. The differences spring from the design of the Java and Objective-C languages. Objective-C lets you attach methods to other classes while Java does not. This changes how class authors organize methods, but doesn't change their basic purpose. As an accomplished Java developer, you don't need a lesson in graphic containers or an explanation of how or when to draw lines. What you need to know is that in Java the string drawing primitives are found in the `java.awt.Graphics` class, and in Cocoa they're in the `NSString` class. You'll also want to know how categories attach a method to another class and how to implement your own.

Terminology and Culture Shock

If you came to Java from the C or C++ world, moving to Objective-C will not be an earth-shaking transition. If, however, you are exclusively a Java programmer, there are going to be things about Objective-C that you will find odd, disappointing, confusing, or even shocking.

There are two major learning hurdles. The first is philosophy. Java is a highly structured language designed to produce robust, predictable code. Java tries to protect the programmer from herself by imposing a litany of rules that encourage good programming practices. In contrast, Objective-C is a minimalist and pragmatic language that affords the programmer immense freedom and liberties. It does little to protect you from common, and potentially disastrous, programming mistakes. The contrast reminds me of the old joke about safety scissors and scalpels: you can't perform surgery with safety scissors, but you also don't have to count your fingers afterwards.

A lot of thought, effort, and academic research have gone into designing languages that "coerce" you into writing good code. Personally, I think this approach is somewhat misguided. Sloppy programming is sloppy programming in any language. Both Java and Objective-C require the developer to be disciplined—just in different ways. You can write applications in Objective-C that are every bit as robust and reliable as Java if you adhere to some consistent practices. These practices are highlighted in each chapter.

The second hurdle is terminology. There are a lot of new terms to learn. Many new terms are synonyms for ones you already know. In the text, a new term like *protocol* (interface) will be followed by its equivalent Java term in parentheses. Once you know that "protocol" is synonymous with "interface," the text will use the term "protocol" exclusively.

Defining Better

Any discussion of two technologies will inevitably lead to a comparison of the two and an attempt to ascertain which is "better." I suppose this is human nature. I try to avoid such comparisons here for a variety of reasons.

Java and Objective-C are, in some respects, radically different languages. In other respects, they are virtually identical. Each has features that allow you to produce good code. Each also has limitations and flaws that make some tasks awkward or even impossible. I enjoy writing in both for very different reasons. I consider Java and Objective-C *comparable* languages, but I don't consider either to be categorically superior.

The problem with various "better" assessments is that they are rarely universal. When someone states that something is better, it typically means "better for me" or "better for this particular application."

I'm sure you could make a compelling argument for why the Mercedes C-class sedan is one of the best vehicles ever made. Your argument could be supported by an impressive list of design choices, engineering specifications, safety features, and so on. It would be a persuasive position—unless you needed to haul a half-ton of bricks up a dirt road. In that context, a luxury Mercedes sedan could quite possibly be the worst vehicle for the task.

Several years ago, I embarked on a project to develop a backup solution for the Macintosh. I initially started the project in Java. This was not surprising, since I considered Java the best programming language ever created. Despite Mac OS X's admirable support for Java, it quickly became evident that I could not develop a compelling solution in Java. A viable commercial application would require a native programming language and the choices were C, C++, and Objective-C. This project was my half-ton of bricks.

Objective-C has not usurped my love of Java. Instead, it has joined it side by side as a capable alternative. There are still situations where Java is unquestionably superior to Objective-C. There are also situations where the opposite is equally true. Rather than obsessing about which tool is best, I focus on which tool is best for the job.

Summary

Objective-C is a mature and powerful language with very real advantages. But you shouldn't have to approach it like a first-year programming student. The rest of this book is dedicated to taking your existing Java knowledge and experience and refocusing it on Objective-C, turning you into a productive Objective-C developer as quickly as possible.

CHAPTER 2

■ ■ ■

Java and C: Key Differences

This chapter highlights the important differences between Java and C. We'll pay particular attention to familiar syntax and keywords that mean substantially different things in C—*faux amis*, as the French would say—and constructs that are foreign to Java. Where Objective-C adds to the C language in an unambiguous way, the similarities between Java and C can be a source of confusion. So the first step in your journey to Objective-C is to become comfortable with C.

Java and C++ are both C derivatives. Both created completely new, sophisticated, object-oriented languages while correcting some of the perceived inadequacies of C. Each imposes and enforces concepts such as constructors, method access, encapsulation, and so forth.

Objective-C takes a radically minimalist approach. Objective-C adds the concept of classes and objects to traditional C by introducing a thin layer of syntax and a handful of keywords—with the emphasis on *thin*. Objective-C does not change or redefine the underlying C language in any significant way. In Java you program in Java. In C++ you program in C++. In Objective-C you program in industry standard C overlaid with some object-oriented extras.

■**Note** I should probably mention that there is also an Objective-C++ language; it overlays C++ with Objective-C objects and features. It's primarily useful to programmers who must integrate legacy C++ code into an Objective-C runtime environment. This book does not discuss Objective-C++, but most of the information about C and Objective-C is applicable.

If you've previously programmed in C, then you can skip this chapter. Since Objective-C *is* C, you won't find any surprises. If it's been a while, you might skim over the sections to remind yourself of the differences.

If you've never programmed in C, there are differences between Java and C that you need to be aware of. Java's syntax is patterned after C, so you are already familiar with the structure of methods, code blocks, conditionals, assignment statements, operators, and so on. Here's a crash course in the key differences between Java and C.

Primitive Types

Primitive types are the atomic types defined by the language and are the building blocks for all computations. Most are the scalar variable types with various sizes, numerical ranges, and formats. In general, the integer and floating-point types in Objective-C are similar to those in Java. Table 2-1 lists the basic numeric variable types for both.

Table 2-1. *Primitive Numeric Types*

Java	Objective-C	C Typedef	Size	Range
boolean			1 bit	false … true
	BOOL		8 bits	NO … YES
byte	char	int8_t	8 bits	-128 … 127
	unsigned char	uint8_t	8 bits	0 … 255
char		int16_t	16 bits	-32768 … 32767
	unichar	uint16_t	16 bits	0 … 65535
short	short int	int16_t	16 bits	-32768 … 32767
	unsigned short int	uint16_t	16 bits	0 … 65535
int	int	int32_t	32 bits	-2147483648 … 2147483647
	unsigned int	uint32_t	32 bits	0 … 4294967295
long	long long int	int64_t	64 bits	-9223372036854775808 … 9223372036854775807
	unsigned long long int	uint64_t	64 bits	0 … 18446744073709551615
float	float	float_t	32 bits	approximately $+/-10^{+/-38}$
double	double	double_t	64 bits	approximately $+/-10^{+/-308}$

C does not have a strict Boolean type. In C, Boolean operators (i.e. == and &&) have integer results. C interprets a zero value as false and any non-zero value as true. This allows you to write the statements if (i!=0) and if (p!=nil) as if (i) and if (p), respectively. The statements are equivalent, but I believe using the more verbose form—even though the language doesn't require it—makes the intent clearer. For convenience and readability, Objective-C defines a BOOL type for declaring Boolean values. The actual type is an unsigned 8-bit integer, but you should treat it as if it were only capable of representing YES (true) or NO (false). The C language also defines a bool type, interchangeable with BOOL, but Objective-C programmers use BOOL almost exclusively.

▓**Caution** One of the side effects of not having a Boolean type is that C control statements accept integer expressions. This makes it easy to use an assignment statement where you meant to write a comparison. Be careful not to write if (i=1) when you mean to write if (i==1). The former means, "assign the value of 1 to the variable i then test to see if that value is not zero."

C's long and short keywords are technically modifiers for the int type, as in short int or long int. Java's long, int, and short are three distinct integer types and aren't used in combination. The int type in C is implied wherever the keywords long or short appear, so short int and short are equivalent. Which you use is a matter of style.

One of Java's significant contributions to programming was to standardize the size of integer types. Traditional C does not specify the size of types like char and int; they would vary from one compiler or system to the next. Modern C has largely standardized on the sizes listed in Table 2-1. To avoid any possible ambiguity, the C standard now includes typedefs (covered later in this chapter) that result in consistent variable sizes. A variable of type int32_t will always be a signed 32-bit integer, regardless of the compiler's preferred word size for int or short int.

Historically, a C int was 16 bits and a long int was 32 bits. As 32- and 64-bit CPUs replaced smaller microprocessors, the standard size of int became 32 bits. For backwards compatibility, long int remained 32 bits and the long long int type was introduced to define a 64-bit integer.

▓**Caution** The size of integers has changed again for 64-bit architectures. If you compile your code for a 64-bit CPU, long int becomes a 64-bit integer—short int, int, and long long int remain the same size. If you need an integer value that will be 32 bits on a 32-bit architecture and 64 bits on a 64-bit architecture, declare it as NSInteger or NSUInteger. These are C typedefs that change size to match the architecture. Pay attention to the APIs to determine the correct type. If a method returns an NSInteger, declare the variable you are assigning it to as NSInteger. It will behave consistently when compiled for either 32- or 64-bit executables.

Java simplified traditional C by eliminating unsigned integer types. In C, integers come in both signed and unsigned flavors. The closest equivalent to the Java char type is C's unichar, but be careful— char is signed and unichar is unsigned. Unsigned integers are fertile ground for subtle programming mistakes, which is probably why Java eliminated them. Here are the most common ones.

Avoid writing nonsense inequality statements, like that shown in Listing 2-1.

Listing 2-1. Nonsense Comparison Statement

```
unsigned int i = 99;
while (i>=0) { … }    // nonsense/always true; i can never be < 0
```

Be aware that the sign bit can be reinterpreted through assignment, as shown in Listing 2-2.

Listing 2-2. *Sign Bit Reinterpretation*

```
int i = -3;
unsigned int j = i;     // j = 4294967293
```

Listing 2-3 illustrates a mix of signed and unsigned types in a comparison. Avoid this or cast one of the values so the types are compatible.

Listing 2-3. *Comparing Mixed Types*

```
int i = -3;
unsigned int j = 3;
if (i<j) { … }     // unpredictable condition
```

Most size, index, and array counts are unsigned. When declaring a variable that will be used as an index into a collection, declare an unsigned integer. Use signed integers just about everywhere else.

Constants

Constants are names assigned to unchanging, well-known values. Programming symbolically is easier and more informative than working with naked numeric values—even when the value is obvious. Modern code libraries and frameworks define thousands of constants, but the ones you use regularly are listed in Table 2-2.

Table 2-2. *Common Constants*

Java	Objective-C	Usage
true	YES	Logical truth
false	NO	Logical untruth
null	nil	Empty or Invalid Object Reference
	NULL	Empty or Invalid Pointer

Technically, nil and NULL are interchangeable. For readability, use nil to set and test Objective-C object references exactly as you would use null in Java. NULL is C's empty pointer constant and is used to set and test pointers. Adopting this convention underscores the distinction between memory pointers and object references in your code.

The const keyword before an integer type means pretty much what final means in Java, but is rarely used to define simple integer constants. Most constants in C are defined using the preprocessor (also described later in this chapter) or using an enumeration statement.

The enumeration, or enum, in Listing 2-4 defines a numeric variable v that can hold one of the integer constants Zero, One, or Two. Unlike Java, v is not an object. It's just an integer. The three constants (Zero, One, and Two) are public symbols with the values 0, 1, and 2 respectively. They can be used in any context in which an integer constant would be acceptable. The variable is often omitted and the enum statement is used only to define the constants.

Listing 2-4. Enumeration

```
enum {
    Zero = 0,    // = 0 optional, enums start at 0 if omitted
    One,
    Two } v;
```

Typedefs

A typedef is a concept foreign to Java, but used extensively in C. In Java, new data structures and functionality are accomplished by creating new classes. In C, you can define your own primitive data types. The program in Listing 2-5 uses an integer value to identify an inventory part.

Listing 2-5. Typedef

```
typedef int PartCode;
PartCode aCode;
int bCode;
```

Placing the typedef keyword before a variable declaration turns it into a *type definition*. Instead of defining an integer variable PartCode, the typedef statement in Listing 2-5 creates a new variable type (PartCode) synonymous with int. Once defined, the new PartCode type can be used instead of the int type. The declarations for aCode and bCode are identical.

Typedefs help to make your code more readable. The function prototype add(PartCode c) is much more descriptive than add(int c). Typedefs also improve maintenance. PartCode can later be redefined as unsigned int or long long int without needing to revise every declaration of a part code variable.

Typedefs are often used with complex declarations such as structs and enums. The typedef statement in Listing 2-6 simultaneously creates a new enum type (Flavor) and three integer constants (Strawberry, Rhubarb, and Apricot). You can now write Flavor favorite = Apricot;, which will assign the value 2 to the variable favorite.

Listing 2-6. enum typedef

```
typedef enum {
    Strawberry,
    Rhubarb,
    Apricot } Flavor;
```

Pointers

Java "protects" you from physical memory by purposefully omitting any programming construct that gives the programmer direct access to arbitrary memory locations. In Java, you only have access to named primitives and references to objects.

C provides no such insulation between your code and physical memory. This gives you a great amount of freedom to access and manipulate data. It also places the responsibility of not overstepping boundaries on you, the programmer.

Think of C pointers as Java object references with two principal differences. A C pointer can point to any kind of value or structure—not just objects. You can declare a pointer to an integer, a float, a complex structure, a function, or even another pointer. Second, a C pointer is always a real memory location in the process's address space, whereas Java's object reference is an abstract and opaque value. Beyond that, most of the programming rules for Java references apply to pointers. For example, passing a pointer as a parameter copies the reference to the value, not the value itself.

Since C provides both values and pointers to values, programming syntax must be used to distinguish between the two. The unary pointer operator (*) can appear in both type definitions and expressions. In a declaration, a pointer operator changes the variable type from a simple variable to a pointer to that type of variable, as shown in Listing 2-7.

Listing 2-7. Using Pointers

```
int i = 1;
int *iptr;
iptr = &i;
*iptr = 2;
```

In Listing 2-7, the variable iptr is a pointer to an integer variable. The *value* of iptr is a memory address where an integer value is stored, not the value of the integer stored there. In other words, it's a reference to a primitive integer value somewhere else in the process's address space.

The ampersand character (&) is the unary "address of" operator. It returns the address of a variable instead of the value of the variable. The iptr = &i statement sets the value of iptr to the memory address, not the value, of variable i.

The unary pointer operator (*) in an expression redirects the reference to the value that the pointer variable points to. In a sense, it's the complement of the unary address of operator. The last statement uses the pointer operator to redirect the assignment to the value pointed to by iptr, rather than the value of iptr itself. In English the statement says, "store the value 2 in the integer variable whose address is contained in iptr." The last statement does not change the value of iptr; it changes the value of the integer variable that iptr points to. After these four statements have executed, the value of variable i will be 2.

Structures

C structures define the organization of a block of memory. Structures, or structs, are constructed from other variable types. Once defined, the collection of variables can be treated as a single unit. A struct statement is very similar to a Java class definition, sans methods. Simple struct declarations, like enums, define a single variable with a given structure. It is far more typical to find a struct in a typedef statement so that the structure definition can be reused by name (see Listing 2-8).

Listing 2-8. Structure

```
typedef struct {
    int key;
    int count;
    } KeyCount;
...
```

```
KeyCount counter;
counter.key = 1;
counter.count = 0;
```

The KeyCount structure shown in Listing 2-8 defines a unit of memory containing two member variables at successive addresses, named key and count. Like Java, C uses the member operator (.) to address a member variable within a structure. More often, a structure is referred to indirectly using a pointer to the structure, like the one in Listing 2-9.

Listing 2-9. Structure Pointer

```
KeyCount *nextCounter = &counter;
nextCounter->count += 1;
```

The variable nextCounter is a pointer to a KeyCount structure. When a variable is a pointer to a structure, the indirect member operator (->) is used to specify a member variable. This is technically shorthand for (*nextCounter).count, but is easier to read and write.

Assigning one structure to another makes a copy of the entire structure. The statement KeyCount save = counter copies both integers in the counter structure to the corresponding integers in the save structure. Method arguments are passed by value, so passing a structure in an argument will make a copy of the entire structure. This differs from Java, which doesn't allow you to copy objects by value. Consequently, most methods declare arguments that are pointers (references) to structures rather than the structure itself. But should you need to pass a structure by value, you have that option.

Object References

If you think a C structure looks a lot like a class and a pointer to a structure acts a lot like an object reference, you are very astute. Objective-C uses C structures to define objects and it uses structure pointers as object references.

An Objective-C class definition essentially defines a C structure. You start by using Objective-C syntax to define the class. Once defined, you can interact with the object using the C syntax for structures and pointers. Both are shown in Listing 2-10.

Listing 2-10. Objective-C Class as C Structure

```
@interface KeyCounter {
    @public
    int key;
    int count;
}
@end

KeyCounter *countObject = …;
countObject->count += 1;
```

Behind the scenes, the structure created for the class includes additional member variables which are used to define the object's class, provide access to its methods, manage memory, and so on. Objective-C even provides an operator that converts a class type into a C struct type, allowing you unfettered access to the internals of an object or to treat the object as a simple C structure. This is rarely used, but underscores the transparency of Objective-C.

If all of this is becoming overwhelming, don't fret. You can largely ignore the details of typedefs, structs, and pointers. To program in Objective-C you need to know that classes are structures, the pointer (*) operator is used to declare a pointer (reference) to an object, and the indirect member operator (->) is used to directly access member variables via an object pointer (reference).

You can successfully program in Objective-C without ever creating your own structures, defining typedefs, or using pointers to variables other than objects. You do, however, need a passing familiarity with these concepts because you *will* encounter them in other Objective-C programs. I anticipate that you will eventually want to explore C types in more detail, if only to utilize libraries with C interfaces.

Arrays

C arrays continue in the vein of things you need to be aware of but probably don't need to use yet. C arrays are not like Java arrays. A C array defines a set of values that occupy successive memory addresses. A C array is not an object, provides no bounds checking, and is often manipulated using pointers.

The statement in Listing 2-11 declares an array of 10 integer variables, then obtains the value of the fourth integer in the array. Like a Java array, an individual element can be addressed using array subscript syntax (array access expression).

Listing 2-11. *C Array of Integers*

```
int numbers[10];
int j = numbers[3];
```

C arrays and pointers are deeply intertwined. In Listing 2-12, the symbol numbers (by itself) evaluates to the address of the first element of the array, equivalent to the expression &numbers[0].

Listing 2-12. *Array and Pointer Interchangeability*

```
int *iptr = numbers;
iptr += 3;
if (*iptr==j) …
```

The pointer iptr in Listing 2-12 is first assigned to the address of the first element in the array. The second statement adjusts the pointer using pointer math. Pointer math (adding or subtracting an integer value from a pointer value) adjusts a pointer so that it points to the nth value after the current address by adding n*sizeof(type) to the pointer's address value. In this example, assuming the size of an integer is 4 bytes, adding 3 to an integer pointer adjusts its memory address by 12 bytes. Afterward, the iptr variable points to the fourth element of the array, and the expressions numbers[3] and *iptr are equivalent.

■**Note** The `sizeof()` operator is a compile-time function that evaluates to the size of the enclosed type in bytes. The argument can be either a type or a variable. Using Listing 2-11 as an example, the expressions `sizeof(int)`, `sizeof(j)`, and `sizeof(numbers[3])` are all equivalent and evaluate to the integer constant 4—the size in bytes of a single 32-bit integer. The expression `sizeof(numbers)` evaluates to 40, or `10*sizeof(int)`, since `numbers` is an array of 10 integers. You will often see expressions such as `(sizeof(numbers)/sizeof(int))` to determine the number of elements in an array.

C pointers and array variables are essentially interchangeable. Arrays are commonly assigned and passed as if they were pointers (the value passed will be the address of the first element of the array). It is also permissible to use the array subscript syntax on a pointer, as in `iptr[3]` = 0. This is equivalent to `*(iptr+3)` = 0.

Objective-C provides an object array class and object wrappers for most primitive types. These act very much like the Java arrays and collections you are familiar with. While you need to be aware of how C arrays are defined and accessed, you can avoid them in favor of object-oriented array classes until you become comfortable with C arrays, memory management, and pointer arithmetic.

static

The `static` keyword in C has some additional meanings and is *not* used the way it is in Java. Java uses static to declare a single persistent class variable within a class declaration. Objective-C does not allow you to declare variables in a class definition. Instead, static variables are declared as global C variables or static variables inside a code block. Listing 2-13 declares two static variables.

Listing 2-13. *Global Static Variables*

```
int scramingZombieHitCount = 1;        // accessible from all modules
static int screamingZombieBounceCount;   // accessible only from this module
```

A variable declaration outside of any method, structure, or class definition creates a global variable, approximately equivalent to a Java static variable. Global variables are pre-initialized to zeros at startup unless explicitly initialized to some other value. In this context, the static keyword only determines the scope of the symbol (all global variables are "static" in the Java sense). Omitting the static keyword makes the symbol globally accessible. Any module in the program can access it by name using an extern statement. Including the static keyword limits the scope of the variable to the file containing the declaration. Thus, `screamingZombieHitCount` can be used directly by any module in the program, while `screamingZombieBounceCount` will only be accessible to the code in this file.

Inside a code block, a variable declared to be static creates a persistent static variable. The scope of the variable is limited to the code block it is declared in. Listing 2-14 shows a static integer that is incremented each time the code block is executed.

Listing 2-14. Static Variable in a Code Block

```
{
    static int hitCount = 0;    // global hit count initialized at startup to 0
    hitCount++;                 // increment global hit count variable
    return (hitCount);          // return updated hit count
}
```

Functions

C is a procedural language with no concept of objects. In C, callable blocks of code are called functions. A C function is equivalent to a static class method in Java; it has no object context. C function names are not scoped within a class or package, they are not inherited, nor can they be overridden. Listing 2-15 shows a C function that compares two Objective-C date objects and returns the earlier of the two.

Listing 2-15. C Function

```
NSDate* earlierDate( NSDate* a, NSDate* b )
{
    if (a==nil)
        return (b);     // returns nil if both a & b are nil
    if (b==nil || [a compare:b]==NSOrderedAscending)
        return (a);
    return (b);
}
```

Function calling syntax is identical to Java: NSDate *first = earlierDate(sometime,whenever).

The earlierDate() function is globally accessible to all modules. A static keyword preceding the function definition would limit its scope to the module being compiled, just as it does for static variables.

extern

A module uses an extern statement to access a global variable or C function defined in another module. An extern statement is typically put in the header file of the module that defines it (see Listing 2-16). This is only necessary for global variables and functions defined in other modules. You do not use extern statements to declare or reference Objective-C classes.

Listing 2-16. External Variable Declaration

```
extern int screamingZombieHitCount;
extern void killAZombie( Zombie *victim );
```

The statement in Listing 2-16 declares that some other module has defined a global integer variable named screamingZombieHitCount (from Listing 2-13) and a C function named killAZombie. The module is compiled *with the assumption* that this variable and function exist in some other module, or modules. The linker is responsible for connecting this module's references to the actual variable location and function address when the application is built.

Preprocessor

The C Preprocessor is a text macro language that is (conceptually) applied to the text of a source file before it is input to the Objective-C compiler. When a source file is compiled, the preprocessor first scans the text of the file, executing all preprocessor directives and performing any text substitutions. Java does not have any comparable functionality.

The important preprocessor statements you should know are #include, #import, #define, and #if. All preprocessor directives are delimited by line breaks. Java and C generally ignore line breaks, treating them no differently than any other whitespace. The C preprocessor processes one line at a time, so preprocessor directives cannot be mixed with Objective-C source code on the same line.

#include and #import

The #include and #import statements insert the contents of another source file into the file being compiled, as shown in Listing 2-17. #include and #import statements can be nested. That is, a file can #include another file, which includes a third file, and so on.

Listing 2-17. #include and #import Directives

```
#include <Cocoa/Cocoa.h>
#import "MyClass.h"
```

The C compiler knows nothing about the classes or symbols defined in other files. To use any class or symbol, the source code being compiled must first define it. This is different than the Java compiler which automatically finds and interprets other .java files to obtain the definitions of other classes.

Clearly, it's impractical to type in the definition of every class or symbol that you plan to use. The C community long ago settled on a simple organization of files to solve this problem. Each module is divided into two files: a *source* file and a *header* file. Objective-C source files, sometimes called implementation files, contain the code for methods and are saved with a .m file extension. The header file, sometimes called the interface file, contains only the class definitions, variables, and constants that the programmer wants to make public for use by other modules.

Source files inevitably begin with a series of #include and #import statements to acquire the definitions that the module requires, like the one shown in Listing 2-17. This is then followed by the code to implement the methods in that module. In practice, this is analogous to Java's import statement. But instead of simply declaring the package names being brought into scope (and leaving Java to go find those definitions), the #import directive inserts the contents of a module's header file to declare the needed classes and constants.

Java requires that an entire class be defined in a single file. While it's possible to include more than one Java class in a file, it is not possible to split a class up across several files.

Objective-C has no such restriction, but defining your entire class in a single source file is a highly recommended arrangement. Objective-C's categories—described in an upcoming chapter—are a formal programming pattern for subdividing a single class into multiple parts. But until you start writing categories, place all of the definitions for a class in a header file named after that class (i.e. MyClass.h), and all of the code that implements the methods of that class in a source file with the same name (i.e. MyClass.m). The MyClass.m file should begin by importing its MyClass.h file. Follow that with #import directives for any other classes the implementation needs to know about. Listing 2-18 shows the beginning of a typical pair of source files for the StringPool class.

Listing 2-18. *First Lines of the StringPool Class Source Files*

```
//  StringPool.h

#include <libkern/OSAtomic.h>
#import <Cocoa/Cocoa.h>

@interface StringPool : NSObject {
@private
    NSHashTable *strings;
    OSSpinLock spinLock;
}
…
```

```
//  StringPool.m

#import "StringPool.h"

#import "InverseHashTable.h"
#import "StringUtilities.h"

@implementation StringPool
…
```

#import is slightly different than #include. #include unconditionally inserts the contents of another file, while #import inserts the file only if it has not already been inserted. #import should be used for all class definition headers because it avoids the possibility of including a header file twice, which will result in a duplicate definition error.

Both #include and #import take a filename delimited by either double quotes or angle brackets. Use brackets when including system headers and use quotes when including files within your own project.

#define

The #define directive creates a text macro, as shown in Listing 2-19. A text macro replaces a token in the source code with the contents of the macro. Macros can include parameters, which look similar to function definitions, and perform complex substitutions. More often, preprocessor macros are simply used to define constants.

Listing 2-19. *Defining Literal Constants*

Java
```
final int MAX_ZOMBIES = 999;
final int MANY_ZOMBIES = MAX_ZOMBIES-100;
```

C

```
#define MAX_ZOMBIES 999
#define MANY_ZOMBIES (MAX_ZOMBIES-100)
```

Once the MAX_ZOMBIES text macro is defined, any subsequent occurrence of the token MAX_ZOMBIES will be replaced with the text "999". The preprocessor will rewrite the statement if (zombieCount>=MAX_ZOMBIES) by replacing the token. The Objective-C compiler will ultimately compile the statement if (zombieCount>=999). The Objective-C compiler never sees the MAX_ZOMBIES symbol, since preprocessor token replacement is performed before the C language compiler phase.

Token substitution is performed on word boundaries and does not occur inside literal strings or comments.

Token substitution is recursive. The code if (zombieCount>MANY_ZOMBIES) would be replaced with if (zombieCount>(MAX_ZOMBIES-100)), which would then be replaced with if (zombieCount>(999-100)). Include parentheses around any preprocessor macros that include operators to avoid unexpected evaluation order.

Also note that preprocessor macros are *not* C language statements. They do not use equal signs for assignment and are not terminated with a semicolon. Doing so would include those symbols in the substituted text. The directive #define MAX_ZOMBIES = 999; would turn the C statement if (zombieCount>=MAX_ZOMBIES) into if (zombieCount>== 999;), ultimately resulting in a compiler error.

#if

The #if directive has no Java analog. An #if directive includes or omits a block of text depending on the value of an expression, as shown in Listing 2-20.

Listing 2-20. #if Preprocessor Directive

```
#if LOG_OUTPUT > 1
    NSLog(@"game now contains %d zombies",zombieCount);
#endif
```

The text between the #if directive and the #endif directive in Listing 2-20 is only compiled if the expression evaluates to a non-zero value. The expression can only use constants that are known at compile time. In this example, the NSLog statement will be compiled only if the LOG_OUTPUT preprocessor macro evaluates to a number greater than one. Otherwise the text is not compiled, just as though the NSLog statement had been commented out.

You can place an #else directive between the #if and #endif directives. The text between the #if and #else is included if the conditional expression is true. The text between the #else and #endif is included if it is false.

#ifdef and #ifndef are two convenient variations of the #if directive. The parameter for each is a single preprocessor macro name. If the macro has been defined (it doesn't matter what its value is), #ifdef includes the text up to the #endif. #ifndef is its opposite, including the text only if that macro name has never been defined. These are often used to alter the code for different environments, as shown in Listing 2-21.

Listing 2-21. #ifdef Preprocessor Directive

```
#ifdef DEVELOPMENT_VERSION
    NSAssert(poolSize<256,@"pool overflow");     // alert developer
#else
    if (poolSize>=256)
        return;    // return immediately if pool overflows
#endif
```

Defining the preprocessor macro DEVELOPMENT_VERSION, either in a source file or via a build setting, will compile the code to throw an assertion (program exception) if the poolSize variable is greater than or equal to 256. If a DEVELOPMENT_VERSION macro has not been defined, the if/return statements are compiled instead.

#if directives can be nested. Text omitted by an #if directive is also ignored by the preprocessor, making it possible to conditionally include files or conditionally define other preprocessor macros.

It is also common to see #if 0 … #endif used to comment out large blocks of unwanted or experimental code.

Initializing Automatic Variables

Java ensures that all variables are initialized to a predictable value before they are used. This is Java's Definite Assignment rule. Similarly, Objective-C initializes all instance variables to zero when an object is created. C initializes all static variables to zero, unless explicitly initialized to some other value.

C does not, however, initialize automatic (local) variables, nor does it require that they be initialized before being used (see Listing 2-22).

Listing 2-22. Uninitialized Automatic Variable

```
{
    int i;
    while (i==0)
        …
}
```

The integer variable i in Listing 2-22 is an automatic (local) variable allocated on the stack frame of the method. C does not require that it be initialized to any value. If not initialized, the value is unpredictable. It will be whatever value previously occupied that word position in the stack or CPU register. Make sure that you initialize automatic variables before you use them.

Labels: break, continue, and goto

The C break and continue statements perform the same function as their Java counterparts.

A Java label identifies a block of code, typically a for or while loop. A Java break or continue statement can optionally specify the label of an enclosing control block, allowing it to exit, or jump to the end of, the named block. C break and continue statements do not accept labels.

In C, execution control is much more permissive. Instead of limiting abnormal flow control to just break and continue statements, C provides the all purpose goto statement. A C label identifies a statement in the code block. The goto statement immediately transfers execution to the code identified by the label. The label and goto statements can appear anywhere within the function or method, as shown in Listing 2-23.

Listing 2-23. break, continue, and goto

Java
```
    int segment[][] = new int[100][100];
    ...
    int optimalLength = 200000;
    int lineLength = 0;
    int bestFit = 0;
lineLoop:
    for (int i=0; i<100; i++) {
        lineLength = 0;
        for (int j=0; j<100; j++) {
            int s = segment[i][j];           // get segment length
            if (s==0)                         // stop at zero length
                break;
            lineLength += segment[i][j];      // accumulated line length
            if (lineLength>optimalLength)     // line too long
                continue lineLoop;
            if (lineLength==optimalLength)    // line perfect fit
                break lineLoop;
            if (lineLength>bestFit)           // remember best fit
                bestFit = lineLength;
        }
    }
return (lineLength);
```

C
```
    int segment[100][100];
    ...
    int optimalLength = 200000;
    int lineLength;
    int bestFit = 0;
    for (int i=0; i<100; i++) {
        lineLength = 0;
        for (int j=0; j<100; j++) {
            int s = segment[i][j];
            if (s==0)
                break;                        // Same as Java
            lineLength += segment[i][j];
            if (lineLength>optimalLength)
                goto nextLine;                // Jump to end of outer loop
            if (lineLength==optimalLength)
                goto stop;                    // Continue after outer loop
```

```
            if (lineLength>bestFit)
                bestFit = lineLength;
        }
    nextLine:
        ;
    }
stop:
    return (lineLength);
```

The code fragments in Listing 2-23 demonstrate the use of break, continue, and goto statements. The statement goto nextLine continues execution at the end of the outer loop's control block and is equivalent to the continue lineLoop statement in Java. The goto stop statement jumps to the statement immediately following the outer loop and is equivalent to the break lineLoop statement.

The nextLine label illustrates a quirk of C labels; they must precede an executable statement. Following it with an empty statement (;) satisfies the requirement.

C labels, unlike Java, are not limited to jumping to the end of code blocks. A goto statement can jump forward or backward in the code stream, and into or out of code blocks at any level. It's possible to construct for, while, do, and case statements using only label, if, and goto statements—although I don't recommend it.

Use goto statements sparingly, if ever. They can solve very tangled code flow problems, but should be used only as a last resort. They are easy to abuse, often defeat code optimization, and can make execution order difficult to analyze.

Summary

This chapter was designed to give you *just enough* C that you can begin programming in Objective-C. Programming in Objective-C liberates you from many of the arcane and mundane aspects of programming in C. Using Objective-C classes you can largely avoid C strings, memory management, arrays, and a raft of other constructs.

This chapter was not, by any stretch of the imagination, a comprehensive C tutorial. The C language is vast—even more so than Java, given that one of Java's goals was to create a simpler and more concise version of C.

While this abbreviated introduction will give you enough knowledge that you can start programming in Objective-C, you will eventually encounter more complex C code or need to interface with C libraries. That will require a deeper understanding of the language. I highly recommend you procure a book on standard C for further reading and future reference.

Now that you understand the salient differences between C and Java, you can begin to explore the additional syntax that defines Objective-C.

CHAPTER 3

■ ■ ■

Welcome to Objective-C

This chapter describes the core Objective-C language and how its syntax differs from Java. Functional differences and more esoteric language features are covered in later chapters.

Objective-C enhances C by adding an additional layer of syntax. It does not redefine C, or limit its capabilities, in any meaningful way. Objective-C syntax is easily recognized. If Objective-C had a logo, it would probably be the "at" sign (@); all Objective-C directives, including string constants, begin with @ (as in @interface, @selector(), @"string"). Other notable traits are the use of square brackets ([…]) to invoke methods and very descriptive method names.

But if you ignore these peculiarities, you won't find any significant discord between the two. Both are object-oriented languages that let you define classes, declare instance variables and methods, instantiate instances of those classes, inherit from subclasses, override methods, invoke methods, pass parameters, and return values. Good Objective-C programming embraces the same design patterns and practices that you are familiar with in Java.

Defining an Objective-C Class

Objective-C classes are defined in an @interface directive. Its implementation is defined in an @implementation directive. This differs from Java's single class definition, which defines both the class's interface and its implementation, as shown in Listing 3-1.

Listing 3-1. Objective-C Class Definition

Java
```
import com.apress.java.SuperClass;

public class NewClass extends SuperClass
{
    int instanceVariable;

    Object method( )
        {
        return (null);
        }


    Object method(Object param )
        {
        return (null);
        }
```

```
}
```

Objective-C
```
#import "SuperClass.h"

@interface NewClass : SuperClass {
    int instanceVariable;
}

-method;
-methodWithParameter:param;

@end

@implementation NewClass

-method
{
    return (nil);
}

-methodWithParameter:param
{
    return (nil);
}

@end
```

Listing 3-1 shows the definition of the NewClass class in Java and an equivalent class in Objective-C. The @interface part of a class definition is typically in a header (.h) file for inclusion by other modules, while the @implementation portion is in a source (.m) file. See the "#include and #import" section of the previous chapter if you need a refresher on C source file organization.

The @interface portion of a class declaration has two parts. The first part contains the instance variable declarations surrounded by braces. This portion is similar to a C struct declaration.

Following the variable declaration are the class's method prototypes. The hyphen prefix indicates that the method is an instance method. A plus prefix denotes a class method, which is similar to a static method in Java.

The @implementation directive contains the actual code for the methods that were described in the @interface section. It is an error to declare a method and not implement it, although the opposite is permitted. One of Java's more elegant design features is that a class file defines both a class's interface and its implementation. In Objective-C, it's the programmer's responsibility to keep the interface and the implementation in agreement.

Both the @interface and @implementation sections are terminated with an @end directive.

Class inheritance works the same way it does in Java. The class NewClass inherits all of the instance variables and methods of the class SuperClass. Declaring a method in NewClass with the same name as a method inherited from SuperClass overrides the inherited method.

■**Caution** Always declare the superclass in the @interface declaration, even when the superclass is NSObject. NSObject is the logical root class in the Cocoa framework, functionally equivalent to Java's Object class. It is not, however, the root class of Objective-C. Objective-C's actual root class, Object, is so primitive that a direct subclass is essentially useless. It is unlikely that you will ever want to create a direct subclass of Object.

Object Pointers

A variable containing a pointer to an Objective-C object is an *object pointer* (reference) or *object identifier*. Both are equivalent to a Java object reference.

Listing 3-2 shows the two ways of declaring an object pointer. An object pointer can be declared as a pointer to a specific class or as a generic object identifier (id). Both contain a pointer to the memory address of an object. The difference is in how they are treated by the compiler.

Listing 3-2. *Object Pointer Declarations*

```
SpecificClass *specificObject;
id anyObject;
```

■**Note** Like Java, Objective-C does not permit a variable to contain the contents of an object, only a pointer (reference) to an object. The declaration SpecificClass object is invalid. This is one case where Objective-C objects and C structures differ; a variable can contain an entire C structure or a pointer to a C structure, but you can only declare a pointer to an Objective-C object.

A pointer to a specific class acts mostly like a Java object reference. The compiler assumes that the pointer refers to an object of that class, or a subclass of that class. It will warn you if you attempt to invoke methods that are not defined or inherited by that class. It will only allow you access to instance variables defined or inherited by that class. The pointer is implicitly compatible with a pointer to any of its superclasses, but not with a pointer to a subclass.

The special object identifier type (id) is a non-specific object pointer (reference). It is *not* the equivalent of a pointer to a base class object, e.g. NSObject *obj (Object obj). The compiler assumes that a variable of type id could be *any* class. The compiler will permit you to invoke any method from any class that's been defined. An object identifier can be assigned to any kind of object pointer, or from any kind of object pointer, with no compiler warning. You *cannot* use an object identifier to directly access an object's instance variables.

If you declared every object pointer as type id, programming would be similar to some scripting languages. The compiler would make no assumptions, allowing you to invoke any method and assign the pointer to any other object pointer variable without complaint. The appropriateness of those methods and assignments would be vetted at run time.

At the other extreme, declaring every reference as a pointer to a specific class results in a programming experience similar to Java. The compiler will only allow method calls to those defined for the pointer's class, and inappropriate assignments will be flagged. The only significant difference is that in Java, a cast from one class to another is checked at runtime; in Objective-C a cast simply suppresses a compiler warning.

Real-world Objective-C is a blend of these two extremes. The id type is used where the class of an object is not known, variable, or indeterminate. Strong, class-specific pointers, are used everywhere else. For example, an NSError object contains a recoveryAttempter object reference. It's the object that will take responsibility for recovering from the error. This variable has an id type since NSError makes no assumptions about its class. Type id allows the property value to be set, assigned, or used to call any method without casting. On the other hand, NSErrors' domain and userInfo variables are declared as pointers to NSString (String) and NSDictionary (Map) objects. There's no ambiguity about what class of objects is stored in these variables or what methods they implement.

All pointer types are functionally identical at runtime. The compiled code retains no pointer type information. The two pointers declared in Listing 3-2 will behave exactly the same way when the code executes.

Sending Messages

Method invocation syntax is the most dramatic difference between Java and Objective-C. A method invocation consists of an object pointer (reference) and the name of the method to execute, surrounded by brackets. Examples are shown in Listing 3-3.

Listing 3-3. *Objective-C Message Syntax*

Java
```
object.method();
object.method(param);
```

Objective-C
```
[object method];
[object methodWithParam:param];
```

Objective-C does not call object methods, as Java does. It sends messages to objects. This is more than a semantic difference.

Java works very much like C or C++ when you call a method. The method name in the statement identifies the method to execute. The parameters of the call are pushed onto the stack along with a return address. Execution flow is then transferred to the method.

Objective-C invokes a method by first pushing the parameters of the method onto the stack. It then calls a central dispatching function, passing it the object pointer and a compact method identifier called a *selector*. This dispatching function uses the two to locate the object's method and transfer execution to the method's code. The method executes and returns, just like any C or Java method.

The difference might seem trivial, or even pointless, but it is the key to Objective-C's dynamism and is critical to several important and unique language features. This will become more evident as you work through the chapters of this book.

To underscore this concept, Objective-C uses different language to describe the process of invoking methods. In Objective-C, you *send* a *message* to an object. The calling object is the *sender* and the object whose method is being invoked is the *receiver*. The term receiver is used extensively in Objective-C, especially in documentation (as in the phrase "… returns the number of Unicode characters in the receiver"). The terms "method" and "message" are often used interchangeably.

Naming Methods

Objective-C method names are verbose, consisting of one or more keywords that naturally describe each parameter. Listing 3-4 shows four hypothetical Objective-C methods with none, one, two, and three parameters, respectively.

Listing 3-4. Named Parameters

```
-method;
-methodWithParameter:parameter;
-methodWithContext:context object:object;
-methodWithDialog:dialog message:message behindWindow:window flags:mode;
```

The first Objective-C declaration in Listing 3-4 defines a method that takes no parameters. This is the Java equivalent of `Object method()`. The second declaration defines a method taking one parameter, equivalent to `Object method( Object parameter )`.

The identifier following the colon is the name of the parameter variable; this is the variable name you will use to reference the variable in the method's code (e.g., `dialog`, `message`, `window`, `mode`). The name of the parameter variable and the keywords that form the method's name are in different name spaces. They can be the same or different. Only the parameter variable name is in scope within the body of the method's implementation.

■**Note** As in Java, parameter names are in the same scope as the object's instance variables. An instance variable (say, `cell`) and a parameter variable with the same name create some ambiguity. Like Java, the symbol name by itself will always refer to the parameter or local variable. The cell instance variable must then be addressed indirectly using `self->cell` (`this.cell`). Unlike Java, the Objective-C compiler will complain with a warning that "the local declaration of 'cell' hides instance variable." To avoid the warning, and any possible ambiguity, most Objective-C programmers choose parameter names that don't conflict with any instance variables, electing to use names like `aCell` or `newCell` instead of just `cell`.

Naming methods in Objective-C is a bit of an art. Objective-C method names are generally constructed using one of the forms shown in Listing 3-5. The listing shows some abstract method names followed by several real-world examples.

Listing 3-5. Method Naming Examples

```
Simple actions:
-action;
-draw;
-play;
-becomeKeyWindow;
```

Action methods with a parameter:
-actionParameter:param;
-drawCell:cell;
-sendEvent:event;

Actions with multiple parameters:
-actionParameter:firstParam secondParameter:secondParam;
-replaceSubview:oldView with:newView;
-postNotificationName:name object:sender;

Methods returning a value:
-value;
-key;
-window;
-stringByExpandingTildeInPath;

Methods with parameters that return a value:
-valuePrepositionParameter:parameter;
-objectForKey:key;
-stringByAppendingString:string;
-numberFromString:string;

Reading and inventing your own names isn't too difficult if you keep the following in mind. The general form for a method name begins with a description of the returned value (if any), followed by the action the method performs, followed by a description of the first parameter (if any). A method named -menuForEvent: can be reasonably assumed to take an NSEvent object as a parameter and return an NSMenu object. Subsequent keywords describe that parameter and often include a preposition such as "in," "to," or "with." The parameter's description is sometimes implied, as in -replaceSubview:oldView with:newView. Avoid including superfluous verbs like "do" or "does."

Objective-C does not the support overloading of method names that differ only in their parameter types the way Java does. But it really isn't necessary. If two Objective-C methods differ only in their parameters, the methods will have different names: -drawRect:rect, -drawCell:cell, -drawPage:page instead of the equivalent overloaded Java functions draw(Rect rect), draw(Cell cell), draw(Page page).

There are no hard and fast rules for naming methods. The principal goal is readability. Objective-C method names lend a refreshing verboseness to code that makes it much more self-explanatory. Listing 3-6 shows two code fragments that extract the substring "Walrus" into a character array.

Listing 3-6. Method Name Example

Java
```
char c[] = new char[20];
String s = "The time has come, the Walrus said ...";
s.getChars(23,29,c,1);
```

Objective-C
```
unichar c[20];
NSString *s = @"The time has come, the Walrus said ...";
[s getCharacters:&c[1] range:NSMakeRange(23,6)];
```

The code phrase getCharacters:c range:NSMakeRange(23,6) is more descriptive than (23,29,c,1). It is clear that the first parameter involves characters and the second parameter is a range. This becomes especially helpful with methods that have many parameters. When Objective-C method names become exceptionally long, the formatting convention is to place each parameter on its own line, horizontally aligning the colons as shown in Listing 3-7. The Xcode editor, as well as other Objective-C–savvy text editors, will do this automatically.

Listing 3-7. Multiline Message

```
NSString *new = [s stringByReplacingOccurrencesOfString:@"Walrus"
                                             withString:@"Carpenter"
                                                options:NSLiteralSearch
                                                  range:NSMakeRange(20,10)];
```

Parameter and Return Types

Like Java, an Objective-C method can return a single value to the caller. The methods presented so far have omitted the return type and the types of the parameters. I did that intentionally to focus on the basics of method declaration and naming. Parameter and return types are specified in parentheses before the method name or parameter variable name, very much like a type cast. Some examples are shown in Listing 3-8.

Listing 3-8. Parameter and Return Types

```
- (id)objectForKey:(id)aKey
- (NSMenuItem*)itemWithTag:(NSInteger)aTag;
- (unichar)characterAtIndex:(NSUInteger)index;
- (NSString*)stringByAddingPercentEscapesUsingEncoding:(NSStringEncoding)encoding;
- (void)runInNewThread;
- (void)addAttribute:(NSString*)name value:(id)value range:(NSRange)aRange;
```

If the type is omitted, the non-specific object identifier type (id) is implied. The declarations -objectForKey:key; and -(id)objectForKey:(id)key; are identical. For clarity, Objective-C programmers invariably specify the types of all parameters and return values, even when the type is id.

A parameter type can be any valid C or Objective-C variable type. Usually they are simple types such as numeric primitives (int), object pointers (id or NSColumn*), or small structures (NSPoint). Method parameters and return values are always passed by copy, so any type that can be assigned using the assignment operator (=) can be passed as a parameter. As mentioned earlier, Objective-C does not allow you to declare a variable to *be* an Objective-C object—you can only declare pointers *to* Objective-C objects. By extension, you cannot pass a copy of an Objective-C object as a parameter, only a copy of the pointer (reference) to the object. Thus, you cannot declare the method -(NSString)description, but you can declare the method -(NSString*)description.

In addition to valid variable types, the return type of a method can also be (void), indicating that it does not return any value. The compiler will warn you if you attempt to use the return value of a void method. It will also warn you if you attempt to return a value from a void method, or fail to return a value from a non-void method.

Method Selectors

An Objective-C method's complete name, sans the parameter variable names and any types, forms its unique identifier. The identifier for the method `-(NSfont*)fontWithFamily:(NSString*)family traits:(NSFontTraitMask)fontTraitMask weight:(NSInteger)weight size:(CGFloat)size` is `fontWithFamily:traits:weight:size:`. This is equivalent to a method signature in Java. The concrete embodiment of this identifier is a numeric constant called a *selector*. Selectors are values of type `SEL`. The Objective-C directive `@selector()` evaluates to the selector value of the method identifier in parentheses, as in `SEL selector = @selector(fontWithFamily:traits:weight:size:)`.

▓Note It's tempting to think of the keywords in a method name as parameter names, but this is not technically accurate. Unlike languages with named parameters, the parameters of an Objective-C method cannot be omitted or rearranged. The methods `-sendMessage:toRecipient:withAttachement:` and `-sendMessage:withAttachement:toRecipient:` are distinct methods with unique signatures.

Selectors are used internally to dispatch messages to objects. They can be used programmatically to send messages, register for messages, perform introspection, and other tricks described in later chapters.

In documentation and in communications between programmers, method names are often written like an invocation with the class name and method identifier. A programmer might write "-[NSFontManager fontWithFamily:traits:weight:size:]" when referring to the fontWithFamily:traits:weight:size: instance method defined by the NSFontManager class. It's nonsense code, but concisely describes the method.

Instance Variables

Instance variables are declared in the `@interface` directive of the class, as was shown in Listing 3-1. This is virtually identical to Java, with the minor restriction that all instance variable declarations are grouped together in a single block. Like Java, instance methods access instance variables as if they were local variables.

▓Note Instance variable and method names traditionally use "camel case"—they begin with a lowercase letter and use uppercase letters to delineate words. Instance variable and method names that begin with an underscore (_) are reserved by the Cocoa framework and should be avoided.

You've also seen how the indirect member operator is used to directly address a member variable in another object, as in `object->value = 1` (`object.value = 1`). In Java you normally wouldn't do that. Good Java practices encourage the use of accessor (getter) and mutator (setter) methods to insulate the variable's implementation from external code. The instance variable would be declared `protected` or `private`, and the methods `int getValue()` and `void setValue( int value )` would be used to get and set its value.

Good Objective-C follows the same practice for all of the reasons Java does and a few more. In Objective-C, the instance variable `int value` would be accessible via the methods `-(int)value` and `-(void)setValue:(int)newValue`. Objetive-C encourages the use of accessor methods so much, the definition and construction of accessor methods has been built into the language in the form of *properties*. How to declare properties is described immediately after the section on the `isa` variable.

■**Note** Objective-C uses the names "value" and "setValue" for the methods that get and set the property `value`, rather than "getValue" and "setValue" which are more common in Java. Technologies that use introspection to identify properties via accessor methods will often accept the "getValue" form as an alternative, but the "value" form for getters is preferred.

---

isa

Every object in Objective-C inherits an `isa` instance variable; `isa` literally defines the class of the object.

At runtime, there is a single instance of a Class object for every class. The Class object defines the behavior for all instances of that class. Every instance of that class refers to its defining Class object via its `isa` variable.

You should not directly access an object's `isa` variable. If you want to get an object's Class, the `-(Class)class` method will return it. You may also find `-(NSString*)className` useful: it returns the name of the object's class as a string.

Several technologies alter an object's `isa` variable (a technique known as "isa swizzling") to dynamicaly alter that object's behavior. Never change the value of an object's `isa` variable yourself, until you have a clear and deep understanding of Objective-C's runtime architecture.

Properties

Objective-C 2.0 adds the `@property` and `@synthesize` keywords for defining object properties and implementing their matching accessor methods. A property is a value that is fetched using an accessor method and set using a mutator method. A property's value is typically stored in an instance variable, but that's not a requirement.

The `@property` directive declares a property of the class. A `@property` directive typically appears in the `@interface` directive. It does not implement the accessor methods or create any instance variables. It is simply a promise that the class implements that property. Listing 3-9 shows the Person class, in both Java and Objective-C. The class defines five properties: tag, firstName, lastName, fullName, and adult.

Listing 3-9. *Property Declarations*

Java
```java
public class Person
{
    int     tag;
    String  firstName;
    String  secondName;
    boolean adult;
```

```
synchronized int getTag( )
    {
    return (tag);
    }

synchronized void setTag( int tag )
    {
    this.tag = tag;
    }

public synchronized String getFirstName()
    {
    return firstName;
    }

public synchronized void setFirstName( String firstName )
    {
    this.firstName = firstName;
    }

public synchronized String getLastName()
    {
    return secondName;
    }

public synchronized void setLastName( String lastName )
    {
    secondName = lastName;
    }

public synchronized boolean isAdult()
    {
    return adult;
    }

public synchronized void setAdult( boolean adult )
    {
    this.adult = adult;
    }

public String getFullName( )
    {
    return (firstName+" "+secondName);
    }
}
```

Objective-C

```objc
@interface Person : NSObject {
    int         tag;
    NSString    *firstName;
    NSString    *secondName;
    BOOL        adult;
}
@property int tag;
@property (copy) NSString *firstName;
@property (copy) NSString *lastName;
@property (getter=isAdult) BOOL adult;
@property (readonly,nonatomic) NSString *fullName;

@end

@implementation Person

@synthesize tag;
@synthesize firstName;
@synthesize lastName = secondName;
@synthesize adult;

- (NSString *)fullName
{
    return ([NSString stringWithFormat:@"%@ %@",firstName,secondName]);
}

@end
```

The @synthesize directive appears in the @implementation of the class. A @synthesize directive tells the compiler to generate the accessor and mutator methods needed to implement the property.

In the absense of a @synthesize directive, it is up to the programmer to implement the methods that sastify the contract declared in the @property directive. Failing to either include a @synthesize directive or implement the expected accessor methods is an error.

■**Note** The special @dynamic directive suppresses the compiler's expectation for the required accessor methods. In some cases (i.e., class extensions, categories, subclassing, dynamically-loaded frameworks), it's possible that the class will implement methods at runtime that the compiler is not aware of. The @dynamic directive tells the compiler not to worry about it; the programmer promises that the expected methods will exist when the program executes. Use of @dynamic is rare.

The first two properties are straightforward. The @property int tag declares that the class Person implements getter and setter methods that satisfy the contract of an integer property named tag. The @synthesize tag directive instructs the compiler to generate the methods -(int)tag and -(void)setTag:(int)newTag for you. The tag property will be stored in the instance variables of the same name.

The second property declaration is similar, but since the property is an object, we're obliged to include a property attribute clarifying how assignments are handled. The copy attribute causes the synthesized setter to make and store a copy of the object that is passed to it (rather than storing a reference to that object). Like tag, the value of the firstName property will be stored in the firstName instance variable.

The third @property directive is identical to the second, except that the name of the property doesn't correspond to any declared instance variables. This is immaterial to the @property directive; that statement is just a promise *that* the class will implement the property, not *how*. The @synthesize lastName = secondName directive implements the required getter and setter methods for the lastName property using the instance variable secondName for storage. Getting the lastName property returns the secondName variable; setting the lastName property replaces the secondName variable with a copy of the value passed to -setLastName:.

■**Tip** If you prefer really compact code, the four @synthesize directives in Listing 3-9 could have been written as @synthesize tag, firstName, lastName=secondName, adult.

The @property (getter=isAdult) BOOL adult directive declares a Boolean property named adult. The gettter= attribute renames the getter method to -(BOOL)isAdult, rather than the default -(BOOL)adult. As in Java, the getter method for a Boolean property traditionally begins with "is" or "has".

The final @property (readonly,nonatomic) NSString *fullName directive declares that the Person object provides a string property named fullName. The property is read-only (it has a getter method but no setter method) and the getter method is not thread safe. In the @implementation section of the class is there no @synthesize directive for fullName. The required getter method is implemented by the programmer.

■**Caution** When implementing accessor methods to satisfy a @property directive, it is up to the programmer to fulfill the implied contract of the declaration. If you omit the nonatomic attribute, it is up to you to ensure the methods are threadsafe. If the copy attribute is specified, the setter methods should make and store a copy of the value, not a reference to the value (unless you can guarantee it to be immutable).

Property Attributes

The example in Listing 3-9 showed some of the common attributes used in property definitions. Table 3-1 describes all of the property attributes that can be included in a @property directive. Multiple properties are seperated by commas.

Table 3-1. *Property Attributes*

Property Attribute	Description
readonly	Declares the property to be immutable. A @synthesize directive for a readonly property will generate a getter method, but no setter method. readonly is mutually exclusive with readwrite.
readwrite	Declares the property to be mutable. This is the default mutability attribute. If neither readonly nor readwrite are specified, readwrite is assumed. readwrite is mutually exclusive with readonly.
copy	Declares that the setter method makes a copy of the object passed to it and stores a reference to that copy, not a reference to the original object. This attribute is only appropriate for object pointer properties—primitive values are always passed by copy. copy is mutually exclusive with assign and retain. Use copy where there is a chance that objects used to set the property might be mutable and you do not want the value of the reciever's property to change if the original object is modified.
assign	Declares that the setter method sets the property by keeping a pointer to the object passed to it. In practical terms, it means that the getter and setter methods are implemented using simple assignment (i.e., self->firstName = name). Use assign in a garbage collection environment where you want to retain the reference to the original object value or the object values are always immutable. assign is typically assumed if no storage attribute is specified, but there are some environments where you must explicitly include assign, copy, or retain. assign is mutually exclusive with copy and retain, and is only appropriate with object pointer properties.
retain	This attribute is like assign, but retains the reference to the object in a managed memory (non-garbage collection) environment. Refer to Part 4 for information about about non-GC memory management.
getter=name	Renames the method used as the getter method. Useful when an alternate form of the default getter method name is desired, such as -isValue, or -getValue. Use this attribute with caution; it can break the standard pattern of getter and setter names such that technologies like Key-Value Coding will not recognize the property.
setter=name	Renames the method used for the setter method. Cannot be used if the readonly attribute is specified. The same caution that applies to getter= applies to setter=.
nonatomic	Declares that the getter and setting methods are not thread-safe. There is no "atomic" attribute; omitting nonatomic implies the property is atomic. If omitted, the @synthesize may wrap the getter and setter methods with code that first obtains an object-specific lock in order to guarantee that accessor methods are well behaved in a multi-threaded environment. It also insures that the object returned is fully realized in the memory space of the executing thread. Use nonatomic whenever your manually-written accessor methods do not provide these safeguards, or when such precautions are not wanted. The thread safety features add a non-trivial amount of runtime overhead to the accessor methods, which may have performance implications. There are exceptions for primitive scalar properties and assign object properties on certain platforms, where the processor guarantees atomic assignments.

The copy attribute is more appropriate with string and collection objects than it is in Java. In Objective-C, string and collection classes have mutable subclasses. So an NSString is not guaranteed to be immutable the way a Java String object is. Making a copy ensures that the property isn't affected by changes to the orginal object used to set the property.

Overriding Properties

Properties are implemented by accessor methods that get and set a value in the receiver. Since they are implemented using methods, subclasses can override those methods, essentially overriding the property.

Overriding a property's accessor methods can be done informally or formally. To do it informally, simply override the appropriate accessor method. To override the setter method implied by @property int tag, just implement a new -(void)setTag:(int)newTag method in your subclass. It doesn't even have to be declared in the subclass's @interface.

To formally override a property, declare a duplicate @property directive in the subclass. The @property directive must be identical to the one in the superclass with one exception: a subclass can declare a property as readwrite when the superclass's property is readonly. This supports the design pattern of a mutable subclass of an immutable superclass. Once declared, the @synthesize directive can be used to reimplement the accessor methods for the subclass or you can implement them yourself.

■**Tip** This is one practical application for the @dynamic directive. Since the superclass already implements the accessor method for the property, the subclass can redeclare the property, use the @dynamic directive to ignore the requirement to reimplement both accessor methods, then override just the getter or setter method.

Accessing Properties

The accessor methods for a property can be invoked like any other method. But formally declared properties carry an additional benefit. Objective-C 2.0 extends the member variable operator (.) to allow easy access to formally defined properties. This so-called "dot syntax" lets you interact with an object's property the way you would address a member variable in Java.

Using the class defined in Listing 3-9, the code in Listing 3-10 sets and accesses several properties of a Person object. The dot syntax is expanded by the compiler to call the appropriate getter or setter method for each property; it does *not* directly access the object's instance variables as it would in Java. This is considered "syntactic sugar," provided to improve readability and reduce clutter. The code produced by Listing 3-10 is identical to the code shown by Listing 3-11.

Listing 3-10. Object Properties via Dot Syntax

```
Person *person = ...;
person.firstName = @"James";
if (person.lastName.length==0)
    person.lastName = @"Smith";
person.tag += 3;
```

Listing 3-11. Dot Syntax Equivalent Code

```
Person *person = ...;
[person setFirstName:@"James"];
if ([[person lastName] length]==0)
    [person setLastName:@"Smith"];
[person setTag:[person tag]+3];
```

Scope

I'll get the bad news out of the way first: there are no packages in Objective-C. All class names, C functions, and global variables share a single name space. Instance variables within a class are encapsulated by that class, and Objective-C does provide control over their scope. Objective-C does not restrict access to class methods, but there are practical ways of emulating the kind of access restrictions that you enjoy in Java.

Class Name Scope

Class names are all public and exist in the same globally accessible name space. To avoid naming conflicts, Objective-C developers have adopted a naming convention for classes that must coexist with others. Classes in a logical group all begin with a common two-character abbreviation. In Apple's frameworks, all of the Core Image classes begin with CI (CIColor, CIFilterShape, CIVector, . . .). Classes for QuickTime begin with QT (QTTrack, QTMovie, QTTimeValue, . . .).

■**Note** If you were wondering, the NS prefix found on Cocoa foundation classes stands for NextStep. NextStep is the Objective-C operating system developed by NeXT Computer. When Apple purchased NeXT in 1996, it adopted NextStep as the core technology for the nascent Mac OS X. In a feat that George Orwell would admire, almost every reference to NeXT and NextStep was redacted from the Mac OS X source code and documentation. But it was virtually impossible to rename every class in the gargantuan framework, so the legacy NS prefix survives to this day.

Classes developed by third parties follow the same convention. The OmniGroup makes an extensive set of application classes available to other developers. The OmniAppKit classes all begin with OA (OAController, OAUtilities, OAScriptMenuItem, . . .). The OmniNetworking classes all begin with ON (ONHost, ONPortAddress, . . .).

In your development, consider the scope of the classes you are creating. If the class will be used only in your application development environment, don't worry about a prefix. Give your classes simple names like Student, BoardGame, Troll, and so on. If you are developing classes that are going to be used by other programmers, even if only within your organization, choose a prefix that is likely to be unique and name your classes accordingly. If your company is Widget Makers, you might name your classes WMToy, WMAlarm, etc. You also don't have to commit to this decision now. The Xcode IDE includes refactoring tools that make renaming your classes relatively painless.

Instance Variable Scope

Access to instance variables is controlled the same way it is in Java, conveniently using the same terminology. Rather than specifying the scope of each variable individually, Objective-C adopts the C++ style of scope directives. The directives @public, @protected, and @private can appear before any variable declaration in the instance variable block of an @interface directive. All variables declared after a scope directive inherit the specified visibility. Listing 3-12 shows four instance variables with varying degrees of visibility.

Listing 3-12. *Instance Variable Scope*

```
@interface Toy : NSObject {
    NSString    *name;
    @public
    int         starRating;
    @protected
    NSRange     recommendedAge;
    int         playCount;
    @private
    NSSet       *toyBox;
}

@end
```

The variable starRating is public. It can be accessed by any code in any context.

The scope of the name, recommendedAge, and playCount variables is protected. Methods defined in this class, or any subclass of this class, have direct access to these variables. Protected is the default scope of instance variables. Variables defined before the first, or in the absence of any, scope directive are protected.

The variable toyBox is private. It can only be accessed by methods defined in this class.

Keep in mind that Objective-C variable scope only *discourages* access to instance variables. If you attempt to use a member variable in a context where you do not have access to it, the compiler will complain. It is still possible to access those variables using introspection or by coercing pointers—Objective-C has no "security" in the Java sense. Also, the variable names are not technically scoped within a name space of the class the way they are in Java. The toyBox instance variable exists for all subclasses of the Toy class. A subclass of Toy cannot declare its own instance variable named toyBox; the compiler will issue a duplicate member error.

Method Scope

Methods are always public, in the Java sense. Objective-C places no runtime restrictions on who can invoke an object's method given a pointer to that object. Although there's no explicit way to restrict a method from being invoked, there are several techniques for hiding methods to discourage their use outside the scope they were intended for.

The simplest technique is to include the method in the @implementation section but omit the method prototype from the @interface directive. Other modules that #import the interface for that class will not be aware of that method's existence, and the compiler will complain if an attempt is made to send that message.

This technique works because a method in the @implementation section implies its own prototype. Once the method appears in the implementation, the compiler knows about the method and will allow you to invoke it just as if it had been predefined in the class's interface. This technique is casual and simple. Its biggest disadvantage is that all undeclared methods must be defined before they can be referenced. This can make source code organization awkward. In some cases of recursion, it makes it impossible.

A similar technique can be applied to @property directives. Earlier, I cagily stated "a @property directive *typically* appears in the @interface directive." A @property directive can also appear in an @implementation. It has the same meaning, but omitting it from the @interface also hides the definition from other modules.

Objective-C categories and extensions are more formal patterns for subdividing the declarations of a class, allowing you to compartmentalize the knowledge about a class. Those techniques and how they can be used to emulate private and protected Java methods are explained in a later chapter.

Finally, it's sometimes useful to create a "helper" class—a class whose purpose is internal to the implementation of another class. A helper class can be entirely declared and implemented in the implementation file of the class that uses it. The helper's interface and implementation are hidden from other classes. If the class requires an instance variable that points to a helper object, use a @class directive—described next—or the type id.

Forward @class Directive

The @class directive declares a class name without defining the class. It permits you to declare a reference to a class without having compiled the @interface for that class. Following a @class directive, you can refer to the class but you cannot compile any code that assumes knowledge about that class— since the compiler has none. You can't send messages to an object of that class, or access any of its properties, until the actual @interface directive for that class is compiled.

As soon as you start declaring variables that are pointers to objects, you'll discover that the compiler requires that those classes be defined before it will allow you to use the class name in a statement. The natural inclination is to just #import the needed class header files for every object you reference in your @interface directive. For smaller projects, that's fine.

For large projects, this becomes a burden on the compiler (translation: it will slow down your development). Every class that uses class A will import its interface (#import "A.h"). If class A has instance variables that point to objects of classes B, C, and D, it will import all of those header files. If classes B, C, and D collectively contain references to classes E through N, their header files will import all of those header files, and so on. As the complexity of your project grows, the effort needed to compile each module grows geometrically.

The @class directive can be used to lighten this load considerably. An @interface directive rarely needs to know anything about a referenced class other than it exists. A typical application of the @class directive is shown in Listing 3-13.

Listing 3-13. Forward @class Directive

```
#import "Vehicle.h"
@class Engine;
@class MoonRoof;
@class Radio;

@interface Car : Vehicle {
    Engine      *engine;
    MoonRoof    *moonRoof;
    Radio       *radio;
}
```

```
- (void)startEngine;
- (void)stopEngine;
- (void)tuneRadio;

@end
```

The Car class contains references to Engine, MoonRoof, and Radio objects. A module that #imports this @interface can use the methods and properties of Car, but knows nothing about the other objects. The @implementation of Car, which presumably will use the other objects, begins by importing the full definition of those classes.

As a rule, I #import the header file for the superclass, the class of all public objects, and the class of objects returned by methods (on the assumption that the caller will use the returned object). All remaining classes in the @interface are declared using @class.

The @class directive also makes it possible to declare classes with circular references. In other words, class A has a reference to class B which has a reference to class A.

self and super

An Objective-C method has access to two predefined variables for referring to itself: self (this) and super (super). They work exactly like their Java counterparts, as shown in Listing 3-14.

Listing 3-14. Use of self and super

```
#import "Person.h"

@interface Voter : Person {
}
- (void)setAdult:(BOOL)isAdult;

@end

@implementation Voter

- (void)setAdult:(BOOL)isAdult
{
    if (isAdult && !self.isAdult)
        [VoterRegistration registerVoter:self];
    [super setAdult:isAdult];
}

@end
```

The self variable is always a pointer to the reciever (the object whose method was invoked). The type of the self variable is a pointer to the class that implemented the method. It can be used to address instance variables defined or inherited by that class (i.e., self->secondName), but not a subclass variable (even if the actual class of the object is a subclass).

■**Caution** Java programmers may initially find this bizarre, but `self` is a modifiable automatic variable and can be reassigned in the body of a method. I'll explain later why you would want to do this. For now, just be careful not to change it inadvertently.

The statement `[self method]` sends an object a message to itself. The equivalent Java statement would be `this.method()` or just `method()`. The pseudo-variable `super` is identical to `self`, but its only practical use is when sending messages. The statement `[super method]` invokes the method defined by the object's superclass and is equivalent to the Java statement `super.method()`.

Class Methods

So far, only instance methods have been defined for classes. To review, an instance method is declared with a minus sign (-) prefix. It defines a message that *instances* of that class will respond to.

A method name that begins with a plus sign (+) defines a class method. As described in the `isa` section, each class creates a single Class object at runtime that defines the identity and behavior for all instances of that class. A class method defines a message that the single Class object will respond to. A class method is (technically) not the equivalent of a static method in Java, although they tend to fill the same role.

A class name, when used in an expression, evaluates to the singleton Class object for that class. To invoke a class method, use the class name as the receiver, as shown in Listing 3-15. Using the class name sends the message to that class's Class object.

Listing 3-15. Class and Instance Method Invocation

```
@interface RandomSequence : NSObject {
    long long int seed;
}

+ (NSNumber *)number;
+ (NSString *)string;

- (NSNumber *)nextNumber;
- (NSString *)string;

@end

...

NSNumber *n = [RandomSequence number];
NSString *s = [RandomSequence string];

RandomSequence *r = ...;
n = [r nextNumber];
s = [r string];
```

■**Note** By convention, class methods are defined first, followed by the instance methods.

The method +(NSNumber*)number defines a class method that returns an NSNumber object. The statement [RandomSequence number] sends the message number to the single Class object that defines the RandomSequence class.

A string method has been defined for both the Class object and instances of the class. The statement [RandomSequence string] sends the string message to the Class object and executes the code in +(NString*)string. The statement [r string] sends the string message to an instance of the RandomSequence class and executes the code in -(NSString*)string. There is no ambiguity or name conflict because -string and +string are implemented for different objects.

In the body of the +(NSNumber*)number method, the self variable refers to the Class object (RandomSignature). This is where Java class methods and Objective-C class methods differ. In Java, a class method has no object context (it has no this variable). In Objective-C, class messages are sent to the Class object the same way messages are sent to regular objects. The statement [self string] in the body of the +(NSNumber*)number method would invoke the class method +(NSString*)string, not the instance method -(NSString*)string. The true equivalent of a static Java method is a C function.

This distinction is important for inheritance. Class objects inherit class methods the same way instance methods are inherited. If class B is a subclass of class A, and class A defines a class method, class B inherits that class method. Class B can also override the class method. Listing 3-16 illustrates this relationship.

Listing 3-16. *Class Method Inheritance*

```
@interface Classy : NSObject

+ (void)greeting;
+ (NSString*)salutation;

@end

@implementation Classy

+ (void)greeting
{
    NSLog(@"%@, world!",[self salutation]);
}

+ (NSString*)salutation
{
    return (@"Greetings");
}

@end


@interface Classic : Classy

+ (NSString*)salutation;
```

```
@end

@implementation Classic

+ (NSString*)salutation
{
    return (@"Hello");
}

@end

…

[Classy greeting];      // Logs "Greetings, world!"
[Classic greeting];     // Logs "Hello, world!"
```

The statement [Classy greeting] sends the greeting message to the Classy Class object. That method sends itself a salutation message and uses the return value to construct the log message "Greetings, world!"

The statement [Classic greeting] sends the greeting message to the Classic Class object. Classic does not define a class method +(void)greeting, but it inherits one from Classy. When +(void)greeting executes in this context, the self variable refers to Classic, not Classy. Sending self the salutation message invokes Classic's overridden -(NSString*)salutation method, and the message logged is "Hello, world!"

■**Note** If the statement in Listing 3-16 was NSLog(@"%@, world!",[Classy salutation]) instead of NSLog(@"%@, world!",[self salutation]), the message would always be "Greetings, world!" That's because Classy is a constant that always refers to the single Classy Class object, while self refers to the Class object receiving the greeting message.

Despite the subtle technical differences, class methods in Objective-C are used for many of the same purposes that static methods in Java are. Methods that return a singleton object, factory methods, object pools, and convenience utilities are common uses for class methods.

Constructing Objects

You might have expected me to explain the syntax for instantiating objects much earlier in this chapter, instead of making you wade through instance variables, explanations about the self variable, and class methods. The reason I didn't is simple: *there is no syntax for instantiating objects*.

True to its minimalist philosophy, Objective-C lets the class designer decide how objects are created and initialized. In the Cocoa framework, that's through a combination of a factory class method and some conventions for writing initializer (constructor) methods.

■**Note** You will see this minimalist pattern repeated again and again. Java defines a specific syntax and enforces pre-determined rules for how objects are created, serialized, copied, and so on. Objective-C, in contrast, provides only the bare essentials and leaves the implementation decisions to the class designers. You can't change how objects are created in Java, but you can in Objective-C. You might not need to do it often, but you can do it with great effect.

Creating an object is a two-step process. First, the memory for the object's structure is allocated. The instance is then initialized. Listing 3-17 shows a rewriting of the RandomSequence class to include two initializers (constructors).

Listing 3-17. Object Initialization

Java
```java
public class RandomSequence
{
    long seed;

    public RandomSequence()
        {
        seed = 1;
        }

    public RandomSequence( long startingSeed )
        {
        seed = startingSeed;
        }

}

...
RandomSequence r1 = new RandomSequence();
RandomSequence r2 = new RandomSequence(-43);
```

Objective-C
```objc
@interface RandomSequence : NSObject {
    long long seed;
}

- (id)init;
- (id)initWithSeed:(long long)startingSeed;

@end

@implementation RandomSequence

- (id)init
{
    self = [super init];
```

```
    if (self!=nil) {
        seed = 1;          // default seed
    }
    return (self);
}

- (id)initWithSeed:(long long)startingSeed
{
    self = [super init];
    if (self!=nil) {
        seed = startingSeed;
    }
    return (self);
}

@end

...
RandomSequence *r1 = [[RandomSequence alloc] init];
RandomSequence *r2 = [[RandomSequence alloc] initWithSeed:-43];
RandomSequence *r3 = [RandomSequence new];
```

The [RandomSequence alloc] statement begins the process by sending an alloc message to the RandomSequence Class object. The root NSObject class implements the +(id)alloc class method, which is inherited by all subclasses. +(id)alloc uses the class reference to allocate the required memory for the new object, sets its isa variable, fills all remaining instance variables with zeros, and returns the pointer to the newly allocated object. At this point, the object exists and is an object of the requested type. However, the object has not yet been initialized.

Next, the init message is sent to the newly created object. This is the message responsible for initializing the object. Once init returns, the object is ready to use.

The three statements in Listing 3-17 that create the objects r1, r2, and r3, demonstrate the common ways to create new objects. Variable r1 is assigned a new object, allocated and initialized without any parameters, equivalent to the Java statement r1 = new RandomSequence().

The r2 variation calls an alternate initializer, passing additional parameters for use in initializing the object. Like Java, you can create whatever additional initializers (constructors) your class needs.

The shorthand form used to create object r3 is functionally identical to the one used to create r1. The root NSObject class implements a +(id)new class method that first calls +(id)alloc and then sends the newly created object the -(id)init method before returning. It's only useful for creating an object that can be constructed using its -(id)init method (i.e., no parameters), but it does save a little code.

■**Caution** Object constructor customization is *always* accomplished by overriding or defining -(id)init... methods for the class. Never override or attempt to intercept the +(id)alloc or +(id)new class methods.

Writing an init Method

To write an Objective-C initializer (constructor), your method must fulfill a four-part contract:

1. The initializer must call its superclass initializer.
2. It must update its `self` variable.
3. It must check for a nil object.
4. It must return the pointer to itself.

The first two parts of the contract are satisfied by the statement `self = [super init]`. It should be obvious that every initializer must call its superclass initializer before proceeding. In Java, this convention is guaranteed by the language. In Objective-C, you're responsible for calling it.

Updating `self` might seem bizarre to a Java programmer, but it's key to something called *class clusters*. Class clusters are explained in detail in Chapter 22. You might be tempted to leave the assignment to `self` out. Don't. The code is actually smaller and faster if you leave it in, and you won't violate the class cluster contract.

■ **Note** The return value for init methods is traditionally `id`. Logically, init should always return a pointer to the class or a subclass. However, declaring the return value as a class pointer type (i.e., `-(BaseClass*)init`) makes it difficult for subclasses. The subclass must call `[super init]` and assign it to `self`. If `[super init]` returns a BaseClass* type value, the subclass can't assign it to `self` without a cast.

The third step is to check for nil. The superclass init method will return nil if, for any reason, it can't create the requested object. For example, nil is returned if the process runs out of free memory and a new object can't be allocated. A class can decide not to construct an object and return nil for any reason. Program defensively; always assume an initializer could return nil.

If the returned object is valid, your initializer should then perform whatever initialization your object requires.

Finally, the initializer must return itself, or nil, if the initialization failed, to the caller.

Study the `-(id)init` method in Listing 3-17. Memorize it. Every object initializer you will ever write should look just like it. You will undoubtedly encounter subtle variations—many programmers combine the first two statements into `if ((self=[super init])!=nil)`—but every well-written init method satisfies the four-part contract for initializers.

Chaining Initializers

Java has special syntax for explicit constructor invocation, whereby a constructor can invoke a specific superclass constructor with parameters (`super(param)`) or an alternate constructor (`this(param)`). Naturally, Objective-C doesn't have any special syntax for this, but the principle is the same.

The class RepeatableSequence, shown in Listing 3-18, is a subclass of RandomSequence, shown in Listing 3-17. The init methods for RepeatableSequence build on the init methods in its superclass as well as the other methods in RepeatableSequence.

Listing 3-18. *Chained Initializers*

Java
```java
public class RepeatableSequence extends RandomSequence
{
    private long restartSeed;

    public RepeatableSequence()
        {
        this(1);
        }

    public RepeatableSequence( long startingSeed )
        {
        super(startingSeed);
        restartSeed = seed;
        }

    void restartSequence( )
        {
        seed = restartSeed;
        }
}
```

Objective-C
```objc
#import "RandomSequence.h"

@interface RepeatableSequence : RandomSequence {
    long long restartSeed;
}

- (id)init;
- (id)initWithSeed:(long long)startingSeed;

- (void)restartSequence;

@end


@implementation RepeatableSequence

- (id)init
{
    self = [self initWithSeed:1];
    return (self);
}
```

```
- (id)initWithSeed:(long long)startingSeed
{
    self = [super initWithSeed:startingSeed];
    if (self!=nil) {
        restartSeed = seed;
    }
    return (self);
}

- (void)restartSequence
{
    seed = restartSeed;
}

@end
```

The -(id)initWithSeed: method invokes its superclass's -(id)initWithSeed: method, passing the initialization parameter to the superclass. After the superclass initialization is finished, it completes its initialization.

The -(id)init method hands off initialization to the -(id)initWithSeed: method. Note that the message initWithSeed: is sent to itself, not to its superclass.

Designated Initializer

When subclassing a class, read the documentation (or comments) about that class. Some Objective-C classes have one or more *designated initializers*. An init method for a subclass should only initialize the superclass using one of its designated initializers.

The documentation for many classes includes an explicit "Subclassing Notes" section that contains important information and caveats for subclass authors.

Convenience Constructors

A very common use of class methods is to provide convenience constructors, sometimes referred to as factories. These are class methods that return a preconfigured object of the same class, ideally using less code than needed to formally create and initialize a new object. Listing 3-19 shows a fragment of the NSDictionary class provided by the Cocoa framework. All of the class methods return a new NSDictionary object.

Listing 3-19. *Class Convenience Constructors*

```
@interface NSDictionary

+ (id)dictionary;
+ (id)dictionaryWithObject:(id)object forKey:(id)key;
+ (id)dictionaryWithDictionary:(NSDictionary *)dict;
+ (id)dictionaryWithObjects:(NSArray *)objects forKeys:(NSArray *)keys;

@end
```

The statement [NSDictionary dictionary] is equivalent to [[NSDictionary alloc] init], and the statement [NSDictionary dictionaryObject:@"Mary" forKey:@"Name"] is equivalent to [[NSDictionary alloc] initWithObject:@"Mary" forKey:@"Name"]. The principal advantage is brevity.

■**Caution** The statement [NSDictionary dictionary] is equivalent to [[NSDictionary alloc] init] only when using garbage collection. In a traditional managed memory environment, these two are quite different. The former returns an autoreleased object while the latter returns a retained object. See Chapter 9 (on garbage collection) and Chapter 24 (on memory management) for a complete explanation.

Convenience constructors are often included to construct objects that would otherwise be awkward to create. For example, the NSString class provides the +(NSString*)pathWithComponents:(NSArray*)components convenience constructor. It takes an array of path components, assembles them into an absolute POSIX path, and returns the result as a single immutable string. Trying to accomplish this using alloc and class init methods would require creating a mutable string buffer, appending all of the components in a loop, then converting the temporary string buffer into an immutable string object. Clearly, the single statement [NSString pathWithComponents:array] is significantly more compact.

Destructors

Like Java, Objective-C objects can optionally override their -(void)finalize method. This message is sent to objects before being destroyed by the garbage collector. Every finalize method must send a finalize message to its superclass immediately before returning.

An example -finalize method is shown in Listing 3-20. Note that finalize methods should be used only for exceptional cleanup and to provide robustness. A well-written program would not rely on the finalize method to close a file; it should have closed the file before allowing this object to become collectable. The finalize code simply protects against the possibility of leaking the resource in unusual circumstances, for example, if the file was left open following a program exception.

Listing 3-20. *Well-Behaved finalize Method*

```
- (void)finalize
{
    if (file!=nil) {
        [file close];
        file = nil;
        }

    [super finalize];
}
```

■**Caution** The finalize message is sent to objects only when running in a garbage collection environment. Objective-C applications using managed memory (sans garbage collection) implement the -(void)dealloc method instead. See Chapter 24 for more details.

What's Missing?

Table 3-2 has a brief list of Java features that you won't find in Objective-C.

Table 3-2. *Missing Java Features*

Feature	Description
Inner/Anonymous Classes	You cannot define a class within a class, or a class within a method. Inner and anonymous classes are typically used as adaptors and for code encapsulation. In Objective-C, these patterns are implemented using informal protocols and code blocks (a recent addition to the C language that allows an executable block of code to be passed as a variable).
Object Arrays	Objective-C has no inherit concept of an object array. Arrays of objects can be handled as a C array of object pointers or using the NSArray collection class.
final	There is no final keyword in Objective-C. You cannot prevent a class or method from being subclassed or overridden. When applied to variables, the keyword const is largely synonymous with final.
abstract	All classes and methods in Objective-C are concrete.
package	There are no packages in Objective-C, so there is no package scope.

Java interfaces, thread synchronization, and exceptions have Objective-C counterparts that are detailed in later chapters.

Many other features of Java, such as serialization, introspection, remote method invocation, and copying, are not defined by the Objective-C language; as it does with constructors, the Cocoa framework implements these features using classes and methods.

In the upcoming chapters, you'll also discover many features and capabilities unique to Objective-C.

CHAPTER 4

Creating an Xcode Project

The last couple of chapters contained a lot of theory and abstract concepts to digest, and the next few chapters contain even more. For me, there's nothing more frustrating than trying to learn a complex topic without any way of exploring each individual concept. To that end, I'll take a brief respite from the theoretical and indulge in the purely pragmatic task of creating a working Objective-C application in Xcode, Apple's free software development kit.

Having a working project that you can tinker with and test on is an invaluable learning experience. As you work through the rest of this book, I encourage you to code small examples of the concepts you are exploring. Add the code to a test project, and step through it using the debugger. A few lines of code can answer a lot of questions.

If you haven't installed Apple's Xcode development tools, do so now. Xcode is available online at http://developer.apple.com/. This tutorial assumes that you are using a Macintosh computer running Mac OS X 10.5 or later and are installing Xcode 3. The term *Xcode* actually refers to two things: Apple's entire suite of development tools, and the Xcode IDE (Integrated Development Environment) application. In this book, *Xcode* refers to the Xcode application and *Xcode development tools* refers to the entire package of development applications, utilities, documentation, example code, and other support material.

Download the Project

This project is a simple desktop application called Scrapbook Words. Give the application a set of letters and it will tell you what words you can spell with them. The code is small (a couple hundred lines), but it dabbles in a number of technologies. It uses collection and string objects, reads data from a file, schedules tasks to run asynchronously in a background thread, communicates between threads using queued messages, and employs controllers and binding to implement a Model-View-Controller design. You can learn more about these specific technologies in the following chapters:

- String objects are examined in Chapter 8.
- Programmatic message sending is explained in Chapter 6.
- Collections are explored in Chapter 16.
- Chapter 20 discusses data model, view, and controller objects (the Model-View-Controller pattern), as well as bindings.
- Threads are covered in Chapter 15.

Before you start, download the finished project files at www.apress.com in the Source Code/Download area. This chapter will walk you through the steps that were used to create this project from scratch, but it does not include every detail. The code excerpts in this chapter are used to illustrate concepts, but aren't necessary complete. Refer to the finished project for the whole implementation. There are a number of ways of working through this chapter:

- Read the chapter to get a feel for Xcode development. Download the finished project and play with it.
- Copy each step in this chapter in Xcode to re-create the project on your own, copying source code from the finished project where needed.
- Use the steps here as the starting point for your own project.

In the following sections, you're going to create a new Xcode project, configure the project, design an application, create controller and data model objects to implement a Model-View-Controller design, and finally add the business logic to produce a working app. Working through this process will take you on a mini-tour of Xcode, Interface Builder, Objective-C, and the Cocoa frameworks. There are few comparisons to Java in this chapter, since this is more about the development tools than the language.

Creating a Project

Once installed, launch the Xcode application.

Start by creating a new project. Choose File ➤ New Project… to open the new project assistant (Apple's term for a wizard). A new project is always based on one of the many templates included. Each template creates a complete project preconfigured for a particular purpose. It's a great head start towards your final goal, so choose the template that most closely describes your end product. Most projects require a non-trivial amount of configuration before they will produce anything useful, so I strongly discourage you from choosing the Empty Project template.

For this project, choose the Cocoa Application template as shown in Figure 4-1. Name the project Scrapbook Words and select a location where the project and its files will be stored. Xcode will create a folder with the name of your project. The folder will contain a similarly named project document and whatever additional resource files are included in the template. This might be nothing for some templates, or scores of items for others.

Figure 4-1. *Choosing a Project Template*

The project window is where all of the project's components are organized and managed. The project window, shown in Figure 4-2, uses the default Xcode layout. You can choose to use an all-in-one window or multiwindow layout in Xcode ➤ Preferences, should one of those better suit your tastes and habits.

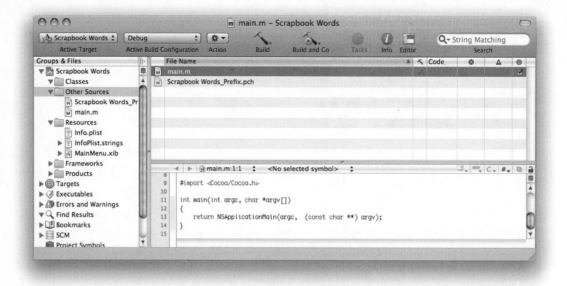

Figure 4-2. *Project Window*

Most templates produce a project that can be immediately built and run, but does nothing useful. The Cocoa application template is no exception. If you like, you can build and launch the application right now (Build ➤ Build and Run).

The Group & Files pane of the project window is where you organize the project's assets. You can create an arbitrarily complex hierarchy of source items by creating new groups and sub-groups, and rearranging items by dragging. You can create new files directly in the project or import existing files. By default, the actual files are all stored in the root project folder. It's possible to organize the physical files into a hierarchy or have them reside outside the project folder, but for even moderately sized projects it's far less complicated if you confine your organizing to the project window.

Getting Started

Before getting started on the principal design, there's some housekeeping to do. For the most Java-like experience, you'll want your application to use garbage collection. As of the writing of this book, garbage collection is opt-in; a new Cocoa project will use legacy memory management unless reconfigured.

Choose Project ➤ Edit Project Settings from the menu. Switch to the Build tab, choose All Configurations and All Settings, and then type **garbage** into the search field. You should see the build setting for Objective-C Garbage Collection as shown in Figure 4-3. Click the value pop-up and change the setting to Required. Build setting changes occur immediately.

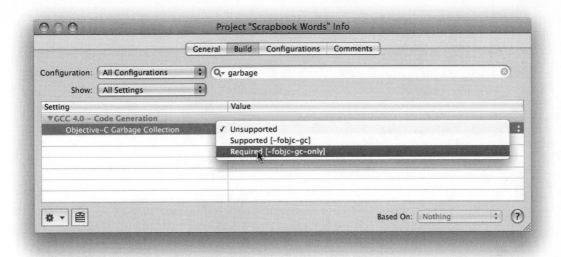

Figure 4-3. *Garbage Collection Build Setting*

Feel free to explore the other build settings while you're here (clear the search field). Build settings are organized into a three-dimensional matrix of values. The first two dimensions are formed by a hierarchical tree of build settings: one set for the project, one set for each target, and a limited set for each file. Each entity can define or override any build setting. Target build settings override those in the project, and file settings override those in the target. Before establishing a build setting, decide if it applies to the entire project, a specific target, or just one file. The third dimension is formed by *build configurations.* Each configuration contains a completely independent set of build settings for each entity in the project. The Cocoa application template comes with two build configurations: Debug and Release. The Debug build configuration has settings that include debugging symbols and disable most code optimizations, suitable for debugging and profiling. The Release build configuration strips symbol information and turns on most code optimizations. You can create your own build configurations, but do so sparingly as it multiplies the build settings you must maintain.

Designing the Application

Now let's move on to the application design. This application will present a graphical user interface, so it adapts the Model-View-Controller (MVC) design pattern. Our data model is simple—a string of letters and a list of words that can be spelled—provided by a string and an NSArray object. The ScrapWordsController class will be our main controller object. The view objects are all subclasses of NSView, provided by the AppKit framework.

The application will present a window with four components, as shown in Figure 4-4. An input field lets the user type the letters they have. An output view lists the words that can be spelled with those letters. The interface is simple; you type letters, you see words.

Figure 4-4. *Scrapbook Words User Interface*

To get the design started, create a ScrapWordsController class. This will be our primary controller object. Click on the Classes group to select it. Either control+click (or right-click) on the group and choose Add ➤ New File…, or choose File ➤ New File… from the main menu. In the New File assistant, choose the Objective-C class template from the Cocoa group. Give it the name ScrapWordsController.m and have it create a matching ScrapWordsController.h file. Click the Finish button and the assistant will create the new files and add them to your project.

The `ScrapWordsController` object will need to do the following:

1. Get the letters the user types from the input text field.
2. Clear the output list whenever the user types something new.
3. Search a list of words for those that can be spelled using those letters.
4. Add each word found to the output list for the user to see.

Listing 4-1 shows the initial version of the ScrapWordsController.h file. The version of ScrapWordsController.h in the finished project has one additional instance variable, which you can ignore for now. It has a letters property that holds the string of letters entered by the user. The NSMutableArray object will contain the list of words that can be spelled. The `wordsController` variable will reference an NSArrayController object that does all of the work needed to bind the data model to the view object that will display the list words—more about that later. Finally, methods are defined to clear and add one word to the output display list, respectively.

Listing 4-1. Initial Version of ScrapWordsController Interface

```
@interface ScrapWordsController : NSObject {
    NSString                *letters;
    NSMutableArray          *words;
    NSArrayController       *wordsController;
}

@property (assign) NSString *letters;
@property (assign) IBOutlet NSArrayController *wordsController;

- (void)removeWords;
- (void)foundWord:(NSString*)word;

@end
```

Designing the User Interface

To get this to work, the application will need an interface window with an input text field and an output list. The user interface will be developed using Interface Builder. Interface Builder is an interface design tool that works closely with Xcode. Interface Builder edits NIB documents. A NIB document contains an archived (serialized) object graph. You can create whatever objects you want in a NIB document. Objects in the NIB are created, configured, and connected together using point-and-click design tools. When the application runs and loads a NIB document, the objects are instantiated, their properties set, and inter-object references are connected together. NIB documents are stored as resource files in the application's bundle.

Note Historically, Xcode projects would include a binary .nib document that Interface Builder would edit directly. Xcode 3 introduced the .xib document type, a more robust and flexible XML-based Interface Builder document. An .xib document is a source document that is compiled into a binary .nib document when the application is built. I refer to all Interface Builder documents generically as NIB documents because that's the language used by Cocoa developers and in the documentation, and they are what will ultimately be loaded by your application.

Double-click on the MainMenu.xib document in the project window; you'll find it in the Resources group. This will launch Interface Builder and open the project's MainMenu NIB document. Interface Builder presents the contents of the MainMenu NIB document in a window as a hierarchical collection of objects, as shown in Figure 4-5. Top-level visual objects in the NIB, like the window and menu bar, are also displayed separately. Content can be edited in either one.

Figure 4-5. *MainMenu NIB Document and Top-Level Visual Containers*

Creating the user interface is as easy as dragging and dropping. Open the Library window (Tools ➤ Library). In the Objects tab, find the Input & Values group under Views & Cells. Drag two Labels and a Text Field from the Library window into the application's window, as shown in Figure 4-6. Arrange their position. Locate the Data Views group and drag a Table View into the window. Resize and arrange the objects and window until these objects are in the same position as those in Figure 4-4. Edit the labels by double-clicking on them.

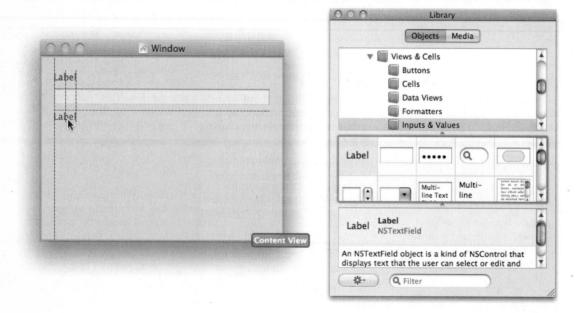

Figure 4-6. *Adding View Objects to the Window*

Properties of objects are edited using a variety of inspector palettes. Choose Tools ➤ Inspector, then select the input text field. The palette presents the properties of the selected object (or objects).

To edit the properties of the Table View object, you must first select it. In the Main Menu document window, dig through the nested hierarchy of view objects to select the Table View objects, as shown in Figure 4-7. An alternate method is to click once on the view in the window. This selects the top level Scroll View object. Clicking on the interior again drills down into the view and selects the Table View object. Clicking again would select a column within the table, and so on.

Figure 4-7. *Editing the Table View Attributes*

Edit the properties of the Table View: set the number of columns to 1. Turn off headers, reordering, and resizing. Turn off column selection.

The view objects should resize when the window does. Open the Size Inspector (Tools ➤ Size Inspector). In that palette, edit the Autosizing settings for the input text field and the scroll view, as shown in Figure 4-8. Decide which edges of the object are anchored to the window, then choose if the horizontal or vertical size changes with the window. You'll want the input field to be anchored top and sides and resize horizontally, and the output list anchored on all sides and resize both horizontally and vertically. The animation previews the effect of the settings.

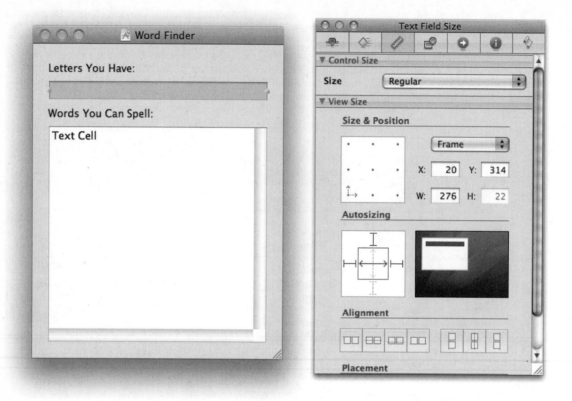

Figure 4-8. *Editing a View Object's Autoresize Attributes*

Adding a Controller

The application will need to create an instance of the ScrapWordsController. It will be connected to other objects in the NIB document, so the NIB document should instantiate the controller as well. From the Library, select the Objects & Controllers group and drag a new Object object into the MainMenu.xib document window, as shown in Figure 4-9. Select the newly created object and switch to the Identity inspector (Tools ➤ Identity Inspector). Set its class to ScrapWordsController. You can type it in or choose it from the pull-down menu; Interface Builder keeps track of the classes you've defined in your project.

Figure 4-9. *Adding a Custom Object to the NIB Document*

When this NIB document is loaded at runtime, it will create an instance of ScrapWordsController, just as if your application had executed the statement `[ScrapWordsController new]`. This is an important concept to grasp. All of the objects in a NIB document represent real objects that will be instantiated when the NIB is loaded. The result is identical to creating new instances of those objects, setting all of their properties, adding them to their container object (for nested objects), and setting references between them. But by using Interface Builder, you save yourself from writing a ton of code.

Making a Binding

In an MVC design, data model objects broadcast changes to view objects whenever they change. View objects update the data model object whenever the user alters the value. This requires connections and communications between the view and data model objects. This application's data model is a couple of simple values (a string and an array) created by the controller object.

There are a variety of ways of connecting the data values to the view objects, but this application is going to use a binding. Bindings are actually a collection of technologies that support the MVC design pattern. A binding connects two objects so that a change in a property of one object is automatically communicated to the other object. The second object can initiate changes that alter the property of the first object. Typically, the first object is a data model object and the second object is a view object. Once bound together, changes to one are automatically reflected in the other. This doesn't require you to write any code. You need only declare the property and bind it to an object.

In Interface Builder, choose the Text Field object (either in the MainMenu.xib or in the Window itself). Bring up the Bindings Inspector (Tools ➤ Bindings Inspector). Expand the text field's Value binding. Bind it to the ScrapWordsController object using a key path of letters, set it to Continuously Update Value, and uncheck the other options so they match the ones shown in Figure 4-10.

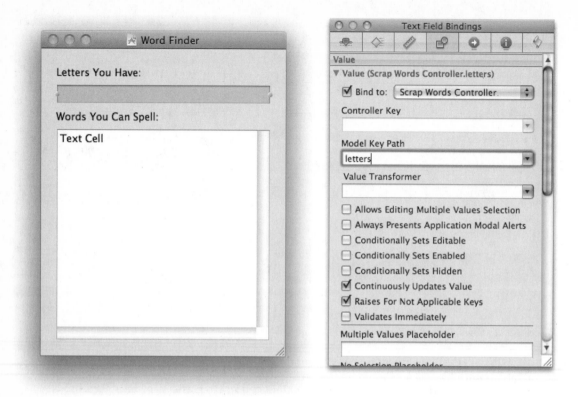

Figure 4-10. Binding the Text Field to the letters Property of ScrapWordsController

This binding is complete. Any change to the controller's letters property (i.e. `[controller setLetters:@"hello"]`, or `controller.letters = @"hello"`) will be immediately reflected in the text field view. Editing the text field will update the value of `letters` in the controller.

If that seems like a lot of magic for so little code, I'll lift the curtain a little and give you a peek at some of what's going on behind the scene. The key thing to keep in mind is that Interface Builder isn't doing anything special. The technologies that allow bindings to work —Key-Value Coding, Key-Value Observing, and controllers—are available to you directly. They can be used individually, or in concert, to implement a wide spectrum of solutions, beyond just making MVC designs easy.

KVC

Key-Value Coding (KVC) allows an object's properties to be accessed interpretatively. It uses a combination of informal protocols (explained in Chapter 5) and introspection. As an example, assume there's a Key-Value Coding–compliant Person class that has three properties: a string `name` property, and `father` and `mother` properties that reference two other Person objects. A person's `name` could be examined using the Key-Value path `@"name"`. Their father's `name` could be addressed with the path `@"father.name"`, and their maternal grandfather's `name` could be accessed using the path `@"mother.father.name"`. KVC is discussed in more detail in the Introspection chapter.

KVO

Key-Value Observing (KVO) is a notification service used to observe changes in an object. The property to observe is specified using a KVC path. Once an object begins observing a property, any change to that property sends a notification to the observer (listener). Unlike Java, this doesn't require the source object to manage a set of listeners or fire notification messages itself—although it can. All it has to do is declare a property. The KVO framework does all the work of managing the list of observers, detecting when the property changes, and sending the appropriate notifications. KVO is explained in Chapter 19.

Controllers

The Cocoa framework defines an NSController class that provide the "glue" between data model and view objects. The Cocoa framework provides a number of useful controllers for arrays, dictionaries (maps), trees, and user preferences. You can subclass NSController should you need to define your own. There's more about controllers in Chapter 20.

Bindings

The bindings framework leverages KVC, KVO, and controllers to create a unified MVC notification and synchronization service. Bindings can be created in Interface Builder or programmatically using the -[NSObject bind:toObject:withKeyPath:options:] method. Bindings are also covered in Chapter 20.

Adding an Array Controller

The binding between the Table View and Array object is, naturally, a little more complicated. To coordinate the display with the data requires two bindings: one binding connects a column in the table view to an array controller. A second binding connects the array controller to the actual array of value objects. The array controller sits between the view and data model objects and maintains state information—like the sorting order and current user selection—that doesn't belong in either the view or the data model. This is often called the Mediated MVC design pattern, because the controller object sits between the view and the data model and mediates their communications.

First, add an instance of NSArrayController by dragging a new Array Controller object from the Library into the NIB document. You'll find Array Controller in the Controllers group. Start by selecting the first, and only, Table Column inside the Table View object. Bind its value to the Array Controller with a controller key of arrangedObjects and a model key path of self. The self key-value path causes the view object to display the value of each object in the collection, rather than a property of each object. This is appropriate because the array contains simple string objects.

Now the array controller needs to be connected to its data model object. Select the newly created Array Controller object in the MainMenu NIB document and set its Content Array binding to ScrapWordsController with a model key path of words. The key-value path words tells the controller that the words property of ScrapWordsController is the data source for the array.

Finally, the ScrapWordsController will need to interact with the array controller object programmatically. To do that, it will need an object pointer (reference) to the instance of the array controller created by the NIB document. This is established using an outlet and a connection. An outlet is just an instance variable that points to another object. The IBOutlet type modifier, as shown in Listing 4-1, turns the object pointer property into a public outlet in Interface Builder. A connection creates a relationship in the NIB so that the instance variable will point to its connected object when the NIB document is loaded.

Object pointers decorated with the IBOutlet keyword automatically appear as outlets in Interface Builder. The IBOutlet keyword can be placed before an instance variable or in a `@property` directive. Select the ScrapWordsController in the MainMenu NIB document and switch to the Connections Inspector. Interface Builder lists wordsController as an outlet of the object. To connect the outlet to the array controller object—i.e., to set the instance variable to point to the address of the array controller object at runtime—drag the outlet's connector to the Array Controller object and release the mouse button, as shown in Figure 4-11.

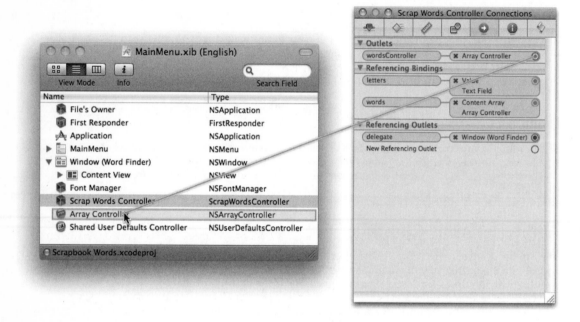

Figure 4-11. *Connecting arrayController Outlet to the Array Controller Object*

The application now has an interface and runs, but it does nothing useful. All of the views and data model object work together, but since nothing happens when you type in the input field, the experience is underwhelming. The application needs business logic.

Getting Down to Business

The application will read in and construct a dictionary of about 200,000 common words. Whenever letters are typed in, it will search for the words that can be spelled using those letters. There are numerous ways of solving this kind of problem, but this application opts for the simple approach: a brute force search of all 200,000 words. This could be time consuming, so the search shouldn't occur on the main UI thread of the application. Otherwise, the application will appear to freeze whenever a new letter is typed.

The solution is to perform the search on a background thread. The search thread will send messages to the main thread whenever it finds a word. This could be accomplished with threads and semaphores, but it's easier to let NSOperationQueue do the heavy lifting for us.

Back in the Xcode project, select the Classes group and add a new Objective-C class file named WordFinder.m, along with its companion WordFinder.h header file. Make the WordFinder a subclass of NSOperation, as shown in Listing 4-2.

Listing 4-2. WordFinder Interface

```
@class ScrapWordsController;

@interface WordFinder : NSOperation {
    ScrapWordsController    *controller;        // reference to controller
    NSArray                 *letterSet;         // set of letters to search
}

+ (NSArray*)words;

- (id)initWithLetters:(NSString*)letters
          controller:(ScrapWordsController*)windowController;

- (void)main;

@end
```

When the user types in some letters, the view object will update the data model by sending a `setLetters:` message to the controller. The implementation of `setLetters:`, shown in Listing 4-3, creates a new WordFinder operation and queues it up to execute. When the WordFinder thread runs, it sends removeWords and foundWord: messages back to the ScrapWordsController on the main thread. All the main application thread has to do is start the operation, then sit idly and wait for the results to come pouring in. The application's interface never blocks and is never unresponsive. The `removeWords` and `foundWords:` methods must modify the data model through the array controller object. The array controller is responsible for keeping the data model, the view, and itself in synchronization.

Listing 4-3. ScrapWordsController Implementation

```
@implementation ScrapWordsController

@synthesize wordsController;

  - (id) init
{
    self = [super init];
    if (self != nil) {
        words = [NSMutableArray new];
        finderQueue = [NSOperationQueue new];
    }
    return self;
}

- (NSString*)letters
{
    return (letters);
```

```
}

- (void)setLetters:(NSString*)newLetters
{
    if (newLetters==nil)
        newLetters = @"";
    if (![letters isEqualToString:newLetters])
    {
        letters = newLetters;

        [finderQueue cancelAllOperations];
        WordFinder *finder = [[WordFinder alloc] initWithLetters:newLetters
                                                controller:self];
        [finderQueue addOperation:finder];
    }
}


- (void)removeWords
{
    NSRange all = NSMakeRange(0,[words count]);
    NSIndexSet *everyItemIndex = [NSIndexSet indexSetWithIndexesInRange:all];
    [wordsController removeObjectsAtArrangedObjectIndexes:everyItemIndex];
}

- (void)foundWord:(NSString*)word
{
    if ([words count]==0 || ![[words lastObject] isEqualTo:word])
        [wordsController addObject:word];
}

@end
```

A skeleton of the WordFinder implementation is shown in Listing 4-4. In brief, it contains a class method to construct and return a singleton array of all possible words. This method is synchronized in case it is invoked from multiple WordFinder threads. The main method is invoked to perform the operation. It simply tests each word against the letters in the set. If successful, it sends a message to the main thread using [controller performSelectorOnMainThread:@selector(foundWord:) withObject:candidate waitUntilDone:YES]. See Chapter 6 for more on sending messages to objects.

Listing 4-4. WordFinder Implementation Skeleton

```
static NSArray *DictionaryWords;            // singleton copy of English word
list

@implementation WordFinder

+ (NSArray*)words
{
    @synchronized(self) {
        if (DictionaryWords==nil) {
            NSMutableArray *words = [NSMutableArray new];
            ...
            DictionaryWords = [NSArray arrayWithArray:words];
        }
```

```
    }

    return DictionaryWords;
}

- (void)main
{
    // Get the list of possible words
    NSArray* possibleWords = [WordFinder words];

    // First, signal to the controller that a new word search has started
    [controller performSelectorOnMainThread:@selector(removeWords)
                            withObject:nil
                            waitUntilDone:YES];

    // Brute force search of every word in the dictionary...
    for ( NSString *candidate in possibleWords ) {
        ...
    }
}

@end
```

The finished application is shown in Figure 4-12. When letters are typed, a search thread is spawned that finds the possible words.

Figure 4-12. *Finished Scrapbook Words Application*

Debugging Your Application

The debugger is an invaluable tool during development, and when learning a language it is also a great sandbox. You can write code and watch it execute, examine results, and even change data. To play with the Scrapbook Words application, make sure the build configuration is set to Debug. Do this in the Build Results window (Build ➤ Build Results). To set a breakpoint, click in the line number margin to the left of the code. Breakpoints are shown as blue tabs, as shown in Figure 4-13. Clicking a breakpoint again disables it. Drag the breakpoint to relocate it, or out of the margin to discard it. Choose Run ➤ Debug to start the application executing under the control of the debugger.

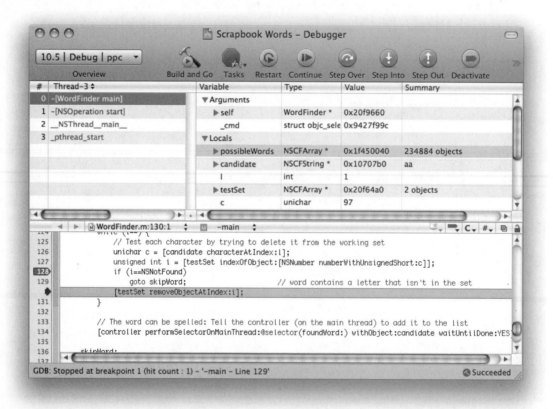

Figure 4-13. *Stopped at a Breakpoint in the Xcode Debugger*

Once stopped at a breakpoint, you can control execution of the application from any source window, using menu commands, or the main Debugger window (Run ➤ Debugger) shown in Figure 4-13. The debugger window also displays the stack and local variables.

Creating Sandbox Applications

When experimenting with code, a sandbox application can be very useful. Follow these steps to quickly create a simple Cocoa application that can be used to exercise code, or even as the foundation for a full-fledged application:

1. Create a new project using the Cocoa Application template.
2. Turn on garbage collection in the build settings.
3. Add a new class to the project. This is your test class.
4. Add an action to the class. An action is a method that takes a single object identifier as its sole parameter and returns an IBAction, as in - `(IBAction)doSomething:(id)sender`. IBAction is synonymous with void, so the action doesn't actually return anything. The `sender` parameter will be the object that sent the action (the button or menu item defined in step 8). It's often ignored.
5. Add your test code to the action method.
6. Open the MainMenu NIB document.
7. Create an instance of your test class in the NIB document.
8. Add a button to the window or a new menu item to a menu.
9. Select the button or menu item and connect its Sent Action to the action method defined in step 4. Do this by dragging the Sent Action connector to your test object, releasing the mouse button, and then choosing the action.

You now have an application that lets you exercise your code when you click the button or choose the test command from the menu. If you need editable parameters, add input text fields, checkboxes, sliders, or even date picker view objects to the window and bind those to IBOutlet properties in your test class. Objective-C bindings perform obvious type conversions automatically. That is, if you bind a text field to an integer property value, the text in the field will be translated into an integer.

Add more test methods, buttons, or menu commands as your needs grow.

An even simpler environment can be created using a Foundation command-line tool:

1. Create a new project using the Foundation Tool template.
2. Turn on garbage collection in the build settings.
3. Add your test code to the main() function.

Foundation tools do not have any graphical user interface and are not linked to the AppKit framework. Thus, they have no access to classes that deal with graphics or the user's login environment. The application's main() function will execute immediately upon running the application.

Summary

By now you should have a feel for how applications are developed using Xcode, and the skill to create your own applications. The basic steps and tools are pretty much the same for almost any project, be it a browser plug-in or an iPhone application. I will warn you that this chapter merely scratched the surface of Xcode. Xcode itself is both broad and deep—entire books have been written about it. Consider this introduction as more of a stroll down the Champs-Élysées than an exhaustive tour of Paris.

Now that you have some grounding in practical development, the next few chapters will delve deeper into specific Objective-C technologies.

CHAPTER 5

■ ■ ■

Exploring Protocols and Categories

Objective-C provides two additional schemes for defining methods: protocols and categories. This chapter will describe both, explain how they differ, show how they are used, and present some design patterns that incorporate them.

Objective-C *protocols* are equivalent to Java interfaces. Protocols are employed just as interfaces are in Java, although less frequently. Objective-C programmers are more likely to use a relaxed form called an *informal protocol*.

Objective-C *categories* add methods to a class, independent of its primary class declaration (@interface). The concept of a category may seem very foreign to a Java developer, but it's really quite simple. Categories are used to isolate or hide portions of a class's implementation, break complex classes into manageable pieces, and attach functionality to a class that would normally be outside its domain.

Protocols

A protocol (interface) is defined using a @protocol directive, as shown in Listing 5-1. The directive lists the methods required by the protocol. Like a Java interface, a protocol doesn't contain any instance variables—only methods.

Listing 5-1. *Game Protocols*

```
@interface VenusAttacks : Game
...
@end

@class Thing;

@protocol Living

- (float)age;
- (float)health;
- (NSDictionary*)healthInfo;

@end
```

```
@protocol Communicating

- (NSArray*)recipientsInRange;
- (void)sendMessage:(NSString*)messsage to:(id<Communicating>)recipient;

@end

@protocol Storing

- (NSDictionary*)inventory;
- (BOOL)giveItem:(Thing*)item to:(id<Storing>)recipient;
- (BOOL)acceptItem:(Thing*)item from:(id<Storing>)recipient;

@end

@interface Thing : NSObject
...
@end

@interface Weapon : Thing
...
@end

@interface Radio : Thing <Communicating>
...
@end

@interface StorageLocker : Thing <Storing>
...
@end

@interface Character : Thing <Living,Communicating>
...
@end

@interface Earthling : Character <Storing>
...
@end

@interface Venusian : Character
...
@end
```

The code in Listing 5-1 defines three protocols for objects in the VenusAttacks adventure game. The protocols (interfaces) are Living, Communicating, and Storing. A class declares the protocols that it implements between angle brackets following the name of its superclass. The StorageLocker class implements all of the methods defined by the Storing protocol. The Character class implements all of the methods defined by both the Living and Communicating protocols.

In Objective-C parlance, StorageLocker *conforms to* the Storing protocol.

When a class conforms to a protocol, it is required to implement all of the methods defined by that protocol. Failing to implement a method defined in a protocol is a compile-time error. Conforming to a protocol implies the prototypes for the methods in that protocol. Thus, it is not necessary for the

StorageLocker class @interface to explicitly declare that it implements the -(NSDictionary*)inventory method; that is already implied by <Storing>.

Like Java Interfaces, protocols are inherited by subclasses and are additive. The Earthling class conforms to the Storing, Living, and Communicating protocols. Venusian objects conform to the Living and Communicating protocols, but not the Storing protocol—Venusians have no pockets.

Protocol names can be combined with a class name in a type expression. The declaration Weapon<Communicating> *weapon = nil defines a pointer to a Weapon class object that is *assumed* to implement the Communicating protocol. The compiler will allow messages from both Weapon and Communicating to be sent to that object.

■**Caution** Unlike Java, Objective-C does not test objects for class or protocol membership during assignment. If you assigned a weapon object pointer to the Weapon<Communicating> *weapon variable, and that object does not conform to the Communicating protocol, that fact will not be discovered until the object is sent a sendMessage:to: message (throwing an unrecognized selector exception).

In Java you can use an interface name as if it were a class type. When you want to declare or cast an object to mean "a reference to *any* class of object that implements said protocol" in Objective-C, combine the protocol name with the id type, as in id<Storing>. When id is used in this form, it loses its normal permissiveness. A variable of this type is assumed to *only* accept messages defined by that protocol.

Protocols can extend and combine other protocols. Listing 5-2 defines the FTLCommunicating protocol, which itself conforms to the Communicating protocol. Any class that conforms to FTLCommunicating must implement all of the methods defined by FTLCommunicating and Communicating. A subprotocol doesn't have to declare any new methods; it can be used simply to aggregate multiple protocols.

Listing 5-2. Subprotocol

```
@protocol FTLCommunicating <Communicating>

- (id)receiveMessageBeforeBeingSent;

@end
```

Each protocol definition is typically saved in its own header (.h) file, which is then imported (#import "Living.h") by classes that conform to or reference it.

Informal Protocol

An informal protocol is a set of methods that a programmer expects an object to implement. The set of methods is not declared in any formal way, which is why Objective-C protocols are sometimes referred to as *formal protocols*, to distinguish them from informal protocols. Informal protocols are little more than a programming convention—hopefully, one documented by the programmer.

Informal protocols are attractive in Objective-C for two reasons. As previously mentioned, Objective-C does not verify the class of an object when an assignment is made. Whether an object does, or does not, implement a protocol or method is ignored until a message is actually sent to the object. This makes it easy to define an object reference that *assumes* an object implements a set of methods, but makes no assurances that it actually does.

Programmatically determining if an object implements a method is also trivial. Combining these two features, you can effortlessly pass around an object of indeterminate aptitude, assessing the capabilities of the object when the need arises.

To illustrate the contrast between a formal protocol (interface) and an informal protocol, consider the task of intercepting a request to close a window. The javax.swing.JWindow class has an addWindowStateListener(WindowStateListener l) method. To register itself as a listener, an object must implement to the WindowStateListener interface in order to pass itself as the parameter in the addWindowStateListener() call. Once registered, the object then receives event callbacks and watches for WINDOW_CLOSING events.

The Cocoa framework takes a much more casual approach to the same problem. An object that wants to intercept the closing of a window sets itself as the window's delegate object. Before a window is closed, NSWindow examines the delegate object to determine if it implements the -(BOOL)windowShouldClose:(id)window method. If it does, it sends the windowShouldClose: message to the object and examines the results. If not, it ignores the delegate and proceeds to close the window.

The -windowShouldClose: method defines an informal protocol: either the object implements -windowShouldClose: or it doesn't. A hypothetical implementation of the window closing logic is shown in Listing 5-3.

Listing 5-3. *Testing for an Informal Protocol*

```
BOOL shouldClose = YES;
if ([delegate respondsToSelector:@selector(windowShouldClose:)])
    shouldClose = [delegate windowShouldClose:self];  // ask delegate for permission
if (!shouldClose)
    return;
```

This programming style has elements of aspect-oriented programming, where common capabilities ("aspects") are scattered across heterogeneous classes. This design pattern is repeated for other window related activities. The window delegate can intervene in the resizing of a window, but only if it implements the -windowWillResize:toSize: method. A delegate is given the opportunity to prepare for a modal dialog sheet, but only if it implements the -window:willPositionSheet:usingRect: method.

Testing an object for class membership, protocol conformance, and method implementation is covered in more detail in Chapter 10.

Combining Formal and Informal Protocols

Starting with Objective-C 2.0, formal and informal protocols can be combined. An example TableDataSource protocol is shown in Listing 5-4. The protocol defines a set of methods that a data model object should implement in order to provide data to a hypothetical Table object.

Listing 5-4. *TableDataSource Protocol*

```
@protocol TableDataSource
@required
- (int)numberOfRowsInTable:(Table*)table;
- (id)table:(Table*)table objectForColumn:(int)col row:(int)row;
@optional
- (void)table:(Table*)table setObject:(id)object forColumn:(int)col row:(int)row;
@end
```

This protocol has two required methods (the number of rows in the data set, and a method to obtain the object for a specific cell) and one optional method (for setting the value of a specific cell). The Table class uses the first two methods to obtain values in the data set, and the third to alter data in the set. If the data source object doesn't implement the final method, Table treats the data set as immutable.

A class that conforms to this protocol must implement all the methods declared after @required, but may choose to implement any or none of the @optional methods. Methods declared before, or in the absence of, either directive are @required by default.

Testing an object to determine if it conforms to the TableDataSource protocol would tell you that the object implements all the @required methods, but not necessarily any of the @optional methods. Those would have to be tested singly.

An important reason for declaring optional methods—besides documenting them—is for the benefit of the compiler. The Objective-C compiler assembles method invocations most reliably when the method has been prototyped. This is explained in more detail in Chapter 6. The TableDataSource protocol provides prototypes for all of the methods, even those that are never implemented.

■ **Note** Prior to Objective-C 2.0, it was common to declare a formal protocol that was never formally adopted by any class, just for the purpose of providing the compiler with method prototypes. Prototypes for informal protocol methods can also be declared using categories, described later in this chapter.

Whether you choose to use formal protocols, informal protocols, or some combination of the two depends on your needs. Formal protocols ensure that all of the methods in the protocol are implemented and conformance can be verified with a single test. Informal protocols are more flexible and dynamic, but may require additional documentation and programmer cooperation.

Categories

A category is a named fragment of a class definition. In Java, a class is defined in a single monolithic statement. In Objective-C, parts of a class definition can be split off into groups of auxiliary methods. Each group is a category. Categories have a variety of applications.

A category is defined just like a class, using @interface and @implementation directives, except that the category is identified using an existing class name followed by the category name in parentheses. Like protocols (interfaces), categories cannot add new instance variables to a class—just methods. Categories can define both instance and class methods.

The code in Listing 5-5 is the controller for a recipe management application. The RecipeBoxController object handles the top-level application commands, like creating new recipe and shopping list documents.

Listing 5-5. *Monolithic Recipe Box Controller*

```
@interface RecipeBoxController : NSObject {
    NSMutableArray*        recipes;
    NSMutableDictionary*   recipeIndex;
}

- (id)init;
```

```
- (Document*)newRecipe;
- (Document*)newShoppingList;
- (Document*)newShoppingListFromRecipes:(NSIndexSet*)recipeIndexes;

@end

@implementation RecipeBoxController

...

@end
```

As the program grows in complexity, it becomes cumbersome to maintain all of the controller methods in a single class definition. Categories are used to subdivide the class definition into manageable modules, as shown in Listing 5-6.

Listing 5-6. Recipe Box Categories

```
@interface RecipeBoxController : NSObject {
    NSMutableArray*         recipes;
    NSMutableDictionary*    recipeIndex;
}

- (id)init;

- (Document*)newRecipe;

@end

@implementation RecipeBoxController

...

@end

@interface RecipeBoxController (ShoppingLists)

- (Document*)newShoppingList;
- (Document*)newShoppingListFromRecipes:(NSIndexSet*)recipeIndexes;

@end

@implementation RecipeBoxController (ShoppingLists)

...

@end
```

After the reorganization, the new recipe document method is still implemented in the primary RecipeBoxController class. All of the methods that create shopping list documents have been sequestered into the ShoppingLists category, which can be compiled as a separate module. Methods defined in the ShippingLists category are first-class citizens of the RecipeBoxController class. They have the same scope and variable access as methods defined in the principal `RecipeBoxController` class. At runtime, the class in Listing 5-5 functions identically to the class and category in Listing 5-6.

Using Categories for Organization

Subdividing a large class into manageable pieces is one use for categories. It is also useful for encapsulating the knowledge or dependencies required by a functional subsection of a class. In the recipe application example, the `ShoppingLists` category implementation would undoubtedly need to import class definitions for shopping lists, ingredient lists, a grocery store editor, and so on. The implementation of the primary `RecipeBoxController` class does not need to know anything about those classes.

Categories allow related methods of a class to be organized into their own module, without requiring any additional classes or complexity. This reduces dependencies and keeps your application design modular. This is particularly useful in collaborative development environments where one programmer might be working on new recipe functionality while another is working on new shopping list features. Both programmers can make changes to the same class while remaining independent of one another.

The Builder pattern is another application for categories. The Builder pattern moves complex object construction outside the class. In Java, the Builder pattern would normally be implemented as a separate class (sometimes called a helper class). In Objective-C, the complex construction code can be isolated from the main class definition via a category.

Hiding Methods

A popular use of categories is to hide portions of a class's interface, typically to discourage the use of methods designed for internal consumption. In Java, methods can be scoped as private or protected, making them inaccessible outside the class. In Objective-C, you can "hide" a set of methods in a category. Listing 5-7 shows how the internal methods of the Toaster class are isolated in the `Private` category.

Listing 5-7. Methods in a Private Category

```
@interface ToasterController : NSObject {
    @private
    float       darkness;
}

- (void)setDarkness:(float)level;
- (void)startToasting;
- (void)stopToasting;

@end

@interface ToasterController (Private)

- (float)darkness;
- (CarrierState)carrierPosition;
- (NSTimeInterval)cycleTime;
- (void)setCycleTime:(NSTimeInterval)cycleTime;
- (void)finishedToasting:(NSTimer*)timer;

@end
```

To make this effective, the declaration of the ToasterController (Private) category is saved in its own header (.h) file. Modules that use the ToasterController class import only the ToasterController.h file, which does not include any of the Private category methods. In the absence of the Private category declaration, the compiler—and by extension the programmer—remains blissfully ignorant of the internal control methods.

■ **Note** By convention, a category is saved in a header file named after the class "+" the name of the category. In the example in Listing 5-7, the ToasterController (Private) category would be saved in the ToasterController+Private.h file.

This could also be done with just two source files. The ToasterController.h file would contain only the primary @interface ToasterController declaration. The implementation (.m) file would begin by importing its header. It would then declare the @interface for the Private category, followed by @implementation directives for both the ToasterController class and its Private category methods. No other module would have knowledge of these internal methods.

This is such a common use of categories that Objective-C 2.0 has added the concept of extensions, described later in this section, which formalizes this technique.

Augmenting Foreign Classes

A feature that will seem almost bizarre to Java developers is that categories can attach methods to *any* class. This permits a class to be extended without subclassing it or altering its original class definition. More importantly, subclasses of the class inherit the category methods.

The NSArray class in the Cocoa framework defines an -(id)lastObject convenience method, approximately equivalent to the statement [array objectAtIndex:[array count]-1]. For symmetry, I wish the NSArray class designers had also included a -(id)firstObject method too. Objective-C grants my wish in Listing 5-8.

Listing 5-8. NSArray Category

```
@interface NSArray (MyCollectionAdditions)

- (id)firstObject;

@end

@implementation NSArray (MyCollectionAdditions)

- (id)firstObject
{
    return ([self objectAtIndex:0]);
}

@end
```

MyCollectionAdditions dynamically alters the behavior of the operating system's NSArray class by inserting a new method. My application can now send the -firstObject message to any NSArray object in my process.

■**Caution** When a category and class both implement the same method, the category's method *replaces* the one in the class. It does not override it; there is no way to invoke the original method. A call to [super method] in the category's code will invoke the superclass's method, not the class's original method. If two or more categories implement the same method for the same class, which gets invoked at runtime is unpredictable.

Besides being able to decorate classes with convenience features, categories are very useful for adding functionality to classes that are outside of their domain. Returning to the example in this book's introduction, the AppKit framework defines the NSStringDrawing category that extends the base NSString class with the additional methods shown in Listing 5-9.

Listing 5-9. NSStringDrawing Category

```
@interface NSString(NSStringDrawing)

- (NSSize)sizeWithAttributes:(NSDictionary *)attrs;
- (void)drawAtPoint:(NSPoint)point withAttributes:(NSDictionary *)attrs;
- (void)drawInRect:(NSRect)rect withAttributes:(NSDictionary *)attrs;

@end
```

All NSString objects inherit these methods. This allows you to write the much more natural and concise [string draw], rather than being forced to write [currentDrawingContext drawString:string].

■**Note** Categories underscore the fact that Objective-C classes are assembled dynamically at runtime. A GUI application that loads the AppKit framework (containing the NSStringDrawing category), injects these additional drawing methods into the base NSString class. An Objective-C command-line utility linked only to the Foundation framework (which contains no graphic drawing classes) does not load the AppKit framework and will not have these methods implemented for its NSString objects.

Categories allow you to implement methods where they are convenient and make sense, without sacrificing good programming practices like encapsulation and modularity.

As you explore various frameworks, you will discover many categories that expand classes with useful methods that would be totally inappropriate to implement in those classes. The NSStringPathExtensions category adds a slew of file system path manipulations to NSString objects. Similarly, the NSURLUtilities category adds URL character-encoding methods to NSString. NSPasteboardSupport adds clipboard copy and paste methods to the NSURL class, and so on.

The important thing to remember is that methods in Objective-C classes are not confined to the domain of the class. When looking for methods in the documentation, don't confine your search to the classes within the domain of responsibility. NSGraphicsContext doesn't implement any drawing methods. The objects that get drawn (NSString, NSImage, NSAttributedString, etc.) each have their own -draw method, some courtesy of categories supplied by NSGraphicsContext.

As you write your own code, strive to break out of the strict Java model of method organization. In Java, a method that encodes a game character's name would naturally be a method in the Character class—because that's the class with the knowledge required to encode a character's name. In Objective-C, consider writing a category that adds your own -(id)encodedCharacterName method to the core NSString class.

■**Caution** Take extra care and consideration when adding a category to the root NSObject class. It may cause unanticipated, and potentially hazardous, side effects. Every Class object (the quasi-object that defines a class at runtime) is also a subclass of NSObject, so any NSObject method becomes both an instance method *and* a class method. This means that the self variable might refer to an instance object or a Class object, depending on the context. Also, an NSObject method cannot send messages to super.

Extensions

Objective-C 2.0 introduces the concept of an extension. An extension is, essentially, an anonymous category. An extension is used to subdivide a class's @interface, but not its @implementation. It is particularly useful for excluding method prototypes from a class's public interface, as described earlier in the "Hiding Methods" section.

The @interface directive of an extension is identical to a category, except that the category name is empty. An extension does not have a separate @implementation. Methods declared in extensions must be implemented in the class's @implementation, along with the rest of the regular class methods (see Listing 5-10).

Listing 5-10. Extension

```
@interface CaseDocument : NSObject {
    @private
    CaseNumber      caseNumber;
}

- (CaseNumber)caseNumber;

@end

@interface CaseDocument ()

- (void)setCaseNumber:(CaseNumber)number;

@end

@implementation CaseDocument

- (CaseNumber)caseNumber { return (caseNumber); }
- (void)setCaseNumber:(CaseNumber)number { caseNumber = number; }

@end
```

It is assumed that the first @interface directive in Listing 5-10 is stored in the CaseDocument.h file, and is imported by other modules that use the CaseDocument class. The @interface for the extension could be in its own header file or part of the CaseDocument implementation file. Either way, the methods in the extension are not publicly known, making the caseNumber property appear immutable to other modules, but mutable within the implementation of the class. When compiling the extension declaration, also compile the original class declaration. The compiler works best when it can relate the extension to the class.

Remember that category and extensions only hide the declaration of methods from the compiler and programmer. At runtime, all of these methods exist and can be discovered using introspection. In the CaseDocument example in Listing 5-10, the caseNumber property will appear to be mutable to technologies like Key Value Observing. Those technologies dynamically examine the object at runtime to determine if it implements a matched pair of getter and setting methods for the caseNumber property—which CaseDocument does. To make caseNumber appear read-only to introspection, the internal setCaseNumber: method should be renamed to something like -(void)assignToCase:(CaseNumber)number. This breaks the naming contract for the property, leaving caseNumber with a getter but no setter.

Summary

As you can see, Objective-C protocols and categories are more flexible and dynamic than Java interfaces. They can declare optional methods, subdivide a class's implementation into multiple modules, and augment other classes with new functionality.

Classes, protocols, and categories exhaust the techniques for declaring methods. The next chapter explains the various ways of invoking them.

CHAPTER 6

■ ■ ■

Sending Messages

Sending messages (calling methods) is fundamental to programming. You already know the basics of Objective-C messages. This chapter delves into the mechanics of how messages are sent, describes three different techniques for invoking methods programmatically, and explains how to write methods that accept a variable number of arguments. It isn't absolutely necessary to understand these topics in detail, but expanding your knowledge makes technologies like notifications, actions, remote invocation, and Key-Value Observing a little more comprehensible.

As briefly explained in Chapter 3, methods in Objective-C are not *called* in the Java sense. Messages are *sent* to objects via a dynamic dispatching function. Sending a message to an object involves (approximately) these steps:

1. The message parameters are assembled and copied onto the stack.

2. A pointer to the receiver and the message selector constant are copied onto the stack.

3. The message dispatch function is called. In Apple's implementation of Objective-C the function called is typically objc_msgSend(), but in general, it's best to ignore the implementation details of the runtime system.

4. If the receiver value is nil, the dispatching function returns immediately.

5. The message dispatch function uses the receiving object's pointer to obtain its isa instance variable. This variable points to the object's Class object, which contains the dispatch table for the class.

6. The selector is used to look up the address of the method's code in the dispatch table.

7. The CPU's program counter is loaded with the address and the method's code begins executing.

8. Execution proceeds until the method ends, and program control returns to the code that originally sent the message.

■**Note** Message dispatching might seem like a convoluted and inefficient procedure, but it is highly optimized. Selectors are constants and the method dispatch tables are cached. In most cases, sending a message takes only a few nanoseconds on modern systems. For performance-sensitive applications, even that can be eliminated (see "Calling Methods Directly" at the end of this chapter). In general, don't be overly concerned about message performance.

A class method receives all of the message parameters as automatic variables, including the receiver and the selector. The self variable contains the pointer to the receiver and the _cmd variable contains the message selector. The _cmd variable is usually uninteresting because it is always the selector for the method.

Compiling Messages

The Objective-C compiler translates each method invocation into the machine instructions that will send the message. In order to emit the correct machine instructions, the compiler must know the size and type of each parameter and the type of the return value.

Java goes to some lengths to ensure that the compiler knows exactly how to construct each method call. Java always has the details of each class, the class of an object reference is always known, and Java method signatures ensure that there is never any ambiguity about the parameter types a method expects. As you might imagine, Objective-C is considerably more lax. This occasionally leads to circumstances where the exact meaning of a method invocation is ambiguous. I'll explain why this can happen and what you can do to rectify it.

Keep in mind that these are exceptional cases. The vast majority of the time, the compiler knows exactly what to do. If the receiver's variable type is a pointer to a specific class and the method prototypes for that class have been compiled, the compiler has all of the information it needs.

However, if the compiler has not compiled a prototype for the method, or the class of the receiver is vague (i.e., id), the compiler must either guess the types of the parameters or arbitrarily choose a method prototype from those it knows about.

Undeclared Methods

The first case arises when a method prototype has never been compiled, either by omitting the class definition or when a class definition is incomplete—the method might be declared in a category of that class or not declared at all. When this occurs, as shown in Listing 6-1, the compiler infers the parameter types from the invocation. In other words, the compiler guesses.

Listing 6-1. Undeclared Method Invocation

```
@class ToasterController;
ToasterController *toaster;
…
[toaster setDarkness:1];
warning: no '-setDarkness:' method found
warning: (Messages without a matching method signature will be assumed
warning:  to return 'id' and accept '...' as arguments.)
```

The code in Listing 6-1 results in a "no method found" compiler warning. The compiler has no knowledge of a method named -setDarkness:. Without any information, it assumes that the parameters of the message are the same types as those in the invocation, and that the method returns an object identifier (object pointer of type id). Assuming that the ToasterController class is the one from the previous chapter, the compiler will generate erroneous code. That's because the parameter in the invocation is an integer, but the actual -setDarkness: method expects a float. Integer and floating-point values are not interchangeable, so the -setDarkness: method will receive a garbage value instead.

The solution to this problem is simple: include the method declaration. The module that includes this code should have used an #import directive, as shown in Listing 6-2. Now the compiler has the method prototype for the class. It knows that the -setDarkness: method takes a float parameter and the compiler correctly promotes the integer constant to a floating-point value before sending the message.

Listing 6-2. Declared Method Invocation

```
#import "ToasterController.h"
ToasterController *toaster;
…
[toaster setDarkness:1];
```

As a rule, never ignore "no method found" compiler warnings. Always import or declare the classes and methods you employ. There's rarely any good reason why you can't include the needed declarations, and it ensures correctly compiled code.

Ambiguous Methods

A subtler problem occurs when the type of the receiver is unknown (type id) or incomplete (defined only by a @class directive), but the compiler has seen at least one method prototype matching its identifier. In these cases, the compiler confidently assumes that the receiver implements the method you invoked—you're the programmer; you must know you're doing, right? It searches through all known method prototypes and compiles the message using the first method identifier matching the statement.

In most cases this works fine. Statistically, method identifiers tend to be unique or functionally identical. In the entirety of the Cocoa framework (which is quite large), there is only one -setLocation: method. There are six different -setTag: methods implemented by varying classes, but they all have the same prototype (-(void)setTag:(int)tag). So it doesn't matter which prototype the compiler chooses to use; the compiled code will be correct.

The problem occurs in the rare case where there are two or more methods with identical identifiers but with different parameter or return types (see Listing 6-3). One such case is the -options message. There are six -options methods defined in the Cocoa framework. Two return pointers to dictionaries, three return integers, and one returns a custom enum value.

Listing 6-3. Ambiguous Method Invocation

```
id mystery;
…
NSDictionary *options = [mystery options];
warning: initialization makes pointer from integer without a cast
```

Listing 6-3 sends the -options message to the mystery object. Without any class information, Objective-C uses the first prototype for -options that it finds. The warning occurs because, again, the compiler has guessed wrong. It used a prototype for -options that returns an integer instead of a pointer to a dictionary object. It is the implied promotion of an integer to a pointer that generates the warning.

To resolve the ambiguity, cast the receiver. Casting the mystery variable in Listing 6-4 tells the compiler to assume that the receiver is an NSTextTab object. The compiler restricts itself to using method prototypes from the NSTextTab class. It compiles the correct code and no spurious warnings are generated. In the second example, the sidekick variable is cast to any class conforming to the Communicating protocol from the previous chapter. Again, the compiler restricts the receiver to methods defined in Communicating.

Listing 6-4. Disambiguating Messages

```
id mystery;
id hero, sidekick;
…
NSDictionary *options = [(NSTextTab*)mystery options];
[(id<Communicating>)sidekick sendMessage:@"Help!" to:hero];
```

If the message is ambiguous because the receiver is a class type that hasn't been defined—it was declared only by a @class directive—the solution is to #import its full declaration.

Coercion

A typecast can be used to intentionally coerce Objective-C into letting you send a method that it doesn't believe the object implements. A Character object does not accept the -giveItem:to: message. If, programmatically, you discover that a Character object is actually an Earthling object (or one of its subclasses), you may want to send it a subclass-specific message. Casting lets you override the compiler's normal assumptions about the receiver and compile the appropriate method invocation, as shown in Listing 6-5.

Listing 6-5. Coercing Method Invocation

```
Character *player;
Earthling *hero;
Thing *secret;
…
if ([player respondsToSelector:@selector(giveItem:to:)])
    [(Earthling*)player giveItem:secret to:hero]; // assume player is Earthling
```

Sending Messages Programmatically

Objective-C makes sending messages to objects very easy—not just using the method invocation syntax discussed up to this point, but programmatically allowing variables to determine what message is sent. The ease by which messages can be composed programmatically has encouraged its adoption of Objective-C in a wide variety of solutions and design patterns. You'll encounter many services that send messages to, or on behalf of, your code using a pointer to the receiver, a selector (SEL), or both. Some examples include the following:

Controls: Every visual control object (button, menu item, checkbox, radio button, slider, …) has an action. An action consists of a target property (the receiver) and an action property (a selector). When the control is activated, it sends the action to the target. See Chapter 20.

Notifications: Timers and notification services send a message to an object when an event occurs. You determine the object and the method to invoke using an object identifier and a selector. See Chapter 18.

Callbacks: Components like a model dialog notify your code by sending your object the message of your choice when the dialog is dismissed.

Delegates: The delegate pattern is used extensively in the Cocoa framework. The delegate is always a variable. Sometimes the message it receives is also variable, determined using a selector you specify. See Chapter 17.

In Java, programmatic method invocation is complex and somewhat cumbersome, involving several introspection objects. Often, Java interfaces are defined just so an object has a well-defined entry point to receive messages. In Objective-C, a simple message is extremely lightweight, requiring only a pointer to the receiver and an integer selector. In reality, message selectors are pointers to internal runtime data structures, resolved by the linker when the program's binary is loaded into memory. From the programmer's perspective, selectors should be treated as opaque integer constants.

There are basically three ways to compose and send a message programmatically. The most common, and quickest, technique is to use one of the -performSelector: methods provided by the root class. The most flexible and Java-like technique is to construct an NSInvocation object. Finally, an Objective-C method can be called directly as a C function. This last technique is popular with performance-sensitive applications.

■**Caution** The cardinal rule for all messages is that the parameters supplied in the message *must* match the type, size, and order of the parameters the method expects. None of the programmatic message-sending techniques provides any kind of type checking, type conversion, promotion, or auto-boxing.

Immediate Messages

The root NSObject class implements a family of -performSelector: methods. You can use them to send any message to an object, exactly as if your code had invoked the method directly. The code in Listing 6-6 shows the -className message being sent to an arbitrary object using a direct message, and then again programmatically using the -performSelector: method.

Listing 6-6. *Sending a Message with -performSelector:*

```
id anything = …;
NSString *name;
name = [anything className];

SEL variableMessage = @selector(className);
name = [anything performSelector:variableMessage];
```

The two invocations of -className in Listing 6-6 are functionally identical. The second is slightly slower because it sends two messages: performSelector: is sent to the object, which then immediately sends itself the className message. The value returned by the className method is passed back to the caller.

Sending a message using -performSelector: is quick, easy, and lightweight. The principle drawback of -performSelector: is that it only accepts none, one, or two object identifiers as parameters and always returns an object identifier as a return value. By casting, you can coerce the compiler to pass or return any pointer value; all pointers are the same size and format. Listing 6-7 shows how to pass an integer pointer instead of an object pointer. The pointer to (address of) the integer is cast to an object identifier so that it agrees with the parameter type of the message. This just mollifies the compiler; no actual value conversion takes place.

Listing 6-7. *Passing Other Kinds of Pointers to -performSelector:*

```
@implementation ShiftyMethods

- (void)incrementAnInteger:(int*)valuePtr
{
    *valuePtr += 1;
}

@end

...

ShiftyMethods *shifty = [ShiftyMethods new];
int i = 1;
[shifty performSelector:@selector(incrementAnInteger:) withObject:(id)&i];
```

If the methods being called expect more parameters, or more exotic parameters such as long long integers, floating point values, or structures, you will have to use one of the other techniques in this chapter.

Table 6-1 lists the basic -performSelector: methods implemented by NSObject. All of these methods are compatible with methods returning some kind of pointer or void. When used with a void method, ignore the value returned by -performSelector:.

Table 6-1. *Immediate Invocation Methods*

Method	Description
-(id)performSelector:(SEL)message	Sends the message specified by the selector to the receiver. The message includes no parameter and returns the object identifier returned by the method.
-(id)performSelector:(SEL)message withObject:(id)firstParam	Sends the message to the receiver. The message includes a single pointer as the first parameter, and returns the returned pointer to the caller.
-(id)performSelector:(SEL)message withObject:(id)firstParam withObject:(id)secondParam	Sends the message to the receiver. The message includes two pointer parameters, returning the returned pointer to the caller.

Deferred Messages

A message can also be queued and sent to an object at some future time. The method might be invoked on a different thread, after some time has elapsed, or just "whenever." To understand how messages are deferred, you need to know a little about run loops.

A run loop is an event queue that executes in its own thread. Every Cocoa application has at least one run loop. The first run loop started is christened the *main run loop* or *main thread.* All user interaction (mouse clicks, keyboard commands, display updates, animation, and so on) is fed to the main run loop and executes in the main thread.

You can create additional threads in your process. Starting a run loop takes over a thread and turns it into an *event driven* thread. A run loop's life is spent pulling an event from its event queue, processing it, and immediately "looping" around to process the next waiting event. If there are no pending events, the thread suspends. You can read more about creating threads and run loops in Chapter 15.

One type of event that can be pushed onto a run loop's queue is a method invocation. It is little more than a reference to an object and the message and parameters the object will receive. When an object message event appears at the top of the event queue, the run loop sends the message to the object.

The root NSObject class implements several methods for queuing a message on a run loop for later execution. The principal ones are shown in Table 6-2.

Table 6-2. *Deferred Invocation Methods*

Method	Description
`-(void)performSelector:(SEL)message withObject:(id)arg afterDelay:(NSTimeInterval)delay`	Queues a message that will be sent to the receiver in the current thread. The message is not queued until after delay seconds have elapsed.
`-(void)performSelectorOnMainThread:(SEL)message withObject:(id)arg waitUntilDone:(BOOL)wait`	Queues a message that will be sent to the receiver on the main thread. If wait is YES, the call will suspend the current thread until the method has finished executing.
`-(void)performSelector:(SEL)message onThread:(NSThread*)thread withObject:(id)arg waitUntilDone:(BOOL)wait`	Queues a message that will be sent to the receiver on the run loop attached to a specified thread. If wait is YES, the call will suspend the current thread until the method has finished executing.
`-(void)performSelectorInBackground:(SEL)message withObject:(id)arg`	Creates and starts a new thread. When the new thread begins executing, the message and arg argument are sent to the receiver which executes in that thread. When the method returns, the thread terminates.

The `-performSelector:withObject:afterDelay:` method pushes the message event onto the run loop of the currently running thread. The delay time is a floating-point value expressed in seconds. The run loop first waits for delay number of seconds to elapse then it queues the event to be executed at the next opportunity. The method does not guarantee the time the message will be sent, just that that message won't be sent any *earlier* than delay seconds in the future. To queue a message to be sent at the run loop's next opportunity, pass a delay of 0.0.

The `-performSelectorOnMainThread:…` and `-performSelector:onThread:…` methods both queue a message to be executed on a particular thread.

As described earlier, the main thread runs the primary run loop of the application. The `-performSelectorOnMainThread:` message is particularly useful to auxiliary threads that need to execute some action in the main thread (say, to update the value of a field in a window). Such methods *must* be performed on the main thread. The background thread can choose to send the message asynchronously by passing NO in the wait argument, or suspend until the deferred message has completed by passing YES.

The -performSelector:onThread: variant queues up a message to be executed on any thread with a run loop. If the target thread passed to this, or implied by the -performSelectorOnMainThread:, method is the same as the currently running thread, the message is immediately sent to the object (using -performSelector:) without any run loop involvement.

All three of the previous methods have an alternate form that accepts an additional mode parameter. Run loops operate in modes. A mode is a filter that ignores certain events in the queue that aren't appropriate in the current mode. Read more about run loop modes in the Threads chapter.

The final -performSelectorInBackground:… method sends a message to an object in a newly created thread. This method does not use run loops. A thread is created for the sole purposes of executing the message, and is destroyed afterwards.

All of these methods provide a single object identifier parameter that will be included with the message. If the method being invoked doesn't expect an argument, the value is ignored; set it to nil.

Object-Oriented Method Invocation

The role of Java's java.lang.reflect.Method class is filled largely by NSMethodSignature and NSInvocation in Cocoa. These classes form a high-level, object-oriented, interface to the method's definition, and a means to invoke it. NSMethodSignature is an immutable description of the method's parameters and return type. NSInvocation encapsulates the receiver, message, parameter values, and return value that constitute an invocation of the method. Think of NSMethodSelector as the method's prototype and NSInvocation as the act of sending the message.

While the simple -performSelector: methods are fast and easy to use, they lack flexibility. NSInvocation can deal with methods that take any kind or number of parameters. This includes everything from a single byte to an entire structure.

To create an NSInvocation object you must first obtain the NSMethodSignature for the method. Any object will return the signature for one of its methods when sent a -methodSignatureForSelector: message. If you don't have a representative object, send the Class object an +instanceMethodSignatureForSelector: message. Once you've obtained the NSMethodSignature for the method, create an NSInvocation object using +invocationWithMethodSignature:.

The target, parameter values, and return value are set individually and persist in the NSInvocation object. This is different than Java. The Method object is passed the target object and all of the parameters in the call to invoke(), which retains no information about the invocation after it returns.

NSInvocation parameter and return values are configured one at a time using -setArgument:atIndex:. Each parameter value is set by passing -setArgument:atIndex: the address of the parameter's value—not the value to be passed. This is true even for object pointer values; pass a pointer *to* the object pointer, *not* the pointer itself. NSInvocation uses its knowledge of the parameter type to copy the value at that address into the parameter stream.

Listing 6-8 demonstrates using NSInvocation to send an NSString object the -substring: message along with the functionally equivalent code in Java.

Listing 6-8. *Object-Oriented Method Invocation*

Java
```
try {
    String prose = "Do nine men interpret?";

    // Get Method for String.substring(int,int)
    Class[] paramTypes = { int.class, int.class };
    Method method = prose.getClass().getMethod("substring",paramTypes);
```

```
    // Invoke prose.substring(3,7)
    Object[] paramValues = { new Integer(3), new Integer(7) };
    String count = (String)method.invoke(prose,paramValues);

    System.out.println(count+" men, I nod.");
    }
catch (Exception e) {
    e.printStackTrace();
    }
```

Objective-C
```
NSString *prose = @"Do nine men interpret?";
NSMethodSignature *signature;
NSInvocation *invocation;
NSString *count;

// Create invocation for -[NSString substringWithRange:] method
signature = [prose methodSignatureForSelector:@selector(substringWithRange:)];
invocation = [NSInvocation invocationWithMethodSignature:signature];
[invocation setSelector:@selector(substringWithRange:)];

// Set range structure as first parameter (after self and _cmd)
NSRange range = NSMakeRange(3,4);
[invocation setArgument:&range atIndex:2];

// Invoke method and extract the return value
[invocation invokeWithTarget:prose];
[invocation getReturnValue:&count];

NSLog(@"%@ men, I nod.",count);
```

Unlike Java's Method object, NSInvocation does not perform any form of parameter type conversion. You must pass -setArgument:atIndex: a pointer to the exact type of variable the method expects. In the Java example in Listing 6-8, the parameter types are given as int.class, but the values passed as parameters are Integer objects. Java knows that the Integer object must be converted into a primitive int value before being passed to the substring(int,int) method. NSInvocation performs no such conversion. If a method expects an int argument, the value passed to -setArgument:atIndex: must be a pointer to a primitive int value (&myValue) that contains the value to send.

Variable parameter indexes start at 2. The first two parameters are always the hidden self and _cmd parameters passed to every method. Use -setTarget: and -setSelector: to configure those two properties. For convenience, -invokeWithTarget: sets the target and invokes the method with a single message.

You might find it odd that you must configure the method that will be sent. After all, you used the method selector to create the invocation object in the first place. That's because the NSMethodSignature isn't associated with a particular message, it only defines the "shape" of the parameters. You can reconfigure NSInvocation to send different messages that all expect the same type, number, and order of parameters. For example, you could create a single NSInvocation object that sends listeners a callback message with four parameters, but lets the clients of your service choose the message they want to receive. The client has the flexibility to create a method with any name they want, as long as it expects the correct parameters. Your code can efficiently reuse a single NSInvocation object for all callbacks.

Calling Methods Directly

Every method you write eventually gets compiled into a static C function. Pointers to these functions populate the dispatch tables of each Class object.

The compiler hides the names of these functions, so you are never exposed to them. But Objective-C will provide the address of each, making it possible to call methods directly—bypassing all of the nominal message dispatch logic. This technique is somewhat technical, but is useful if you ever need to invoke Objective-C methods from some other programming language or where message dispatching has a significant impact on performance.

The method -methodForSelector: returns the implementation—the address of the method's code—that will execute when the receiver is sent that message. The class method +instanceMethodForSelector: returns the address of the code that will nominally execute when an instance is sent that message. I've chosen my words here very carefully. An *individual* object can be modified so that the code executed when sent a message is different than the code executed by another object of the same class, or even the code that the Class object assumes each instance will execute. Don't casually assume that the method implementation address for one object is the same as that for another instance, or equal to the address returned by -[Class instanceMethodForSelector:]. The safest practice is to query an individual object for its implementation address and only use that address for that object. Read Chapter 26 (the "isa Swizzling" section) to get a better idea about how and why an object's methods might be dynamically altered.

The C function generated for each method expects a receiver object pointer (self) and a selector (_cmd) as the first two parameters. Any remaining parameters mirror those defined by the method. Listing 6-9 demonstrates calling a method via its implementation address.

Listing 6-9. *Calling a Method As a C Function*

```
@interface BezierPathMapper : NSObject {
    NSBezierPath *path;
}
@property (assign) NSBezierPath *path;

- (BOOL)containsAnyPoint:(NSPoint*)pointArray pointCount:(unsigned int)count;

@end

@implementation BezierPathMapper

@synthesize path;

- (BOOL)containsAnyPoint:(NSPoint*)pointArray pointCount:(unsigned int)count
{
    if (path==nil)
        return NO;

    // Get function address of -[NSBezierPath containsPoint:]
    typedef BOOL (*containsPointPtr)(id self, SEL _cmd, NSPoint point);
    containsPointPtr containsPointImpl =
        (containsPointPtr)[path methodForSelector:@selector(containsPoint:)];

    // Test every point in array by sending the path -containsPoint:
    unsigned int i;
    for (i=0; i<count; i++)
```

```
        if (containsPointImpl(path,@selector(containsPoint:),pointArray[i])!=NO)
            return YES;
    return NO;
}
```

@end

The -containsAnyPoint:pointCount: method of BezierPathMapper tests a sequence of coordinates to see if any reside inside its path property. The method begins by getting the implementation address of the path's -containsPoint: method. The crazy syntax you see surrounding this is how you declare a pointer to a function in C. The type consists of a complete function prototype describing the function's parameters and return type (BOOL foo(id self, SEL _cmd, NSPoint point)), with the name of the function replaced with a pointer declaration ((*containsPointPtr) replaces foo). The result is a variable that points to a function with that prototype. In a typedef statement, it results in a new pointer type. In Listing 6-9, a typedef is used so the entire function prototype doesn't have to be repeated when casting the value returned by -methodForSelector:. C allows a function pointer variable to be used as a function name, just as if there was a function named "containsPointImpl."

The receiver and selector parameters must be included in the call. While the selector is often ignored, it's always good programming practice to pass the selector constant of the method being called. Since this technique bypasses the dispatcher's nil receiver test, this code must first make sure that the function is never called for a nil path object—that would most likely cause the program to crash.

The code in Listing 6-9 is principally to demonstrate the technique. It's unlikely to result in any significant performance gains, even when testing thousands of points—mostly because the computations performed by -[NSBezierPath containsPoint:] probably far outweigh the trivial overhead of sending the message. Nevertheless, if the code executed by the method was very fast, and it was called millions of times, this technique could save valuable CPU time.

It should also be noted that calling a method directly might be simpler and faster than trying to use an NSInvocation, particularly in situations where the method being called has well-understood parameters.

Variable Arguments

One trick that Java doesn't have is variable arguments. Granted, Java 1.5 added variable argument syntax, but that's just syntactic sugar for the way Java has always handled variable arguments. The programmer (pre-Java 1.5) or the compiler (Java 1.5 and later) first creates an array to contain the variable arguments, populates it with the parameters (wrapping primitive values in objects), and then passes the single array object to the method.

Variable arguments in Objective-C are far more direct and raw: the sender may supply whatever additional parameters they want in the message. The additional parameters are unaltered and are pushed onto the stack exactly like any other parameter. The method parses the list of parameters programmatically when it executes. The type, order, and meaning of those parameters are agreed on by convention. Objective-C doesn't impose any restrictions on them, nor does it supply any type information about them. It's up to the caller to supply the kind of parameters the method is expecting.

■**Note** Objective-C "borrows" variable arguments from C. Everything in this section applies equally to plain old C functions.

To declare a variable argument list, follow the last parameter variable name with a comma and three periods (an ellipsis, but don't use the Unicode ellipsis character). When invoked, the named parameters may be followed by additional comma-separated parameters. There is no limit on the number or kind of additional parameters. The parameters sent to the method form a kind of data stream. The values of each parameter are extracted serially using special library functions. The process is loosely analogous to using a java.io.ObjectInputStream to read a sequence of serialized values.

Two commonly used Cocoa methods that accept variable arguments are demonstrated in Listing 6-10. The +[NSArray arrayWithObjects:...] method creates a new NSArray object pre-populated with the objects passed as parameters. The +[NSString stringWithFormat:...] method creates strings using a format string. The format string includes placeholders that are replaced with the values of the additional parameters. The example code shown in Listing 6-10 returns the string "Dark toast will take 45 seconds."

Listing 6-10. *Variable Argument Methods in Cocoa*

```
@interface NSArray

+ (id)arrayWithObjects:(id)firstObj, ...

@end

@interface NSString

+ (id)stringWithFormat:(NSString*)format, ...

@end

...

int toastTimes[] = { 8, 22, 35, 45, 60, 90 };
NSArray *toastDescriptions = [NSArray arrayWithObjects:@"Warm",
                                     @"Light",
                                     @"Medium",
                                     @"Dark",
                                     @"Very dark",
                                     @"Burnt",
                                     nil];

int level = 3;
int secs = toastTimes[level];
NSString *desc = [toastDescriptions objectAtIndex:level];

return [NSString stringWithFormat:@"%@ toast will take %d seconds.",desc,secs];
```

A method with variable arguments must assume the number and type of the parameters in the list. The parameter list doesn't include any type information or end-of-list indicator; it's just a raw sequence of bytes formed when the parameter values were pushed onto the stack. Consequently, the method must either assume the parameter types or infer them using information supplied in the named parameters.

The two Cocoa methods shown in Listing 6-10 demonstrate the two most common solutions to this problem. The +arrayWithObjects: method assumes that all of the additional parameters will be object pointers and the list is terminated by a final nil parameter.

The +stringWithFormat: method uses the format parameter to infer the sequence of parameter values that follow. The format string is scanned for format specifications. The first specification (%@) is an object formatter. This tells +stringWithFormat: that the first additional parameter is a pointer to an object. The %@ is replaced with the -description (toString()) value of the object. The next specification encountered is %d, indicating that the next parameter is a signed int (d stands for decimal). It extracts one int from the parameter stream and continues, until all of the format specifications in the string have been replaced.

In both cases, a programmer's agreement exists between the method and the caller. +arrayWithObjects: assumes that only object pointers are passed, terminated with a nil pointer. +stringWithFormat: assumes that the additional parameter agrees with the value types implied by the placeholders in the format string.

■**Caution** The compiler has no type information about variable parameters, so it assumes that all values are of the correct/expected type. The parameter 1 will pass an integer and 1.0 will pass a float. To remove any doubt, cast the parameter as in [NSString stringWithFormat:@"float %f, int %d, char %c",(float)34,(int)34,(char)34]. This will force the compiler to convert the parameter to the expected type before pushing onto the stack.

Writing your own variable argument method is not difficult, but it does require a little planning. You must design the method so the type and number of the additional parameters is known or can be inferred. Listing 6-11 rewrites the containsAnyPoints:pointCount: method to use a variable argument list, instead of an array of pointers.

Listing 6-11. *Variable Argument Implementation*

```
@interface BezierPathMapper : NSObject {
    NSBezierPath *path;
}
@property (assign) NSBezierPath *path;

- (BOOL)containsAnyOfCountPoints:(unsigned int)count, ...;

@end

@implementation BezierPathMapper

@synthesize path;

- (BOOL)containsAnyOfCountPoints:(unsigned int)count, ...
{
    va_list varList;
    BOOL    hit = NO;
    NSPoint point;

    va_start(varList,count);
    while (count!=0) {
        point = va_arg(varList,NSPoint); // copy next point
```

```
        if ([path containsPoint:point]) {
            hit = YES;
            break;
        }

        count--;
    }
    va_end(varList);

    return hit;
}

@end

...

if (![mapper containsAnyOfCountPoints:5,
      NSMakePoint(0.0,1.0),
      NSMakePoint(1.0,0.0),
      NSMakePoint(1.0,0.0),
      NSMakePoint(0.0,0.0),
      NSMakePoint(0.5,0.5)]) {
    NSLog(@"no points in path");
}
```

The new method is passed a list of NSPoint structures directly as parameters. The initial count parameter tells the method how many NSPoint parameters to expect.

To implement variable arguments in your method, follow these steps:

1. Follow the last parameter variable name in the method declaration with ", ...".
2. Define a va_list automatic variable.
3. Call va_start() with the va_list variable and the last named parameter. The parameter is just used to tell the variable argument functions where the additional parameters begin.
4. Call va_arg() with the va_list variable and the *type* of the next parameter. The value returned is a copy of the parameter.
5. When finished, call va_end().

It is not necessary to retrieve all of the parameters before calling va_end(). Calling va_arg() for more parameter values than were passed is unpredictable and should be avoided.

Unimplemented Methods

Possibly even more interesting than how messages are sent is what happens when an object is sent a message it doesn't implement. If you don't do anything special, the results are similar to Java; the runtime throws an "unrecognized selector" exception.

But before that exception is thrown, the object is given the opportunity to handle the message in some other way. When the message dispatch function finds that an object doesn't implement that method, it converts the message into an NSInvocation object. It then passes that NSInvocation to the object's -forwardInvocation: method.

The root NSObject's -forwardInvocation: simply sends itself a -doesNotRecognizeSelector: message, which (unless overridden) throws the unrecognized selector exception. A class can override -forwardInvocation: and intercept unimplemented messages.

As the name implies, -forwardInvocation: is designed to redirect or forward a message to another object. The StandIn class in Listing 6-12 shows how this is accomplished. The object responds normally to all of the methods it implements or inherits. When sent a message it does not implement, it receives a -forwardInvocation: message. StandIn passes the message, and all of the call's parameters, to its actor object. If actor doesn't implement the message, it will either throw an exception or forward the invocation.

Listing 6-12. Forwarding an Unimplemented Message

```
@interface StandIn : NSObject {
    id   actor;
}
@property (assign) id actor;

@end


@implementation StandIn

@synthesize actor;

- (void)forwardInvocation:(NSInvocation*)invocation
{
    if (actor==nil)
        [self doesNotRecognizeSelector:[invocation selector]]; // does not return

    [invocation invokeWithTarget:actor];
}

- (NSMethodSignature*)methodSignatureForSelector:(SEL)sel
{
    NSMethodSignature *signature = [super methodSignatureForSelector:sel];
    if (signature==nil)
        signature = [actor methodSignatureForSelector:sel];
    return signature;
}

@end
```

It's also necessary to override -methodSignatureForSelector:. The message dispatcher first sends the object -methodSignatureForSelector: and uses the returned object to create the invocation argument passed to -forwardInvocation:.

Through a little sleight-of-hand, any value returned by the method invoked by -invokeWithTarget: will be returned to the code that originally sent the message. For this to work, it's important to return immediately after sending the -invoke message. The return value will still be in the registers or on the stack, so the caller gets them as if your handler had explicitly returned them.

You can do lots of interesting things with -forwardInvocation::

- Wrap one object in a logger object that intercepts and records the invocation of interesting messages.

- Implement "synthetic" messages that are handled by other methods in your class. Imagine creating a generic database record object that catches any property message it receives (i.e., -saleDate, -setSaleDate:) and automatically translates it into a record query. Instead of coding date = [record getDateFieldWithKey:@"SaleDate"], you could simply write date = [record saleDate], without ever writing a -saleDate method. NSManagedObject and CALayer are examples of classes that implement synthetic properties.

- Create an object that forwards the message to a hierarchy of other objects, like a responder chain. Chapter 20 talks about responder chains. The proxy object would search a collection of other objects looking for one that implements the message.

-forwardInvocation: will not work with variable argument methods because the NSInvocation object won't include a copy of the extra parameters.

Summary

While conceptually similar to Java methods, Objective-C messages are subtly different. Really start thinking in terms of *sending messages*, rather than *calling method*. Objective-C's lightweight method dispatching makes it easy to send methods programmatically. Not only can a class send messages dynamically, but it can also respond to them dynamically. The ease and efficiency by which messages can be manipulated is why dynamic messages play such a key role in so many Objective-C solutions.

CHAPTER 7

■■■

Making Friends with nil

Dealing with nil (null) references is an inevitable part of programming. This chapter will explain how nil and NULL pointers are handled in Objective-C, and some of the surprising consequences. Learning to use nil object pointers to your advantage can substantially simplify—rather than complicate—your design.

nil (null) and NULL references are sometimes treated more harshly in Objective-C than they are in Java, but are at other times permitted—embraced, even. Java is very consistent in its treatment of null; use of a null reference is universally considered a programming error and throws a java.lang.NullPointerException object at runtime. Runtime exceptions typically terminate the Java application, but can be caught, potentially recovering from the misstep.

In Objective-C, the consequences of using a nil or NULL reference are mixed. Accessing the memory at or near address 0—which is what happens if you attempt use a pointer with a nil value—causes a memory address violation. Address violations are detected by the hardware and cause a SIGBUS signal to be sent to the process, resulting in its immediate termination. A system CrashReporter daemon usually catches the SIGBUS signal and prepares a crash report document, detailing the state of the process before it was terminated. While it's technically possible for an application to intercept some signals, the ability to recover from a SIGBUS signal is extremely limited.

■**Note** The Objective-C constants nil and NULL are technically interchangeable. By convention, nil (defined by Objective-C) is used with object pointers and NULL (the traditional C constant) is used for all other pointer types. Thus, you would write `MyClass *object = nil` and `int *iPtr = NULL`.

Just as you do in Java, you should avoid direct access of member variables using object pointers (`int i = object->iVar`) or values via a pointer (`int i = *intPtr`) without first ensuring the pointer variable contains a valid address. The code in Listing 7-1 demonstrates some typical coding strategies for avoiding NULL pointer references.

Listing 7-1. Avoiding a NULL Pointer Reference

```
- (void)expandSize:(NSSize*)size
{
    if (size!=NULL) {
        area.height += size->height;
        area.width += size->width;
    }
}

- (BOOL)deleteAllReferencesToKey:(id)key error:(NSError**)outError
```

```
{
    ...

    if (!successful && outError!=NULL)
        *outError = [NSError errorWithDomain:NSPOSIXErrorDomain
                                        code:errno
                                    userInfo:nil];

    return successful;
}
```

Messages to nil Are Safe

In stark contrast, sending a message to a nil object pointer is not only allowed, it's encouraged! In Chapter 6, I ignored a very important step of the message dispatch function:

4.   If the receiver value is nil, the dispatching function returns immediately.

This condition makes it perfectly safe to send any message to a nil object pointer. When the message receiver is nil, the dispatch function does nothing and returns immediately. More importantly, it explicitly returns a value of zero, nil, or NO for senders that are expecting a return value.

Unlike typical Java code, it is not necessary to test an object pointer for nil before sending it a message. In fact, it's redundant since the test is performed for every message.

The code in Listing 7-2 is a fragment from our mythical Venus Attacks adventure game and shows how nil receivers can simplify code. The TacticalDisplay object draws a map on the display, but only if a map object is present. It also superimposes an optional location highlight drawn in either cyan or a custom color. The Java code in the paint() method uses traditional condition statements to handle the cases where there is no map object, or the map object doesn't provide a location highlight shape, or the color of the location highlight isn't set.

Listing 7-2. *Using nil Objects to Simplify Code*

Java
```
package com.apress.java;

import java.awt.*;
import javax.swing.*;

public class TerrainMap
{
    private Color customLocationColor;
    private Shape locationHighlightShape;

    public void paint( Graphics graphics )
        {
        // ... draw the map
        }
```

```java
    public Color getCustomLocationColor() { … }

    public Shape getLocationHighlightShape() { … }
}

public class TacticalDisplay extends JComponent
{
    private TerrainMap terrainMap;

    public TerrainMap getTerrainMap( ) { … }

    public void paint( Graphics graphics )
        {
        super.paint(graphics);
        Graphics2D g2 = (Graphics2D)graphics;

        …
        graphics.setColor(Color.CYAN);       // default location color

        TerrainMap map = getTerrainMap();
        if (map!=null) {
            map.paint(graphics);

            Shape locationShape = map.getLocationHighlightShape();
            if (locationShape!=null) {
                Color customColor = map.getCustomLocationColor();
                if (customColor!=null)
                    graphics.setColor(customColor);

                g2.draw(locationShape);
                }
            }

        }
}
```

Objective-C
```objc
#import <Cocoa/Cocoa.h>

@interface TerrainMap : NSObject
{
    NSBezierPath    *locationHighlightPath;
    NSColor         *customLocationColor;
}

@property (assign) NSBezierPath *locationHighlightPath;
@property (assign) NSColor *customLocationColor;

- (void)drawRect:(NSRect)dirtyRect;
```

```objc
@end

@implementation TerrainMap

@synthesize locationHighlightPath, customLocationColor;

- (void)drawRect:(NSRect)dirtyRect
{
    // ... draw the map
}

@end


@interface TacticalDisplay : NSView
{
    TerrainMap *terrainMap;
    ...
}

@property (copy) TerrainMap *terrainMap;

- (void)drawRect:(NSRect)dirtyRect;

@end

...

@implementation TacticalDisplay

@synthesize terrainMap;

- (void)drawRect:(NSRect)dirtyRect
{
    ...
    [[NSColor cyanColor] setStroke];        // set default location color

    TerrainMap *map = [self terrainMap];
    [map drawRect:dirtyRect];
    [[map customLocationColor] setStroke];
    [[map locationHighlightPath] stroke];
}

@end
```

The Objective-C version leverages the power of nil object pointers. A message sent to a nil pointer does nothing. Since any message sent to nil returns nil, a nested call that sends a message to the object returned by the previous message also does nothing. If the map object pointer in Listing 7-2 is nil, none of the subsequent messages are sent. If the map does exist, but the message -customLocationColor returns nil, then the -setStroke message is ignored and no custom color is set. If the -locationHighlightPath message returns nil, the -stroke message is ignored and no location is drawn.

■**Caution** While a message sent to nil does nothing, this does not exclude side effects of parameters. Parameters to a message are assembled and pushed onto the stack *before* the message is dispatched. Messages sent or other side effects—such as post-incrementing a value—in the parameter expressions will still occur. One reason to explicitly compare a receiver to nil and skip the message if it's equal would be to avoid undesirable side effects of assembling the parameters.

nil Returns Zero

A nil receiver always returns nil or 0 to the caller as long as the caller is expecting the message to return one of the variable types in Table 7-1. The compatible variable types are essentially any pointer or scalar.

Table 7-1. nil Message Return Values

Return Type	Returned Value
id	nil
Pointer to any type	NULL
BOOL	NO
(unsigned) char	'\0'
(unsigned) int	0
(unsigned) long int	0L
(unsigned) long long int	0LL
float	0.0f
double	0.0
long double	0.0

Callers expecting a message to return a structure are *not* compatible with nil receivers. In those cases, you must avoid sending messages to nil just as you would in Java. A simple example is shown in Listing 7-3. Structures are exchanged through the use of special "copy pad" registers that are not part of the return value. The obscure exception to this rule is when the entire structure is returned in a register. The mechanism for that is described in the "Mac OS X ABI Function Calling Guide," available at http://developer.apple.com/, and is architecture dependent.

Listing 7-3. *Avoid Sending nil Messages That Return Structures*

```
NSView *headsUpDisplay = [self headsUpDisplay];
NSRect hudRect = NSMakeRect(0.0,0.0,0.0,0.0);

if (headsUpDisplay!=nil)
    hudRect = [headsUpDisplay visibleRect];
if (hudRect.size.width>0.0 && hudRect.size.height>0.0) {
    ...
}
```

Designing With nil

Embracing nil receivers in Objective-C will change how you write code and design classes. This section will show how to take advantage of nil receivers to simplify your code and will introduce three design patterns that leverage nil. Abstractly, this is about adopting the programming principle of "letting the data make the decision" first articulated by Charles Moore, computer science pioneer and inventor of the FORTH language. The principle avoids writing conditional statements that branch to handle exceptional cases, in favor of data and expressions that incorporate those cases.

Contrast the two code snippets in Listing 7-4. The code is part of a recipe management program. The makeLists method assembles a list of recipes planned for the week, along with a shopping list of ingredients that must fit within the current budget. If the cost of all ingredients exceeds the budget, ingredients for meals later in the week are omitted.

The program uses a number of classes, many of which have optional properties that must be considered. There might not be a Budget object, in which case there are no budgetary restrictions on the grocery list. There might not be any meals in the planner, in which case the resulting lists will be empty. A meal might not have a recipe property (some meals might be take-out), in which case it would go in the list of meals but would not add any ingredients to the shopping list.

Listing 7-4. *Letting nil Receivers Make Decisions*

Java

```
package com.apress.java;

import java.util.*;


public class Ingredient
{
    public double getCost( ) { ... }
}


public class Recipe
{
    protected ArrayList ingredients;

    public synchronized List<Ingredient> getIngredients() { ... }
}
```

```java
public class Meal
{
    protected Recipe recipe;

    public synchronized Recipe getRecipe() { ... }
    public synchronized void setRecipe( Recipe recipe ) { ... }
}


public class Budget
{
    public void planExpendature( double amount ) { ... }
    public boolean isOverBudget( ) { ... }
}


public class RecipeBox
{
    protected ArrayList meals;

    public synchronized Budget getMealBudget() { ... }

    public synchronized List<Meal> getMeals() { ... }
    public synchronized void setMeals( List<Meal> meals ) { ... }

    public void makesLists( )
        {
        ArrayList mealList = new ArrayList();
        ArrayList shoppingList = new ArrayList();

        Budget budget = getMealBudget();
        List meals = getMeals();
        if (meals!=null) {
            boolean isOverBudget = false;
            for ( Meal meal: getMeals() ) {
                Recipe recipe = meal.getRecipe();
                if (recipe!=null) {
                    List<Ingredient> ingredients = recipe.getIngredients();
                    for (Ingredient ingredient: ingredients) {
                        if (budget!=null) {
                            budget.planExpendature(ingredient.getCost());
                            if (budget.isOverBudget())
                                isOverBudget = true;
                        }
                    }
                }
                mealList.add(meal);
```

```
            if (!isOverBudget)
                shoppingList.addAll(recipe.getIngredients());
            }
        }
    }
}
```

Objective-C
```objc
#import <Cocoa/Cocoa.h>

@interface Ingredient : NSObject

@property (readonly) double cost;

@end


@interface Recipe : NSObject {
    NSMutableArray *ingredients;
}

@property (assign) NSMutableArray *ingredients;

@end


@interface Meal : NSObject {
    Recipe *recipe;
}

@property (assign) Recipe* recipe;

@end


@interface Budget : NSObject

- (void)planExpenditure:(double)amount;
- (BOOL)isOverBudget;

@end


@interface RecipeBoxController : NSObject {
    NSMutableArray *meals;
}

@property (assign) NSMutableArray *meals;
@property (readonly,copy) Budget *mealBudget;

- (void)makeLists;
```

```
@end

@implementation RecipeBoxController

…

- (void)makeLists
{
    NSMutableArray *mealList = [NSMutableArray new];
    NSMutableArray *shoppingList = [NSMutableArray new];
    NSMutableArray *affordableGroceryList = shoppingList;

    Budget *budget = [self mealBudget];
    for (Meal *meal in [self meals]) {
        for (Ingredient *ingredient in [[meal recipe] ingredients])
            [budget planExpenditure:[ingredient cost]];
        if ([budget isOverBudget])
            affordableGroceryList = nil;
        [mealList addObject:meal];
        [affordableGroceryList addObjectsFromArray:[[meal recipe] ingredients]];
    }
}

@end
```

The Java approach uses traditional conditions that branch to each case. The Objective-C approach largely lets the presence or absence of objects dictate its behavior. If the budget object is nil, the -planExpenditure: message is never sent and the -isOverBudget message always returns NO. If a meal's recipe property is nil, no ingredients are processed. If the budget is exceeded, the affordableGroceryList pointer is set to nil, and shoppingList stops receiving -addObjectsFromArray: messages.

To begin designing with nil, start with these three principles: property accessors, absent behavior, and consistency with nothing.

Property Accessors

You probably already adhere to the Java practice of writing accessor methods for all of your class properties. Objective-C just gives you one more reason to continue that practice.

Since nil objects always return nil or 0, all property accessor methods that get or set one of the types in Table 7-1 are safe to use with a nil receiver. In Listing 7-4, the expression [meal recipe] can be called whether meal points to a Meal object or nil. In contrast, the expression meal->recipe would cause the application to crash if meal was nil. Similarly, the statement [meal setRecipe:recipe] does nothing if meal is nil.

Absent Behavior

Design optional behavior around the presence or absence of an object. In the presence of an object, the object executes messages. In its absence, nothing happens. Simple examples are

- *Logger object*: Messages sent to the logger are logged, or ignored if the logger is nil.

- *Listener object*: Status and update messages are sent only if a listener has been established. Setting the listener to nil suppresses the updates.

- *Delegate object*: Query the delegate if set, or use default answers if not. This is a combination of the absent behavior and consistency with nothing design, discussed next.

Listing 7-5 shows a simple FIFO stack class that can operate in a thread-safe manner, but only if the application needs it to be thread safe.

Listing 7-5. *Absent Object Behavior*

```objc
@interface AutoSafeFIFO : NSObject {
    NSMutableArray  *stack;
    @private
    NSLock          *lock;
}

- (void)push:(id)object;
- (id)pop;
- (BOOL)hasObjects;
- (void)makeThreadSafe;

@end

@implementation AutoSafeFIFO

- (id) init
{
    self = [super init];
    if (self != nil) {
        stack = [NSMutableArray new];
    }
    return self;
}

- (void)push:(id)object
{
    [lock lock];
    [stack addObject:object];
    [lock unlock];
}

- (id)pop
{
```

```
    id object = nil;

    [lock lock];
    if ([stack count]!=0) {
        object = [stack objectAtIndex:0];
        [stack removeObjectAtIndex:0];
    }
    [lock unlock];

    return object;
}

- (BOOL)hasObjects
{
    [lock lock];
    BOOL answer = ([stack count]!=0);
    [lock unlock];

    return answer;
}

- (void)makeThreadSafe
{
    lock = [NSLock new];
}

@end
```

The lock object is initially nil, so all messages sent to lock and unlock it do nothing. This provides the best performance, but at the expense of thread safety. To operate safely in a multi-threaded environment, the -makeThreadSafe method sets the lock property to a real NSLock object. Once set, the lock and unlock messages are now sent to the NSLock object, providing the desired thread synchronization.

Consistency With Nothing

Design your class properties so that a value of nil or 0 is consistent with the concept of a "nothing" object. Usually this means defining properties that express positive, rather than negative, attributes—which is a good practice in general. In Listing 7-5, the AutoSafeFIFO class defines -(BOOL)hasObjects. You might have been tempted to define a -(BOOL)isEmpty method instead. But if the receiver were nil, isEmpty would return NO implying that the nil object had objects, which it clearly does not.

No Free Rides

Objective-C's treatment of nil receivers can make your code simpler, safer, and more elegant. It does not, however, mean that nil is universally acceptable any place an object pointer is. As you've already seen, trying to use a nil object pointer to access member values will result in abrupt program termination. Most method parameters that accept an object pointer generally expect an object, not nil. The exceptions are usually documented.

For example, most Cocoa collection classes—just like Java—do not allow nil objects to be stored as values or used as keys. So while it's perfectly safe to send the -addObject: message to a nil receiver, the statement [array addObject:nil] will throw a runtime exception (assuming array isn't nil, of course).

Summary

Coming from a Java background, I can tell you that embracing nil receivers takes some getting used to. There is a subconscious, nearly autonomic tendency to design and write code that avoids null references at every step. Learning to use nil objects to your advantage will take some practice, but is ultimately rewarding.

PART 2

■■■

Translational Technologies

CHAPTER 8

■ ■ ■

Strings and Primitive Values

Java and Objective-C take very similar approaches to primitive values. Both have direct language support for primitive scalar values (i.e., numbers) and arrays. Both provide a set of "wrapper" objects that encapsulate primitive values when they need to be treated as objects. Both provide syntax for declaring string object literals.

This chapter describes the classes used to "wrap" primitive values in objects and the string classes. The balance of the chapter focuses on converting and formatting strings.

Wrapping Scalar Primitives

Like Java, Objective-C variables can be broadly divided into primitive scalar values and object reference values. To pass an integer value to a method that expects an object, you must "wrap" or "box" the primitive value in an object that encapsulates the original value. Like Java, Objective-C provides a set of classes specifically for wrapping primitive C variable types. The scalar value types were listed in Chapter 2 Table 8-1 lists the wrapper objects for those same types.

Table 8-1. *Primitive Scalar Type Wrapper Classes*

Java Type	Java	Objective-C
boolean	new Boolean(x)	[NSNumber numberWithBool:x]
byte	new Byte(x)	[NSNumber numberWithChar:x]
char	new Character(x)	[NSNumber numberWithUnsignedShort:x]
short	new Short(x)	[NSNumber numberWithShort:x]
int	new Integer(x)	[NSNumber numberWithInteger:x]
long	new Long(x)	[NSNumber numberWithLongLong:x]
float	new Float(x)	[NSNumber numberWithFloat:x]
double	new Double(x)	[NSNumber numberWithDouble:x]

I'm sure that you'll notice a pattern in Table 8-1. Where Java has individual classes for each scalar type, Objective-C uses the single NSNumber class to encapsulate all numeric types. Internally, NSNumber stores a copy of the primitive value in its original form.

The parallel set of constructor methods for unsigned integers was omitted from Table 8-1 for brevity, but all follow the same form: -[NSNumber numberWithUnsignedChar:], -[NSNumber numberWithUnsignedShort:], and so on.

Scalar Type Conversion

Getting the original primitive value from a wrapper in Objective-C, or obtaining an equivalent primitive value of a different type, is much as it is in Java. The NSNumber class has several conversion methods that return the best possible representation of the original value. These are listed in Table 8-2.

Table 8-2. *Primitive Type Conversion*

Java Type	Java	Objective-C
boolean	value.booleanValue()	[value boolValue]
byte	value.byteValue()	[value charValue]
char	value.charValue()	[value unsignedShortValue]
short	value.shortValue()	[value shortValue]
int	value.intValue()	[value integerValue]
long	value.longValue()	[value longLongValue]
float	value.floatValue()	[value floatValue]
double	value.doubleValue()	[value doubleValue]

Because the single NSNumber class performs all primitive scalar type conversions, type conversion is orthogonal in Objective-C; any NSNumber object will return its value as a BOOL, char, integer, or floating-point value. This symmetry is broken in Java, where the Boolean class does not include an intValue() method, the Character class does not include a boolValue() method, etc. Conversion generally follows the rules for native type conversions in C. That is, asking an NSNumber for its intValue is no different than casting the original value to int, as in (int)original. No exceptions are raised (thrown) if the requested type cannot represent the original value.

Converting Strings to Scalars

In Java, each wrapper class has several methods for parsing strings and interpreting its scalar value, returning either a primitive type or an object. For example, the java.lang.Integer class has a string constructor (Integer(String)), a static method that takes a string and returns an integer primitive (parseInt(String)), and a static method that takes a string and returns an Integer object (valueOf(String)). The Boolean, Character, Short, Float, and Double classes contain similar methods.

In Objective-C, the NSString class implements the same scalar conversion methods listed in Table 8-2. Send a string object the -intValue message to interpret it as an integer. Send it -floatValue to interpret it as a float. To convert a string into an NSNumber object, create one from the converted value, as in [NSNumber numberWithInt:[string intValue]].

Hexadecimal strings can be converted using the NSScanner object. NSScanner is a general purpose utility class for parsing strings. To convert a string containing a hexadecimal number into an integer, create a scanner for the string then parse it using the -[NSScanner scanHexInt:] method, as illustrated in Listing 8-1.

Listing 8-1. *Converting a Hexadecimal String Into an Integer*

```
unsigned int i;
NSScanner *scanner = [NSScanner scannerWithString:@"cafe1234"];
[scanner scanHexInt:&i];
```

NSFormatter provides yet another, and progressively more sophisticated, means of converting a string into a number. While typically used to turn numbers into strings, NSFormatters are bidirectional and will convert strings back into scalar values as well. NSFormatters are discussed later in this chapter in the "Formatting" section.

The Cocoa framework classes contain no general purpose numeric conversion for arbitrary radixes, like Java's java.lang.Integer.parseInt(String s, int radix). Formatting conversions support octal, decimal and hexadecimal only. Arbitrary base conversion can be accomplished using the C library function strtol(...). This would require converting the Objective-C string object into a C string—covered later in this chapter—and then passing that to the strtol(...) function, or one of its relatives.

Wrapping Arrays

In Java, arrays are already objects so the language doesn't need a wrapper class for them. Native arrays in Objective-C are not objects, but they can be wrapped with the NSData class. NSData provides a generic wrapper for any amorphous block of memory. NSData is particularly convenient for insolating you from the underlying C memory allocation functions, letting you create and manage large structures and native C arrays as if they were objects.

NSData encapsulates an immutable array of bytes. The NSMutableData subclass manages a modifiable array of bytes. NSData provides methods to obtain the size and starting address of the byte array. NSMutableData extends NSData with methods to adjust the size of the array, and the ability to append, replace, and remove bytes. Table 8-3 lists the common ways of creating NSData objects.

Table 8-3. *Common NSData Constructors*

Method	Purpose
+[NSData dataWithBytes:length:]	Creates a new NSData object that contains a copy of the memory at the given address and length.
+[NSData dataWithBytesNoCopy:length:]	This constructor wraps an NSData object around a block of memory allocated using one of the C malloc(…) functions—low level C memory management. The object assumes responsibility for the memory block and releases it when the object is destroyed. This is a most efficient way to turn a C allocated block of memory into an Objective-C object.
+[NSData dataWithBytesNoCopy:length:freeWhenDone:]	If the freeWithDone: argument is YES, this method is equivalent to +[NSData dataWithBytesNoCopy: length:]. If the argument is NO, it wraps an existing block of memory with an NSData object. The new object simply refers to the original address and length given to it during construction. It is the responsibility of the programmer to ensure that the memory it refers to is valid for the lifetime of the NSData object. This constructor is particularly useful in avoiding the performance penalty of making a copy of the data.
+[NSData dataWithContentsOf…:]	Creates an NSData object that contains a copy of the raw data contained in the target. This family of convenience constructors includes +dataWithContentsOfFile:, +dataWithContentsOfURL:, and so on.
+[NSData dataWithData:]	Creates a new NSData object that's a copy of an existing NSData object.
+[NSMutableData data]	Creates a zero-length NSMutableData object.
+[NSMutableData dataWithLength:]	Creates a mutable byte array wrapper of the given length, filled with zeros.

Since NSMutableData is a subclass of NSData, all of the NSData constructors apply equally to NSMutableData, such as using [NSMutableData dataWithData:data] to create a mutable copy of an existing NSData object. In fact, the +data constructor is actually defined by NSData, where it has limited utility.

In principle, the contents of an NSData object are immutable. In reality, there is nothing (beyond hardware) that prohibits its contents from being modified. The -[NSData bytes] method returns the address of the first byte in the array. Once obtained, there is nothing preventing you from modifying any of the values at that address. I prefer to construct NSData objects for memory that I do not intend to modify, and NSMutableData objects for modifiable memory, but there's nothing that dictates this in practice.

NSData objects treat their contents as a single contiguous byte array. You will often want to treat it as something else—an array of some other type or a structure. Listing 8-2 demonstrates the use of NSMutableArray to store an array of NSPoint structures.

Listing 8-2. Using NSMutableData to Wrap an Array of Structures

```
NSArray *objects = ...          // array of objects with a coordinate
unsigned int count = [objects count];
NSMutableData *data = [NSMutableData dataWithLength:count*sizeof(NSPoint)];
NSPoint *points = (NSPoint*)[data bytes];
unsigned int i;
[data retain];
for (i=0; i<[objects count]; i++) {
    points[i] = [[objects objectAtIndex:i] coordinate];
}
[data release];
```

The code in Listing 8-2 allocates an empty array of bytes large enough to contain count number of NSPoint structures. Once allocated, the address of the array is cast as a pointer to an NSPoint structure. C pointers are interchangeable with array variables, so the pointer is used to address the individual elements of the array. This technique will work for a single structure or an array of any type.

■**Caution** In Listing 8-2 you'll notice two odd statements: [data retain] and [data release]. Due to a quirk of Objective-C 2.0's garbage collector, the variable (points) that points to the interior of the NSData object is *not* sufficient to keep the object from being recycled by the garbage collector immediately following the [data bytes] statement. These extraneous statements prevent the NSData object from being collected by keeping its object reference in scope. This is only a problem for transient NSData objects. If the NSData object was returned from this function, stored in a globally reachable variable, or referenced in any other way following the for loop, it wouldn't be a problem. The -retain and -release methods are for traditional memory management and do nothing when running in a garbage collection environment. See Chapter 9 for an explanation and for an alternate solution, described in the "GC vs. Non-GC Pointers" section of that chapter.

Wrapping Arbitrary Values

C allows you to define your own memory structures and variable types using struct and typedef declarations. Consequently, there's more that can be wrapped than just the integer and float types supplied by the language. That's the job of NSValue.

NSValue wraps any C data type. This includes all non-object types defined by the language or the programmer. The principal method for creating NSValue objects is +[NSValue valueWithBytes:objCType:]. This method is passed the address of the value—not the value itself—and an Objective-C type value. The type value is generated using the Objective-C @encode() directive. This evaluates to a constant C string that formally identifies the type of the value. From this information,

NSValue determines the size of the value and makes a copy of it. Listing 8-3 shows how an arbitrary C structure is wrapped in an NSValue object and than added to a collection.

Listing 8-3. Wrapping an Arbitrary Structure in NSValue

```
typedef struct {
    int         population;
    long long   hectares;
    BOOL        landLocked;
} CountryStats;

...

CountryStats stats;
stats.population = 195450000;
stats.hectares = 859250000;
stats.landLocked = NO;

NSValue *value = [NSValue valueWithBytes:&stats objCType:@encode(CountryStats)];
NSMutableArray *array = [NSMutableArray array];
[array addObject:value];

...

CountryStats lastStats;
value = [array lastObject];
[value getValue:&lastStats];
return (lastStats.population);
```

The key points in Listing 8-3 are as follows:

- An NSValue is constructed by passing it the address of the value, not the value itself.
- The size of the value is implied by the Objective-C type generated by the @encode( ) directive.
- Once encapsulated, NSValue can be treated like any other object.
- To examine the value stored in NSValue, send it the -getValue: message—again passing the address of the variable to be overwritten with a copy of the value stored in the object.

NSValue has several convenience constructors for commonly used structures, such as +valueWithPoint:(NSPoint)point, +valueWithRange:(NSRange)range, +valueWithSize:(NSSize)size, and so on. Note that these all take a copy of the original value, not an address.

NSNumber is actually a subclass of NSValue. In a way, everything in NSNumber can be considered convenience methods for dealing with native data types. Internally, NSNumber uses NSValue to store its value. You can send an NSNumber or NSValue object an -objCType message to determine the type of its original value.

Wrapping nil

Objective-C provides the NSNull class as an object placeholder for nil values. This provides an object that can be stored in collections, archived (serialized), or otherwise used to represent "nothing" where nil is unacceptable.

The method +[NSNull nil] returns the singleton instance of NSNull created by the Objective-C runtime. The single NSNull object is immutable and immortal.

Listing 8-4 demonstrates a simple technique for writing a method that accepts an object, an instance of NSNull, or nil—treating the last two equally.

Listing 8-4. Method That Accepts an Object, nil, or NSNull

```
- (void)doSomethingWithObject:(id)object {
    if (object==[NSNull null])
        object = nil;
    …
}
```

Strings

Strings are the odd duck in both Java and Objective-C. They are so fundamental to programming that both languages include special syntax for declaring string literals. Yet beyond declaring string literals, the languages provide little direct support for strings, expecting the programmer to manipulate them as objects. The exception to this is Java's string concatenation operator (+), which Objective-C does not include. This section covers string literals, string comparison, string manipulation, converting strings to and from scalar values, and complex formatting.

At many levels, strings in Objective-C follow the familiar patterns they do in Java. All Objective-C strings are objects of class NSString. NSString characters are represented internally using Unicode. NSString objects are immutable. Literal Objective-C string objects are written using the @"*string*" directive. Table 8-4 lists common string operations and their Objective-C counterparts.

Table 8-4. Common String Classes and Methods

Java	Objective-C
"string"	@"string"
java.lang.String	NSString
java.lang.StringBuffer	NSMutableString (although not thread safe)
java.lang.StringBuilder	NSMutableString
Object.toString()	-[NSObject description]
new String(byte[],String)	+[NSString stringWithCString:(const char*)cString encoding:(NSStringEncoding)enc]

String.length()	-[NSString length]
String.charAt(int)	-[NSString characterAtIndex:(int)index]
String.equals(String)	-[NSString isEqualToString:(NSString*)string]
String.compareTo(String)	-[NSString compare:(NSString*)string]
String.compareToIgnoreCase(String)	-[NSString caseInsensitiveCompare: (NSString*)string]
String.concat(String)	-[NSString stringByAppendingString:(NSString*)string]
String.substring(int)	-[NSString substringFromIndex:(int)index]
String.substring(int,int)	-[NSString substringWithRange:(NSRange)range]
String.toLowerCase()	-[NSString lowercaseString]
String.toUpperCase()	-[NSString uppercaseString]
String.trim()	-[NSString stringByTrimmingCharactersInSet:↵ (NSCharacterSet*)set]
String.format(String,Object…)	+[NSString stringWithFormat:(NSString*)format, …]

You will find many other analogous methods in String and NSString. NSString tends to prefer more generic methods that handle a wide variety of cases, where the Java classes implement many simplistic methods. A good example is java.lang.String.trim(). The Objective-C equivalent is -stringByTrimmingCharactersInSet:, which takes an NSCharacterSet object as a parameter. To accomplish exactly what String.trim() does, use [string stringByTrimmingCharactersInSet:↵ [NSCharacterSet characterSetWithRange:NSMakeRange(0,0x20+1)]]. While more verbose, it has the advantage of being able to trim any arbitrary set of characters from a string. If you do this a lot, use a Category to add your own -trim method to NSString, as explained in Chapter 5.

■**Note** Modern Objective-C development tools coalesce identical literal strings when your application is built. No matter how many times the string literal @"Welcome" appears in your application, every occurrence will refer to a single instance at runtime.

There are, however, several key differences between String and NSString that you need to be aware of:

- There are subclasses of NSString.
- A string object *might* be mutable.

- There are two kinds of strings: Objective-C strings and C strings.
- The additional operator (+) will not concatenate two strings.
- Objective-C string literals *do* follow the C language's compile-time string concatenation syntax. The literal string expressions @"Hello" @", World!" and @"Hello, World!" are identical.

NSString follows a consistent pattern in the Cocoa class framework; when a class has immutable and mutable variants, the mutable class is the subclass of the immutable class. This has three important consequences. First, the class for mutable string objects is the NSMutableString subclass. Use NSMutableString where you would use java.lang.StringBuilder.

The second consequence is that any NSString pointer or parameter *could* potentially contain a reference to a mutable subclass. In Java, the java.lang.String class is final and cannot be subclassed, guaranteeing that all String objects are immutable. To dynamically create a string requires first constructing a StringBuffer object, then converting that into a String object using toString(). In Objective-C, you can use NSMutableString to assemble a string then simply return it or use it as a regular NSString object. If you do not modify it thereafter, it's indistinguishable from an immutable string. In the situation where you must guarantee that a string object is immutable, construct a copy of the suspicious string object using [NSString stringWithString:possiblyMutableString]. Also, see Chapter 12 for information about copying objects.

The last consequence is more of a benefit. Since NSMutableString is a subclass of NSString, it inherits all of the methods of NSString. This includes methods added to NSString by categories.

Converting Objects to Strings

Just as every Java object inherits a toString() method, every Objective-C object inherits the -(NSString*)description method. Its purpose and use is virtually identical to toString() in Java. Notably:

- The base class implementation of -[NSObject description] returns a string containing the name of the object's class and its address. Unless overridden, this is an object's default description.
- String formatting functions and the debugger send objects a -description message whenever they need their string representation.
- -[NSString description] returns itself.
- -[NSNumber description] returns a string representation of the original value.
- Many classes override -description to provide a more informative string representation. For example, the collection classes return a string describing all of the objects in the collection—recursively sending -description to each object.

C Strings

Finally, there's the added confusion of having two types of strings: Objective-C string objects and traditional C strings. A C string is just the address of an array of characters, and is more of a programming convention than a defined entity. The C language's only concession to strings is the syntax for declaring a literal string ("hi!"), equivalent to allocating a null-terminated array of characters (char string[] = { 'h', 'i', '!', '\0' }).

■**Tip** As a Java programmer, you will undoubtedly compile an Objective-C program and encounter the message "`warning: initialization from incompatible pointer type`" or "`warning: passing argument from incompatible pointer type`." This is typically because you omitted the '@' before an Objective-C string literal. Instead of declaring a literal string object (@"`Hello`", of type `NSString*`), you declared a literal C string ("`Hello`", of type `const char*`). Don't feel bad. Even after years of Objective-C programming, I still make this mistake about once a week.

Converting C Strings into NSString Objects

While you can program for ages in Objective-C without ever touching a C string, inevitably the day will come when you need to interact with C functions that expect or return C strings. The principal methods for constructing a new NSString object from a C string are listed in Table 8-5. These are very similar to the Java constructors for creating String objects from byte or character arrays.

Table 8-5. *Constructing NSString Objects from Character Arrays*

Java	Objective-C
new String(byte[],String)	+stringWithCString:(const char *)cString encoding:(NSStringEncoding)enc
	+stringWithUTF8String:(const char*)utf8String
new String(char[],int,int)	+stringWithCharacters:(const unichar*)chars length:(int)length

Traditional C strings use 8-bit char values, are typically encoded using ASCII, and are terminated with a single null ('`\0`') character. This is by far the most common representation of C strings. To create an NSString from a traditional C String, use [`NSString stringWithCString:cString encoding:NSASCIIStringEncoding`]. Because of the null termination character, the length of the string is implied. If the string is encoded using some other encoding, specify that encoding instead. The documentation for NSStringEncoding lists the encodings supported by the Cocoa framework.

The other popular 8-bit encoding is UTF-8, which consists of Unicode characters translated into a stream of 8-bit bytes. Most UTF-8 strings are also null terminated. The +`stringWithUTF8String:` message will create an NSString object from a null-terminated UTF-8 character array and is equivalent to [`NSString stringWithCString:utf8String encoding:NSUTF8StringEncoding`].

Finally, you may occasionally encounter arrays of Unicode characters—the true equivalent of a Java char. Use the +[`NSString stringWithCharacters:(const unichar*)chars length:(int)length`] method to construct an NSString object from the array. You will have to supply the constructor with the number of characters in the array.

There are other NSString constructors for more specialized situations. Consult the NSString documentation for the details.

Converting NSString Objects into C Strings

Converting the characters in an NSString into a char or unichar array mirrors the methods in Table 8-5. Table 8-6 lists the common methods of extracting the characters in an NSString along with some convenience converters.

Table 8-6. *Extracting Characters from NSString Objects*

Java	Objective-C
getBytes(String)	-getCString:(char*)buff maxLength:(int)len encoding:(NSStringEncoding)enc
	-cStringUsingEncoding:(NSStringEncoding)enc
	-UTF8String
	-fileSystemRepresentation
	-dataUsingEncoding:(NSStringEncoding)enc
getChars(int,int,char[],int)	-getCharacters:(unichar*)buffer range:(NSRange)range
toCharArray()	-getCharacters:(unichar*)buffer

When converting an NSString into a C string you have the option of allocating the char array yourself and then using -getCString:maxLength:encoding: to extract the characters into it, or letting the string object allocate a character array for you using -cStringUsingEncoding:, -UTF8String, or -fileSystemRepresentation. These three methods allocate a temporary character array buffer, extract the characters into it, terminate it with a null character, and return the address of the first character. The -dataUsingEncoding: method returns an NSData object containing the encoded string. Only -dataUsingEncoding: is a true substitute for Java's getBytes(String) method, because it's the only one that returns an object.

■ **Caution** The lifetime of the C string pointer returned by -cStringUsingEncoding: et al is tied to the lifetime of the string object. The temporary string buffer is released when the string object is destroyed. Do not continue to use the pointer after the string object reference has gone out of scope, or the garbage collector might recycle the object—destroying its temporary C string buffer—prematurely.

The -cStringUsingEncoding:, -UTF8String, and -fileSystemRepresentation messages are extremely convenient for passing an NSString object to any method or function that expects a traditional C string. Listing 8-5 demonstrates how temporary C strings can be generated and passed to a traditional C function. The -fileSystemRepresentation method should be used when the string object is a file or path name. If the string only contains ASCII characters, -UTF8String and -cStringUsingEncoding:NSASCIIStringEncoding are equivalent.

Listing 8-5. *Passing NSString Object as C Strings*

```
NSString *filePath = @"/tmp/somefile.dat";
NSString *fileMode = @"w+";
...
FILE *file = fopen([filePath fileSystemRepresentation],[fileMode UTF8String]);
```

The length of an encoded string will often be different—typically longer—then the number of Unicode characters in the NSString object. Either of the `-lengthOfBytesUsingEncoding:(NSStringEncoding)enc` or `-maximumLengthOfBytesUsingEncoding:(NSStringEncoding)enc` methods can be used to determine the number of 8-bit characters that will be needed to contain the encoded string. The latter is faster, but often overestimates the number of bytes required. Neither method includes the terminating null character in its count. An example of extracting a C string with a specific encoding into a dynamically allocated buffer is shown in Listing 8-6.

Listing 8-6. *Extracting a C String from an NSString*

```
NSString *unicodeString = …

int len = [unicodeString lengthOfBytesUsingEncoding:NSWindowsCP1250StringEncoding];
NSMutableData *buffer = [NSMutableData dataWithLength:len+1];
[unicodeString getCString:(char*)[buffer bytes]
                maxLength:len+1
                 encoding:NSWindowsCP1250StringEncoding];
// [buffer bytes] now contains a null-terminated C string version of unicodeString
// encoded using the Windows Central and Eastern European character set.
```

If the Unicode characters of a string cannot be represented by the requested encoding, the previous messages will return NO or NULL. You can preflight the conversion using `-canBeConvertedToEncoding:(NSStringEncoding)enc`, or consider using `-dataUsingEncoding:(NSStringEncoding)enc allowLossyConversion:(BOOL)flag`. Passing YES for allowLossyConversion will always return an encoded string, omitting or simplifying any characters that can't be encoded. Also be aware that NSNonLossyASCIIStringEncoding along with the family of NSUTF…StringEncoding encodings can represent the entire range of Unicode characters and will always return a successfully encoded string.

The last two methods, `-getCharacters:(unichar*)buffer range:(NSRange)range` and `-getCharacters:(unichar*)buffer`, are the complements to `+stringWithCharacters:length:`. Both extract Unicode values into a unichar array. These methods do not perform any encoding. The number of unichar characters extracted will always be the same as the source range.

Formatting Strings

Creating strings from other values can be accomplished in a dizzying number of ways, but by far the most versatile method is `+[NSString stringWithFormat:(NSString*)format, …]`. The Java counterpart is java.lang.String.format(String,Object…). It has the same purpose and use, but the format specifiers in the formatting string are slightly different.

Similar to Java, the format string parameter is a template of the resulting string, embedded with format specifiers (i.e., %d) that are replaced using the values in the argument list. Unlike Java, the values in the variable argument list are either object pointers or primitive values that are not wrapped in objects. In fact, wrapping them in objects severely limits the utility of `-stringWithFormat:`. Avoiding the need to convert primitive values into objects makes -stringWithFormat: much more convenient—and efficient—to use. So much so, that you'll find yourself using it in many places where you would have used java.lang.StringBuffer or some other technique.

Format specifiers follow this generalized syntax:

`%[argument_index$][flags][width][.precision][length]conversion`

The only significant difference is the optional length modifier, which Java doesn't need. The common conversion format specifiers and their Java equivalents are listed in Table 8-7.

Table 8-7. *Format Conversion Specifiers*

Java	Java Type	Objective-C	Objective-C Type	Replaced With
%s/%S	object	%@	object	object's -description (toString())
		%p	any pointer	hexadecimal memory address
		%s	char*	Null-terminated ASCII C string
		%S	unichar*	Null-terminated Unicode C string
		%c	char	8-bit ASCII character
%c	char	%C	unichar	16-bit Unicode
%d	any integer	%d/%D/%i	int	signed decimal value
		%u/%U	unsigned int	unsigned decimal value
%o	any integer	%o/%O	unsigned int	octal value
%x/%X	any integer	%x/%X	unsigned int	hexadecimal value
%e/%E	float, double	%e/%E	float, double	value in scientific notation
%f	float, double	%f/%F	float, double	decimal value
%g/%G	float, double	%g/%G	float, double	decimal value or scientific notation
%a/%A	float, double	%a/%A	float, double	hexadecimal value
%%		%%		Literal '%' character

The most notable difference is Objective-C's use of the %@ conversion specifier for object descriptions; this replaces Java's %s specifier. Use %@ for all Objective-C strings and object arguments. All other format specifiers expect a primitive scalar or pointer. The flags, width, and precision modifiers all behave much as they do in Java.

Variable argument lists in C provide no type or size information about the individual arguments. The mechanics are explained in the Variable Arguments section of Chapter 6. The type and size of each argument is inferred from the length and conversion specifier found in the format string. This imposes two important restrictions.

The first restriction is on the optional argument index modifier: you can't "skip" arguments. Take the statement [NSString stringWithFormat:@"%d-%3$d",1,2,3] as an example. The format string provides no information about the type or size of the second variable parameter. Without it, the formatter doesn't have enough information to extract the third variable argument, so the format operation fails.

The second restriction is that the combination of the length modifier and the conversion specifier *must* agree with the type of the parameter. The formatter blindly assumes that each argument agrees with the type implied by the specifier, and will interpret it accordingly. This is the single most common cause of garbled strings, and can occasionally cause catastrophic runtime errors (say, trying to interpret an integer as a pointer to an object). Table 8-8 lists the length modifiers and the argument type that each implies. If the length modifier is omitted, the argument type is assumed to be compatible with the type listed in Table 8-7.

Table 8-8. *Conversion Length Modifiers*

Modifier	Applicable Conversions	Argument Type
hh	d, i, o, u, x, X	char, unsigned char
h	d, i, o, u, x, X	short int, unsigned short int
l	d, i, o, u, x, X	long int, unsigned long int
ll, q	d, i, o, u, x, X	long long int, unsigned long long int
L	a, A, e, E, f, F, g, G	long double

To format a char as an unsigned numeric value, use the specifier %hhu. To format a 64-bit long long integer in hexadecimal, use the specifier %llx or %qx. If you are unsure if the type of an argument will match its specifier, force it using a typecast, as in [NSString stringWithFormat:@"%hi",(short int)i].

In 32-bit CPU architectures, the long int type is 32-bits, so int and long int mean the same thing. Nevertheless, it's good programming practice to match the correct length modifier (%ld) when passing a long int argument, even though the simpler form (%d) is compatible.

Objective-C string formatting does not provide format specifiers for Boolean values, dates, or times. The -[NSDate description] method returns the date and time using an ISO-like international format. If that's sufficient, the date object can be formatted using %@. For more complex date formatting, use NSDateFormatter, the results of which can then be inserted into a format string using %@. When formatting Boolean values, I typically use a trinary conditional expression, as in [NSString stringWithFormat:@"%@",(t?@"YES":@"NO")].

This is by no means a comprehensive exploration of formatting strings. The Cocoa framework implements the IEEE printf specification, with some additional Objective-C–specific extensions. This IEEE standard is extensive and includes many obscure options, features, and specifiers. The "Format

Specifiers" section of "String Programming Guide for Cocoa"[1], published by Apple, and "Standard 1003.1,"[2] published by the IEEE and The Open Group, contain complete descriptions.

NSFormatter

The NSFormatter class is the abstract base class for objects used to convert value objects into strings and vice versa. Don't confuse it with the java.util.Formatter class. Java's Formatter is where the formatting logic described in the previous section is implemented. Cocoa's NSFormatter class defines an abstract interface for creating formatter objects. NSFormatter objects perform the conversion between what the user sees and types and (potentially) complex values such as currency, calendar dates, and clock times. NSFormatter objects are intended to encapsulate features such as normalization, localization, and user display preferences—transformations too complex for simple format specifiers. They can be used in isolation or attached to certain view objects, where they are invoked automatically to translate between the data model and the view.

The Cocoa framework provides two concrete implementations: NSNumberFormatter and NSDateFormatter. If you have the need, you can subclass NSFormatter and create your own.

Significant changes have been made to some NSFormatter classes over the years. For backwards compatibility, these classes may exhibit legacy behavior unless configured otherwise. Review the NSFormatter behavior for your programming environment. For the best experience, use the modern behavior when available. If this is not the default, Listing 8-7 shows how to set the modern behavior before you begin using them.

Listing 8-7. Setting Modern Formatting Behavior

```
// Send these two messages before creating any date or number formatter objects.
// A good place to do this is in your application initialization.
// This will set the behvior mode for all new date & number formatter objects.
[NSDateFormatter setDefaultFormatterBehavior:NSDateFormatterBehavior10_4];
[NSNumberFormatter setDefaultFormatterBehavior:NSNumberFormatterBehavior10_4];

// Or, you can individually set the behavior of each date & number
// formatter after it is created.
NSDateFormatter *dateFormatter = [NSDateFormatter new];
[dateFormatter setFormatterBehavior:NSDateFormatterBehavior10_4];

NSNumberFormatter *numberFormatter = [NSNumberFormatter new];
[numberFormatter setFormatterBehavior:NSNumberFormatterBehavior10_4];
```

Formatters are configured with the desired formatting options, and then repeatedly used to convert values. The `-(NSString*)stringForObjectValue:(id)value` method uses the currently configured format to turn an object value into a string. The `-(BOOL)getObjectValue:(id*)object forString:(NSString*)string errorDescription:(NSString**)error` performs the opposite conversion, returning a value for the given string. It returns YES if the conversion was successful. If unsuccessful, it returns NO and creates an error object describing the problem.

---

[1] Apple, Inc., "String Programming Guide for Cocoa," http://developer.apple.com/documentation/ Cocoa/Conceptual/Strings/index.html, 2008.

[2] The IEEE and The Open Group, "The Open Group Base Specification Issue 6, IEEE Std 1003.1," http://www.opengroup.org/onlinepubs/009695399/functions/printf.html, 2004.

NSNumberFormatter

NSNumberFormatter formats decimal numbers. It implements two convenience methods: -stringFromNumber: and -numberFromString:. The easiest way to configure a formatter is to use one of the predefined formatting styles using -setNumberStyle:. Styles take into account the user's language, cultural conventions of the user's locale, and their global display preferences. Table 8-9 lists some of the predefined number format styles.

Table 8-9. Predefined Number Formatting Styles

Style	Use for
NSNumberFormatterDecimalStyle	Decimal numbers
NSNumberFormatterCurrencyStyle	Local currency
NSNumberFormatterPercentStyle	Percentages
NSNumberFormatterScientificStyle	Scientific notation
NSNumberFormatterSpellOutStyle	Natural language (i.e., "twenty-two")

If one of the predefined styles is insufficient, you can configure a formatter using a *number format pattern*. Number format strings use the Unicode Number Format Patterns standard (Unicode Technical Standard #35[3]), and should not be confused with the format specifiers used by -stringWithFormat: and similar methods. Number format patterns form a template describing how many significant digits to display, what punctuation to use, and may contain alternate templates for zero and negative values. Table 8-10 shows some sample number format patterns and the resulting string when formatting numbers for an English-speaking user in the US. Table 8-11 shows the same results for a user in Spain.

Table 8-10. Example Number Format Patterns in English (US)

Number Format	7	1234.56	0	-0.98765
#,##0.5	7.0	1,234.6	0.0	-1.0
#,##0.###;zero;#,##0.###-	7	1,234.56	zero	0.988-
000000.0000	000007.0000	001234.5601	000000.0000	-000000.9876
00.0%	700.0%	123456.0%	00.0%	-98.8%

---

[3] Mark Davis, "Unicode Technical Standard #35, Locale Data Markup Language," http://unicode.org/reports/tr35/tr35-6.html, 2006.

Table 8-11. *Example Number Format Patterns in Spanish (Spain)*

Number Format	7	1234.56	0	-0.98765
#,##0.5	7,0	1.234,6	0,0	-1,0
#,##0.###;zero;#,##0.###-	7	1.234,56	zero	0,988-
000000.0000	000007,0000	001234,5601	000000,0000	-000000,9876
00.0%	700,0%	123456,0%	00,0%	-98,8%

Finally, you can take extremely fine-grained control over the formatting by individually setting any of the nearly forty properties of NSNumberFormatter directly.

Number format styles localize the results automatically. The format strings localize some elements for you, like the decimal separator character, but not all. Individually setting the various NSNumberFormatter properties gives you the ultimate control, but ignores the localization and display preferences set by the user.

NSDateFormatter

Similar to NSNumberFormatter, NSDateFormatter is a specialized formatter for translating calendar dates and clock times. It can also be configured using predefined styles, a date format pattern, or through individual properties. The predefined styles are listed in Table 8-12, along with the results for an English-speaking user in the United Kingdom.

Table 8-12. *Predefined Date Formatting Styles in English (UK)*

Date Style	February 15, 2005
NSDateFormatterShortStyle	15/02/2005
NSDateFormatterMediumStyle	15 Feb 2005
NSDateFormatterLongStyle	15 February 2005
NSDateFormatterFullStyle	Tuesday, 15 February 2005

Unicode Technical Standard #35 also defines date format patterns. They are very similar to the date and time format specifiers supported by java.util.Formatter. Objective-C string formatting does not attempt to support even simple date and time formatting, electing to delegate that to the more capable NSDateFormatter class. Some simple date format patterns are shown in Table 8-13. The results are for an English speaking user in the USA.

Table 8-13. *Example Date Format Patterns in English (US)*

Date Format	February 15, 2005 1:40:59 PM
yyyy-MM-dd 'at' HH:mm	2005-02-15 at 13:40
EEEE MMMM d, yyyy	Tuesday February 15, 2005
'millisecond' A 'of Julian day' g	millisecond 49259000 of Julian day 2453417
QQQQ	1st quarter

Summary

The string and wrapper classes in Objective-C aren't conceptually much different than those in Java. The wrapper classes are more generic and can wrap more than just the built-in value types. Unlike Java, Objective-C strings can be subclassed. This means that they *might* be mutable, but generally aren't, and can usually be treated the same way they are in Java. Remember to use %@ instead of %s in format strings, and use the NSFormatter classes for sophisticated value conversion.

CHAPTER 9

■ ■ ■

Garbage Collection

Garbage object collection is most notable for what you, the programmer, don't have to do. In a perfect world, you just ignore the mechanics of garbage collection and let the run time system take care of the details. But there are situations when you do need to pay attention to garbage collection. Weak references and finalize methods require some understanding of what causes objects to become garbage and how they get collected.

Garbage collection in Objective-C 2.0 is broadly similar to what you experience in Java. Most of the time, you simply forget about it and "just works." Objective-C's garbage collector is on a par with modern Java implementations. It's a conservative, multi-generational, garbage collector that runs in the background on a separate thread. It handles all of the typical programming problems, like circular references, with aplomb. It's efficient, and rarely gets in the way of your application.

Later in the chapter you'll learn how to write -finalize methods and use weak references. If you write only "pure" Objective-C—you only deal with objects and object pointers—that's probably all you'll need to know and you can skip to the next chapter when you've learned what you want. You'll only need to read further if you step outside Objective-C into the wilderness of C pointers.

The devil, as the saying goes, is in the details. Objective-C's garbage collection is complicated by C's permissive—some would say anarchic—memory access. Without the strict isolation between the programmer and physical memory imposed by Java, there is no possible way of determining definitively what objects are being referenced and which ones aren't. Objective-C uses a best effort approach that balances efficiency with convenience. There are, however, subtle holes in this approach that can cause objects to leak or be prematurely collected. Learning how to recognize and avoid these situations is the focus of the last half of this chapter.

THE THEORY OF GARBAGE COLLECTION

Modern garbage collection systems function by determining the graph of reachable objects. This is the set of objects that your application has references to, or can obtain a reference to via some other reference. The graph starts with the root set of objects. This includes the object pointers in global (static) variables, the object pointers in every thread's stack, and any object pointers in CPU registers. The set is then expanded by adding in all of the objects referenced by the root objects, and all of the objects referenced by those objects, and so on, until there are no more object references that aren't in the set. This forms the complete set of reachable objects. Any objects *not* in that set are eligible to be collected and destroyed.

To cause an object to be collected involves nothing more than clearing—sometimes referred to as "forgetting"—all reachable references to that object. The object falls outside the set of reachable objects and gets collected.

Choosing to Use Garbage Collection

Objective-C garbage collection is not universally available. Not all development and runtime environments support it, and when they do it is often not the default memory management service. As of this writing, Objective-C garbage collection is a feature, not a standard. Review the capabilities of your deployment environment (platform and operating system versions) to determine if garbage collection is supported. If it is, make sure it is enabled for your project—see Chapter 4 for an example. If garbage collection is not available, you will have to resort to using traditional Objective-C memory management. This is explained in more detail in Chapter 24.

In most runtime environments, such as a Cocoa application, the garbage collector is started automatically for you. If you are building a command-line tool that uses Objective-C, you must start the garbage collector by calling the C function objc_startCollectorThread() at the earliest reasonable point in your tool's startup.

Writing Code with Garbage Collection

Choosing to use garbage collection or not will dictate your coding style. It's possible to write Objective-C code that will function in both a GC (garbage collected) and non-GC (managed memory) runtime environment, but it's complicated and rarely necessary to do so. An example would be a plug-in framework that is loaded dynamically by other applications—some using GC, others not. For straightforward application development, write all of your code assuming either garbage collection or managed memory. This chapter provides guidance on writing Objective-C in a garbage collection environment. Chapter 24 explains traditional managed memory.

The common ways of creating new objects in Objective-C are as follows:

```
[SomeClass new]
```

```
[[SomeClass alloc] init]
```

```
[[SomeClass alloc] initWith:…]
```

```
[SomeClass someConvenienceConstructor]
```

These are identical to the ways objects are created in a non-GC environment. In a GC environment, you're pretty much done. You don't have to do anything else once the object is created; the garbage collector will take care of it when you no longer reference it.

Note If you are reading code that was written for a non-GC environment, you'll see objects sent the messages -retain, -release, and -autorelease. In a garbage-collected environment, these messages are ignored. If you are porting code from a non-GC to a GC environment, you can safely remove all -retain, -release, and -autorelease messages. In addition, the -retainCount and -dealloc messages are blocked. The value returned by -retainCount is meaningless. An object's -dealloc method will never be executed, even if you try to send it a -dealloc message yourself—which you should never do anyway.

Properties and hand-coded setter methods in a GC environment should use simple assignments. Listing 9-1 shows a property and a manually implemented setter method that was written assuming garbage collection. For contrast, an implementation appropriate for a non-GC environment is also included. Both implementations have equivalent behavior and are thread safe.

Listing 9-1. GC and Non-GC Property Implementations

GC Environment
```
@interface Doll : NSObject {
    NSColor *hairColor;
    NSColor *eyeColor;
}
@property (assign) NSColor *hairColor;
@property (assign) NSColor *eyeColor;

@end

@implementation Doll

@synthesize hairColor;

- (NSColor*)eyeColor
{
    return eyeColor;
}

- (void)setEyeColor:(NSColor*)color
{
    eyeColor = color;
}

@end
```

Non-GC Environment
```
@interface Doll : NSObject {
    NSColor *hairColor;
    NSColor *eyeColor;
}
@property (retain) NSColor *hairColor;
@property (retain) NSColor *eyeColor;

@end

@implementation Doll

@synthesize hairColor;

- (NSColor*)eyeColor
{
    @synchronized(self) {
        return [[eyeColor retain] autorelease];
    }
}
```

```
- (void)setEyeColor:(NSColor*)color
{
    @synchronized(self) {
        if (eyeColor!=color) {
            [eyeColor release];
            eyeColor = [color retain];
        }
    }
}

@end
```

Writing Finalize Methods

When all references to an object are gone, the object is eligible to be collected and destroyed. In Objective-C, just as in Java, the garbage collector sends each collectable object a -finalize message before it is destroyed. The rules for well-behaved finalize methods are very similar to those in Java, so I'll just summarize them here:

- Don't attempt to perform time-consuming clean-up or resource recovery. That should be done before the object is forgotten.

- Don't disconnect object graphs or set instance variables to nil in an attempt to help the garbage collector (it's redundant).

- Don't attempt to remove the object from collections or view hierarchies (it's redundant).

- All weak references to the object will be disconnected *before* it is sent a -finalize message.

- It's generally safe to send messages to other objects, but keep it to a minimum.

- Objects may be finalized in any order, so your object should be prepared to receive messages (from other collectable objects) before *or* after receiving -finalize.

- Objects receiving the -finalize message should not attempt to resurrect collectable objects or attempt to resurrect themselves by creating a strong reference to self.

- Only one -finalize message is sent to each object.

- An object's -finalize methods must be thread safe.

Creating Weak References

There are situations where your application wants to maintain a reference to an object but does not want to prevent the garbage collector from collecting it. The typical situation is a cache or pool of objects (let's say they are graphic images) that are used by many other objects. A single cache or pool of resource objects makes it convenient for individual objects to obtain references to those common resource objects. When all of the objects in the application are done with a resource, they all "forget" the object.

Ideally, the resource object should now be reclaimed, but the single reference from the pool to the object keeps the resource object from being collected.

This is solved using a *weak reference*. A weak reference is a pointer to an object that the garbage collector does *not* traverse when building the set of reachable objects. From the garbage collector's perspective, it is not a reference and does not prevent the object from being collected.

In Java, weak references are established via java.lang.ref.WeakReference objects. To create a weak reference, a WeakReference object is created to hold the reference to the weakly referenced object, as shown in Listing 9-2. In Objective-C, appending the __weak modifier to any object pointer creates a weak reference.

Listing 9-2. *Creating Weak References*

Java
```
String name = "Clarence";
WeakReference weakName = new WeakReference(name);
name = null;

...

name = (String)weakName.get();
if (name!=null) {
    // ... name has not been collected
    }
```

Objective-C
```
__weak NSString *name = @"Clarence";

...

if (name!=nil) {
    // ... name has not been collected
    }
```

A __weak object pointer is set to nil by the garbage collector whenever it determines that there are no other strong references to that object and the object is eligible for collection. The garbage collector guarantees that all __weak references to an object are set to nil before the object is finalized and destroyed.

For the sake of clarity, all non-weak references are *strong* references. Objective-C does not support soft references or phantom references. Nor are there any reference queues, so your objects are not notified when the garbage collector decides to collect an object.

To make it easy to manage groups of objects via weak references, both Java and Objective-C provide specialized collections that hold weak references to a set of objects, gracefully removing them when they are collected. These are listed in Table 9-1.

Table 9-1. *Weak Collection Classes*

Weak Java Collection	Weak Objective-C Collection
	NSHashTable
WeakHashMap	NSMapTable
	NSPointerArray

The NSHashTable implements a general-purpose set collection. It is largely consistent with the traditional NSMutableSet class, but can be programmed with different "personalities" that define how it treats each element of the set. One of the more useful options is to configure the set to use weak references to all of its objects using the constructor [NSHashTable hashTableWithWeakObjects]. This creates a mutable set of objects that can be collected if they lack any strong references. When collected, an object simply disappears from the set.

Similarly, NSMapTable is a mutable dictionary (map) of key/value pairs. Unlike java.util.WeakHashMap, an NSMapTable can be created with strong or weak references to its keys, and strong or weak references to its values, as listed in Table 9-2. A key/value pair in the collection is removed if either object is collected.

Table 9-2. *NSMapTable Constructors*

Constructor	Key Pointers	Value Pointers
[NSMapTable mapTableWithStrongToStrongObjects]	strong	strong
[NSMapTable mapTableWithWeakToStrongObjects]	weak	strong
[NSMapTable mapTableWithStrongToWeakObjects]	strong	weak
[NSMapTable mapTableWithWeakToWeakObjects]	weak	weak

Finally, the NSPointerArray collection is similar to the NSMutableArray collection, except that it permits items in the collection to be nil (or NULL). It is intended to be used with generic pointers—normally outside the scope of garbage collection—but can be programmed to use weak object pointers using the constructor [NSPointerArray pointerArrayWithWeakObjects]. When an object is collected, its pointer entry in the collection is set to nil. This does not alter the number of items in the collection, just its content.

See Chapter 16 for more about collection classes.

Creating Strong References

You can programmatically create a strong reference by dynamically promoting an object pointer to the root set of objects, even if your application does not maintain a strong reference to it. This might be useful, for example, if you created an autonomous controller that performs actions on its own—possibly responding to notifications or C callbacks, which are themselves weak references—and you don't need a reference to it. The code in Listing 9-3 prevents an object from being garbage collected using the -disableCollectorForPointer: method. To make the object collectable again, balance each -disableCollectorForPointer: message with an -enableCollectorForPointer: message.

Listing 9-3. Preventing an Object from Being Collected

```
EventDaemon *eventDaemon = [EventDaemon new];
[[NSGarbageCollector defaultCollector] disableCollectorForPointer:eventDaemon];
eventDaemon = nil; // EventDaemon will not be collected
```

The __strong type modifier is the counterpart to __weak. All object pointers and identifiers (id) in Objective-C are __strong by default. Declaring them __strong is redundant, but permissible. The __strong modifier exists principally for use with other types of pointers that are neither __strong nor __weak, allowing you to use Objective-C's garbage collector to manage non-object memory allocations. See the "Allocating Collectable Memory" section of this chapter, and the section on using garbage collection to manage Core Foundation structures in Chapter 24.

Encouraging Garbage Collection

You normally do not need to interact with the garbage collection system directly. If you do, the NSGarbageCollection class provides an object-oriented interface to the service. As in Java, there are methods that will encourage the garbage collector to start collecting objects. These methods don't force the garbage collector to do anything—for example, it might have just finished collecting objects, so collecting again would be waste of time. It just suggests to the GC that it might be an opportune time to do so.

In addition, you can temporarily disable garbage collection in Objective-C by sending the -disable message. You might do this during an extremely performance-sensitive section of code, but I won't suggest leaving it off for very long. Send an -enable message to resume collection. The common methods for controlling the garbage collector are listed in Table 9-3.

Table 9-3. Garbage Collector Control Methods

Method	Description
+[NSGarbageCollector defaultCollector]	Returns the singleton instance of NSGarbageCollector for your process.
-[NSGarbageCollector disable]	Turns off garbage collection.
-[NSGarbageCollector enable]	Starts garbage collection again after sending -disable. Each -disable must be balanced by one -enable.
-[NSGarbageCollector collectIfNeeded]	Suggests that the garbage collector begin a collection cycle if the memory consumption thresholds have been exceeded.
-[NSGarbageCollector collectExhaustively]	Suggests that the garbage collector begin a complete and thorough collection cycle.

GC vs. Non-GC Pointers

Garbage collection in Java is both determinate and homogenous; all references refer to objects. In Objective-C, pointers can point to just about anything. They can point to objects, blocks, structures on the stack, structures within other structures, elements of an array, or even be filled with random meaningless values. It is demonstrably impossible, therefore, to determine with absolute certainty the set of reachable objects.

Objective-C's solution to this is to ignore most pointers and pay attention only to pointers that (should) reference objects. This results in a mixture of memory management techniques. Objective-C objects use the garbage collector, while conventional C memory allocations are managed using their traditional design patterns.

This section explains which pointers are naturally managed by the garbage collection service, which ones aren't, and what control you have over that. It also highlights situations where non-managed pointers can be a problem and how to deal with them.

Write Barriers

Objective-C keeps track of the pointer references that it manages using a technique called a *write barrier*. The compiler replaces all assignments to __strong and __weak pointers with a fast function call that makes the assignment and registers the pointer with the garbage collection system. Remember that all Objective-C object pointers are __strong by default. Every object pointer assignment is registered with the garbage collector, which uses that information to determine the set of reachable objects.

Allocating Collectable Memory

You can also have the garbage collector manage any pointer to an allocated block of memory by explicitly typing it as __strong or __weak, then setting the pointer to a managed block of memory. The garbage collector will treat the pointer like any other object reference and dispose of the memory once it's no longer reachable. This technique has two prerequisites:

- *All* pointers to the memory allocation must be typed __strong (or __weak, as appropriate).

- Allocate the memory using NSAllocateCollectable(int size, int options).

- If the contents of the collectable memory block contain __strong or __weak pointers, the options parameter of NSAllocatableCollectable should be NSScannedOption. Otherwise, pass 0. Listing 9-4 demonstrates the allocation of an arbitrary block of memory that will be managed by the garbage collector. Note that this is a rewriting of the code fragment from the last chapter that used an NSMutableData object to contain the array.

Listing 9-4. *Allocating Garbage Collected Memory Blocks*

```
- (__strong NSPoint*)pointsForObjects:(NSArray*)objects
{
    __strong NSPoint *points;
    unsigned int count = [objects count];
    unsigned int i;

    points = (NSPoint*)NSAllocateCollectable(count*sizeof(NSPoint),0);
    for (i=0; i<[objects count]; i++) {
        points[i] = …
    }
    return points;
}
```

Garbage Collection Pitfalls

Here's a short collection of the most common garbage collection–related hazards and how to resolve them.

Interior Pointers

Pointers that point to structures inside a collectable object do not prevent that object from being collected. If the object is prematurely collected, the pointer becomes invalid. The example shown in Listing 9-5 demonstrates this problem.

Listing 9-5. *Interior Pointer*

```
NSData *data = [NSData dataWithData:originalData];
const char *bytes = [data bytes];
```

Let's assume that the data variable in Listing 9-5 is never referenced again. Immediately following these two lines of code, the NSData object could be collected leaving the bytes variable pointing to invalid memory. The reason is because the [data bytes] statement is the last reachable reference to the NSData object in the method. The Objective-C compiler can be *extremely* aggressive about reclaiming automatic variables. The compiler could very likely assign both data and bytes to the same CPU register, since their lifetimes don't overlap. Thus, by the time the bytes assignment is complete, the NSData object pointer is gone and the object becomes collectable.

The solution is to reference the data object at least once after the last use of any interior pointers. It doesn't matter how the reference is accomplished. This includes sending it gratuitous -retain and -release messages. I personally prefer this technique, because these messages are used for classic memory management and they scream, "I'm doing memory management here," which is true.

An alternative solution is to use a collectable memory block, described earlier in the Allocating Collectable Memory section.

Opaque Pointers

Objects assigned to pointers that are neither __strong nor __weak (i.e., not write barrier protected) are not considered by the garbage collector. This can be a problem when passing an object via a void* or some other opaque pointer type. Listing 9-6 demonstrates the problem in passing a dictionary object as the context for a message that will be sent at some later time. The void* to the object does not prevent it from being collected before the message is sent.

Listing 9-6. *Assigning an Object to an Opaque Pointer*

```
NSDictionary *info = …;
[NSApp beginSheet:sheetWindow
    modalForWindow:window
     modalDelegate:delegate
    didEndSelector:@selector(sheetDidEnd:returnCode:contextInfo:);
       contextInfo:(void*)info];

…

- (void)sheetDidEnd:(NSWindow*)sheet
         returnCode:(int)returnCode
        contextInfo:(void *)contextInfo
{
    NSDictionary *info = (id)contextInfo;
    id value = [contextObject objectForKey:@"Value"];
    …
}
```

In the first part of Listing 9-6, a dictionary is created to pass one or more values to the modal sheet completion method designated in the didEndSelector: parameter. However, since the contextInfo: parameter is not a __strong pointer, the NSDictionary object becomes unreachable—in the eyes of garbage collector—immediately following the beginSheet:… message.

There are two simple solutions to this problem. The first is to use the Core Foundation functions CFRetain(id) and CFRelease(id) to give the object a non-zero retain count. As mentioned earlier, Objective-C's garbage collector coexists with traditional C memory management. CFRetain increments the retain count of the object—as if the object were also in use by C code—preventing it from being collected. A more object-oriented solution would be to use +[NSGarbageCollector disableCollectorForPointer:] to prevent the object from being collected, and +[NSGarbageCollector enableCollectorForPointer:] in the model sheet completion method to make it collectable again.

Enumerating Weak Collections

Care must be taken when enumerating through collections of weak object pointers. Their contents, and element count, can spontaneously change as objects are collected. This can cause enumerator objects and for(;;) loops to behave erratically.

To avoid this, either use Objective-C's fast enumeration or create a temporary immutable collection that uses strong references until your enumeration is finished. Fast enumeration is covered in Chapter 16.

Uninitialized Stack References

Due to the way that the Objective-C garbage collector detects strong references in automatic variables on the stack, it can be tricked into thinking that an uninitialized automatic variable contains a strong reference. You can religiously initialize all automatic variables, or simply call the C function `objc_clear_stack(0)` occasionally. It should be called at the lowest reasonable stack frame—ideally from the thread's top-level loop. When the function is called, all of the methods on the stack should have as few uninitialized automatic variables as possible. If the thread is running a run loop, you don't need to do this. Each run loop automatically calls `objc_clear_stack(0)` for you.

Other Pitfalls

There are other, progressively more obscure, situations that can cause objects to leak or be prematurely collected. If you believe you are having problems with garbage collection, review the *Garbage Collection Programming Guide* published by Apple.[1]

Design Patterns to Avoid

Here are a few programming patterns that should be avoided when writing programs that use garbage collection:

- You cannot override, intercept, or send the `-release`, `-dealloc`, or `-retainCount` methods.

- Delegate, parent, and observer references are often described as "weak" when using managed memory because they are not retained—to avoid circular retains. These are not, in fact, weak references and should not be typed as __weak. The garbage collector has no problem dealing with circular references.

- Do not use the lifetime of an object to manage an expensive resource. Often, an object will be created just to manage a large buffer or pool of computed objects. Once all of the references to the object are released, it releases the underlying resource. When using garbage collection, implement your own reference counting or create a dictionary (map) that contains each client object as keys and a reference to the resource as values. Each client object should remove itself from the collection when finished with the resource, allowing the resource to be collected when the last client is removed.

- Don't use allocation zones for Objective-C objects. The garbage collector requires that all managed objects be allocated in the default zone.

Debugging

There are also a couple of debugging aides. If the `OBJC_PRINT_GC` environment variable is set to YES, the garbage collection framework will print diagnostic information to the console.

If you believe that a pointer is, or is not, being protected by a write barrier, the `-Wassign-intercept` compiler flag will help you discover where write barriers are being inserted into your code.

---

[1]Apple, Inc., *Garbage Collection Programming Guide*, `http://developer.apple.com/documentation/Cocoa/Conceptual/GarbageCollection/`, 2008.

Summary

At the surface, Objective-C garbage collection is on a par with Java's—you just need to turn it on. Strong and weak references are concepts Java programmers are comfortable with, and behave almost identically in Objective-C. You just need to be careful when working with other pointer types, as non-object pointers are not normally managed for you, and be conscious of the pitfall that can occur when working with pointers that are not managed by the garbage collector.

CHAPTER 10

Introspection

Introspection (reflection) is the act of exploring information *about* an object, often referred to as its metadata: the class of the object, the methods it implements, what properties it declares, the protocols (interfaces) it conforms to, and so on. The common questions ("What class is this object?," "Can I treat this object as a specific class?," and "Does this object implement a specific method?") are all easy to answer. This chapter will first tell you how to answer those common questions. It will then look into the deeper exploration of objects and classes.

This chapter will also explore Key-Value Coding, a technology closely related to introspection. Key-Value Coding, or KVC, allows you to access the properties of an object symbolically. As a trivial example, take a Person class that has NSString *name, Person *mother, and Person *father properties. KVC would allow you to get a person's name with the path @"name", and the name of their mother with the path @"mother.name". KVC isn't introspection; KVC won't tell you what properties an object implements. But it is so closely related to introspection that it's useful to understand what it can do for you. You might prefer to use KVC rather than perform your own introspection. You'll also want to know how to design your classes so that they work with KVC.

For reasons both pragmatic and philosophical, Objective-C introspection techniques focus more on discovering individual traits than determining what class an object is, and then inferring what methods and properties it has from that. If you want to know if an object can open a URL, you should determine if the object implements an -openURL: method. This is preferable to testing its class against those that you believe implement an -openURL: method. The fewer assumptions you make about an object's class, the more robust and flexible your code will be. Here are the most common questions you'll want to ask about an object:

- Does this object implement a specific method?

- Is this object an instance of a specific class?

- Is this object an instance of a specific class, or any subclass of that class?

These three questions are the easiest to answer in Objective-C. They are listed in order of efficiency and speed. Determining if an object implements a particular method, rather than if it's a member of a class, has two advantages. It more directly addresses the question of the object's functionality, and it's considerably more efficient.

This isn't to say that you shouldn't test an object's class. There are many valid reasons to do so. But if you are testing an object's class to *infer* that it implements some method, consider testing the more direct assertion.

Testing for Methods

Java doesn't have a simple, concise method for determining if an object implements a specific method. Instead, Java programs tend to create classes and interfaces that implement functional groups of methods. The programmer then tests an object for membership in those classes or interfaces. This works well in Java because of its strong type checking and strict inheritance model.

Objective-C's class structure is much more relaxed and dynamic, so the assumptions one can make in Java are not as applicable. The preferred method of determining if an object implements a particular method is to test that directly, as shown in Listing 10-1.

Listing 10-1. Testing for the Implementation of a Specific Method

Java
```
Method method = null;
try {
    Class objectClass = object.getClass();
    Class[] paramTypes = { };
    method = objectClass.getMethod("intValue",paramTypes);
    }
catch (Exception e) {
    }
if (method!=null)
    … // object can convert itself into an int
```

Objective-C
```
if ([object respondsToSelector:@selector(intValue)])
    … // object can convert itself into an int
```

The -respondsToSelector: message takes a selector constant and returns YES if the receiver responds to (implements) that method. The parameter can be a selector constant generated using the @selector() directive, or a value of type SEL. Listing 10-2 demonstrates using -respondsToSelector: to selectively send messages to a group of listeners. The method sends a notification to all of its listeners that implement a specific method. This allows each listener to receive specific messages simply by electing to implement those methods. The listener is ignored when the sender broadcasts a message that it doesn't implement.

Listing 10-2. Sending a Message Only to Objects That Implement It

```
- (void)updateListenersUsingSelector:(SEL)sel
{
    for ( id listener in listeners ) {
        if ([listener respondsToSelector:sel])
            [listener performSelector:sel withObject:self];
    }
}
```

Sending the message -updateListenersUsingSelector:@selector(startingChat:) sends every listener that implements the -startingChat: method a notification. The practice of recognizing object roles based on what methods they implement is called an *informal protocol*, and was described in more detail in Chapter 5.

Testing Class Membership

Java's instanceof operator tests an object to determine if it is an instance of a class, a subclass of that class, implements an interface, or a subinterface of that interface. True to its minimalist roots, the Objective-C language has no membership operator. Instead, the class framework implements the methods listed in Table 10-1 in the root NSObject class.

Table 10-1. *Class and Protocol Membership Tests*

Message	Tests
-isKindOfClass:(Class)class	The object is an instance of the class, or a subclass of the class.
-isMemberOfClass:(Class)class	The object is a specific class.
-conformsToProtocol:(Protocol*)protocol	The object adopts the protocol, or inherits from a class that adopts the protocol.

Objective-C treats class membership and protocol (interface) adoption differently, both internally and syntactically. So there is no single equivalent to the instanceof operator. Use -isKindOfClass: when testing for class membership, and -conformsToProtocol: when testing for protocol adoption. Listing 10-3 illustrates the different methods and syntax to use for each. The Class object for a specific class is usually obtained by sending a -class message to either the class itself, or any instance of that class. Use the @protocol() directive to generate a protocol identifier constant.

Listing 10-3. *Testing and Casting Class Membership and Protocol Adoption*

Java
```
Object object = …

if (object instanceof MyClass) {
    MyClass myObject = (MyClass)object;
    …

if (object instanceof MyInterface) {
    MyInterface myObject = (MyInterface)object;
    …
```

Objective-C
```
id object = …

if ([object isKindOfClass:[MyClass class]]) {
    MyClass *myObject = object;
    …

if ([object conformsToProtocol:@protocol(MyProtocol)]) {
    id<MyProtocol> myObject = object;
```

Key-Value Coding

As mentioned at the beginning of this chapter, Key-Value Coding is not an introspection technology per se; it won't describe what properties an object supports. KVC is, however, so intimately entwined with introspection that it's difficult to relate it to any other topic.

KVC is a powerful tool that's the foundation for many other technologies such as Key-Value Observing, bindings, and scripting. Before implementing your own property introspection solution, first consider if KVC already solves your problem. Designing your properties to be compatible with KVC gives your objects the greatest interoperability with other technologies. This section will explain the basics of Key-Value Coding, along with techniques to make your classes KVC compliant.

In its simplest terms, Key-Value Coding allows you to access (get and set) the properties of an object using a string (key) that identifies the property by name. For example, an object's name property could be set using [object setValue:@"Earnest" forKey:@"name"], and is equivalent to [object setName:@"Earnest"]. If that was all KVC could do, it would have some limited utility. KVC gets really interesting when property names are combined into paths and applied to collections.

The best explanation is an example. Listing 10-4 shows the objects that might make up a school management program. It defines Person, Student, Parent, Teacher, and Period classes. Student, Parent, and Teacher objects are all subclasses of Person.

Rachael, one of the teachers, is planning a family field trip that will include all of the students in her homeroom, along with their siblings and stepsiblings. She needs the names of her homeroom students and their siblings.

Listing 10-4. *Using KVC to Access Object Properties*

Java
```java
package com.apress.java.school;

public class Person
{
    public String name;
}

public class Parent extends Person
{
    public ArrayList<Student> children;
}

public class Teacher extends Person
{
    public ArrayList    periods;
    public Period       homeroom;
}

public class Student extends Person
{
    public ArrayList<Parent>    parents;
    public ArrayList            classes;
    public Period               homeroom;
}
```

```java
public class Period
{
    public ArrayList<Studen>    students;
    public Teacher             teacher;
}

...

// Assemble the names of siblings from the students in Rachael's homeroom Class
Teacher teacher = School.teacherWithName("Rachael");
Period homeroom = teacher.homeroom;
HashSet siblingNames = new HashSet();
for ( Student student : homeroom.students ) {
    for ( Parent parent : student.parents ) {
        for ( Student child : parent.children ) {
            if (!siblingNames.contains(child.name)) {
                siblingNames.add(child.name);
            }
        }
    }
}
return siblingNames;
```

Objective-C
```objc
@class Period;

@interface Person : NSObject {
    NSString *name;
}
@end

@interface Parent : Person {
    NSMutableArray *childen;
}
@end

@interface Teacher : Person {
    NSMutableArray  *periods;
    Period          *homeroom;
}
@end

@interface Student : Person
{
    NSMutableArray  *parents;
    NSMutableArray  *classes;
    Period          *homeroom;
}
@end
```

```
@interface Period : NSObject {
    NSMutableArray  *students;
    Teacher         *teacher;
}
@end

...

// Assemble the set of siblings from the students in Rachael's homeroom Class
Teacher *rachael = [School teacherWithName:@"Rachael"];
return [rachael valueForKeyPath:
  @"homeroom.students.@distinctUnionOfArrays.parents.@unionOfArrays.children.name"];
```

The Java implementation uses a traditional procedural solution to iterate through the students in Rachael's class, their parents, and their children, and assemble a set of unique names. The Objective-C solution leverages the power of KVC. Each identifier in the path addresses a property of the receiver or preceding object. Properties that are collections of objects apply the remainder of the path to each item in the collection, assembling the results into a new collection. Thus, the path children.name returns a collection populated with the name property of each Student object in the children property. Special path operators, such as @distinctUnionOfArrays, perform transformations or calculations on the results. In this example, the return value is reduced to a single array of unique objects, eliminating any duplicate names and collections of collections.

More importantly, a list view object on the screen, or a scripting property, could be bound using that same path. The list would display, or the scripting property would return, the result of the search without writing a single line of code.

Using Key-Value Coding

Using Key-Value Coding is straightforward. The root NSObject class defines the -valueForKey:(NSString*)key and -valueForKeyPath:(NSString*)path methods. Send either of these methods to retrieve an object's property value. Mutable values can be set by sending either -setValue:(id)value forKey:(NSString*)key or -setValue:(id)value forKeyPath:(NSString*)path. A *key* is a single property name, while a *key path* may be a simple property name or a complex path of multiple property names and operations. Primitive property values are automatically converted to and from NSNumber or NSValue objects.

Table 10-2 lists some of the KVC operations implemented by the Cocoa framework. An operator transforms the result of the path that follows the operator. All of the operators in Table 10-2 transform a collection (set or array) of values.

Table 10-2. Key-Value Coding Path Operators

Operator	Results
@count	Count of objects
@avg	Numeric average of values
@max	Largest value in a collection
@min	Smallest value in a collection

@sum	Numeric sum of the values in a collection
@distinctUnionOfArrays	Single array of unique objects from a collection of arrays
@distinctUnionOfObjects	Array of unique objects
@distinctUnionOfSets	Single set of unique objects from a collection of sets
@unionOfArrays	Single array of objects from a collection of arrays
@unionOfObjects	Single array of objects
@unionOfSets	Single set of objects from a collection of sets

You will most likely use KVC indirectly when working with technologies like Key-Value Observing, binding, and scripting. These all use KVC paths to identify the property being observed, bound, or scripted. For your objects to work with these technologies, you'll want them to be KVC compliant.

Designing KVC-Compliant Classes

Most properties you define will be KVC compliant without any additional work. At a minimum, simply declaring an instance variable—like NSString *name in Listing 10-4—defines a KVC-compliant property. KVC will use instance variable introspection to find and use the property.

If you follow the practice of using @property declarations, these too will be KVC compliant. Just avoid non-standard getter and setter names. KVC prefers accessor methods, and will use them over an instance variable with the same name. If you implement your own accessor methods, they must follow the standard getter and setter patterns. Table 10-3 lists the acceptable accessor method names for use with KVC. Replace the italicized *Property* in each with the actual name of your property (paying attention to case). Implement exactly one getter for immutable properties, and one of the getters and a setter for mutable properties.

Table 10-3. KVC-Compliant Single Value Accessor Names

Method Name	Role
-*property*	Getter
-get*Property*	Getter
-is*Property*	Boolean getter
-set*Property*:	Setter

Properties that are arrays or sets (i.e., @property NSArray *teachers or @property NSSet *teachers) are automatically Key-Value Coding–compliant. To implement a KVC-compliant collection property that is *not* one of the standard array or set types, you will need to implement a number of special methods. To implement a custom array property, implement these methods:

`-(unsigned int)countOf`*Property*

Implement at least one of

- `-(`*Class*`*)objectIn`*Property*`AtIndex:(NSUInteger)index`

- `-(`*NSArray*`*)`*property*`AtIndexes:(NSIndexSet*)indexes`

For improved getter performance, you can optionally implement

- `-(void)get`*Property*`:(id*)array range:(NSRange)range`

Mutable properties must implement at least one of the following:

- `-(void)insertObject:(`*Class*`*)object in`*Property*`AtIndex:(NSUInteger)index`

- `-(void)insert`*Property*`:(NSArray*)objects atIndexes:(NSIndexSet*)indexes` (better performance)

Mutable properties must implement at least one of the following:

- `-(void)removeObjectFrom`*Property*`AtIndex:(NSUInteger)index`

- `-(void)remove`*Property*`AtIndexes:(NSIndexSet*)indexes` (better performance)

For improved performance, a mutable property may optionally implement any of the following:

- `-(void)replaceObjectIn`*Property*`AtIndex:(NSUInteger)index withObject:(`*Class*`*)object`

- `-(void)replace`*Property*`AtIndexes:(NSIndexSet*)indexes with`*Property*`:(NSArray*)objects`

In each of these methods, the italicized *Property* name is replaced with the name of the property being defined, as in `-(NSUInteger)countOfTeachers`. Note that if you choose a singular property name, consistently use the singular—not the plural—form when constructing KVC-compliant method names. Replace *Class* with the class of the property object, as in `-(Teacher*)objectInTeachersAtIndex:(NSUInteger)index`.

To implement a custom set property, implement these methods:

`-(NSUInteger)countOf`*Property*

`-(NSEnumerator*)enumeratorOf`*Property*

`-(`*Class*`*)memberOf`*Property*`:(`*Class*`*)object`

Mutable properties must implement at least one of the following:

- `-(void)add`*Property*`Object:(`*Class*`*)object`

- `-(void)add`*Property*`:(NSSet*)objects`

Mutable properties must implement at least one of the following:

- `-(void)removePropertyObject:(Class*)object`

- `-(void)removeProperty:(NSSet*)objects`

For improved performance, a mutable property may optionally implement

- `-(void)intersectProperty:(NSSet*)set`

Custom Key Values

In addition, named properties can be implemented programmatically by overriding `-(id)valueForUndefinedKey:(NSString*)key` and `-(void)setValue:(id)value forUndefinedKey:(NSString*)key`. These message are sent to an object whenever an attempt is made to get or set a property that KVC doesn't recognize. Your code can translate the name or synthesize a value. KVC also defines a standard for validating properties. Consult the *Key-Value Coding Programming Guide* published by Apple for additional details.[1]

Inspecting Classes

This section describes the primary functions for obtaining information about a Class. The next few sections will describe how to perform the most common and useful introspections. More advanced developers are encouraged to read the *Objective-C 2.0 Runtime Reference* published by Apple.[2]

Just as in Java, advanced introspection begins with the Class object. Class introspection in Java is neatly and logically organized into a class hierarchy starting with the java.lang.Class class, and working down through java.lang.reflect.Method, java.lang.reflect.Field, and so on.

In Objective-C, this is where things get a little obscure. Up until now, I've discussed the single Objective-C Class object that defines each class, and is referenced by each object's isa variable. This was somewhat misleading. There actually isn't a Class class, in the strictest sense. The Class *type* is a C structure pointer to the opaque objc_class structure. Readers with a particularly keen eye will have noticed that references to Class, like those in Table 10-1, are always just Class not Class*, as they would be for a true Objective-C object pointer.

I could get away with this deception because a pointer to an objc_class structure responds to messages much like any Objective-C object. This is why you can send it messages using Objective-C method invocation syntax, as in [MyClass new].

So the Class type exists in a kind of twilight zone between a real class and a C structure, generally behaving as an object, but without any formal class definition. Deeper introspection into classes and objects involves C functions that take an objc_class structure pointer and return information about it. This information will often be in the form of other C structures or C strings. This isn't particularly difficult, but be aware that you're stepping outside the bounds of object-oriented programming and into the bowels of the Objective-C runtime system.

---

[1] Apple, Inc., *Key-Value Coding Programming Guide*, http://developer.apple.com/documentation/Cocoa/Conceptual/KeyValueCoding/, 2009.
[2] Apple, Inc., *Objective-C 2.0 Runtime Reference*, http://developer.apple.com/documentation/Cocoa/Reference/ObjCRuntimeRef/, 2008.

■**Note** Objective-C's runtime system is designed to be completely transparent. Unlike Java's java.lang.ClassLoader—the internals of which are shrouded in secrecy—the functions by which Objective-C classes are created, registered, modified, instantiated, and sent messages are all directly available through the Objective-C runtime API. Advanced programmers who want to implement scripting languages, or dynamically define and augment classes at runtime, have unfettered access to the same APIs used by the Cocoa frameworks.

Table 10-4 lists a few functions that are useful in exploring information about classes. The first four functions in the table translate names into Class or Protocol pointers, and back again. This is how you could obtain a Class reference from nothing but a name. The second four functions are just wrappers that perform the same functions, taking and returning Objective-C string objects. The wrapper function simply calls one of the first four, converting the strings for you. Finally the class_getSuperclass(Class) function returns a class's superclass reference, or Nil if the class is the root class. It's equivalent to sending the -superclass message to an object.

Table 10-4. *Functions for Inspecting Classes*

Function	Returns
objc_getClass(const char*)	Class with that name
class_getName(Class)	The name of the Class
objc_getProtocol(const char*)	Protocol with that name
protocol_getName(Protocol)	The name of the Protocol
NSClassFromString(NSString *name)	Class with that name
NSStringFromClass(Class)	The name of the Class
NSProtocolFromString(NSString *name)	Protocol with that name
NSStringFromProtocol(Protocol*)	The name of the Protocol
class_getSuperclass(Class)	Superclass of Class

Listing 10-5 shows how to iterate through the classes an object inherits.

Listing 10-5. *Walking Up the List of Superclasses*

Java
```
Class objClass = object.getClass();
while (objClass!=null) {
    ...
    objClass = objClass.getSuperclass();
}
```

Objective-C
```
Class class = [object class];
while (class!=Nil) {
    ...
    class = class_getSuperclass(class);
}
```

■**Note** Objective-C defines the `Nil` constant for use with Class pointers. Use `Nil` with Class pointers exactly as you would use `nil` with object pointers.

Exploring Protocols

Formal protocols (interfaces) are defined separately from classes. You may want to know what protocols a class conforms to, or the methods that a protocol declares. The functions in Table 10-5 will identify the protocols that a class conforms to, and let you explore those protocols. If you just want to know if an object conforms to a specific protocol, use the -[`NSObject conformsToProtocol:`] method described earlier.

Table 10-5. *Protocol Introspection Functions*

Function	Returns
objc_getProtocol(const char*)	The protocol with that name
NSProtocolFromString(NSString*)	Same as objc_getProtocol, but accepts an Objective-C string object
class_copyProtocolList(Class,unsigned int*)	The list of protocols the class conforms to
protocol_conformsToProtocol(Protocol*,Protocol*)	YES if the protocol conforms to another protocol
protocol_getName(Protocol*)	The name of the protocol
protocol_isEqual(Protocol*,Protocol*)	YES if the protocols are equivalent

class_copyProtocolList returns a NULL-terminated C array of Protocol pointers. This block of memory must be released using the free(void*) function when you are finished with it. The number of protocols in the array is returned in the unsigned integer located at the address passed in the second parameter. If that parameter is NULL, no count is returned. You can use either the returned count or the NULL-terminating pointer to determine the length of the list, as shown in Listing 10-6.

Listing 10-6. *Listing the Protocols of a Class*

```
unsigned int protocolCount;
Protocol **protocols = class_copyProtocolList(class,&protocolCount);
NSMutableString *list = [NSMutableString new];
unsigned int i;
for (i=0; i<protocolCount; i++) {
    Protocol *p = protocols[i];
    if (i!=0)
        [list appendString:@", "];
    [list appendFormat:@"%s",protocol_getName(p)];
}
if (protocolCount!=0)
    NSLog(@"Class %s implements the protocols: %@",class_getName(class),list);
free(protocols);
```

Points of interest in Listing 10-6: the name returned by protocol_getName and class_getName are C strings, formatted using the %s format specifier. The list variable is a string object, formatted using %@. Protocol is a structure type, not an opaque pointer type like Class and Method. As such, references are declared as pointers to Protocol (Protocol*), rather than just the type (Class, Method). Confusing, isn't it?

Exploring Methods

I've already shown you how to easily determine if an object implements a specific method. Using the functions in Table 10-6 you can obtain a list of all of the methods a class implements. From a Method value you can get a method's name, selector, implementation address, and parameter information.

Table 10-6. *Common Method Introspection Functions*

Function	Returns
class_copyMethodList(Class,unsigned int *)	NULL-terminated Method array
class_getClassMethod(Class,SEL)	Method if selector was sent to the class
class_getInstanceMethod(Class,SEL)	Method if selector was sent to an instance of class
method_getName(Method)	Selector constant for Method
sel_getName(SEL)	Name for selector

NSStringFromSelector(SEL)	Name for selector
NSSelectorFromString(NSString*)	Selector for name
class_getMethodImplementation(Class,SEL)	Address of code that implements selector
method_getImplementation(Method)	Address of code that implements Method

The class_copyMethodList function works similarly to class_copyProtocolList. It returns a NULL-terminated array of Method references, which should be released using free(void*) when done. The class_getClassMethod function obtains a single Method for a specific selector constant. Note that these functions only return the methods defined by that class, not inherited by that class. To discover inherited methods, you must examine all of its superclasses.

The two functions class_getClassMethod and class_getInstanceMethod consider the difference when sending a message to class object ([MyClass message]), or an instance of the class ([myObject message]). Class and instance methods are implemented for different objects, so the results of the two functions will be different.

The method_getName function, despite its name, returns the selector constant associated with the Method—not the name of the method. To turn the selector into a name, call sel_getName or NSStringFromSelector. To do the opposite, call NSSelectorFromString.

An example of these functions in action can be found in Listing 10-7.

Listing 10-7. *Listing the Methods Implemented by a Class*

```
unsigned int methodCount;
Method *methods = class_copyMethodList(class,&methodCount);
NSMutableString *list = [NSMutableString new];
unsigned int i;
for (i=0; i<methodCount; i++) {
    Method m = methods[i];
    if (i!=0)
        [list appendString:@", "];
    [list appendFormat:@"%s",sel_getName(method_getName(m))];
}
if (methodCount!=0)
    NSLog(@"Class %s implements the methods: %@",class_getName(class),list);
free(methods);
```

The functions class_getMethodImplementation and method_getImplementation both do the same thing: they return the execution address of the code that implements the method. The Sending Messages chapter explained how to call a method directly using its implementation address.

With a Method reference, there are a score of C functions for examining its parameter list, the types and sizes of each parameter, and so on. Instead of diving into these functions, I encourage you to use the method -[NSObject methodSignatureForSelector:] to obtain an NSMethodSignature object. NSMethodSignature substantively represents all of the information embodied by the Method structure, but in an object-oriented interface. If you have a need to stick with the C functions, refer to the Objective-C 2.0 Runtime Reference document.

With an NSMethodSignature object, you can get the type of each argument (i.e., its @encode() constant) using -getArgumentTypeAtIndex:. The message -methodReturnType returns the C type of the method's return value. To invoke a method using NSMethodSignature, use it to create an NSInvocation object. This was also demonstrated in Chapter 6.

Exploring Properties

In Objective-C 2.0, the @property directive attaches metadata to the class that is available to the programmer at runtime. These are called *formal properties*. Naturally, the set of properties will overlap instance variables and methods, since most properties are implemented using instance variables along with getter and setting methods. Table 10-7 lists the common methods for examining the formal properties of a class.

Table 10-7. Common Formal Property Introspection Functions

Function	Returns
class_copyPropertyList(Class,unsigned int *)	NULL-terminated array of objc_property_t structure pointers
protocol_copyPropertyList(Protocol*,unsigned int *)	NULL-terminated array of objc_property_t structure pointers
class_getProperty(Class,const char*)	objc_property_t structure for a named property
protocol_getProperty(Protocol*,const char*,BOOL,BOOL)	objc_property_t structure for a named property
property_getName(objc_property_t)	name of property
property_getAttributes(objc_property_t)	attribute string that describes the property

The …_copyPropertyList and …_getProperty functions obtain an array or a single property description. You can inspect the properties for a class or a protocol. Lists must be released using free(void*).

The function property_getName returns the name of the property. The property_getAttributes function returns a string that describes the property. The description includes an encoded form of the property's type, attributes, and name. The string always begins with a T followed by the @encode() constant for its type. Attributes such as readonly, copy, and retain add R, C, and & characters, respectively. Other attributes are also represented. A V and the property's formal name follow the type and attributes. A few examples are listed in Table 10-8. Note that BOOL values are always encoded as signed characters.

Table 10-8. Example Property Attribute Descriptions

Property Declaration	Attribute String
@property int someInt;	Ti,VsomeInt
@property id (assign) anyObject	T@,VanyObject
@property(readonly) int ceiling;	Ti,R,Vceiling
@property(getter=isRunning) BOOL running;	Tc,GisRunning,Vrunning
@property(nonatomic,readonly,copy) id safe;	T@,R,C,Vsafe

Exploring Instance Variables

The introspection functions for instance variables follows the same pattern as those for methods, protocols, and properties. There are functions, listed in Table 10-9, to obtain a list of Ivar structures that describe all instance variables defined by a class, or just one. The functions ivar_getName, ivar_getOffset, ivar_getTypeEncoding will reveal the name, byte offset within the object's structure, and type of each Ivar—but these latter two should not generally be used to access the variable. To get or set an instance variable, call object_getIvar(id,Ivar) or object_setIvar(id,Ivar,id). The value returned or passed is an object that is converted, as needed, to the actual type of the variable (a.k.a. auto-boxing).

Key-Value Coding is implemented using these low-level instance variable introspection functions. If you need to programmatically get or set the value of instance variables, you might find it easier to use the higher-level KVC methods. Listing 10-8 demonstrates setting the name instance variable to the string @"Hugh" via introspection, and is equivalent to the statement object->name = @"Hugh".

Listing 10-8. Programmatically Setting an Instance Variable

```
Ivar ivar = class_getInstanceVariable([object class],"name");
object_setIvar(object,ivar,@"Hugh");
```

As an alternative to object_getIvar and object_setIvar, the functions object_getInstanceVariable(id,const char*,void**) and object_setInstanceVariable(id,const char*,void*) get or set instance values directly, without using intermediate objects. Both return, as a side effect, the Ivar describing the variable they identified as the target. The getter function accepts the address of a pointer, which will be set to point to the actual variable in the object, and the setter function accepts a pointer to a value to copy into the object.

Table 10-9. *Common Instance Variable Introspection Functions*

Function	Returns
class_copyIvarList(Class,unsigned int*)	NULL-terminated array of Ivar pointers
class_getInstanceVariable(Class,const char*)	Ivar pointer describing the named variable
ivar_getName(Ivar)	Name of the variable
object_getIvar(id,Ivar)	The value of the object's variable as an object
object_setIvar(id,Ivar,id)	Nothing; Sets the value of the object's variable
object_getInstanceVariable(id,const char*,void**)	Ivar of the named variable and a pointer to its value
object_setInstanceVariable(id,const char*,void*)	Ivar of the named variable, copying a new value into it

Summary

There are many other methods and functions for manipulating the structures that define classes and objects at runtime. The functions highlighted in this chapter let you perform the common forms of introspection, through which you can examine almost every aspect of an object and its class. If you need to dig even deeper (no pun intended), I highly recommend reading Apple's *Objective-C 2.0 Runtime Reference*.[3]

---

[3] Apple, Inc., *Objective-C 2.0 Runtime Reference*, http://developer.apple.com/documentation/Cocoa/Reference/ObjCRuntimeRef/, 2008.

CHAPTER 11

■ ■ ■

Files

File systems are essential to virtually every computer operating system. It's where the operating system itself, applications, documents, and other information persist. Conceptually, files are very simple: a file is a named sequence of bytes, organized hierarchically in a file system.

You'd think this would be a short chapter, but it's not. Probably because of their importance, file systems have been the focus of much development. They have steadily evolved over the decades and are now quite complex. Files have sophisticated permissions, attributes, and multiple data forks. There are device files, memory files, serial communication files, and symbolic link files. File systems incorporate advanced caching, asynchronous data transfer, journaling, and change tracking. Much of this complexity has spilled into APIs and objects that interface with the file system.

There are more details to contend with when using files in Objective-C than there are in Java. To be portable, Java tries to hide or abstract as many of the underlying file system details as possible. Objective-C exposes all of the underlying POSIX file system details in all their glory. On the other hand, Objective-C provides many more high-level methods that allow you to read, write, or access the contents of an entire file with as little as a single statement.

This chapter will cover the basics of file and path names, how to process files in a directory, the manipulation of file metadata, and various ways of reading and writing data files. Along the way, it will also touch on some alternate APIs.

File System APIs

The functions, classes, and methods you use to interact with the file system are collectively referred to as the file system's application programming interface (API). In Java, the file system API is neatly organized in the java.io package. Not so in Objective-C. The Objective-C Cocoa framework provides a simple interface to the file system that's adequate for most needs. Parallel to that is the Core Services framework. Core Services provides numerous advanced file system functions along with a set of C APIs that mimic the original file services of the classic Macintosh operating system (often referred to as the Carbon API). Underneath both of these APIs is the core BSD API. These are the C functions that actually implement most of the file services in Mac OS X. Much of the Cocoa and Core Services are just compatibility APIs that do little more than call a BSD function to get the work done.

A conceptual difference between Objective-C and Java is that much of Java is organized around abstract classes that read and write serial data (java.io.Reader, java.io.Writer, java.io.InputStream, java.io.OutputStream), with subclasses that work with data files. Objective-C (and C) tend to use purpose-built functions for working with data files, and reserve the use of data stream classes for network ports and communication pipes. There is some overlap, but much less than in Java.

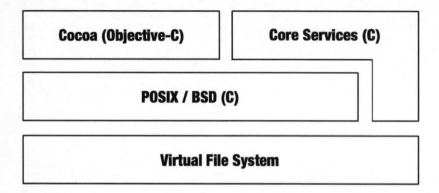

Figure 11-1. File System API Organization in Mac OS X

Every Objective-C process has a singleton instance of the NSFileManager class, obtained by sending [NSFileManager defaultManager]. NSFileManager implements most of the global file system methods. This chapter presents Objective-C solutions to common file system tasks whenever possible, but a few useful features are only available through C functions in the Cocoa, Core Services, or BSD frameworks.

A Java virtual machine can be hosted on a variety of computing platforms, all with different underlying file systems. Consequently, the Java file APIs tend to be general and make as few assumptions as possible. The Objective-C and BSD APIs, in contrast, unambiguously assume a POSIX-compatible file system. You will find no variable that's equivalent to java.io.File.pathSeparatorChar in Objective-C. All file and directory paths in Objective-C are POSIX paths and the path component separator is, and will always be, a single '/' character. The Core Services framework largely assumes an HFS+ file system, although mostly for compatibility with legacy code, as most of the HFS+ file specifiers and data structures are simply translated into BSD calls.

While the programming interfaces explicitly assume a POSIX file system, the underlying file services framework allows for a great deal of latitude on how file system API calls are translated into action. Ultimately, all file system calls make some change to the contents of a volume—a logical partition of a physical storage device. The format of that volume can vary dramatically. The HFS+ volume format is the native format for the Mac OS X operating system, but the BSD file system framework is perfectly happy to work with UFS volumes, Samba volumes, AppleShare volumes, Windows volumes, and so on. The file system APIs you call are automatically translated into the appropriate action for the format of the volume through a plug-in architecture called the Virtual File System (VFS). The only time you would need to be conscious of this is when dealing with obscure features that are foreign to the volume format being used. For example, a UFS volume might not support access control lists and the file names on HFS+ volumes may, or may not, be case sensitive. You can usually ignore the implementation details of the underlying volume format; just be aware that some features might not be implemented by every volume format supported by the operating system.

Identifying Items in the File System

This section explains the basic rules for how items in a file system are named and how to construct paths to those items. It also details how to get and set the working or default directory. In addition to string paths, files are also identified using URL objects and aliases. This section explains how file URLs and aliases are used and how to convert them to string paths. Finally, Mac OS X defines a number of standard directories whose location can be requested symbolically, avoiding the need to hard-code paths to system resources that might change in the future or are variable by nature. This section describes the functions used to obtain those directory paths.

File and Path Names

Welcome to POSIX File Names 101. Let's start with a quick review of the basics, so there's no confusion later. To work with any entity on a volume you must identify it by name. A file name can be just about any string, with the restriction that it can't contain the '/' path separator character, be one of the reserved names ("." or ".."), be an empty string, or be too long (no more than 255 Unicode characters). The string @"notes.txt" is a valid file name.

A path is one or more concatenated names, delineated by the '/' path separator character. The string @"james/Documents/Publications" is a path. The last element of a path names a file. All of the names before the final one must name directories or some other kind of file system container, such as a mount point.

■**Note** Objective-C file classes are built on POSIX file concepts, and inherit many of the notions of the original UNIX operating system. Most important is the concept that *everything is a file*. In UNIX, the file system is not a concrete collection of data files on a disk drive, but an abstract naming system for identifying any source of serial data. "Files" in UNIX can be data files, directories, network sockets, serial ports, semaphores, random number generators, blocks of RAM, logical console devices, and so on. Think of the term "file" as being the base class of any named entity in the file system hierarchy. Directories, data files, and FIFO pipes are all specialized subclasses of a "file." This terminology percolates through the APIs. For example, the -[NSFileManager removeFileAtPath:handler:] method deletes much more than just data files. If passed the path to a directory, it will delete it and every item it contains. It would also delete a named socket or semaphore. In this book, I adhere to the UNIX nomenclature of "file" to mean virtually any named entity in a file system—it just gets too confusing otherwise. When referring to an actual document file on a volume, I'll use the term *data file*.

Paths can be *absolute* or *relative*. A path that begins with a '/' is an absolute path specifying a series of directories beginning at the root directory of the file system. Otherwise, the path is a relative path specifying a series of directories starting in the current working directory. Some file system functions recognize paths that begin with a tilde, as in "~/Documents/Publications", to mean an absolute path beginning with the home directory of the current user.

For better or worse, the UNIX naming convention of extensions has followed us into the twenty-first century. File name extensions intimate the kind of information a file contains. They are typically short identifiers—three or four alphabetic characters—appended to the end of a file name following a period (.). The extension of the name @"Outline.doc" is @"doc", and the extension of the name @"Letter to Jake 2.0.pages" is @"pages".

Java's java.io.File object is largely the fundamental object used to identify files in the file system. A File object can be created for nonexistent files. Path manipulations are accomplished by extracting properties of a File or creating new File objects based on an existing File object. For example, the parent directory of a path can be determined by creating a File object to the path then calling getParent().

Objective-C does not have an object that can represent abstract or nonexistent files. Strings are used to represent file names and paths. How you assemble path or file name strings is entirely up to you. You can use any of the string manipulation methods, but there are a few provided by the Cocoa framework specifically for working the paths. The methods are attached to the NSString class via the NSPathUtilities category. The commonly used ones are listed in Table 11-1. Listing 11-1 illustrates the contrast between Java and Objective-C path manipulation. As an example, both the Java and Objective-C methods in Listing 11-1 generate a path to a nonexistent file.

Table 11-1. *Path and File Name Methods of NSString*

Method	Description
+(NSString*)pathWithComponents:(NSArray*)components	Constructs a path from an array of file names. To construct an absolute path, set the first element in the array to the string @"/".
-(NSArray*)stringsByAppendingPaths:(NSArray*)paths	Appends the file names in the array to the path in the receiver.
-(NSString*)pathComponents	Decomposes the path into individual file names, returned in an array. If the path is absolute, the first element in the array is @"/".
-(BOOL)isAbsolutePath	Returns YES if the path is absolute (begins with @"/").
-(NSString*)lastPathComponent	Extracts the last file name from a path.
-(NSString*)stringByDeletingLastPathComponent	Removes the last file name in the receiver's path.
-(NSString*)stringByAppendingPathComponent:(NSString*)str	Appends an additional name to end of a path.
-(NSString*)pathExtension	Extracts the extension from that last name in a path.
-(NSString*)stringByDeletingPathExtension	Removes the extension, if any, from the last name in a path.
-(NSString*)stringByAppendingPathExtension:(NSString*)str	Appends a new extension to the last name in a path.
-(NSString*)stringByAbbreviatingWithTildeInPath	If the receiver's path begins with the current user's home directory path, it is replaced with the shorthand @"~".
-(NSString*)stringByExpandingTildeInPath	Replaces the @"~" at the beginning of the receiver's path with the path to the current user's home directory, or replace @"~account" with the path to the home directory of user "account".
-(NSString*)stringByStandardizingPath	Simplifies and normalizes the path of the receiver.

Most of these methods are self-explanatory. None of them modifies the receiver. As the -stringBy… method names imply, each returns a new string object with the results of the transformation. The first few convert arrays of names into complete paths and vice versa. The bulk of the methods extract, delete, or append a single name or file name extension to an existing path. The -stringByStandardizingPath method "normalizes" a path string by replacing the @"~" or @"~user" shorthand with an explicit path, replacing any relative path references and symbolic links with their physical (nonsymbolic) equivalent, and removing any extraneous path elements. In short, it's a "cleanup" method that reduces a path to its simplest, most explicit, form.

Listing 11-1. *Generate a Path to a Nonexistent File*

Java
```java
public String autoName( String parentDir, String baseName, String ext )
{
    int suffix = 0;
    File parentFile = new File(parentDir);
    File testFile = new File(parentFile,baseName+"."+ext);
    while (testFile.exists()) {
        suffix += 1;
        testFile = new File(parentFile,baseName+"-"+suffix+"."+ext);
    }
    return testFile.getAbsolutePath();
}
```

Objective-C
```objc
- (NSString*)autoNameInDirectory:(NSString*)parentDir
                            name:(NSString*)name
                       extension:(NSString*)ext
{
    int suffix = 0;
    NSString *testPath = [parentDir stringByAppendingPathComponent:name];
    testPath = [testPath stringByAppendingPathExtension:ext];
    while ([[NSFileManager defaultManager] fileExistsAtPath:testPath]) {
        NSString *newName = [NSString stringWithFormat:@"%@-%d",name,++suffix];
        testPath = [parentDir stringByAppendingPathComponent:newName];
        testPath = [testPath stringByAppendingPathExtension:ext];
    }
    return testPath;
}
```

Working Directory

Every process maintains a default directory path, referred to as the *current directory* or *working directory*. This is the directory used to resolve relative paths. All relative paths are concatenated with the current working directory path to obtain the file's explicit path. Table 11-2 shows the two NSFileManager methods used to get and change the current working directory path in Objective-C.

Table 11-2. Working Directory Messages

Method	Description
-(NSString*)currentDirectoryPath	Returns the current working directory path
-(BOOL)changeCurrentDirectoryPath:(NSString*)path	Sets the working directory path

If the path specifies an accessible directory in the file system, this method sets the current working directory to the one identified by the path and returns YES. Otherwise, it does nothing and returns NO.

The equivalent functionality in Java is accomplished by setting the "user.dir" system property. The only significant difference is that the user.dir property is just a string and isn't evaluated until a file operating needs to resolve a relative path. The -changeCurrentDirectoryPath: method qualifies the path and rejects the change if the path is unusable. Listing 11-2 modifies the current working directory so that it refers to a "temp" subdirectory, but only if that subdirectory exists.

Listing 11-2. Changing the Current Working Directory

Java
```
String workingPath = System.getProperty("user.dir");
File testFile = new File(workingPath,"temp");
if (testFile.exists()) {
    System.setProperty("user.dir",testFile.getAbsolutePath());
}
```

Objective-C
```
NSString *current = [[NSFileManager defaultManager] currentDirectoryPath];
NSString *temp = [current stringByAppendingPathComponent:@"temp"];
[[NSFileManager defaultManager] changeCurrentDirectoryPath:temp];
```

The initial current directory for a Mac OS X process is inherited from the environment of the process that started it. For a command-line tool, it will be the working directory of the shell that launched the tool. For application bundles, the OS normally sets the working directory to the directory that contains the application bundle before launching the process.

File URLs

A few major versions ago, the Cocoa framework began to adopt Universal Resource Locators (URLs) as the preferred identifier object for data sources. For example, the original -[NSDocumentController openDocumentWithContentsOfFile:display:] method has been deprecated in favor of -openDocumentWithContentsOfURL:display:error:. This has increased the flexibility of many classes, as URLs can refer to data from a variety of sources—not just data files in the file system. But it also means that you many need to convert a file system path into a URL and back again.

Java's java.net.URL object can refer to a file, but is not typically used in conjunction with the java.io.* classes. About the only concession to URLs, or more correctly URIs (Universal Resource

Identifiers) is in the java.io.File class. It supports constructing a File object from a URI and the File.toURI() and File.toURL() methods for obtaining the URL of a File. Table 11-3 lists the basic methods for converting between paths and file URLs in Cocoa.

Table 11-3. *File Related NSURL Methods*

Method	Description
+(NSURL*)fileURLWithPath:(NSString*)path	Creates a file URL to a given file.
-(BOOL)isFileURL	Returns YES if the receiver is a file scheme URL.
-(NSString*)path	If the receiver is a file scheme URL, -path returns the file system path to the item.

Creating and Deleting Directories

The method -[NSFileManager createDirectoryAtPath:withIntermediateDirectories:attributes:error:] creates a new directory. If the withIntermediateDirectories: parameter is YES, any missing intermediate directories are also created. For example, if the path /Users/daphne/Music exists, sending -createDirectoryAtPath:withIntermediateDirectories:attributes:error: with a path of @"/Users/daphne/Music/Albums/Cocteau Twins" and YES for withIntermediateDirectories: would create an Albums directory within Music, and then create a Cocteau Twins directory within Albums. In this mode, the message is equivalent to the java.io.File.mkdirs() method. If withIntermediateDirectories: was NO, it would return an error, as the parent directory would be expected to exist. That would be equivalent to calling java.io.File.mkdir(). The attributes: parameter is a dictionary of attributes to be set. See the "File Properties" section later in this chapter for information about attribute dictionaries.

Delete a directory, like any file, using -[NSFileManage removeItemAtPath:error:].

Locating Special Directories

It's generally considered bad form to hard-code paths to well-known directories as string constants. These have a habit of changing over time, breaking your application in the process. The Mac OS X operating system defines a number of directories with specific purposes. In addition, it defines a set of domains that form a hierarchy that define the scope of the resource. For example, a font is installed by placing a font file in the Fonts folder. A user has a Fonts folder, all users have a shared Fonts folder, the system has a Fonts folder, and the network has a Fonts folder. Which Fonts folder the font is copied into determines its scope.

Special directories are located by calling NSSearchPathForDirectoriesInDomains(…) with three arguments: a constant describing the well-known directory, a bit mask of acceptable domains, and a flag to automatically expand the "~" shorthand in returned paths. Listing 11-3 shows how to use NSSearchPathForDirectoriesInDomains(…) to get the path of the user's desktop directory.

Listing 11-3. *Locating the User's Desktop Directory*

```
NSArray *paths = NSSearchPathForDirectoriesInDomains(NSDesktopDirectory,
                                                     NSUserDomainMask,
                                                     YES);
if ([paths count]>0) {
    NSString *desktopPath = [paths objectAtIndex:0];
    …
}
```

NSSearchPathForDirectoriesInDomains(…) returns an array containing the paths of the directory in each of the requested domains, in the order they should be searched, from the most specific to the most general. Table 11-4 lists the commonly used directory constants. The domain argument can be any combination of the domains in Table 11-5 OR'd together, or the constant NSAllDomainsMask.

Table 11-4. *Common Directory Constants*

Directory Constant	Description (example path)
NSApplicationDirectory	Applications (/Applications)
NSLibraryDirectory	User resources such as fonts, preferences, and log files (~/Library)
NSUserDirectory	The folder containing all home folders (/Users)
NSDocumentDirectory	Documents (~/Documents)
NSDesktopDirectory	The desktop (~/Desktop)
NSCachesDirectory	Cache files (~/Library/Caches)
NSApplicationSupportDirectory	Ancillary files used by an application (/Library/Application Support)
NSDownloadsDirectory	The download folder (~/Downloads)

Table 11-5. *Directory Domains*

Domain	Description
NSUserDomainMask	The current user
NSLocalDomainMask	The users of this system
NSSystemDomainMask	The entire system
NSNetworkDomainMask	All systems on the local network

There are also two special-purpose functions that return variable paths. NSHomeDirectory() returns the path to the current user's home directory. NSTemporaryDirectory() returns a path to directory specifically set aside for creating temporary files.

Requesting a File from the User

Prompting the user to select a file interactively is remarkably similar in Java. Java uses the JFileChooser class to choose an existing file or allow the user to enter the name of a new file. Cocoa supplies the NSSavePanel class to enter a new file name and its NSOpenPanel subclass to select an existing one. Listing 11-4 shows equivalent code for prompting the user to choose a single data file or directory from the file system.

Listing 11-4. *Choosing a Single File*

Java
```
JFileChooser chooser = new JFileChooser();
chooser.setFileSelectionMode(JFileChooser.FILES_AND_DIRECTORIES);
chooser.setMultiSelectionEnabled(false);
int result = chooser.showOpenDialog(null);
if (result==JFileChooser.APPROVE_OPTION)
    return chooser.getSelectedFile().getAbsolutePath();
return null;
```

Objective-C
```
NSOpenPanel *panel = [NSOpenPanel openPanel];
[panel setCanChooseFiles:YES];
[panel setCanChooseDirectories:YES];
[panel setAllowsMultipleSelection:NO];
NSInteger result = [panel runModal];
if (result==NSFileHandlingPanelOKButton)
    return [panel filename];
return nil;
```

Each class has numerous properties that determine the type of items that can be selected. Filtering and other dynamic customization is done through the NSSavePanel delegate. To filter items in the display, create an object that implements the -(BOOL)panel:(id)sender shouldShowFilename:(NSString*)filename method and set it as the delegate property of the panel object. See the Delegate Methods section of the NSSavePanel documentation for a complete list of the informal protocols a delegate object can implement.

While the Objective-C code in Listing 11-4 is equivalent to the Java code, it isn't the preferred method for presenting a file dialog. The code in Listing 11-5 will suspend the entire application until the user chooses a file. If a file selection is associated with a window, it is much more desirable to use a sheet—a model child window attached to a specific window—so that the high-level application interface isn't blocked. Listing 11-5 starts a model sheet with the same panel used in Listing 11-4. The beginSheet… message returns immediately so that the main application run loop continues uninterrupted. When the user makes a selection in the sheet, the message specified in the didEndSelector: parameter is sent to the modalDelegate: object. These can be any object and message you choose, as long as the method arguments match those defined by the informal protocol.

Listing 11-5. *Using a File Selection Sheet*

```
NSOpenPanel *panel = [NSOpenPanel openPanel];
[panel setCanChooseFiles:YES];
[panel setCanChooseDirectories:YES];
[panel setAllowsMultipleSelection:NO];
[panel beginSheetForDirectory:nil             // use default directory
                         file:nil             // don't preselect any file
               modalForWindow:documentWindow  // sheet attached to this window
               modalDelegate:self
               didEndSelector:@selector(myOpenDidEnd:returned:context:)
                  contextInfo:NULL];

...

- (void)myOpenDidEnd:(NSSavePanel*)sheet returned:(int)code context:(void*)ignored
{
    if (code==NSOKButton) {
        NSString *file = [sheet filename];
        …
    }
}
```

Symbolic Links, Hard Links, and Aliases

The Mac OS X operating system provides three types of files that reference another file. The first are symbolic links. These are special files that contain the path to another directory in the file system. Generally, a symbolic link acts as if it *were* the directory to which it refers. For example, the directory /Users/hannah/Documents/Updates contains the file Monday.doc, and the file /Users/hannah/Public/New is a symbolic link containing the path /Users/hannah/Documents/Updates. In this situation, the paths /Users/hannah/Documents/Updates/Monday.doc and /Users/hannah/Public/New/Monday.doc are functionally equivalent and refer to the same file.

NSFileManager provides methods for creating symbolic links and obtaining their contents. Most file operations traverse symbolic links transparently. A path that ends with a symbolic link usually refers to the link file itself, not the directory that it refers to. For example, the statement [[NSFileManager defaultManager] removeItemAtPath:@"/Users/hannah/Public/New" error:NULL] would delete the symbolic link file, not the Updates folder. The notable exception is the -[NSFileManager fileAttributesAtPath:traverseLink:] method. Its second BOOL parameter determines if it will return the attributes of the symbolic link file or the attributes of the file the symbolic link refers to. Table 11-6 lists the methods for creating and reading the contents of symbolic links.

Table 11-6. NSFileManager Symbolic Link Methods

Method	Description
`-(BOOL)createSymbolicLinkAtPath:(NSString*)path withDestinationPath:(NSString*)destPath error:(NSError**)error`	Creates a symbolic link file at path that refers to the file at destPath.
`-(NSString*)destinationOfSymbolicLinkAtPath:(NSString*)path error:(NSError**)error`	Extracts the path that the symbolic link file refers to.

One of the primary purposes of `-stringByStandardizingPath`, described in Table 11-1, is to replace any symbolic links in the path with their originals. Using the previous example, passing `@"/Users/hannah/Public/New/Monday.doc"` to `-stringByStandardizingPath` would return `@"/Users/hannah/Documents/Updates/Monday.doc"`.

The second kind of file that stands in for another is an alias file. The concept and data structure are inherited from the classic Macintosh operating system. An alias file contains a serialized AliasRecord structure. To use them, you must read the contents of the file and resolve the alias using Core Services functions. The advantage of aliases is that they are quite intelligent. For example, if you create an alias to a document file, that document file can later be renamed and moved to another directory on the same volume and the alias will still locate it. Furthermore, if the original file was on an external or network volume, an alias can automatically remount the volume restoring access to the original file.

From the perspective of the Cocoa and BSD frameworks, alias files are just plain data files and are not automatically recognized or resolved. The exceptions are a few very high-level file classes such as NSOpenPanel, which was just discussed. NSOpenPanel has a resolvesAliases property that, if set, will automatically resolve any alias the user selects, returning the item the alias refers to rather than the alias file itself. Some basic functions for using alias records are described later in this chapter.

Finally, some volume formats support hard links. A hard link describes two or more files in the file system that share the same content. Changing the data of one changes both. Unlike aliases and symbolic links, hard-linked files are peers and each is indistinguishable from a regular file. One file does not "point" to the other file; both files encapsulate the same physical data on the volume. In practice, hard linked files aren't used that often. The NSFileManager method for creating a hard link is `-(BOOL)linkItemAtPath:(NSString*)srcPath toPath:(NSString*)dstPath error:(NSError**)error`. To "break" a hard link, delete one of the files. Deleting a hard-linked file doesn't dispose of any data, because it is still contained in the other file.

Working With the Contents of a Directory

Discovering files by reading the contents of a directory is a common programming task. This is usually done to perform some action on each file in the directory, possibly recursively processing the files contained in any subdirectories of the directory as well. The former constitutes a shallow examination of the directory, while the latter is a deep examination.

The three basic methods of obtaining the contents of a directory are listed in Table 11-7. `-contentsOfDirectoryAtPath:…` returns just the immediate contents of the directory as an array of file names (not paths). `-subpathsOfDirectoryAtPath:…` returns an array of complete paths to each file in the directory, any subdirectories of the directory, sub-subdirectories, and so on.

Table 11-7. NSFileManager Directory Content Methods

Method	Returns
`-(NSArray*)contentsOfDirectoryAtPath:(NSString*)path error:(NSError**)error`	Shallow list of files in the directory
`-(NSArray*)subpathsOfDirectoryAtPath:(NSString*)path error:(NSError**)error`	Deep list containing the path of every file enclosed by the directory
`-(NSDirectoryEnumerator*)enumeratorAtPath:(NSString*)path`	A directory item enumerator

The -enumeratorAtPath: method returns a stateful NSDirectoryEnumerator object that's ready to iterate through the items in the directory. The enumeration can be shallow, deep, or an arbitrary mixture by strategically sending the enumerator object the -skipDescendents message. Listing 11-6 shows code that iterates through a hierarchy of directories, processing all "txt" files, but ignoring the contents of any directory with a "private" extension.

Listing 11-6. Recursively Processing Directory Contents

Java

```java
scanDirectory("/Users/ann/Documents");

…

void scanDirectory( File directory )
{
    File[] files = directory.listFiles();
    for ( File file: files ) {
        if (file.isFile()) {
            if (file.getName().endsWith(".txt"))
                scanTextFile(file);
        }
        else if (file.isDirectory()) {
            if (!file.getName().endsWith(".private"))
                scanDirectory(file);
        }
    }
}

void scanTextFile( File textFile )
{
    …
}
```

Objective-C

```
NSString *path = @"/Users/ann/Documents";
NSDirectoryEnumerator *e = [[NSFileManager defaultManager] enumeratorAtPath:path];
while ( (path=[e nextObject])!=nil ) {
    NSString *type = [[e fileAttributes] objectForKey:NSFileType];
    if ([type isEqualToString:NSFileTypeRegular]) {
        if ([[path pathExtension] isEqualToString:@"txt"])
            [self scanTextFile:path];
    }
    else if ([type isEqualToString:NSFileTypeDirectory]) {
        if ([[path pathExtension] isEqualToString:@"private"])
            [e skipDescendents];
    }
}

…

- (void)scanTextFile:(NSString*)textFilePath
{
    …
}
```

The most significant difference between the Java and Objective-C code in Listing 11-6 is that the Java solution used a recursive method, while the linear Objective-C loop delegated directory recursion to the NSDirectoryEnumerator object.

File Properties

A file's properties, or metadata, are information about a file. Java's java.io.File object is the principal interface for obtaining the properties of a file. It implements a variety of specific methods (i.e., boolean isFile(), long lastModified(), long length()) that describe the various properties of the file. Objective-C has a single -[NSFileManager fileAttributesAtPath:traverseLink:] method that accepts a file path and returns an immutable dictionary containing all salient properties of the file. The traverseLink: argument determines what to do if the path specifies a symbolic link file. If YES, the attributes returned will be for the file the symbolic link refers to; if NO, the attributes describe the symbolic link file.

To examine a particular property, retrieve its value from the dictionary collection. An example using the attributes of a file was already demonstrated listing 11-6. The keys are string constants to values that are NSNumber, NSDate, or NSString objects. Table 11-8 lists the property methods in java.io.File and their Objective-C equivalent. Some are methods, while others are keys into the attribute dictionary.

Table 11-8. *File Attribute Keys*

java.io.File Method	Objective-C Method or Key	Description
exists()	-[NSFileManager fileExistsAtPath:]	File exists
canRead()	-[NSFileManager isReadableFileAtPath:]	File is readable
canWrite()	-[NSFileManager isWritableFileAtPath:]	File is writable
	NSFilePosixPermissions	integer containing user, group, and global read/write/execute permission bits
isFile()	NSFileType	True if type is NSFileTypeRegular
isDirectory()	NSFileType	True if type is NSFileTypeDirectory
isHidden()	LSCopyItemInfoForURL(…)	Launch Services API provides display information
lastModified()	NSFileModificationDate	NSDate file was last modified
length()	NSFileSize	logical length of file
	NSFileCreationDate	NSDate file was created
	NSFileOwnerAccountID	Account number of file's owner
	NSFileOwnerAccountName	Account name of file's owner
	NSFileGroupOwnerAccountID	Group number of file's group
	NSFileGroupOwnerAccountName	Group name of file's group

The type of a file is determined by examining its NSFileType attribute. The attribute value will be one of NSFileTypeDirectory, NSFileTypeRegular, NSFileTypeSymbolicLink, NSFileTypeSocket, NSFileTypeCharacterSpecial, NSFileTypeBlockSpecial, or NSFileTypeUnknown. Detailed information about an item's display name, whether the file's extension should be hidden from the user, or if the entire file should be hidden, is available through various Launch Services functions. See the NSFileManager documentation for a complete list of file attribute keys.

Most file attributes can be modified using the -[NSFileManager setAttributes:ofItemAtPath:error:] method. You provide a dictionary containing the attributes you want modified and a file path. Some attributes, such as NSFileType and NSFileSize, cannot be modified using -setAttributes:…. The security policy may conditionally inhibit modification of other attributes, such as NSFileOwnerAccountID.

The method returns YES if all attributes changes were effected successfully. If it returns NO, the changes were indeterminate.

High-Level File Operations

Objective-C applications tend to deal with files in a holistic fashion, rather than the more traditional approach of opening the file, reading some or all of its data, and closing it again. Application classes, like the document management classes, tend to favor reading an entire file into a single data object. The typical life cycle of a document file is to be read—in its entirety—into a single NSData object, edited, and then written back out, overwriting the original file.

In modern file systems, it is also difficult to "correctly" perform even simple operations, such as copying a file. Extended metadata, access control lists, file ownership, multiple data forks, display properties, and remote file copying protocols are just a few of the seemingly endless details that must be considered just to duplicate a file.

To spare you from these burdens, the Cocoa framework provides a number of high-level methods that correctly perform a variety of atomic actions on whole files. The common ones are listed in Table 11-9.

Table 11-9. *Common High-Level File Operations*

Method	Description
-[NSFileManager contentsAtPath:]	Returns the contents of the entire file as an NSData object
+[NSData dataWithContentsOfFile:]	Creates a new NSData object with the contents of a file
+[NSData dataWithContentsOfMappedFile:]	Creates a virtual memory region mapped to the data in a file
-[NSData writeToFile:atomically:]	Writes the contents of the data object to a file
+[NSString stringWithContentsOfFile: encoding:error:]	Creates a new NSString object with the contents of a file
-[NSString writeToFile:atomically:encoding:error:]	Writes the contents of a string to a file
-[NSFileManager copyItemAtPath:toPath:error:]	Copies a file
-[NSFileManager moveItemAtPath:toPath:error:]	Moves or rename a file
-[NSFileManager removeItemAtPath:error:]	Deletes a file
-[NSFileManager contentsEqualsAtPath:andPath:]	Compares the contents of two files or two directories
-[NSWorkspace performFileOperation:source: destination:files:tag:]	Moves, copies, links, or trashes a set of files

There are numerous methods for reading the entire contents of a file into an NSData or NSString object, not all of which are listed here. Look for subtle variations of these methods in the NSData and NSString documentation if the ones in Table 11-9 don't satisfy your needs. Write methods that accept an atomically: parameter can optionally perform a so-called "safe save"; they write the data to a temporary file, exchange the temporary file with the destination file, then delete the original file. If anything unexpected happens during the save, the original file is not lost.

NSFileManager methods that copy, move, or delete a file, or compare two files, work equally well on data files and directories.

The -performFileOperation:source:destination:files:tag: of NSWorkspace can also be used to move, copy, or link files depending on the constant passed in the operation parameter. These operations are equivalent to methods provided by NSFileManger. Its one exceptional talent is the NSWorkspaceRecycleOperation operation that will move files to the trash. Moving a file to the trash is actually a complex procedure best left to the operating system.

NSWorkspace

The NSWorkspace class provides a number of high-level file- and user-related functions that are only relevant within the context of a graphical application. For example, the method -[NSWorkspace iconForFile:] will return an NSImage object with the file's icon and -[NSWorkspace launchApplication:] will launch a different GUI application. This information is not available to daemons or processes that aren't running in the context of a graphical interface. So you can't use NSWorkspace in a daemon, but you can use NSFileManager. Additional file display details are available through the Launch Services API, visited at the end of this chapter. This is the kind of information that you would use javax.swing.filechooser.FileSystemView to obtain.

Random File Access

Should you need a more traditional open-read-write-close interface to files, Cocoa provides the NSFileHandle class, roughly equivalent to java.io.RandomAccessFile. NSFileHandle is more general than RandomAccessFile because it's essentially an object wrapper for a BSD file descriptor. A "file" in a POSIX file system can be a data file, a serial communication port, or a pipe. By extension, an NSFileHandle object can be used to interact with all of those constructs. The basic NSFileHandle methods are listed in Table 11-10.

Table 11-10. *File Methods*

RandomAccessFile	NSFileHandle	Description
new RandomAccessFile(…,"r")	+fileHandleForReadingAtPath:	Opens a file for reading
new RandomAccessFile(…,"w")	+fileHandleForWritingAtPath:	Opens a file for writing
new RandomAccessFile(…,"rw")	+fileHandleForUpdatingAtPath:	Opens a file for reading and writing

close()	-closeFile	Closes file
getFD()	-fileDescriptor	Returns underlying file descriptor
length()		use -seekToEndOfFile or get attributes
readFully(byte[])	-readDataOfLength:	Reads some number of bytes
read(byte[])	-availableData	Reads as much data as is available
	-readInBackgroundAndNotify	Reads available data asynchronously
	-readToEndOfFileInBackgroundAndNotify	Reads all data asynchronously
	-waitForDataInBackgroundAndNotify	Waits for data to become available
getFilePointer()	-offsetInFile	Current file position
seek(long)	-seekToFileOffset:	Sets file position
--	-seekToEndOfFile	Sets file position to length
setLength()	-truncateFileAtOffset:	Sets the file's logical length
skipBytes()		use -seekToFileOffset:
write(byte[])	-writeData:	Writes bytes

The asynchronous methods return immediately after spawning a new thread that will ultimately perform the action. When the action is complete, your application receives a notification. In the case of the read actions, the notification contains the acquired data. Notifications are covered in Chapter 18. There are also asynchronous notifications specifically for when NSFileHandle is used to wrap a communications socket file. See the NSFileHandle documentation for additional details and the specific notifications sent.

For more fine-grained control, you can turn to the BSD file functions. You can perform all file operations using BSD functions, or obtain the file descriptor from the NSFileHandle object when you need to perform specialized actions.

NSFileManager Delegate

Like many Objective-C objects, NSFileManager supports the delegate pattern. Your delegate object can pre-flight specific actions and intercept, or attempt to recover from, certain failures. Table 11-11 lists the messages that, if implemented, the file manager will send to your delegate object.

NSFileManager employs both persistent and ephemeral delegates. The object set as the delegate of the singleton NSFileManager object receives relevant messages about general file manager operations. A few NSFileManager methods accept a temporary delegate object, designated as its *handler*. These are -copyPath:toPath:handler:, -movePath:toPath:handler:, -removeFileAtPath:handler:, and -linkPath:toPath:handler:. In these methods, the delegate messages are sent to the handler object instead of the global delegate.

Table 11-11. *NSFileManager Delegate Methods*

Method	Receiver	Sent
-fileManager:willProcessPath:	handler	Before attempting to copy, move, delete, or create a hard link to a file
-fileManager:shouldCopyItemAtPath:toPath:	delegate	Before copying a file
-fileManager:shouldMoveItemAtPath:toPath:	delegate	Before moving a file
-fileManager:shouldRemoveItemAtPath:	delegate	Before deleting a file
-fileManager:shouldLinkItemAtPath:toPath:	delegate	Before creating a hard link
-fileManager:shouldProceedAfterError:	handler	After an error copying, moving, deleting, or linking a file
-fileManager:shouldProceedAfterError:↵ copyingItemAtPath:toPath:	delegate	After an error copying a file
-fileManager:shouldProceedAfterError:↵ movingItemAtPath:toPath:	delegate	After an error moving a file
-fileManager:shouldProceedAfterError:↵ removingItemAtPath:	delegate	After an error deleting a file
-fileManager:shouldProceedAfterError:↵ linkingItemAtPath:toPath:	delegate	After an error creating a hard link

The should…AtPath: methods are sent before the action begins and permit your delegate the opportunity to prohibit the action from occurring. You can use this to monitor the file manager's progress or filter the items that it processes. The shouldProceedAfterError:… methods are sent when an action encounters an error processing an item, allowing your handler to log the offense, recover from the failure, or ignore it.

Alternate APIs

This chapter has concentrated on the Objective-C classes and methods that interact with the file system. These are adequate for most purposes, but a lot of important functionality is only available through the Core Services and BSD APIs.

There is a lot of overlap between the functionality of the various frameworks. For example, the Core Services framework provides the FSCopyObjectSync function that is roughly equivalent to -[NSFileManager copyItemAtPath:toPath:error:]. However, it also includes FSCopyObjectAsync, which performs the copy in its own thread. So which API you choose to use will largely depend on the special features or capabilities you need.

The Core Services framework is actually a framework of frameworks that include basic file I/O functions. The subframeworks of interest are the Carbon Core and Launch Services frameworks. The Carbon functions provide basic file functions in addition to backwards compatibility with applications written for the classic Macintosh OS. Launch Services provide functions instrumental when a user is interacting with the file system. This includes information about a file's visibility, it's display name, icon, what application will launch when the user opens a document, what applications are capable of opening a given document, and so on. Some common Core Services functions are listed in Table 11-12. As a rule, the file system functions in the Carbon framework all begin with "FS" and Launch Servcies functions begin with "LS."

■ **Note** Every file in the classic Macintosh OS had two forks: a data fork and a resource fork. While the resource fork is assumed to have a specific structure, the essential fact is that every file is potentially two files. When you open a file using the Carbon functions, you specify not only the file to open but which fork. The API was later generalized to support any number of file forks. But in practice, only the two original forks are consistently supported. The data fork is the unnamed fork of the file, and is the fork accessed by the BSD functions and Cocoa methods. The virtual file system may emulate multi-fork files on file systems that don't inherently support them by creating additional, invisible, files to accommodate the data. BSD and Cocoa functions can access a file's resource fork using a synthetic path name of the form `file.data/rsrc`. The syntax essentially treats every data file as a directory containing an arbitrary number of named fork files.

Table 11-12. Core Services

Function	Description
FSPathMakeRef	Creates an FSRef from a POSIX path
FSRefMakePath	Returns the POSIX equivalent to the FSRef
FSMakeFSRefUnicode	Creates a new FSRef from a parent FSRef and file name
FSCompareFSRefs	Determines if two FSRef structures refer to the same entity
FSGetCatalogInfo	Gets the catalog information about a file
FSGetCatalogInfoBulk	Gets the catalog information for many files at once

FSSetCatalogInfo	Changes the catalog information for a file
FSGetVolumeInfo	Gets information about a volume
FSSetVolumeInfo	Changes information about a volume
FSCreateFileUnicode	Creates a new, empty file
FSDeleteObject	Deletes a file
FSExchangeObjects	Swaps the data contents of two files
FSCreateFork	Creates a data or resource fork
FSOpenFork	Opens a data or resource fork
FSReadFork	Reads data from a file
FSWriteFork	Writes data to a file
FSGetForkPosition	Gets the current file position
FSSetForkPosition	Changes the file position
FSGetForkSize	Gets the file's logical length
FSSetForkSize	Changes the file's logical length
FSFlushFork	Writes any cached changes to physical media
FSCloseFork	Closes the file
FSNewAlias	Creates an alias record to a file
FSResolveAlias	Gets the file best described by an alias record
FSResolveAliasFile	Gets the file best described by an alias file
FSMatchAliasBulk	Gets the list of all files that could be described by an alias record
LSCopyDisplayNameForRef	The file name that should be displayed to the user
LSCopyItemInfoForRef	Gets display properties for a file (invisible, bundle, …)
LSGetExtensionInfo	Gets the file extension and display information for a file
LSGetApplicationForItem	Gets the application that will launch when the user opens the file

Many Core Services functions accept or return an FSRef (file system reference) data structure. An FSRef is an opaque and nonportable structure that uniquely identifies a file in the file system. You cannot interpret the contents of the structure (the opaque part), nor can you use the structure outside the memory address of the current process (the nonportable part). So don't even think about trying to save it to disk or copy it to another process. There are no calls to initialize or dispose FSRef structures, so they can be declared as uninitialized variables, set, used, copied by value, and eventually just forgotten. FSRefMakePath and FSPathMakeRef are the principal functions for converting a C path string into an FSRef structure and vice versa.

The sample code in Listing 11-7 starts with a POSIX path in an Objective-C string object and converts that into a portable alias record. The record is stored in a structure allocated by the FSNewAlias function. A "handle" is just a pointer to a pointer. The alias is later resolved and turned back into a path string, suitable for use in NSFileManager messages. In the process, the code illustrates converting an Objective-C path string to and from an FSRef structure. Note that code in Listing 11-7 could have saved the first step of converting the path into an FSRef by using the FSNewAliasPath function instead, but was included to illustrate this common practice.

Listing 11-7. Objective-C Path to Alias

```
NSString *path = @"/Users/james/Desktop";
OSStatus err;

// Convert a POSIX path string into an alias record
FSRef pathRef;
AliasHandle aliasHndl;
err = FSPathMakeRef((const UInt8*)[path fileSystemRepresentation],&pathRef,NULL);
if (err!=noErr)
    /* error */;

err = FSNewAlias(NULL,&pathRef,&aliasHndl);
if (err!=noErr)
    /* error */;

/* success */

…

// Resolve aliasHndl and get its POSIX path string
FSRef originalRef;
Boolean aliasWasUpdated;
err = FSResolveAlias(NULL,aliasHndl,&originalRef,&aliasWasUpdated);
if (err!=noErr)
    /* error */;

NSMutableData *pathBuffer = [NSMutableData dataWithLength:2048];
char *pathBytes = (char*)[pathBuffer bytes];
err = FSRefMakePath(&originalRef,(UInt8*)pathBytes,[pathBuffer length]);
if (err!=noErr)
    /* error */;
```

```
NSFileManager *fm = [NSFileManager defaultManager];
NSString *originalPath = [fm stringWithFileSystemRepresentation:pathBytes
                                                   length:strlen(pathBytes)];

/* success */
```

Table 11-12 lists only a tiny fraction of the functions implemented in the Core Services framework. There are many variations of the functions listed, and hundreds of others. Core Services provides functions to get and set volume information, mount and eject volumes, receive file system notifications, track changes in real time, record optical media, and perform operations on remote volumes—just to name a few. Your best resource for these specialized functions is the Mac OS X documentation.

Underneath all of these frameworks are the core BSD functions that implement the underlying file system. These are the traditional open(…), read(…), write(…), close(…) functions that have been around since the origin of UNIX. Entire books have been written about this API, they are amply documented, and there are numerous on-line tutorials and resources—so I won't bother going into details. If you have an NSFileHandle object and need to apply a BSD function to the underlying file, send it the -fileDescriptor message. The integer returned is the BSD file descriptor token used to identify the open file. If you already have a BSD file descriptor, you can wrap it in an NSFileHandle using [[NSFileHandle alloc] initWithFileDescriptor:fd].

Summary

You should now have a good grounding in the basic file I/O facilities of Objective-C, the Cocoa framework, and Mac OS X. The principal differences are the use of strings instead of java.io.File objects to manipulate paths, attribute dictionaries instead of File object properties, and the reliance on C functions for advanced features. Beyond that, you won't find that the basic file-related tasks (reading data files, writing data files, deleting files) changes in any significant way.

CHAPTER 12

■ ■ ■

Serialization

Serialization is the process by which the properties of an object, or objects, are converted into a transportable series of bytes that capture their internal state and relationships. The serialized data can be saved or transmitted to another process or system, where the data can later be used to re-create the original set of objects.

Object serialization is one of the defining features of Java. It is largely implemented by the Java runtime. True to its minimalist nature, object serialization is not part of the Objective-C language. Object archiving (serialization) is accomplished by a set of classes that implement the serialization process, and a protocol (interface) that an object must implement in order to be archived (serialized).

Java's biggest advantage is that serialization is part of the language. All of an object's member variables are serialized automatically. In Objective-C, nothing about an object is serialized until the programmer provides the code to do it. Beyond that, the steps you must take to prepare an object for serialization, serialize, and de-serialize it are remarkably similar. Both Java and Objective-C let you customize the serialization process, and each provides some means for dealing with forward and backward compatibility.

This chapter covers Objective-C archiving (serialization) and Objective-C serialization—not to be confused with Java serialization. It explains the different types of archiving that Objective-C provides, and what steps you must take to make your class archivable. It will also cover common archiving problems and how to solve them. Finally, it will briefly describe the support for Objective-C serialization and XML documents—alternate forms of serialization—along with how to make simple in-memory copies of objects.

Archiving

What you think of as serialization in Java is called *archiving* in Objective-C; a graph of objects is *encoded* into a non-human-readable stream of binary data. This architecture-independent data can later be *decoded* to instantiate an equivalent graph of objects. What Objective-C calls *serialization* is slightly different and is described later in this chapter.

In Java, the classes largely responsible for serializing objects are java.io.ObjectOutputStream and java.io.ObjectInputStream. These take object references and primitive values and "flatten" them into a serial java.io.OutputStream, or read serialized data from a java.io.InputStream and turn it back into objects. For an object to be included in the stream, it must implement the java.io.Serializable interface. The Java runtime uses introspection to automatically encode the object's instance variables. You can influence this using Java's transient keyword or by customizing the serialization process.

In Objective-C, the classes that implement serialization are subclasses of NSCoder. Conceptually, NSCoder implements the functionality of both ObjectOutputStream and ObjectInputStream. The NSCoder base class implements abstract methods used to encode and decode objects, but subclasses of NSCoder may elect to implement only half of its functionality. Like Java, Objective-C classes that support archiving must conform to the NSCoding protocol (interface). Unlike Java, NSCoding is not an empty protocol; it declares two methods, -initWithCoder: and -encodeWithCoder:, that must be implemented by the class. The -encodeWithCoder: message is sent to archive the receiver. -initWithCoder: is an alternate -init method, sent to initialize a new object created during decoding.

Archive Types

Objective-C actually provides three different types of archiving, listed in Table 12-1.

Table 12-1. *Archive Types*

Type	NSCoder Class	Description
Keyed Archive	NSKeyedArchiver, NSKeyedUnarchiver	Archives object properties using key/value pairs. This is the preferred method for archiving document data or other persistent objects.
Sequential Archive	NSArchiver, NSUnarchiver	Archives objects by writing property values in a specific order. Its use is deprecated as a persistent storage format.
Distributed Objects	NSPortCoder	Archives objects using sequential encoding for exchange with other threads, processes, and remote systems.

Keyed archiving associates each property value with a "key" string assigned by the programmer. Java serialization is similar, but the keys are always the names of the member variables. It is a particularly flexible and robust format that tolerates changes to the class definition. By using keys, the order in which the properties are encoded in the stream is irrelevant. This permits you to add new properties, or reorder existing properties, without breaking compatibility with archives created using an older version of the class. You can also provide forward compatibility, allowing older versions of your application to decode an archive written by a newer version. Keyed archiving produces more serialized data, but is ultimately much more flexible and stable. For this reason, it's the recommended archive format for document data or any set of objects that are intended to be stored on persistent media for later reconstitution.

Sequential archiving encodes unadorned values into the data stream in a predetermined order. No property names or keys are used to identify the values, nor does it include any type information. To reconstruct the object, the values must be decoded in the same order. While fast and compact, the data format is "fragile." Any change to the order, number, or type of values will make it incompatible with an archive data stream created by a different version. Objective-C addresses this problem by using class versions. A newer version of a class can recognize and assimilate archive data created by an older version. While providing backward compatibility, it does not provide forward compatibility and the solutions tend to be awkward. For these reasons, sequential archiving is not recommended for document data or other persistent objects. However, that's not to say that sequential archiving isn't used.

Distributed objects uses sequential archiving—with a few extra wrinkles—to quickly and efficiently exchange objects with other processes. It might be another thread in the same process, another process on the same system, or a remote system half way around the world. The encoding and decoding technique remains the same, only the data transport changes. Because distributed objects uses sequential archiving, it is subject to all of the same disadvantages. However, version differences between processes are often limited or can be tightly controlled. For example, a client application might launch a helper process and communicate with it using distributed objects. The helper executable is part of the application's resource bundle, so is guaranteed to contain the same version of the classes being used by the client—making data compatibility immaterial.

Documentation for Objective-C archiving will repeat, ad nauseam, that sequential archiving is deprecated and you should implement keyed archiving instead. That *is* true for data model objects that you intend to store in document files, preferences, or other persistent locations. However, distributed objects uses sequential archiving. To use your objects in a distributed environment, your classes must implement sequential archiving, and understanding distributed objects requires a firm grasp of archiving. This chapter will explain how to implement both. The features that distinguish distributed objects from plain sequential archiving are described in Chapter 13.

Archive Coders

Using the archive coder classes to encode and decode objects isn't all that much different than it is in Java. Listing 12-1 shows how to archive (serialized) and unarchive a single object in both Java and Objective-C.

Listing 12-1. Archiving and Unarchiving an Object

Java
```java
Object something = …
ByteArrayOutputStream outStream = null;
ObjectOutputStream objectEncoder = null;
try {
    outStream = new ByteArrayOutputStream();
    objectEncoder = new ObjectOutputStream(outStream);
    objectEncoder.writeObject(something);
    objectEncoder.close();
}
catch (IOException ioException) {
    ioException.printStackTrace();
}
byte[] bytes = outStream.toByteArray();

…

ByteArrayInputStream inStream = null;
ObjectInputStream objectDecoder = null;
try {
    inStream = new ByteArrayInputStream(bytes);
    objectDecoder = new ObjectInputStream(inStream);
    something = objectDecoder.readObject();
    objectDecoder.close();
}
catch (Exception exception) {
    exception.printStackTrace();
}
```

Objective-C

```
id something = …
NSData *bytes = [NSKeyedArchiver archivedDataWithRootObject:something];

…

something = [NSKeyedUnarchiver unarchiveObjectWithData:bytes];
```

The Objective-C code in Listing 12-1 is particularly brief because NSKeyedArchiver and NSKeyedUnarchiver provide convenience methods that create a temporary coder object, encode or decode a single object, and return the result. There are also a pair of methods that will write or read the data directly to a file. The Objective-C code in Listging 12-2 more closely parallels the Java code in Listing 12-1. This is the form you would use if you needed to customize the coder before encoding or decoding any objects, or if you needed to encode multiple root objects.

Listing 12-2. Archiving and Unarchiving Multiple Objects

```
id something = …
id somethingElse = …

NSKeyedArchiver *archiver;
NSMutableData *bytes = [NSMutableData data];
archiver = [[NSKeyedArchiver alloc] initForWritingWithMutableData:bytes];
// customize |archiver| here...
[archiver encodeObject:something forKey:@"Something"];
[archiver encodeObject:somethingElse forKey:@"Alternate"];
[archiver finishEncoding];
// |bytes| now contains the encoded object stream

…

NSKeyedUnarchiver *unarchiver;
unarchiver = [[NSKeyedUnarchiver alloc] initForReadingWithData:bytes];
// customize |unarchiver| here...
something = [unarchiver decodeObjectForKey:@"Something"];
somethingElse = [unarchiver decodeObjectForKey:@"Alternate"];
[unarchiver finishDecoding];
```

Archives and Documents

The NSDocument classes are designed to work hand-in-hand with archiving to implement a simple, and seamless, document storage solution for your application. The basic concept is that your document's data model will consist of a graph of archivable objects. To save your document in a file, those objects are archived into an NSData object that is then written to disk. To open the document again, the document's data file is read into a new NSData object and unarchived to re-create your document's data model.

Listing 12-3 demonstrates the minimal implementation for an NSDocument object that can read and write its content to a document file. This tiny bit of "glue" is all that's required to implement all of the standard document commands (Open…, Save, Save As…, Revert) in a Cocoa application.

Listing 12-3. *Using Archiving to Implement a Document Class*

```
@interface SimpleDocument : NSDocument {
    id   dataModel;
}

@end

@implementation SimpleDocument

- (NSData*)dataOfType:(NSString*)typeName error:(NSError**)outError
{
    return [NSKeyedArchiver archivedDataWithRootObject:dataModel];
}

- (BOOL)readFromData:(NSData*)data
              ofType:(NSString*)typeName
               error:(NSError**)outError
{
    dataModel = [NSKeyedUnarchiver unarchiveObjectWithData:data];
    return (dataModel!=nil);
}

@end
```

Adding Keyed Archive Support to Your Class

As in Java, classes are not archivable by default. Your class must conform to the NSCoding protocol and implement the -initWithCoder: and -encodeWithCoder: methods. An example is shown in Listing 12-4. The Java equivalent is omitted, because in the simple case there's no Java code to write.

Listing 12-4. *Class Supporting Keyed Archiving*

```
typedef struct {
    unsigned int buildingNo;
    unsigned int roomNo;
} RoomIdentifier;

@interface ScheduledEvent : NSObject <NSCoding> {
    @private
    NSDate          *startTime;
    NSTimeInterval  duration;
    RoomIdentifier  room;
}

@end
```

```
@implementation ScheduledEvent

- (id)initWithCoder:(NSCoder*)decoder
{
    self = [super init];
    if (self != nil) {
        startTime = [decoder decodeObjectForKey:@"Start"];
        duration = [decoder decodeDoubleForKey:@"Duration"];
        room.buildingNo = [decoder decodeInt32ForKey:@"Room.building"];
        room.roomNo = [decoder decodeInt32ForKey:@"Room.number"];
    }
    return self;
}

- (void)encodeWithCoder:(NSCoder*)encoder
{
    [encoder encodeObject:startTime forKey:@"Start"];
    [encoder encodeDouble:duration forKey:@"Duration"];
    [encoder encodeInt32:room.buildingNo forKey:@"Room.building"];
    [encoder encodeInt32:room.roomNo forKey:@"Room.number"];
}

@end
```

ScheduledEvent objects can now be archived using the NSKeyedArchiver class. The code in Listing 12-4 only supports keyed archiving, so the object still isn't usable with a sequential archive or distributed objects. The basic steps for creating an archivable class are as follows:

- Conform to NSCoding, or subclass a class that conforms to NSCoding.

- Implement an -initWithCoder: method that initializes the new object using the data in the decoder. If the class inherits NSCoding, the method should begin with self = [super initWithCoder:decoder].

- Implement an -encodeWithCoder: method that encodes the object. If the class inherits NSCoding, the method should begin with [super encodeWithCoder:coder].

- Encode or decode all persistent member variables by sending the appropriate -encode… or -decode… message to the coder object. Complex variables, like structures, must be decompiled into their constituent primitive values. The coding methods are listed in Table 12-2.

NSCoding methods for use with keyed archivers should only send the -encode…:forKey: and -decode…ForKey: messages. Classes that encode sequential archives or are used as distributed objects should only send the -encode…: and -decode… messages. How a class supports both is described a little later.

Table 12-2. Encoding Methods

Objective-C Type	Keyed Encoder	Sequential Encoder
id	encodeObject:forKey:	encodeObject:
NSInteger	encodeInteger:forKey:	
int	encodeInt32:forKey:	
long long int	encodeInt64:forKey:	
BOOL	encodeBool:forKey:	
byte array	encodeBytes:length:forKey:	encodeBytes:length:
double	encodeDouble:forKey:	
float	encodeFloat:forKey:	
NSPoint	encodePoint:forKey:	encodePoint:
NSRect	encodeRect:forKey:	encodeRect:
NSSize	encodeSize:forKey:	encodeSize:
any C type		encodeValueOfObjCType:at:

The values you choose for keys are entirely arbitrary. You can choose to use any keys you like, they just have to be consistent and unique within the scope of the object.

Unlike typical Java serialization, *you* are in control of what values are encoded and how they are interpreted when decoded. You are free to choose how your object is represented in the data stream. As an example, take a publishing application that has an ink color object. The object's -encodeWithCoder: method could simply encode all of the properties of the ink color (amount of Cyan, Magenta, Yellow, Black, and so on) *or* it could encode just the Pantone® name of the color. When the object is decoded, it would use the color's name to initialize itself with equivalent color values. Techniques like this can make the encoded version of your objects more transportable and durable.

■**Caution** Avoid sending messages to object pointers returned by -decodeObject... within the scope of your -initWithCoder: method. Circular references may cause the object pointer returned by -decodeObject… to refer to a partially initialized object.

Both NSCoding methods receive an NSCoder object. This can be the same object, but is often different. In the case of a keyed archive, -initWithCoder: will receive an NSKeyedUnarchiver object and -encodeWithCoder: will receive an NSKeyedArchiver object. NSKeyedArchiver only implements the -encode…:forKey: methods and any attempt to send it any of the -decode… messages will raise an exception. NSKeyedUnarchiver only implements the complementary set of -decode…ForKey: methods.

Adding Sequential Archive Support to Your Class

Adding sequential archive support, which includes distributed objects, is almost identical to adding keyed archive support, with two exceptions:

- Sequential archiving uses the sequential encoding methods in Table 12-2.

- The order and type of properties encoded in -encodeWithCoder: must exactly match the order and type that they are decoded in -initWithCoder:. Unlike keyed encoding, you cannot ignore values or decode them in a different order than they were encoded.

You'll notice that there are far fewer sequential encoding methods. Most obvious is the lack of methods for encoding the primitive C types. That's because sequential encoders provide the catch-all -encodeValueOfObjCType:at: method. This takes an encoded C variable type string (generated using the @encode() directive), and the address of a variable. To encode the duration property in Listing 12-4, you would write [encoder encodeValueOfObjCType:@encode(NSTimeInterval) at:&duration]. While it's conceivable to pass the type string of any C type—say, for an arbitrary structure like @encode(RoomIdentifier)—coders normally only implement the primitive types defined by the language. In the previous example, NSTimeInterval is synonymous with double so @encode(NSTimeInterval) and @encode(double) are interchangeable. You can encode an entire array of primitive values using -encodeArrayOfObjCType:count:at:.

Supporting Both Keyed and Sequential Archiving

But what if you want your class to support keyed archiving, sequential archives, and distributed objects? It's easy: send the coder an -allowsKeyedCoding message to determine if it supports keyed archiving, and then use the appropriate coder methods. An expanded implementation of the ScheduledEvent class that supports *both* keyed and sequential archiving is shown in Listing 12-5.

Listing 12-5. Class Supporting Keyed and Sequential Archiving

```
- (id)initWithCoder:(NSCoder*)decoder
{
    self = [super init];
    if (self != nil) {
        if ([decoder allowsKeyedCoding]) {
            startTime = [decoder decodeObjectForKey:@"Start"];
            duration = [decoder decodeDoubleForKey:@"Duration"];
            room.buildingNo = [decoder decodeInt32ForKey:@"Room.building"];
            room.roomNo = [decoder decodeInt32ForKey:@"Room.number"];
        } else {
            startTime = [decoder decodeObject];
            [decoder decodeValueOfObjCType:@encode(NSTimeInterval) at:&duration];
```

```
        [decoder decodeValueOfObjCType:@encode(unsigned int) at:&room.buildingNo];
        [decoder decodeValueOfObjCType:@encode(unsigned int) at:&room.roomNo];
      }
    }
    return self;
}

- (void)encodeWithCoder:(NSCoder*)encoder
{
    if ([encoder allowsKeyedCoding]) {
        [encoder encodeObject:startTime forKey:@"Start"];
        [encoder encodeDouble:duration forKey:@"Duration"];
        [encoder encodeInt32:room.buildingNo forKey:@"Room.building"];
        [encoder encodeInt32:room.roomNo forKey:@"Room.number"];
    } else {
        [encoder encodeObject:startTime];
        [encoder encodeValueOfObjCType:@encode(NSTimeInterval) at:&duration];
        [encoder encodeValueOfObjCType:@encode(unsigned int) at:&room.buildingNo];
        [encoder encodeValueOfObjCType:@encode(unsigned int) at:&room.roomNo];
    }
}
```

Sequential coders do not implement any of the …forKey: methods, and attempting to send one will raise an exception. Similarly, keyed coders don't implement any of the sequential methods, so make sure you know which kind of coder you are using.

If you want to programmatically limit your object's archive support, you can conditionally raise an exception in your -encodeWithCoder: method. The class in Listing 12-6 supports both keyed and sequential archiving, but will not allow itself to be copied through a distributed objects connection. This is equivalent to overriding your Java object's writeObject(ObjectOutputStream) method and throwing a NotSerializableException.

Listing 12-6. Programmatically Limiting Archive Support

```
- (void)encodeWithCoder:(NSCoder*)encoder
{
    if ([encoder isKindOfClass:[NSPortCoder class]])
        [NSException raise:NSInvalidArchiveOperationException
                    format:@"%@ not distributable",[self className]];

    if ([encoder allowsKeyedCoding]) {
        // Keyed encoding...
    } else {
        // Sequential encoding...
    }
}
```

Archiving Complications

As with almost everything in software engineering, the simple cases are easy; it's the boundary conditions that get tricky. Archiving (serialization) is no exception. There are a number of confounding issues to deal with. Java and Objective-C handle most in a similar fashion. These include transient values, compatibility between saved data and different class versions, shared objects, objects outside the object graph, and duplicate objects.

Transient Properties

Java provides the transient keyword to mark instance variables that should not be included in the serialized data stream. In Objective-C, the solution is to simply ignore the property during encoding and decoding. Listing 12-7 shows a modified version of the ScheduledEvent class that includes a screen coordinate property that holds the position where the scheduled event was last displayed. This value is irrelevant when the event object is stored in a document, so it's omitted from the data stream.

Listing 12-7. Transient Properties

Java
```
public class ScheduledEvent implements Serializable {
    Date                    startTime;
    double                  duration;
    RoomIdentifier          room;

    transient java.awt.Point    lastScreenPopupPosition;

    …

}
```

Objective-C
```
@interface ScheduledEvent : NSObject <NSCoding> {
    NSDate          *startTime;
    NSTimeInterval  duration;
    RoomIdentifier  room;
    NSPoint         lastScreenPopupPosition;
}

@end

@implementation ScheduledEvent

…

- (void)encodeWithCoder:(NSCoder*)encoder
{
    [encoder encodeObject:startTime forKey:@"Start"];
    [encoder encodeDouble:duration forKey:@"Duration"];
    [encoder encodeInt32:room.buildingNo forKey:@"Room.building"];
    [encoder encodeInt32:room.roomNo forKey:@"Room.number"];
    // do not encode lastScreenPopupPosition
}

@end
```

Duplicate Objects

The object that you use to create an archive is called the *root object*. It forms the anchor point in an undirected graph of objects that include all of the objects the root object refers to, any objects those objects refer to, and so on. The object graph might be simple, like an array or tree, but can also form loops and circular references. If the encoder blindly followed every object reference, multiple references to a single object would encode the object's data multiple times, and circular references would cause infinite recursion. Java's java.io.ObjectOutputStream and Objective-C's NSCoder classes solve this problem almost identically. The first time an object is sent to the coder via the -encodeObject: message, the coder recursively sends that object an -encodeWithCoder: message to encode its data in the stream. The coder also remembers that object instance. All subsequent -encodeObject: messages that refer to the same object simply insert a reference to the original object in the data stream. When decoding, all -decodeObject messages return a pointer to the instance of the single unarchived object. You don't have to do anything to get this behavior; it's just good to know how it works.

Decoding an archive can unintentionally create duplicate objects. This can happen if encoded objects refer to objects in a shared pool. The decoder will create new instances of every unique object in the data stream. This leaves your application with duplicates of the shared objects. There are several of ways of dealing with this. One is to use an encoding scheme like the Pantone color example given earlier; encode some symbolic representation of the object, and then obtain its actual contents from a common resource. Another solution is to override the -(id)awakeAfterUsingCoder:(NSCoder*)decoder method. This message is sent to an object after it has been decoded. The object identifier returned by the method replaces the decoded object. The default implementation returns self (i.e., no replacement), but if you override it you can return any equivalent object instead. Listing 12-8 demonstrates an Attendee class that avoids creating duplicate Attendee objects and adds any new Attendee objects to the common pool.

Listing 12-8. *Decoding Shared Objects*

```
@interface Attendee : NSObject <NSCoding> {
    NSString        *name;
    NSString        *uuid;
    NSMutableSet    *scheduledMeetings;
}

@end

@implementation Attendee

- (id)initWithCoder:(NSCoder*)decoder
{
    self = [super init];
    if (self != nil) {
        name = [decoder decodeObjectForKey:@"Name"];
        uuid = [decoder decodeObjectForKey:@"UUID"];
        scheduledMeetings = [decoder decodeObjectForKey:@"Meetings"];
    }
    return self;
}
```

```
- (void)encodeWithCoder:(NSCoder*)encoder
{
    [encoder encodeObject:name forKey:@"Name"];
    [encoder encodeObject:uuid forKey:@"UUID"];
    [encoder encodeObject:scheduledMeetings forKey:@"Meetings"];
}

- (id)awakeAfterUsingCoder:(NSCoder*)decoder
{
    ScheduleAssets *assets = [ScheduleAssets sharedAssets];
    Attendee *existingAttendee = [assets attendeeWithUUID:uuid];
    if (existingAttendee==nil) {
        // Add this attendee to the pool of attendees
        [assets addAttendee:self];
    } else {
        // Replace this attendee with the one that already exists
        self = existingAttendee;
    }
    return self;
}

@end
```

Limiting the Object Graph

Sometimes archiving a root object archives much more than you intended. Archiving a root object normally archives all of the objects it refers to. In our hypothetical scheduling application, a ProjectMeeting object associates a meeting with a project task. It would be convenient to archive a ProjectMeeting object and send it vie e-mail to a team member inviting them to the meeting. The problem is, the ProjectMeeting object in Listing 12-9 contains a reference to the ProjectTask object the meeting relates to. The task object would naturally contain a reference to its project, that would contain references to all of the project's tasks, its milestones, the team members working on the project, the other meetings scheduled for the project, and so on. In short, our attempt to send someone a single meeting object would result in archiving the entire project scheduling system, possibly even the application itself.

Objective-C's solution is to conditionally encode objects. The graph of objects that gets encoded consists only of non-conditional objects added to the stream using -encodeObject: or -encodeObject:forKey:. Conditional objects are encoded using -encodeConditionalObject: or -encodeConditionalObject:forKey: (see Listing 12-9). These objects are included in the archive if, and only if, they have been *unconditionally* encoded at least once. If all of the inclusions of the object are conditional, the object is omitted from the archive. When the graph is decoded, the -decodeObject… requests for the omitted object return nil.

Listing 12-9. *Encoding Conditional Objects*

```
@interface ProjectMeeting : ScheduledEvent {
    NSString    *meetingDescription;
    ProjectTask *task;
}

@end
```

```objc
@implementation ProjectMeeting

- (id)initWithCoder:(NSCoder*)decoder
{
    self = [super initWithCoder:decoder];
    if (self != nil) {
        meetingDescription = [decoder decodeObjectForKey:@"Description"];
        task = [decoder decodeObjectForKey:@"Task"];
    }
    return self;
}

- (void)encodeWithCoder:(NSCoder*)encoder
{
    [super encodeWithCoder:encoder];
    [encoder encodeObject:meetingDescription forKey:@"Description"];
    [encoder encodeConditionalObject:task forKey:@"Task"];
}

@end
```

The code in Listing 12-9 solves the problem by conditionally encoding the reference to its ProjectTask object. If you archive a single ProjectMeeting object, the ProjectTask object is never unconditionally encoded and is omitted. When unarchived, the statement [decoder decodeObjectForKey:@"Task"] returns nil. The resulting object wouldn't be connected to the project scheduling data model, but would be sufficient for inviting someone to the meeting.

When the scheduling system server archives the entire project data model, it will encode the project, its tasks, milestone, and team member objects unconditionally. When it gets to the ProjectMeeting objects, the conditional object references are encoded normally because the ProjectTask objects have been unconditionally encoded elsewhere in the graph. When the project data model is unarchived the next day, the ProjectMeeting's reference to its ProjectTask is restored.

Encoding an object conditionally is usually appropriate when the object pointer is a __weak reference, or when the object is a delegate, a parent, owner, or container.

Class Version Compatibility

The problem with persistent data is that it's persistent. It could persist for days or even years, while your application continues to evolve. Eventually, your class will attempt to decode an archive written by an earlier version of itself. On occasion, it might even be necessary to decode an archive created by some later version of the same class.

Java addresses compatibility using a combination of class versions and key/value encoding. Java's class versions are used strictly to inhibit the decoding of data that might be incompatible with the class. Java serialization also uses key/value encoding, just like an Objective-C keyed archive. But in Java's case the keys are always the names of the instance variables. Java will automatically restore the variables in common with its predecessors, and simply ignore variables not encoded in the data stream. More complicated compatibility problems require that you implement a custom readObjects(ObjectInputStream) method. I'm going to skip the lengthy details, because this isn't a book about Java.

■**Note** *Backward compatibility* is the ability of a newer version of a class/application to interpret data created by an older version. *Forward compatibility* is the ability of an older version of a class/application to, at least partially, interpret the data created by a newer version.

How you provide backward, or forward, compatibility in Objective-C depends on the archive type.

Forward and Backward Compatibility in Keyed Archives

Keyed archives confer one huge advantage: flexible compatibility between class versions. An improved version of the ScheduledEvent class, shown in Listing 12-10, has changed a little from the initial version in Listing 12-4. It contains a new time zone object and the duration value has been replaced with an end time object.

Listing 12-10. *Forward and Backward Compatibility in a Keyed Archive*

```
@interface ScheduledEvent : NSObject <NSCoding> {
@private
    NSDate          *startTime;
    NSDate          *endTime;
    NSTimeZone      *timeZone;
    RoomIdentifier  room;
}

@implementation ScheduledEvent

- (id)initWithCoder:(NSCoder*)decoder
{
    self = [super init];
    if (self != nil) {
        if ([decoder containsValueForKey:@"TimeZone"])
            timeZone = [decoder decodeObjectForKey:@"TimeZone"];
        else
            timeZone = [NSTimeZone localTimeZone];

        startTime = [decoder decodeObjectForKey:@"Start"];
        if ([decoder containsValueForKey:@"End"]) {
            endTime = [decoder decodeObjectForKey:@"End"];
        } else {
            NSTimeInterval duration = [decoder decodeDoubleForKey:@"Duration"];
            endTime = [startTime addTimeInterval:duration];
        }
```

```
        room.buildingNo = [decoder decodeInt32ForKey:@"Room.building"];
        room.roomNo = [decoder decodeInt32ForKey:@"Room.number"];
    }
    return self;
}

- (void)encodeWithCoder:(NSCoder*)encoder
{
    [encoder encodeObject:startTime forKey:@"Start"];
    [encoder encodeObject:endTime forKey:@"End"];
    [encoder encodeObject:timeZone forKey:@"TimeZone"];
    [encoder encodeInt32:room.buildingNo forKey:@"Room.building"];
    [encoder encodeInt32:room.roomNo forKey:@"Room.number"];

    [encoder encodeDouble:[endTime timeIntervalSinceDate:startTime]
                forKey:@"Duration"];

}

@end
```

The implementation in Listing 12-10 provides both forward and backward compatibility with its initial version. That is, the new version of the class can decode archives created by the original version, and the original version can decode archives created by the new version. This is accomplished through judicious use of archive keys.

The new version of ScheduledEvent has a time zone object that the old version lacks. The new version uses the -containsValueForKey: method to determine if the archive it's decoding contains a value for that key. If it does, it reads the value. If not, it assumes that the archive was created by an earlier version of the class and supplies a reasonable default. An old version of the class reading a newer archive ignores the value, knowing nothing about time zones.

The replacement of the duration variable with endTime requires a little more work. Again, -initWithCoder: uses [decoder containsValueForKey:@"End"] to determine if the archive contains an "End" value. Modern archives would, but old archives wouldn't. The new class assumes that a missing "End" value implies that it's reading an older version of the archive; it uses the "Duration" value written by the old version to construct an equivalent endTime object.

To provide forward compatibility, it archives the endTime value twice. Once as an NSDate object and again as an NSTimeInterval compatible with the class's original duration value. An alternate way of maintaining compatibility would be to not encode the endTime object at all and continue to encode the "Duration" value, compatible with the old version. This would be the preferred solution when the new property is logically equivalent to the old one, and easily converted.

Here are a few tips for maintaining backward, and potentially forward, compatibility in keyed archives:

- Test for the existence of keys added in later versions of the class. The absence of a key indicates the archive was created with an earlier version.

- If a value changes type, encode it using a new key.

- The integer and floating point decoding methods perform some modest type conversion. All of the integer encoding and decoding methods are interchangeable, as are the floating-point methods. Thus, you can encode a number as a 32 bit integer, then decode it as a 64-bit integer and vice versa.

- Initialize values for missing keys with something reasonable.

- For forward compatibility, continue to write the keys and values that earlier versions of the class expect, or translate newer values into values compatible with older classes.

- Consider inserting a "version" value, or any other kind of hint, that would help future classes determine how the archive values should be interpreted. The statement [encoder encodeBool:YES forKey:@"isTimeZoneSavvy"] would inform future decoders that this archive was created with a version of the class that understands time zones.

Backward Compatibility in Sequential Archives

In a sequential archive, backward compatibility is accomplished using class versions, somewhat similar to Java. In Java, each class is automatically assigned a class version—that amounts to a hash code of the class definition. By default, the Java runtime will only reconstruct an object if its version exactly matches the one used to create the serialized data. So any change to the class makes it incompatible with serialized data from a previous version. This is extremely limiting, but very safe. The programmer can override this by declaring a permanent serialVersionUID constant for the class. It is up to the programmer to ensure that all versions of the class with the same serialVersionUID are compatible.

Objective-C uses class versions, but in an entirely different way. Every class has a version property that the coder includes in the archive. Objective-C does not care if the version of your class is different than the one being decoded. At decode time, your class can query the coder to determine the version of the class that was used to encode the archive. You can use this information to decode the values in a way that is compatible with your previous versions.

For this to be effective, you must assign each functionally different version of the class a unique version number, and the version property of the class must be set before any archives are encoded. By default, the version of every class is 0. Listing 12-11 shows the implementation of the ScheduledEvent class from Listing 12-5, rewritten to provide backward compatibility. Keyed archive support has been removed for clarity.

Listing 12-11. Backward Compatibility in a Sequential Archive

```
+ (void)initialize
{
    [ScheduledEvent setVersion:1];  // second version
}

- (id)initWithCoder:(NSCoder*)decoder
{
    self = [super init];
    if (self!=nil) {
        startTime = [decoder decodeObject];
        if ([decoder versionForClassName:@"ScheduledEvent"]==1) {
            endTime = [decoder decodeObject];
            timeZone = [decoder decodeObject];
        } else {
            NSTimeInterval duration;
            [decoder decodeValueOfObjCType:@encode(NSTimeInterval) at:&duration];
            endTime = [startTime addTimeInterval:duration];
            timeZone = [NSTimeZone localTimeZone];
        }
```

```
        [decoder decodeValueOfObjCType:@encode(unsigned int)
                                at:&room.buildingNo];
        [decoder decodeValueOfObjCType:@encode(unsigned int)
                                at:&room.roomNo];
    }
    return self;
}

- (void)encodeWithCoder:(NSCoder*)encoder
{
    [encoder encodeObject:startTime];
    [encoder encodeObject:endTime];
    [encoder encodeObject:timeZone];
    [encoder encodeValueOfObjCType:@encode(unsigned int) at:&room.buildingNo];
    [encoder encodeValueOfObjCType:@encode(unsigned int) at:&room.roomNo];
}
```

The +initialize class method is used to set the version of the class before any instances of the class are created. See Chapter 21 for more about the +initialize method. At decode time, the object queries the coder to discover the version number of the class used to create the archive, and adjusts its decoding accordingly.

Every time the encoding of your class changes, you must establish a new class version and update the decoder to handle all of the earlier formats you want to support. Class versioning cannot provide forward compatibility. That would require a time machine.

Class Replacement

Sometimes the changes to an application involve more than just adding or redefining member variables. Refactoring an application might involve renaming or retiring classes altogether. This is a problem when attempting to decode an archive written by an earlier incarnation of the application, because the class recorded in the archive no longer exists. This problem can often be solved using class substitution during encoding or decoding.

Class Substitution During Decoding

Let's say that our scheduling application has been refactored, completely eliminating the ScheduledEvent class. It has been replaced by an AbstractEvent class with MeetingEvent, ProjectEvent, and HolidayEvent subclasses. Any attempt to decode an archive containing a ScheduledEvent object will fail, because there is no ScheduledEvent class for the decoder to create. There are three solutions, and all of them involve creating a stand-in ScheduledEvent class that exists solely to provide backward compatibility.

The first solution is to implement a shell ScheduledEvent class with a legacy -initWithCoder: method. It would also override the -awakeAfterUsingCoder: method as described earlier in the "Duplicate Objects" section. In the latter method, an equivalent object would be created to replace the original.

A more direct approach takes its queue from class clusters—see Chapter 22—to perform an object substitution directly in the -initWithCoder: method, as shown in Listing 12-12. When the coder attempts to initialize a newly created ScheduledEvent object, the constructor destroys the temporary object and creates a new object with the correct class instead.

Listing 12-12. *Replacing a Class During Decoding*

```
@interface ScheduledEvent : NSObject <NSCoding>
@end

@implementation ScheduledEvent

- (id)initWithCoder:(NSCoder*)decoder
{
    self = [super init];
    if (self != nil) {
        // read the properties of the obsolete ScheduledEvent
        NSDate *startTime = [decoder decodeObjectForKey:@"Start"];
        NSTimeInterval duration = [decoder decodeDoubleForKey:@"Duration"];
        RoomIdentifier room;
        room.buildingNo = [decoder decodeInt32ForKey:@"Room.building"];
        room.roomNo = [decoder decodeInt32ForKey:@"Room.number"];

        // replace it with an equivalent MeetingEvent object
        id replacement = [MeetingEvent new];
        [replacement setStartTime:startTime];
        [replacement setEndTime:[startTime addTimeInterval:duration]];
        [replacement setRoom:room];
        self = replacement;
    }
    return self;
}

- (void)encodeWithCoder:(NSCoder*)encoder
{
    [NSException raise:NSInvalidArchiveOperationException
                format:@"ScheduledEvent obsolete"];
}

@end
```

It's also possible for the unarchiver's delegate object to perform decode-time object substitution without requiring the object's cooperation. When an object is decoded, the unarchiver's delegate object is sent an -unarchiver:didDecodeObject: message. The delegate may elect to return a different object than the original, thereby replacing it. The unarchiver must be customized by setting its delegate property prior to decoding any objects. Use the code in Listing 12-2 as a template for creating a customized decoder. Chapter 17 explains delegate objects in more detail.

■**Caution** Object replacement during decoding won't work reliably if objects contain circular references. Circular references cause objects to be constructed recursively. The object reference returned to the nested constructor will be the partially initialized object, *before* it has finished executing -initWithCoder: or been sent the -replacementObjectForCoder: message. The second object created will refer to the original object even after the first object has replaced itself.

Class Substitution During Encoding

In other situations, a class might not want to archive itself. The class may be a private subclass of a class cluster—see Chapter 22 for more about class clusters. Or, it might want to archive itself as though it were a different class for forward compatibility with earlier designs. Whatever the reason, a class can choose to "pretend" to be another class during encoding, or provide a completely different object that will be encoded in its place. There are three ways to accomplish encode-time substitution.

The first is to override the -classForCoder method. This message is sent to an object during encoding. The class of the object in the archive is determined by the returned value. The base class implementation returns [self class], which causes objects to be recorded with their actual class. If an object's -classForCoder method returns a different class, that's the class that will be created when the object is decoded. Note that the data encoded in the -encodeWithCoder: method must be compatible with the class returned by -classForCoder:. -classForCoder affects all archive types. If you only want to limit class substitution to a particular archive type, override -classForArchiver, -classForKeyedArchiver, or -classForPortCoder instead. If not overridden, these methods return the value of -classForCoder.

The second technique allows an object to substitute a completely different object to be encoded in its place. This is accomplished by overriding -replacementObjectForCoder, which normally returns self (thus encoding the original object). If it returns a different object, that proxy object is encoded instead. -replacementObjectForCoder: will perform this substitution for all archive encodings, but the alternate methods -replacementObjectForKeyedArchiver:, -replacementObjectForArchiver:, or -replacementObjectForPortCoder: can be overridden to perform replacement only for particular archive types. By default, the first two of these methods invoke -replacementObjectForCoder:. The -replacementObjectForPortCoder: method is a critical mechanism in distributed objects. Its default implementation substitutes a remote proxy object for the original. See Chapter 13 for the reasons you would want to override it.

As if that wasn't enough flexibility, the encoder's delegate object can also perform object substitution by implementing an -archiver:willEncodeObject: method. The delegate can return a replacement object, performing substitutions ad hoc without the need to modify the class being encoded.

Objective-C Serialization

In Objective-C parlance, *serialization* converts a set of data objects into a transportable byte stream, often in a human-readable format. There are two standard forms of serialization in Objective-C: property lists and XML. Property lists are simplistic, but very convenient, and form the foundation for the user defaults (preferences) service. Cocoa's XML support includes the familiar DOM and event-based XML parsing and encoding. Objective-C serialization does not encode arbitrary objects as archiving does. Property lists are limited to property-list objects, and XML DOM encoding is restricted to the XML document object model classes.

Property Lists

A property list is a text or binary representation of the values in one or more property-list objects. Property-list objects are, self referentially, those objects that can be encoded into a property list. Table 12-3 lists all the property-list objects.

Table 12-3. *Property-List Objects*

Object Class	Description
NSDictionary	Key/value mapping of property-list objects
NSArray	Sequential list of property-list objects
NSString	A string
NSNumber	An integer, floating-point, or Boolean value
NSDate	A date and time
NSData	Any arbitrary byte array

Property lists are used for a variety of purposes. They are used to store user defaults, as described in Chapter 26. They are also particularly convenient for encoding collections of simple values for persistence or interpretation by other applications.

Typically, a property list is a dictionary of key/value pairs containing property-list objects, which can include other arrays and dictionaries. This allows property-list objects to form arbitrarily complex trees, the leaf values consisting of strings, numbers, dates, or opaque data. Virtually any object can be stored in a property list by first archiving the object, and then storing the resulting NSData object in the property-list tree. Listing 12-13 creates a tree of property-list objects and serializes it into a property list.

Listing 12-13. *Generating a Property List*

```
NSArray *attendees = [NSArray arrayWithObjects:
    @"Randy",
    @"Joy",
    @"Douglas",
    @"Heather",
    @"Jon",
    nil];
NSDictionary *invitation = [NSDictionary dictionaryWithObjectsAndKeys:
    @"X-Prize Launch Strategy",                      @"Description",
    [NSDate dateWithString:@"2009-04-02 10:00:00 -0700"],   @"StartTime",
    [NSNumber numberWithInt:55],                     @"Duration",
    attendees,                                       @"Attendees",
    @"Room 312",                                     @"Location",
    nil];
NSData *data = [NSPropertyListSerialization dataFromPropertyList:invitation
                format:NSPropertyListXMLFormat_v1_0
                errorDescription:NULL];
```

```
data now contains:
<?xml version="1.0" encoding="UTF-8"?>
<!DOCTYPE plist PUBLIC "-//Apple//DTD PLIST 1.0//EN"
 "http://www.apple.com/DTDs/PropertyList-1.0.dtd">
<plist version="1.0">
<dict>
    <key>Attendees</key>
    <array>
        <string>Randy</string>
        <string>Joy</string>
        <string>Douglas</string>
        <string>Heather</string>
        <string>Jon</string>
    </array>
    <key>Description</key>
    <string>X-Prize Launch Stratagy</string>
    <key>Duration</key>
    <integer>55</integer>
    <key>Location</key>
    <string>Room 312</string>
    <key>StartTime</key>
    <date>2009-04-02T17:00:00Z</date>
</dict>
</plist>
```

The Objective-C interface for encoding and decoding property lists is the NSPropertyListSerialization class. It provides three methods:

`+dataFromPropertyList:format:errorDescription:` encodes objects into a property list.

`+propertyListFromData:mutabilityOption:format:errorDescription:` decodes a property list.

`+propertyList:isValidForFormat:` determines if the data contains a valid property list.

For all transformations, you must specify the format of the property list. The possible formats are listed in Table 12-4.

Table 12-4. *Property List Formats*

Format	Description
NSPropertyListXMLFormat_v1_0	XML representation of property values
NSPropertyListBinaryFormat_v1_0	Compact binary representation of property values
NSPropertyListOpenStepFormat	Deprecated ASCII format; can be used for reading legacy .plist files, but cannot be use to encode new property lists

Both NSDictionary and NSArray accept a -writeToFile:atomically: or -writeToURL:atomically: message. This will serialize their content and write the resulting XML property list to a file or URL. These messages can succeed only if the collection contains property-list objects; any non-property-list objects will cause the operation to fail and return NO. Do not confuse these methods with -writeToFile:atomically: and -writeToURL:atomically: implemented by NSData and NSString. These latter methods write the *raw* contents of the object to a file—not a property list.

The complements of the -writeTo…:atomically: messages are the +[NSArray arrayWithContentsOfFile:], +[NSArray arrayWithContentsOfURL:], +[NSDictionary dictionaryWithContentsOfFile:] and +[NSDictionary dictionaryWithContentsOfURL:] convenience constructors. These methods create a new collection, populated by interpreting the contents of a property list.

Property-list collection objects created by decoding a property list are, by default, immutable— irrespective of the mutability of those originally used to create the property list. To create mutable property-list objects, use +[NSPropertyListSerialization propertyListFromData:mutabilityOption:format:errorDescription:] and pass either NSPropertyListMutableContainers or NSPropertyListMutableContainersAndLeaves in the mutabilityOption: parameter. The former will return mutable collection objects with immutable leaf values. The latter will cause all objects in the tree to be mutable, where possible. This option does not affect NSNumber or NSDate objects, which are inherently immutable. You can also create a top-level mutable collection by explicitly creating one, as in [NSMutableDictionary dictionaryWithContentsOfFile:propertyFilePath].

XML

Like Java, the Cocoa framework provides a set of classes for creating, manipulating, encoding, and decoding XML files. While XML-formatted property lists are an expedient way to encode very simple values into XML, the NSXML classes can interpret any XML- or HTML-formatted data.

As with Java, Objective-C can digest an entire XML document producing a document object model (DOM). Or it can interpret an XML stream incrementally using an event-driven parser. While many of the details are different, the overarching interface that Java and Objective-C provide for XML processing is almost identical.

Listing 12-14 shows the code used to create a document object model from an XML file, and then encode that DOM back into an XML file.

Listing 12-14. XML Using Document Object Models

Java
```
String filePath = …
Document document = null;
DocumentBuilderFactory factory = DocumentBuilderFactory.newInstance();
factory.setValidating(false);
factory.setNamespaceAware(true);
try {
    DocumentBuilder builder = factory.newDocumentBuilder();
    document = builder.parse(new File(filePath));
}
catch (Exception e) {
    e.printStackTrace();
}

…
```

```
try {
    Source source = new DOMSource(document);
    Result result = new StreamResult(new File(filePath));
    Transformer transformer = TransformerFactory.newInstance().newTransformer();
    transformer.transform(source,result);
}
catch (Exception e) {
    e.printStackTrace();
}
```

Objective-C
```
NSString *filePath = …
NSXMLDocument *document;
NSURL *furl = [NSURL fileURLWithPath:filePath];
document = [[NSXMLDocument alloc] initWithContentsOfURL:furl
                                       options:NSXMLNodePreserveAll
                                         error:NULL];

…

NSData *xmlData = [document XMLData];
[xmlData writeToFile:filePath atomically:YES];
```

Objective-C coding is somewhat simpler, because the NSXMLDocument class provides the DOM translator automatically. To transform an XML or HTML file into a document object model, simply initialize a new NSXMLDocument object with the contents of the XML source. Similarly, transforming an existing DOM into its XML representation is simply a matter of asking the NSXMLDocument for its NSData representation. An alternate method, -[NSXMLDocument XMLDataWithOptions:], accepts a set of flags that influence how the XML is encoded.

Objective-C event-driven XML parsing parallels its Java cousin SAX (Simple API for XML). In Java, you create a custom object that implements the org.xml.sax.ContentHandler interface. This interface defines a number of callback methods (startDocument(), startElement(String,String,String,Attributes), characters(char[],int,int), etc.) that are invoked as each XML element is parsed. Your implementation of these methods would typically use the parsed content to create custom data model objects or feed the information to another object.

In Objective-C the process is nearly identical, except that delegate methods—defined by an informal protocol—receive the parsing events. To parse an XML file using Objective-C, implement the appropriate delegate methods (-parserDidStartDocument:, -parser:didStartElement:namespaceURI:qualifiedName:attributes:, -parser:foundCharacters:, and so on) in your class. Create an instance of the NSXMLParser object using -initWithData: or -initWithContentsOfURL: to specify a source for the XML. Set your custom object as the delegate of the parser ([xmlParser setDelegate:myParser]) and then send it a parse message to begin decoding.

Copying Objects

Archiving and serialization essentially copy an object. If you just need to efficiently copy an object, Objective-C provides the -copy message that will duplicate an object in almost exactly the same way as Java's Object.clone() method. In addition, Objective-C defines a protocol for obtaining mutable copies of immutable objects.

Copying an object may produce a *shallow* copy or a *deep* copy. Which depends on the nature of the object. A shallow copy is the default in both Java and Objective-C. A shallow copy creates a new object whose instance variables contain the same values as the original. It's shallow because the duplicate object will refer to all of the same objects that the original does. For references to immutable objects, that's the preferred result as it avoids unnecessary object duplication. For mutable objects, however, changing a property value affects the value of the copy too. To be truly independent of the original, the copied object must recursively copy any mutable objects it refers to. This is called a deep copy.

In Java, a clonable object must implement java.lang.Cloneable. If you do nothing else, calling Object.clone() will produce a shallow copy of the object. If the object needs to perform a deep copy, it must override Object.clone() and perform whatever additional duplication is required.

Objective-C is very similar. For an object to be copyable, it must conform to the NSCopying protocol and implement the -copyWithZone: method. To perform a shallow copy, -copyWithZone: can call NSCopyObject(...) to produce and return a duplicate of the object. If a deep copy is needed, additional copy operations or other memory management should be performed before returning. Listing 12-15 shows a simple object that performs a deep copy of itself.

Listing 12-15. Copying Objects

Java

```java
public class StormTrooper implements Cloneable
{
    ArrayList evilOrders;

    public Object clone() throws CloneNotSupportedException
    {
        try {
            StormTrooper clone = (StormTrooper)super.clone();
            clone.evilOrders = (ArrayList)this.evilOrders.clone();
            return (clone);
        }
        catch (CloneNotSupportedException e) {
            throw new InternalError(e.toString());
        }
    }

}
```

Objective-C

```objc
@interface StormTrooper : NSObject <NSCopying> {
    NSMutableArray  *evilOrders;
}

@end
```

```
@implementation StormTrooper

- (id)copyWithZone:(NSZone*)zone
{
    StormTrooper *clone = NSCopyObject(self,0,zone);
    if (clone!=nil)
        clone->evilOrders = [evilOrders copy];
    return (clone);
}

@end
```

To copy an object that conforms to NSCopying, send it the -copy message. The object will send itself a -copyWithZone: message, or raise an exception if the object doesn't conform to NSCopying. Do *not* customize object copying by overriding -copy.

NSCopyObject creates a new object. If an object inherits from a class that already implements -copyWithZone: it should create the copy by sending its superclass -copyWithZone:, as in MyClass *clone = [super copyWithZone:zone], and then proceed with any subclass-specific copying.

NSCopyObject is convenient, but you don't have to use it. You can elect to create and initialize an equivalent object using any means available. For example, you could create a new object using something like [[[self class] alloc] init], and then initialize the new object so that it is equal to the original. You could pull an already created object from a pool of similar objects and set its properties to match. An immutable object may elect to return self, instead of actually making a copy.

Objective-C also defines an interface for obtaining mutable copies of immutable objects. If you implement a copyable immutable class that has a mutable subclass, you should follow this design:

- The immutable superclass should also conform to NSMutableCopying and implement -mutableCopyWithZone:.

- In the immutable superclass, -mutableCopyWithZone: should create an instance of the mutable subclass, duplicate the relevant data, and return the new instance.

- In the mutable subclass, -mutableCopyWithZone: should mimic -copyWithZone:, returning a mutable copy of itself.

Your object will now intelligently respond to the -mutableCopy message.

Summary

Objective-C archiving fills the role of Java serialization. Creating an archivable class requires a little more work up front, but follows the same basic pattern as it does in Java. It is not difficult to provide backward, and potentially forward, compatibility with archived data. Objective-C provides the added benefit of restricting the graph of encoded objects to just those relevant to the root object, and there is a flexible framework for substituting and simplifying objects during encoding and decoding.

Objective-C serialization is, as you've now discovered, not the equivalent of Java serialization, but it does provide a simple and convenient means of encoding data using XML. You also learned the basics of making in-memory copies of objects.

With a firm understanding of message dispatching and object archiving, you can now appreciate the simplicity of distributed objects, discussed in the next chapter, which combines these two features to great effect.

CHAPTER 13

∎∎∎

Communicating Near and Far

Communication is a very broad term. In an abstract sense, sending an Objective-C object a message is "communicating" with that object. At the other extreme, burning a file to a compact disc that's later read by another program "communicates" data to that application. This chapter focuses on communication technologies that exchange data directly between objects via an independent agent or service.

Within that scope, communications can be roughly divided into three domains: the exchange of messages between objects in the same process, the exchange of messages between objects in different processes, and the exchange of data over a network. This chapter will survey the common Objective-C technologies used for all three, although the details of some are covered in other chapters. The groups overlap somewhat. There are technologies that are used almost exclusively to exchange messages between objects running in the same process, but that can also be used to send messages to other processes, and vice versa. So take a moment to familiarize yourself with all of them before settling on a solution.

Communicating Within a Single Process

There are several technologies for exchanging messages with objects in your process's memory address space. Fundamental Objective-C message dispatching is one, but this section is going to review the following technologies that send messages to an object on behalf of another object:

- Deferred messages
- Notifications
- Key-Value Observing
- Distributed Objects

Deferred messages were discussed in Chapter 6. Deferred messages are sent using the -performSelector:… family of methods. This is the simplest form of inter-object communication. It queues up an Objective-C message that will be sent to an object at some later time. The message is usually sent in the same thread, but some variants will send it to the object in a different thread.

Notifications send NSNotification objects to the objects interested in receiving them. An NSNotification is a named message container that can include whatever arbitrary information you want to provide the receivers. Notifications are Objetive-C's embodiment of the Provider/Subscriber pattern, and are described in Chapter 18. The most notable differences between notifications and other communication techniques is that notifications are a one-to-many communications path, and the provider and subscriber objects aren't required to have any direct knowledge of each other. Notifications are distributed through NSNotificationCenter objects. The sender describes the nature of the notification it wants to distribute, and the receiver describes the types of notifications it would like to receive. The notification center matches the senders to the receivers and delivers the requested notifications.

Key-Value Observing (KVO) is a specialized notification service that communicates changes about an object's properties. An *observer* object can attach itself to a particular property of another object. Once attached, any change to that property is immediately sent to the observer in the form of an `-observeValueForKeyPath:ofObject:change:context:` message. Key-Value Observing is particularly attractive because there are no prerequisite design requirements on the part of the object being observed—other than it must implement a KVO-compliant property. Thus, your object can request to be notified about changes to virtually any property of any object. Key-Value Observing is described in Chapter 19.

Distributed objects (DO) is usually employed to send messages between objects in separate processes or across networks to other systems. However, it can also be used to send messages between threads of the same process. This use of distributed objects is an easy way of adding asynchronous message processing to your design. Inter-thread DO is described and demonstrated in the next section.

Communicating with Other Processes

Communicating with other processes is severely limited by the fact that an address in the local process's memory address space is meaningless to any other process. To exchange information with another process, all data must be in, or converted into, a transportable form that is meaningful outside the process. This usually takes the form of byte arrays that are interpreted serially by the receiving process. Fortunately, in the previous chapter you just learned about two key technologies that perform this transformation for objects—archiving and serialization.

Ports, pipes, and sockets are the low-level tools for exchanging blocks of bytes between processes. Ports refer to Mach kernel ports, the fundamental mechanism by which messages are sent to the kernel and, by extension, other processes. Technically, *all* extra-process communications are performed through Mach ports, since that's the only means by which a process can communicate with the outside world. Layered on top of ports are the POSIX concepts of pipes and sockets. Pipes are, conceptually, a unidirectional serial communications conduit with a process connected to each end. Bytes injected into the pipe by one process instantly appear as readable data to the other. Sockets are unidirectional or bidirectional communications conduits between two processes. While pipes are limited to two processes running on the same system, sockets can be connected—via data networks or another transport medium—to a process running on a completely different computer system, possibly quite remote. Sockets are more packet oriented, sending and receiving discrete blocks of information rather than individual bytes.

Distributed notifications and distributed objects are the two principal high-level inter-process communications technologies. These are both object-oriented facilities that automatically archive or serialize object data so that it can be transported to another process or system. Ports, pipes, or sockets are employed to transport the serialized data.

This section will briefly describe the Objective-C interfaces to ports, pipes, and sockets. It will then touch on distributed notifications before getting to distributed objects. Distributed objects are the apex of object-oriented inter-process communications, and consume most of the rest of this chapter.

Low-Level Communications

Objective-C has four key classes that represent a source of serial or sequential data:

- NSPort
- NSPipe
- NSStream
- NSFileHandle

There is a huge amount of overlap between the capabilities and functionality of these classes. It's possible, for example, to connect to a BSD socket using NSPort, NSPipe, and NSFileHandle. All allow you to send and receive serial data through the conduit. Which you use will be dictated largely by the context of where you need them. A data source that will be processed by a run loop must be a subclass of NSPort. The POSIX pipes that connect processes (better known as standard in, standard out, and standard error) can be either NSPipe or NSFileHandle objects. Network services provide NSStream objects for communicating with the connected process.

NSPort

NSPort is the base class that connects a data source to a run loop. Messages pushed onto the port are processed by the run loop. NSMachPort is a subclass that connects to a Mach kernel port for direct process-to-process communications. NSSocketPort can be connected to BSD pipes or sockets providing equivalent functionality between processes and systems. NSPorts are the foundation for distributed objects, several of which are demonstrated in the "Distributed Objects" section later in this chapter.

NSMachPort is extremely efficient and the most common type of port used by run loops. User events, system events, deferred messages, timer events, and many other low-level messages are all processed by an application through its run loop. Most events are pushed onto the run loop's Mach port by the system or from within the application. Mach ports can also be used to send messages between processes. The one limitation is the security model of the operating system. All Mach kernel ports exist within a domain called a *bootstrap namespace*. A bootstrap namespace is created for each user that logs into a Mac OS X system. A process can only connect with the Mach ports in its namespace and its parent namespaces. Thus, an application could use Mach ports to establish communications with another process started by the same user, or a system daemon, but not with a process started by another user.

NSSocketPorts are used when a run loop needs to communicate with a process outside its bootstrap namespace or possibly with another computer system. NSSocketPorts can be connected to a variety of different sources; the two most useful are BSD pipes and sockets. A pipe can be a named pipe in the file system. File system names are public to all processes, and provide a means for two processes in different bootstrap namespaces to communicate. Network sockets allow two processes to exchange data using a network transport protocol. The advantage is that the other process could be running on the same machine or one thousands of miles away. The disadvantage is that network ports are typically accessible from outside the computer system, which might not be appropriate for some communications and has security implications.

NSPipe

NSPipe is little more than a wrapper for a pair of NSFileHandle objects. An NSPipe is used to interact with BSD pipes. Often, these are the traditional standard in, standard out, and standard error pipes that connect processes. Listing 13-1 shows how to launch an executable and capture the text output of the new process.

Listing 13-1. Capturing Standard Out

```Java
ProcessBuilder pb = new ProcessBuilder("/bin/echo","Hello, Objective-C");
try {
    Process echo = pb.start();
    InputStream stdOut = echo.getInputStream();
    int c = (int)' ';
    System.out.print("echo says:");
```

```
        do {
            System.out.print((char)c);
            c = stdOut.read();
        } while (c!=(-1));
    } catch (IOException e) {
        e.printStackTrace();
    }
```

Objective-C

```
NSTask *echo = [NSTask new];
NSPipe *stdOut = [NSPipe pipe];
[echo setLaunchPath:@"/bin/echo"];
[echo setArguments:[NSArray arrayWithObject:@"Hello, Objective-C"]];
[echo setStandardOutput:stdOut];
[echo launch];

NSFileHandle *outStream = [stdOut fileHandleForReading];
NSData *output = [outStream readDataToEndOfFile];
NSLog(@"echo says: %@",[NSString stringWithCString:[output bytes]
                                     length:[output length]]);
```

In Java, the java.lang.Process object creates the required java.io.InputStream or java.io.OutputStream objects and provides them to you. In Objective-C, everything is backwards. You create the NSPipe or NSFileHandle object you want to communicate through, then pass it in a -setStandardInput:, -setStandardOutput:, or -setStandardError: message. This must be done before the process is launched. When launched, NSTask will connect the pipe or file handle you provided to the actual pipe attached to the process. Also note that the terminology is reversed. In Objective-C, the standardOut property is the standard out of the process (i.e., the process's output). In Java, java.lang.Process.getInputStream gets the InputStream connected to the process's standard out. In other words, pipe identities in Objective-C are from the perspective of the process. In Java, they are from the perspective of the parent process.

To get the actual input data, the NSFileHandle for reading is obtained from the pipe. It's possible to bypass using NSPipe altogether, as the -setStandardInput:, -setStandardOutput:, and -setStandardError: messages all accept NSFileHandle objects too. So the code in Listing 13-1 could be easily rewritten to set an NSFileHandle as its connection to standard out. The effect would be the same.

NSFileHandle

NSFileHandle is the general purpose wrapper for a POSIX file. When used with pipes and sockets, they become stream interfaces. NSFileHandle methods were described in the Files chapter. When used with a pipe file, methods that don't make sense on a serial data—particularly -offsetInFile, -seektoFileOffset:, and -seekToEndOfFile—should not be used. Unidirectional output pipes should not be sent any -read… messages, and unidirectional input pipes will not accept the -writeData: message.

As with Java InputStreams, the logical end of file (EOF) condition only exists when the input side of the pipe is closed. Thus, the -[NSFileHandle readDataToEndOfFile] method in Listing 13-1 suspends until the other end of the pipe is closed, even if all of the data in the pipe has already been read.

The NSFileHandle methods -readInBackgroundAndNotify, -readToEndOfFileInBackgroundAndNotify, and -waitForDataInBackgroundAndNotify become particularly useful when used with pipes and sockets. These messages create a new thread that waits for data to appear in the pipe, and then posts a notification which your application can observe. -waitForData…

merely notifies you that data has become available, but doesn't read any of it. -readInBackground… immediately reads what's available and supplies that in the notification. -readToEndOfFile… waits until the pipe is closed, then sends a notification containing all of the remaining data in the pipe.

NSStream

Where NSFileHandle is a generic wrapper that can be used with data streams, NSStream is a specialized class designed exclusively for use with serial data streams. NSStream has two usable subclasses: NSInputStream and NSOuputStream. These are the closest Objective-C equivalents of java.io.InputStream and java.io.OutputStream. The base NSStream class defines the methods common to both subclasses (i.e., -open, -close, -streamStatus). Naturally, NSInputStream defines a -read:… method and NSOutputStream defines a -write:… method, along with other methods applicable only to input or output streams.

Like their Java counterparts, NSInputStream and NSOutputStream can be connected to a variety of sources including pipes, sockets, data files, and memory buffers. But instead of defining explicit subclasses for each variation, Objective-C presents a single class that operates in different modes. The object you use might actually be a private subclass, but that's an implementation detail that should be ignored. Table 13-1 shows the Java stream classes and the equivalent NSInputStream or NSOutputStream constructor.

Table 13-1. *Creating Stream Objects*

Java	Objective-C
new ByteArrayInputStream(bytes)	[NSInputStream inputStreamWithData:bytes]
new FileInputStream(path)	[NSInputStream inputStreamWithFileAtPath:path]
new ByteArrayOutputStream()	[NSOutputStream outputStreamToMemory]
new ByteArrayOutputStream(size)	[NSOutputStream outputStreamToBuffer:buffer capacity:size]
new FileOutputStream(path)	[NSOutputStream outputStreamToFileAtPath:path append:NO]

The specific Java subclasses include methods applicable to that type of data stream. For example, the java.io.ByteArrayOutputStream includes a toByteArray() method that retrieves the collected output data as a byte array object. The NSStream classes relate stream-specific information via their properties dictionary. To obtain the data collected by an NSOutputStream initialized with +outputStreamToMemory, obtain the stream's NSStreamDataWrittenToMemoryStreamKey property, like this:

```
NSData *bytes = [outStream propertyForKey:NSStreamDataWrittenToMemoryStreamKey];
```

Similarly, the current file position for a stream attached to a data file can be examined, or modified, by manipulating the stream's NSStreamFileCurrentOffsetKey property; the value is an NSNumber object. These are the only two stream properties of general interest. Other properties are concerned with network socket configuration.

Like Java, other services may create and return specialized subclasses of NSInputStream or NSOutputStream—subclasses that you can't, or shouldn't attempt to, create yourself. These opaque subclasses are usually how NSStreams are attached to pipes, or how network socket ports are obtained.

A significant difference between NSFileHandle and the NSStream classes is the way asynchronous data is processed. NSFileHandle has methods that create a temporary thread that waits for data to become available, and then sends a notification. NSStream objects are designed to work within run loops to provide event-driven stream processing without the need to create additional threads. To take advantage of this, you must attach the stream to a working run loop, as shown in Listing 13-2.

Listing 13-2. *NSStream Event Handling*

```
NSInputStream *inStream = …
MyStreamHandler *delegate = [MyStreamHandler new];

[inStream setDelegate:delegate];
[inStream scheduleInRunLoop:[NSRunLoop currentRunLoop]
                    forMode:NSDefaultRunLoopMode];
[inStream open];

…

@implementation MyStreamHandler

- (void)stream:(NSStream*)stream handleEvent:(NSStreamEvent)eventCode
{
    switch (eventCode) {
        case NSStreamEventHasBytesAvailable:
        {
            uint8_t buffer[1024];
            NSUInteger length;
            length = [(NSInputStream*)stream read:buffer
                                        maxLength:sizeof(buffer)];
            if (length!=0) {
                // do something with data in buffer[]...
            }
            break;
        }
        case NSStreamEventEndEncountered:
        {
            // do something at end-of-stream...
            break;
        }
        case NSStreamEvent…:

            …
            break;
    }
}

@end
```

Once scheduled, the run loop will send stream event messages to your delegate, just as it dispatches other kinds of events. Using stream events is the most efficient, and the preferred, method for stream data processing. It is possible to poll the stream by repeatedly sending it -hasBytesAvailable messages in a tight loop, but this would most likely be a horrific waste of CPU resources.

High-Level Communications

The high-level communication frameworks are an object-oriented interface for exchanging messages and objects. There are two principal high-level communication facilities:

- Distributed Notifications
- Distributed Objects

These frameworks use the low-level communication classes described in the previous section to perform the actual data exchange, shielding you from most of the unpleasant details. The high-level frameworks all have some form of registry or automatic discovery to connect the sender with the receiver. Most of the time, the client and remote service need only agree on a common identifier; the framework will take care of connecting the two.

Distributed Notifications

Distributed notifications are described in the Chapter 18, but there's not much to tell. Distributed notifications are just like regular notifications, with two key differences:

- Notifications are broadcast to all processes.
- Notification content is restricted to property-list objects.

Distributed notifications use Mach ports, which limits them to communicating with processes in the same bootstrap namespace. They use serialization to convert the data into a form suitable for inter-process exchange, so the notification's name, source object, and information must all be property-list objects, as described in the section "Objective-C Serialization" in Chapter 12. Listing 13-3 shows how to send a notification to any number of observer processes running on the same system.

Listing 13-3. Sending a Distributed Notification

```
NSDictionary *info = [NSDictionary dictionaryWithObjectsAndKeys:
    @"Meeting Reminder",                               @"Message",
    @"X-Prize Launch Stratagy",                        @"Description",
    [NSDate dateWithString:@"2009-04-02 10:00:00 -0700"], @"StartTime",
    @"Room 312",                                       @"Location",
    nil];
[[NSDistributedNotificationCenter defaultCenter]
                            postNotificationName:@"PSEventReminder"
                                          object:@"com.apress.schedule"
                                        userInfo:info];
```

Distributed notifications are extremely easy to post and subscribe to. For self-contained, infrequent, unidirectional, broadcast-style messages, they are by far the simplest inter-process communication solution.

Distributed Objects

Distributed Objects (DO) is the apex of inter-object communications, and is equivalent to Java's Remote Method Invocation (RMI) technology. Distributed objects is more flexible and easier to use than RMI, making it a convenient solution to a wide variety of design problems. This section will describe the basics of how distributed objects works, several different ways of establishing a connection to a remote object, how to send and receive messages, and how you can influence object exchange between processes.

How Distributed Objects Works

Using Remote Method Invocation in Java generally involves the following:

1. Create an interface that defines the methods your remote object implements.
2. Create a class that implements the interface in step 1.
3. Execute the rmic utility to generate a _Stub class from the implementation class.
4. Make all objects that are passed to, or returned from, methods in the interface Serializable.
5. Start the rmiregistry process.
6. Create an instance of the implementation class in your server process.
7. Register that object as a named service.
8. In your client process, request the proxy object for the service.
9. Call methods of the proxy object to invoke those same methods on the instance of the object in the server process.

Using distributed objects in Objective-C follows the same general workflow, except that Objective-C eliminates steps 3 and 5, and makes steps 1, 2, 4, and 7 optional. In Objective-C, the minimum required to use distributed objects is:

1. Vend any object via a connection object attached to a run loop.
2. The client requests the proxy object for the vended object from the connection.
3. The client sends the proxy object messages.

The key differences are that you don't have to do anything special to create a proxy of a remote object—Objective-C creates proxy objects spontaneously—and objects do not have to be archivable in order to be passed to, or returned from, remote messages. Although there can be advantages to making objects archivable, as explained in the "Passing Objects by Copy" section.

Listing 13-4 contrasts Java RMI with Objective-C distributed objects. The complete source code and projects for these demonstrations is available at http://www.apress.com/ in the Source Code/Downloads area. Shell scripts to compile and run the examples are included. To try the Objective-C examples one at a time, open and build the Xcode project. Open a Terminal window and cd to the build directory that contains the Greeter and Guest executables. Run the commands from the shell using ./Greeter or ./Guest. You will want to open multiple windows to play with communications between processes, or copy the executable to another computer on the same network to experiment with network connections. Type Control-C to stop a running server process.

The Java implementation is functionally similar to the Objective-C version. Both examples run in two separate processes: a Greeter server and a Guest client. The Greeter process creates and publishes a single Greeter object. The client application connects to the remote process by looking up the Greeter service by name. It obtains a proxy for the Greeter object that exists in the server and interacts with it.

The output from these programs is shown in Listing 13-5. The server and client form a one-to-many relationship. You can start as many client processes as you like; they will all connect and interact with the single Greeter object.

Listing 13-4. *Remote Method Invocation*

Java: Greeter and Guest Classes

```java
public interface Greeter extends Remote {
    public void sayHello( ) throws java.rmi.RemoteException;
    public void greetGuest( Guest listener ) throws java.rmi.RemoteException;
    public String sayGoodbye( ) throws java.rmi.RemoteException;
}

public class GreeterImpl extends UnicastRemoteObject implements Greeter {

    private static final long serialVersionUID = 9990100926135399924L;

    public static void main(String[] args)
    {
        String greeterServiceURI = makeServiceURI(null,null);

        try {
            Greeter greeter = new GreeterImpl();
            System.out.println("Starting Greeter service at "+greeterServiceURI);
            Naming.rebind(greeterServiceURI,greeter);
        } catch (Exception e) {
            e.printStackTrace();
        }
    }

    public static String makeServiceURI( String host, String name )
    {
        if (host==null)
            host = "localhost";
        if (name==null)
            name = "JavaGreeter";
        return "rmi://"+host+"/"+name;
    }

    public GreeterImpl() throws RemoteException
    {
        super();
    }

    public void sayHello() throws RemoteException
    {
        System.out.println("Greeter "+getClass().getName()
                        +" was asked to sayHello()");
    }
```

```
    public void greetGuest(Guest guest) throws RemoteException
    {
        System.out.println("Greeter "+getClass().getName()
                            +" was asked to greetGuest("+guest+")");
        guest.listen("I'm pleased to meet you, "+guest+"!");
    }

    public String sayGoodbye() throws RemoteException
    {
        System.out.println("Greeter "+getClass().getName()
                            +" was asked to sayGoodbye()");
        return "It was a pleasure serving you.";
    }

}

public class Guest implements Serializable {

    private static final long serialVersionUID = -4784697253827363366L;

    public static void main(String[] args)
    {
        String greeterServiceURI = GreeterImpl.makeServiceURI(null,null);

        try {
            System.out.println("Looking up greeter at "+greeterServiceURI);
            Greeter greeter = (Greeter)Naming.lookup(greeterServiceURI);
            Guest guest = new Guest();

            greeter.sayHello();
            greeter.greetGuest(guest);
            String lastWord = greeter.sayGoodbye();
            System.out.println("Greeter's final response was \""+lastWord+"\"");
        }
        catch (Exception e) {
            e.printStackTrace();
        }
    }

    public void listen( String message )
    {
        System.out.println(getClass().getName()+" heard \""+message+"\"");
    }
}
```

Objective-C: Greeter Program
```
@class Guest;
```

```objc
@interface Greeter : NSObject

- (void)sayHello;
- (void)greetGuest:(Guest*)guest;
- (NSString*)sayGoodbye;

@end

@implementation Greeter

- (void)sayHello
{
    NSLog(@"Greeter %@ was asked to sayHello",self);
}

- (void)greetGuest:(bycopy Guest*)guest
{
    NSLog(@"Greeter %@ was asked to greetGuest:%@",self,guest);
    [guest listen:[NSString stringWithFormat:@"Pleased to meet you, %@!",guest]];
}

- (NSString*)sayGoodbye
{
    NSLog(@"Greeter %@ was asked to sayGoodbye",self);
    return @"It was a pleasure serving you.";
}

@end

int main (int argc, const char * argv[])
{
    NSConnection *connection = [NSConnection defaultConnection];
    [connection setRootObject:[Greeter new]];
    if ([connection registerName:SERVICE_NAME_DEFAULT]) {
        NSLog(@"Starting Greeter service '%@'",name);
        [[NSRunLoop currentRunLoop] run];          // never returns
    }
    return 0;
}
```

Objective-C: Guest Program

```objc
@interface Guest : NSObject

- (void)listen:(NSString*)message;

@end

@implementation Guest

- (void)listen:(NSString*)message
{
    NSLog(@"%@ heard \"%@\"",self,message);
}
```

```
@end

int main (int argc, const char * argv[])
{
    NSConnection *connection = nil;

    NSLog(@"Connecting to greeter '%@' via Mach ports",name);
    connection = [NSConnection connectionWithRegisteredName:SERVICE_NAME_DEFAULT
                                                       host:nil];
    Greeter *greeter = (Greeter*)[connection rootProxy];
    Guest *guest = [Guest new];

    [greeter sayHello];
    [greeter greetGuest:guest];
    NSString *lastWord = [greeter sayGoodbye];
    NSLog(@"Greeter's final response was \"%@\"",lastWord);

    return 0;
}
```

Listing 13-5. *Output of Greeter Demonstration*

Java GreeterImpl:
```
$ java com.apress.java.rmi.GreeterImpl
Starting Greeter service at rmi://localhost/JavaGreeter
Greeter com.apress.java.rmi.GreeterImpl was asked to sayHello()
Greeter com.apress.java.rmi.GreeterImpl was asked to talkBackTo(Guest@e9cb75)
com.apress.java.rmi.Guest heard "I'm pleased to meet you, Guest@e9cb75!"
Greeter com.apress.java.rmi.GreeterImpl was asked to sayGoodbye()
```

Java Guest:
```
$ java com.apress.java.rmi.Guest
Looking up greeter at rmi://localhost/JavaGreeter
Greeter's final response was "It was a pleasure serving you."
```

Objective-C Greeter:
```
$ ./Greeter --mach
Starting Greeter service 'ObjCGreeter'
Greeter <Greeter: 0x1011bf0> was asked to sayHello
Greeter <Greeter: 0x1011bf0> was asked to greetGuest:<Guest: 0x1014bc0>
Greeter <Greeter: 0x1011bf0> was asked to sayGoodbye
```

Objective-C Guest:
```
$ ./Guest --mach
Connecting to greeter 'ObjCGreeter' via Mach ports
<Guest: 0x1014bc0> heard "I'm pleased to meet you, <Guest: 0x1014bc0>!"
Greeter's final response was "It was a pleasure serving you."
```

Java and Objective-C remote method invocations are, conceptually, quite similar: a server process instantiates an object that implements a service. One or more client processes connect to the service and obtain a proxy object. The proxy object doesn't implement any of the server's code. Instead, the proxy forwards any method invocations through the connection to the server process, where the desired method is actually executed. Any parameters and return values are similarly encoded and transported through the connection.

There are two significant differences between the Java and Objective-C implementations. The first is how proxy objects are created. In Java, you must first design an interface that defines the methods for the server object, along with a class that implements them. The Java rmic compiler then creates a special _Stub class suitable for use as a proxy object. The client process obtains the proxy object and invokes its methods, which are forwarded back to the server for execution.

Objective-C provides the NSProxy class. This is a very special class, because it is *not* a subclass of NSObject. NSObject and NSProxy are both subclasses of the root Object class. Most of what you consider to be base-class methods are defined in NSObject, not Object. Consequently, NSProxy inherits no methods—which makes it perfect for what it does.

NSProxy overrides the -forwardInvocation: method described in Chapter 6. Since it implements almost no methods, virtually any method you send it will end up invoking -forwardInvocation:. NSDistantObject, the useable subclass of NSProxy, connects an NSProxy with an NSConnection. Any message sent to the proxy object is archived and transported through the NSConnection for execution by the remote process. By leveraging Objective-C's unimplemented method handling, a lightweight proxy object can be spontaneously created for *any* Objective-C object. This means that you can share virtually any object through an NSConnection.

■**Caution** NSProxy objects do not contain any of the instance variables of the objects they stand in for. For convenience, proxy object pointers are often cast as a pointer to the actual object type. Be careful not to directly access any instance variable of the object using a pointer to its proxy, as in distantObject->value. This will most certainly have disastrous results. Use property accessors instead ([distantObject value] or distantObject.value) as these translate into messages, or use the object identifier type (id) which inherently prohibits direct variable access. When designing distributed objects, program defensively. Make all instance variables @protected or @private and provide accessor methods for all public properties.

The other significant difference is how parameters and return values are exchanged. In Java, all parameters and return values are passed by copy, and must therefore be serializable. It also means that the classes that implement those values must exist in the server. Find the "Guest heard 'I'm pleased to meet you, Guest!'" message for both Java and Objective-C in the example output in Listing 13-5. In the Java version, the message is emitted by the server process. The client statement greeter.greetGuest(guest) serialized a copy of the Guest object and sent it to the server. When the Greeter executed guest.listen("I'm pleased to meet you, guest!"), the listen(...) method executed on the server's local copy of the guest object.

In the Objective-C output, the "Guest heard 'I'm pleased to meet you, Guest!'" message is emitted by the client. That's because Objective-C's default is to pass values by reference. The [greeter greetGuest:guest] statement passed a reference to the guest object to the server. The server's -greetGuest: method received a proxy NSDistantObject to the instance of Guest that exists in the client. When the server sends the message [guest listen:@"I'm pleased to meet you, guest!"], the message invocation is intercepted, archived, and sent back to the client for execution, where the output appears.

This allows you to pass virtually any object to a remote method. The object doesn't have to be archivable, you just need to be aware that the receiver will get a proxy to the original object, spontaneously created by NSDistantObject. If you need objects to be passed by copy, you can do that by making them conform to NSCoding and implement sequential archiving, as described in Chapter 12.

Your object will also have to implement code to decide under what circumstances it should be passed by copy or by reference. All of that is explained in the "Passing Objects by Copy" section.

Making a Connection

Using distributed objects is kind of like dating; you first have to find a suitable partner before you can begin a conversation. You can use a third-party matchmaking service, or you can do it yourself if you have firsthand knowledge about the other's existence.

    Java's java.rmi.Naming class performs the role of matchmaker, allowing the server process to publish its existence. For the client, it locates the desired server process and returns a proxy object. Through the proxy object, the client is connected to the server.

    In Objective-C, NSConnection is the central actor that connects two processes via distributed objects. NSConnection does not, by itself, provide any registration services—although it does provide convenience constructers to commonly used ones. To establish a connection between a server and a client, you must create an NSConnection object that uses two unidirectional NSPort objects, or one bidirectional NSPort object. The NSConnection uses the NSPort objects to communicate data and invocation information to the remote process. The general arrangement is shown in Figure 13-1. The solid arrows are object references within the process. The hollow arrows show the direction of data exchanged through some port or socket.

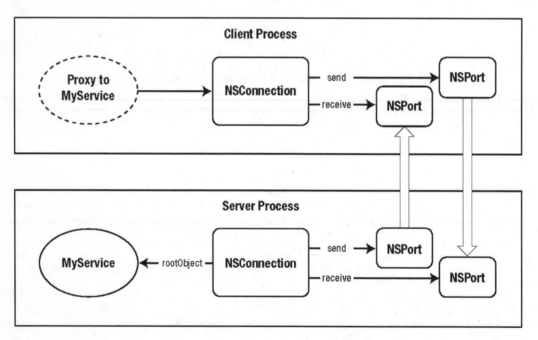

Figure 13-1. *Objects in an NSConnection*

    How you create your NSConnection object depends on the type of connection you want to create. You can create NSPort objects directly, or obtain connected NSPort objects from a registration service, and then use those to create an NSConnection. There are also some facilities that will create a preconfigured NSConnection object for you. Four common NSConnection configurations are listed in Table 13-2.

Table 13-2. Common NSConnection Configurations

Connection Type	How to Create It
Two objects in the same process	Create two NSPort objects, then use those to create an NSConnection.
Connection via Mach ports	Let +[NSConnection connectionWithRegisteredName:host:] create a preconfigured NSConnection for you.
Connection via IP socket	Obtain an NSPort from NSSocketPortNameServer and use it to create an NSConnection.

The role of matchmaker is usually performed by one of the NSPortNameServer subclasses. Each name server provides a registration and discovery service for a particular class of ports. NSMachBootstrapServer registers Mach message ports. The scope of Mach ports is limited to the bootstrap namespace of the current process. NSSocketPortNameServer registers TCP ports on a local area network. Services registered with NSSocketPortNameServer are accessible by any computer on the local network.

Once the NSConnection object is created, the server object is vended. This makes the object available to any clients that connect to the server's NSConnection. This is done using -[NSConnection setRootObject:]. Once set, the client sends its NSConnection a -rootProxy message to obtain the NSDistantObject of the server's root object. Any other object the client and server need to exchange is accomplished by sending messages to the server's root object. The server can change its rootObject at any time, but that doesn't affect any proxy objects clients have previously obtained.

The demonstration project includes examples of four common connection methods. You can try them out using the command's mode argument. Each is described below.

Inter-thread Connection

Distributed objects' focus is inter-process communications, but DO works just as well between threads in the same process. Using DO, it is relatively easy to create a class that receives and executes messages in its own thread, making powerful multi-threaded services as easy to use as simple objects. It also provides a flexible deployment environment for remote services. A service designed to run on a remote computer could just as easily run in a separate process on the same machine, or as a thread in the local process for testing. The client's interface to all three would be identical.

Creating an inter-thread connection is simple. Create two generic NSPorts to provide the communications, and use those to create the NSConnection objects, as shown in Listing 13-6. To run this example in the demonstration project, issue the command ./Guest --thread.

Listing 13-6. *Inter-Thread DO Connection*

```
NSPort          *receivePort = [NSPort port];
NSPort          *sendPort = [NSPort port];
NSConnection    *clientConnection;
NSConnection    *serverConnection;

clientConnection = [NSConnection connectionWithReceivePort:receivePort
                                             sendPort:sendPort];

serverConnection = [NSConnection connectionWithReceivePort:sendPort
                                             sendPort:receivePort];
[serverConnection setRootObject:[Server new]];
[serverConnection runInNewThread];

…

id server = [clientConnection rootProxy];
[server doSomething];
```

Note that the port order is reversed in serverConnection. The client's receive port is connected to the server's send port, and vice versa. The -runInNewThread method detaches a new thread, running its own run loop, attached to the connection. There are lots of variations to this code. Some programmers prefer to create their own thread, pass it the NSPort objects, and let the server object create its NSConnection. It doesn't matter, as long as the end result is the same.

Mach Ports Connection

Mach ports provide extremely efficient inter-process communications within the scope of a single user or with a system process. The NSMachPortNameServer registers server processes by name, and any client can connect to it easily. The code for both client and server are shown in Listing 13-7. Try it yourself by executing the demonstration commands ./Greeter --mach and ./Guest --mach in separate terminal windows.

Listing 13-7. *DO Connection Through Mach Ports*

Server
```
NSConnection *connection = [NSConnection defaultConnection];

[connection setRootObject:[Server new]];
if ([connection registerName:@"Server"])
    [[NSRunLoop currentRunLoop] run];
```

Client
```
NSConnection *connection = [NSConnection connectionWithRegisteredName:@"Server"
                                                         host:nil];

id server = [connection rootProxy];
[server doSomething];
```

The server creates it server object and registers it with its public name. The client uses the convenience constructor -connectionWithRegisteredName:host: to obtain an NSConnection, preconfigured with NSPorts connected to the Mach ports registered under the name @"Server".

It's also possible that both server and client could be running in two threads of the same process. The service, registered with the NSMachBootstrapServer, would be accessible to other processes, but could just as easily be connected from another thread.

Network Connection

The flexibility of distributed objects becomes particularly keen when used to interact with objects over a network. The NSSocketPortNameServer provides registration and discovery services accessible from all the systems on a local area network, as shown in Listing 13-8. The ./Greeter --network and ./Guest --network demonstrations can be run on the same computer, or on multiple computers on the same network.

Listing 13-8. *DO Connection Through Local Network*

```
Server
NSSocketPort *port = [NSSocketPort new];
NSConnection *connection = [NSConnection connectionWithReceivePort:port
                                                 sendPort:nil];
[connection setRootObject:[Server new]];
if ([[NSSocketPortNameServer sharedInstance] registerPort:port name:@"Server"])
    [[NSRunLoop currentRunLoop] run];
```

```
Client
NSPort *port = [[NSSocketPortNameServer sharedInstance] portForName:@"Server"
                                                 host:@"*"];
NSConnection *connection = [NSConnection connectionWithReceivePort:nil
                                                 sendPort:port];
id server = [connection rootProxy];
[server doSomething];
```

The network version is just a subtle variation on the previous themes. Here, the server and client interact directly with the NSSocketPortNameServer to register and obtain NSSocketPort objects directly. The ports are then used to create NSConnection objects.

NSSocketPortNameServer will locate any computer on the local network that has registered a @"Server" service if the host is @"*". The host parameter can also be a specific machine domain name or an IP address if you want to connect with a specific target machine.

BSD Pipe Connection

The final example is a bit more exotic. It demonstrates connecting two processes using a named BSD pipe "file" in the file system. A pipe file looks like a data file, but is actually a live buffer between two processes. Bytes written to the "file" immediately appear as data to the other process, but are never written to any storage device. This demonstrates the flexibility of distributed objects. Essentially any communications conduit that can be connected to an NSPort can be used to create an NSConnection. Since you can create your own subclasses of NSPort, the possibilities are unlimited.

The project commands that demonstrate this technique are ./Greeter --socket and ./Guest --socket. The code can be found in the Greeter_main.m and Guest_main.m files.

Run Loops

Run loops are the engine that drives distributed objects. Run loops are described in more detail in Chapter 15.

In the server examples above, the last step is to start a run loop that will process the events received by its NSPort object. To receive and dispatch asynchronous messages, an NSConnection must be driven by a run loop. Messages sent by clients are pushed onto the server's NSPort. The run loop pops them off one at a time and dispatches them to the root object.

It's obvious that the server must use a run loop. What's not obvious is that the client is also running a run loop. When the client sends a synchronous message (i.e., [server doSomething]), it pushes the message onto the NSPort and then starts a temporary run loop to wait for the response. The server receives the message and replies by sending a message back to the client. The client's temporary run loop pops the reply off its NSPort and returns to the sender.

Look again at the code for the Greeter and Guest example in Listing 13-4. Consider the possibility that Greeter keeps a reference to the proxy Guest object and uses it to send another -listen: message *after* -greetGuest: has returned. If the client process was not running a run loop, the -listen: message would sit in the client's NSPort forever, never to be executed. Since the method is synchronous, the Greeter object would hang, waiting for the Guest object to respond—or at least until the NSConnection timed out.

To implement asynchronous, bidirectional, messaging between distributed objects, both processes must have active run loops.

Asynchronous Messages

As alluded to earlier, messages sent through an NSProxy can be synchronous or asynchronous. To create an asynchronous message, add the oneway keyword to the return value of the method's interface.

```
- (oneway void)doSomething;
```

The message will be sent to the remote object, but execution will return immediately to the sender. oneway methods should always have a void return type. As mentioned in the "Run Loops" section, the client must be running its own run loop if it expects to receive any asynchronous replies from the server. The oneway modifier, along with the other parameter modifiers described later, only affect messages sent through NSProxy objects. The behavior of regular Objective-C messages (i.e., [object doSomething]) does not change.

Passing Objects by Copy

Objects passed in parameters or returned from messages can be exchanged with the remote object by copy or by reference. Sending an object by reference entails creating an NSDistantObject proxy for the object and sending that to the receiver.

To pass an object by copy, the object is archived using sequential archiving, then reconstructed at the receiving end. This places three requirements on the class. First, the class must conform to NSCoding and implement sequential archiving, as described in the Serialization chapter. Second, the code for the class must exist in the receiving process—otherwise, there's no way to instantiate the object.

Finally, the class must override its -replacementObjectForPortCoder: method to decide when it should be copied and when it should be passed by reference. Objective-C can provide hints to the class with the bycopy and byref modifiers. These type modifiers augment object parameters and return values in the method's implementation, as in

```
- (bycopy ProjectStatus*)statusForProject:(byref Project*)project { …
```

The demonstration project includes an implementation of -replacementObjectForPortCoder: for the Guest object, shown in Listing 13-9.

Listing 13-9. Guest Class bycopy Implementation

```
- (id)replacementObjectForPortCoder:(NSPortCoder*)coder
{
    if ([coder isBycopy])
        return self;
    return [super replacementObjectForPortCoder:coder];
}
```

From the perspective of distributed objects, *all* objects are passed by copy. The archived copy of the object is produced using sequential archiving. As you learned in Chapter 12, an NSPortCoder encoder will first invoke -replacementObjectForPortCoder: to allow an object to substitute a different object in the archive. NSObject's default implementation substitutes an NSDistantObject for the object. The distributed objects framework does not perform the substitution of proxy objects for their originals; each object individually decides whether to copy itself or provide a proxy object.

The code in Listing 13-9 makes the by-copy decision for the Guest object based on the hint embedded in the method definition. If the argument or return value type includes the bycopy keyword, the NSPortCoder used to archive the object will return YES when sent -isBycopy. -isBycopy will return NO if the byref modifier, or no modifier, was specified. Or you can test -isByref, which always returns !isBycopy.

Alternatively, you can choose to ignore the recommendation of the coder and return self, [super replacmentObjectForPortCoder:coder], or any other functional substitute. Some objects, like NSString, elect to always send themselves bycopy, ignoring any byref hint. By default, subclasses of NSObject always send themselves by reference, even when the method requests bycopy. Your code can use any criteria to make its decision. An object might send itself by copy if the NSPortCoder is connected to a service over a network, but choose to send a reference if connected to another process in the same system.

Passing Pointers

Passing C pointers as parameters presents another problem. Pointers can't be copied by value—since the local address will be meaningless to the receiving process. Nor is there any way to create the equivalent of a proxy object for a remote structure. Distributed objects solves this problem by copying the value of the structure the pointer parameter points to— unless the pointer is NULL, in which case it simply sends NULL to the receiver.

```
- (void)rectToLocalCoordinates:(NSRect*)rectangle;
```

When the -rectToLocalCoordinates: message is sent to a distant object, the contents of the NSRect structure are copied, verbatim, to the remote process and the C pointer the receiver gets points to a local copy allocated by distributed objects. When the method returns, the (possibly modified) contents of the NSRect structure are copied back to the sender, and the temporary copy is destroyed.

This isn't particularly efficient, but it's safe. For methods that only reference the contents of the structure, or ignore its original content, Objective-C provides the parameter modifiers listed in Table 13-3.

Table 13-3. *Pointer Parameter Type Modifiers*

Modifier	Effect
in	Structure is copied to receiver, but not back to the sender.
out	Structure is not copied to the receiver, but the modified structure is copied back to the sender upon return.
inout	Structure is copied to the receiver, then back again when the method returns. This is the default.

Use the in modifier for parameters that pass information to the receiver, when the receiver doesn't use the pointer to modify the contents of the structure. An example method would be

```
- (BOOL)isValidPoint:(in NSPoint*)inPoint;
```

Use the out modifier for parameters used to point to an uninitialized structure that will be filled in by the receiver. An example method would be

```
- (void)getSize:(out NSSize*)outSize;
```

The inout modifier is the default. Including it won't change the method, but makes your intent clear.

■**Caution** Structures are sent by copy to the receiver. The structure can only contain primitive values. It cannot, for obvious reasons, contain pointers to other structures or objects. If the structure is that complex, it will need to be reengineered as an object or first translated into some portable format, before it can be used with distributed objects.

Pointer value modifiers are also applicable to method return values. There are similar problems with parameters that are pointers to pointers. These, and other esoteric cases, are discussed in the Remote Messaging section of *The Objective-C 2.0 Programming Language.*[1]

Is it an Object or a Proxy?

The NSObject protocol defines a special method, -isProxy, for determining whether an object is actually an NSProxy object. It will return YES if the object reference is *not* an instance of NSObject, or a subclass of NSObject. It's impossible to determine if an object is a proxy using any of the -class, -className, -isMemberOfClass:, or -isKindOfClass: methods; the proxy will simply forward these messages to the original object, which will return the obvious answer. Use -isProxy, for example, to determine if it's safe

---

[1] Apple, Inc., *The Objective-C 2.0 Programming Language*, http://developer.apple.com/documentation/Cocoa/Conceptual/ObjectiveC/Articles/ocRemoteMessaging.html, 2009.

to directly access the member variables of an object, as in `if (![character isProxy]) character->hitCount++`.

Networking

There are a number of classes for communicating over a network. Two worth mentioning are Network Services, which assist in registering and locating services on a network, and the URL Loading System, which implements various network protocols such as HTTP and FTP.

Network Services

Network Services doesn't have a good analog in Java. It works kind of like java.rmi.Named, in that it will publish services on a local area network, and make it easy for remote clients to browse and connect with those services. However, network services is much more generic. It's built on Bonjour, also know as Zeroconf. The NSSocketPortNameServer class, demonstrated earlier, uses network services to register and find distributed object services on the network.

Network Services has two principal classes. An NSNetService object represents a single service. Much like NSConnection, the server and client process each creates an NSNetService object to either publish the service or connect with an existing service. NSNetServiceBrowser performs the role of matchmaker. An NSNetServiceBrowser object will help your application discover services immediately available to it. It can describe all of the resources available, search out specific services, and connect with them.

There are three operational phases to using network services:

1. Publication
2. Discovery
3. Resolution

Publication is the act of registering your service so that it is publicly visible to other processes and computers on the network. You must first create a socket, such as an NSSocketPort, by which clients can communicate with your service. You then create a NSNetService object, connected to that port, that describes the service. You then publish the service by sending the NSNetService object a `-publish` or `-publishWithOptions:` message. Once published, remote clients can find, connect, and communicate with your service.

Use the NSNetServiceBrowser class to find services on your network. You start by creating an instance of NSNetServiceBrowser and then configure it to find the types of services you are interested in. The browser goes to work and reports services as it discovers them.

Once you know about a remote service, by browsing or some other means, the last step is to resolve it. Again, you create an NSNetService object and configure it with the information it needs to locate the remote service. You then send it a `-resolveWithTimeout:` message. The NSNetService object then proceeds to establish a connection. When successful, the message `-getInputStream:outputStream:` will return the input and output stream objects, through which you can communicate with the remote service.

Network service publishing and discovery can be very time consuming, and new services can appear and disappear spontaneously. Consequently, virtually all network services methods execute asynchronously. The results are communicated through a delegate object that you provide. For example, the `-resolveWithTimeout:` message returns immediately, but starts the resolution process in the background. When finished, your delegate object will receive either a `-netServiceDidResolveAddress:` message or a `-netService:didNotResolve:` message if the resolution failed.

The *NSNetServices Programming Guide*[2] provides detailed information about how Network Services work, along with copious code examples.

URL Loading

Both Java and Objective-C provide a set of classes that assist in accessing the services and entities identified by Uniform Resource Locators (URLs). Both have built-in support for the HTTP, HTTPS, FTP, and FILE protocols. URL protocols are often complex, but these classes conveniently internalize those intricacies so that you can interact with them easily. This makes it possible to send a web server request to a URL, such as http://www.apress.com, and receive the response with just a few lines of code.

The organization and roles of URL classes in Java and Objective-C are almost identical, although Objective-C is a little more granular. The NSURL (java.net.URL) class defines a single URL. NSURLConnection (java.net.URLConnection) manages the communications with the remote service described by the URL. Objective-C decomposes Java's single URLConnection object into three objects; NSURLConnection is only concerned with the state of the connection. The request parameters are encapsulated in NSURLRequest, and the service's reply is contained in an NSURLResponse. Any data—the "body" of the request or response—are exchanged through streams or events.

This section will illustrate several common URL loading techniques and how they contrast with similar Java implementations.

Trivial URL Request

The simplest URL interaction is to just obtain the contents of a URL. This can be easily accomplished in either language, as shown in Listing 13-10.

Listing 13-10. Trivial URL Request

```Java
try {
    URL url = new URL("http://www.apress.com/");
    Reader inStream = new InputStreamReader(url.openStream());
    int c;
    System.out.print("URL Response: ");
    while ((c=inStream.read()) != -1)
        System.out.print((char)c);
    inStream.close();
} catch (Exception e) {
    e.printStackTrace();
}
```

```Objective-C
NSURL *url = [NSURL URLWithString:@"http://www.apress.com/"];
NSURLRequest* request = [NSURLRequest requestWithURL:url];
NSURLResponse *response = nil;
```

---

[2] Apple, Inc., *NSNetServices and CFNetServices Programming Guide*, http://developer.apple.com/documentation/ Networking/Conceptual/NSNetServiceProgGuide, 2008.

```
NSData *data = [NSURLConnection sendSynchronousRequest:request
                                     returningResponse:&response
                                                 error:NULL];
NSLog(@"URL response: %@",[NSString stringWithCString:[data bytes]
                                                length:[data length]]);
```

The Java code takes advantage of the convenience method java.net.URL.openStream(), which creates an URLConnection object, initiates the request, and returns an InputStreamReader object connected to the response stream. The Objective-C code is a little more complex to set up, first requiring the creation of an NSURLRequest object. With that accomplished, the entire transaction is performed using the +[NSURLConnection sendSynchronousRequest:returningResponse:error:] class method. A transient NSURLConneciton object is created, the request is sent, and the response is returned in two objects: An NSURLResponse object containing the reply headers and an NSData object containing the response body.

Asynchronous URL Request

URL interaction in Java is inherently synchronous. If the URL data being loaded takes a long time to obtain, the code in Listing 13-10 would block until the data was received. This might be appropriate if the time it took to load the URL was inconsequential. Often, it is not. To avoid hanging the main application, the code in Listing 13-10 could be executed in its own thread. In Java, this would be the preferred solution.

In Objective-C, the natural way to use an NSURLConnection is asynchronously. Most NSURLConnection methods initiate asynchronous operations—synchronous operations are the exception. Just like NSStream, described earlier in this chapter, NSURLConnection communicates its progress by sending messages to its delegate. The code for reading the contents of a URL asynchronously is shown in Listing 13-11.

Listing 13-11. Asynchronous URL Request

```
@interface URLGetter : NSObject {
    NSMutableData   *body;
    NSURLConnection *connection;
}

- (void)loadURL:(NSString*)string;

@end

@implementation URLGetter

- (void)loadURL:(NSString*)string
{
    NSURL *url = [NSURL URLWithString:string];
    NSURLRequest *request = [NSURLRequest requestWithURL:url];
    // allocate buffer to store the received data
    body = [NSMutableData data];
    connection = [NSURLConnection connectionWithRequest:request
                                               delegate:self];
}
```

```
- (void)connection:(NSURLConnection*)connection didReceiveData:(NSData*)data
{
    [body appendData:data];
}

- (void)connection:(NSURLConnection*)connection
didReceiveResponse:(NSURLResponse*)response
{
    // The response headers and metadata were successfully received
    // Successive responses preceed each new body, so reset the buffer
    [body setLength:0];
}

- (void)connectionDidFinishLoading:(NSURLConnection*)connection
{
    // URL loading is complete; NSURLConnection is closed, |body| is complete
}

- (void)connection:(NSURLConnection*)connection didFailWithError:(NSError*)error
{
    // URL failed to load; reason is in |error|
}

@end
```

The +connectionWithRequest:delegate: convenience constructor creates an NSConnection object and immediately initiates the request. The response is communicated to the delegate object through a sequence of events. The NSURLConnection must be created within the context of an active run loop.

■**Tip** When an NSURLConnection is created from a NSURLRequest, the connection makes a deep copy of the request object. Subsequent changes to the request do not influence the connection. The NSURLRequest object can be immediately modified and used to create another connection without affecting any previously created connections.

The delegate receives a -connection:didReceiveResponse: message once the initial headers and metadata have been read and assembled into an NSURLResponse object. Following that, zero or more -connection:didReceiveData: messages pass the balance of the content to the delegate. Finally, a -connectionDidFinishLoading: message signifies that the transaction is complete. At any point, the receipt of a -connection:didFailWithError: message indicates that the request did not complete successfully, and why.

It's possible to receive multiple -connection:didReceiveResponse: messages if the service redirects the request to another URL, which essentially restarts the connection.

Writing to a URL

So far, only the most basic requests have been made. To define a more complex request, or to include additional data with the request, requires more granular object construction. An example that posts a byte array containing form data to an HTTP server is shown in Listing 13-12.

Listing 13-12. *Posting Form Data to an HTTP Server*

```Java
public byte[] submitForm( byte[] formData )
{
    byte[] response = null;
    try {
        URL url = new URL("http://localhost/form.jsp");
        HttpURLConnection connection = (HttpURLConnection)url.openConnection();
        connection.setDoOutput(true);
        connection.setRequestMethod("POST");
        // (configure any additional headers or properties here)

        OutputStream requestStream = connection.getOutputStream();
        requestStream.write(formData);

        InputStream responseStream = connection.getInputStream();
        ByteArrayOutputStream buffer = new ByteArrayOutputStream();
        int c;
        while ( (c=responseStream.read()) != -1)
            buffer.write(c);
        response = buffer.toByteArray();
    } catch (Exception e) {
        e.printStackTrace();
    }
    return (response);
}
```

```Objective-C
- (NSData*)submitForm:(NSData*)formData
{
    NSURL *url = [NSURL URLWithString:@"http://localhost/form.jsp"];
    NSMutableURLRequest* urlRequest = [NSMutableURLRequest requestWithURL:url];
    [urlRequest setHTTPMethod:@"POST"];
    [urlRequest setHTTPBodyStream:[NSInputStream inputStreamWithData:formData]];
    // (configure any additional headers or properties here)

    NSURLResponse *response = nil;
    NSData *responseData = [NSURLConnection sendSynchronousRequest:urlRequest
                                                returningResponse:&response
                                                            error:NULL];

    return responseData;
}
```

The two significant differences between Objective-C and Java are as follows:

- In Java, the URLConnection object is used to configure the request. In Objective-C, you create an NSMutableURLRequest in order to customize the request.
- Java's URLConnection creates OutputStream and InputStream objects, connected to the request data and response data streams, respectively. Objective-C is completely reversed. Instead of getting an OutputStream to write request data to, you supply an input stream object that the NSURLConnection will read in order to obtain the request data.

Downloading a URL

The Cocoa framework provides a handy utility class specifically designed to download files from a URL. You construct an NSURLDownload object very much like you would an NSURLConnection object, but in addition to a request object you also supply a destination file path. The download will start automatically and send your delegate object either a -downloadDidFinish: message if successful, or a -download:didFailWithError: message if not. The code for a simple downloader class is shown in Listing 13-13.

Listing 13-13. Simple File Downloader Class

```
@interface FileDownloader : NSObject

- (void)downloadURL:(NSString*)source toPath:(NSString*)destination;

@end

@implementation FileDownloader

- (void)downloadURL:(NSString*)source toPath:(NSString*)destination
{
    NSURL *url = [NSURL URLWithString:source];
    NSURLRequest *urlRequest = [NSURLRequest requestWithURL:url];
    NSURLDownload *download = [[NSURLDownload alloc] initWithRequest:urlRequest
                                                           delegate:self];
    [download setDestination:destination allowOverwrite:YES];
    // download starts automatically
}

- (void)download:(NSURLDownload*)download didFailWithError:(NSError*)error
{
    // download failed
}

- (void)downloadDidFinish:(NSURLDownload*)download
{
    // download finished successfully
}

@end
```

NSURLDownload supports a number of other delegate methods for monitoring the progress of the download, responding to authentication challenges, and for interactively deciding on a destination file path. It also supports resumption of an interrupted download through the `-initWithResumeData:delegate:path:` constructor.

Caches and Cookies

Like Java, Objective-C URL connections support local caches and cookies. In Java, caching is configured using java.net.URLConnection.setUseCaches(boolean) and cookies are handled automatically.

Objective-C provides a per-process cache manager that will keep frequently requested data in memory or on disk for improved performance. You can influence how a request uses the cache in two ways. The first is to specify the NSURLRequestCachePolicy when the NSURLRequest is created, or by setting the policy of the NSMutableURLRequest before the request is sent. The policy can choose to use an optimal default—the recommended choice—or choose from a number of policies, from ignoring all cached data to only responding with cached data. More sophisticated cache management can be performed by implementing the `-connection:willCacheResponse:` method in your NSURLConnection delegate object. This message is sent to the delegate before storing any received data in the cache. It can permit it to be stored as is, prevent it from being stored, or provide altered data to store in its place.

Cookies are automatically supplied from a system-wide cookie storage service. The default is to handle cookies according to the user-selected security policy. You can disable cookies for a single request by creating an NSMutableURLRequest object and sending it `[request setHTTPShouldHandleCookies:NO]`. You can also change the cookie policy, but doing so changes the policy for all processes on the system.

Summary

Objective-C provides a variety of communication technologies, which reflect the wide range of communication problems facing modern applications. From simple notifications to distributed objects, the solution you choose will depend on the kind of problem you're trying to solve. In most cases, Objective-C solutions will parallel the ones you're familiar with in Java, although the implementation details may vary substantially.

CHAPTER 14

■ ■ ■

Exception Handling

Exception handling in Objective-C is almost identical in capacity with that in Java. Objective-C is, naturally, more casual about exceptions and makes none of the demands that Java does. You can design and write code using Objective-C exceptions exactly as you would in Java, completely ignore them, or settle somewhere in between. This chapter will briefly compare the similarities between Objective-C and Java exception handling—of which there are many—and then explain some of the subtle differences. Later sections will discuss assertions and alternatives to exceptions.

Using Exceptions

Creating, throwing, and catching exceptions are virtually identical in Objective-C and Java. Listing 14-1 shows some simple exception handling.

Listing 14-1. Exception Handling

Java
```java
public class Tosser
{
    public void catcher( ) throws Exception
    {
        try {
            System.out.println("Tosser.catcher(): trying");
            thrower();
        } catch ( SpecificException se ) {
            System.out.println("caught SpecificException: "+se);
        } catch ( Exception e ) {
            System.out.println("caught Exception: "+e);
            throw e;
        } finally {
            System.out.println("Tosser.catcher(): finished");
        }
    }

    public void thrower( ) throws Exception
    {
        throw new Exception("thrower() does not work");
    }

}
```

Objective-C

```objc
@interface Tosser : NSObject

- (void)catcher;
- (void)thrower;

@end

@implementation Tosser

- (void)catcher
{
    @try {
        NSLog(@"%s trying",__func__);
        [self thrower];
    } @catch ( SpecificException *se ) {
        NSLog(@"caught SpecificException: %@",se);
    } @catch ( NSException *e ) {
        NSLog(@"caught NSException: %@",e);
        @throw e;
    } @finally {
        NSLog(@"%s finished",__func__);
    }
}

- (void)thrower
{
    @throw [NSException exceptionWithName:@"MyException"
                                  reason:@"-thrower does not work"
                                userInfo:nil];
}

@end
```

The similarities are much more pronounced than the differences. Specifically, the @try, @catch, and @finally blocks have the same syntax, order, and execution flow that the try, catch, and finally blocks do in Java. You throw exception objects using the Objective-C @throw directive exactly as you would with Java's throw statement. Caught exceptions can be processed or re-thrown in the same way.

If you want to employ exceptions in Objective-C the way you do in Java, you're welcome to do so. The capabilities of Objective-C exceptions are so close to that of Java's that you probably won't notice any significant difference. There are, however, some differences—mostly in what Objective-C will allow you to do that Java doesn't. The next section explains exactly what those differences are and what impact they might have on your design.

Exception Handling Differences

Objective-C is much more relaxed about exceptions than Java. One could argue that it's too relaxed, but that's an academic debate. Most of the differences between Java and Objective-C exception handling fall outside the bounds of what Java allows.

No Catch or Specify

The Java language has a "Catch or Specify" rule that requires you to either declare the exceptions that a method throws or catch those exceptions within the body of the method. Objective-C doesn't check to see if your code catches exceptions, and it doesn't even have syntax for declaring what exceptions a method throws. This is mostly because (due to the dynamic nature of class methods) it has no way of knowing. To use Java parlance, all Objective-C exceptions are *unchecked exceptions*.

Throw Any Object

Objective-C can throw or catch any object, unlike Java, which requires the object of a throw statement to implement the Throwable interface. If an NSString object is sufficient to convey all of the information you want about an exception, then the following code is perfectly valid:

```
@throw @"Something went wrong";
```

Your code may, for example, throw an exception if an NSOperation failed. But instead of throwing an NSException that referenced the NSOperation, you could throw the NSOperation object itself. What you throw will, of course, depend on what you're trying to accomplish, but you aren't limited to NSException and its subclasses.

■**Note** Speaking of subclasses, there are very few subclasses of NSException. In Java, you create different types of exceptions by subclassing java.lang.Exception. NSExceptions have a name property, and it is far more common to identify the type of an exception using its name than its class. That's not to say that you shouldn't subclass NSException. I often do, but it's limited to situations where I want to add functionality to the NSException object or I want to create a broad category of exceptions. The Cocoa framework defines commonly used exception names, which you can find in the *Introduction to Exception Programming Topics for Cocoa.*[1]

If you can throw any kind of object, you might be wondering what the exact role of the NSException class is. For starters, NSException is purpose built for conveying the details of an exception. It contains useful information, like a stack trace and exception description, and it can participate in the unhandled exception mechanism described later in this section. Originally, NSException was the only mechanism for throwing exceptions. See the Legacy Exceptions section towards the end of the chapter for the details. Because of this, many older frameworks are *only* prepared to catch NSExceptions. If you throw an object that might not be caught by your code, make sure it is an NSException object.

---

[1] Apple, Inc., *Introduction to Exception Programming Topics for Cocoa*, http://developer.apple.com/documentation/Cocoa/Conceptual/Exceptions/, 2007.

Re-Throw an Exception

Objective-C includes a convenient syntax for re-throwing the exception caught in a catch block, as shown in Listing 14-2.

Listing 14-2. Re-throwing an Exception

```
@try {

    …

} @catch (NSException *exception) {

    …

    @throw;
}
```

An empty @throw directive re-throws the exception caught by its enclosing catch block. In Listing 14-2, the statement @throw is identical to @throw exception.

Catch Order

Like Java, the order of catch blocks must be from the most specific to the most general. Said another way, a catch block the catches a particular class cannot be followed by a catch block that catches a subclass of that class. Catch blocks are tested in sequential order, and the first catch block would prevent the later one from ever executing.

In Java, improperly ordered catch blocks result in a fatal compiler error. The Objective-C compiler merely issues a warning—and it can only issue that warning if it knows the class's pedigree. Take the code in Listing 14-3 as an example.

Listing 14-3. Out of Order catch Blocks

```
@class MysteryException

…

@try {
    …
} @catch ( NSObject *anything ) {

    …

} @catch ( MysteryException *exception ) {

    …

}
```

The second catch block will never be executed, because MysteryException is a subclass of NSObject. But this code won't generate a compiler warning. That's because the @class statement lets the compiler know that the MysteryException class exists, but doesn't tell anything about it. As a rule, include the class definition for all objects you intend to catch.

Chaining

The NSException class does not have a cause property, like the one in java.lang.Throwable. Instead, NSException objects have a dictionary (map) object that allows you to provide arbitrary context for the exception. If you want to throw an exception that references another exception, include it—along with any other pertinent details—in the exception's info dictionary, as shown in Listing 14-4.

Listing 14-4. Chaining Exceptions

Java
```
try {
    ...
} catch ( Exception e ) {
    throw new SpecificException("encountered exception",e);
}
```

Objective-C
```
@try {
    ...
} @catch ( NSException *exception ) {
    NSDictionary *userInfo = [NSDictionary dictionaryWithObject:exception
                                                forKey:@"RootCause"];
    @throw [SpecificException exceptionWithName:@"MySpecialException"
                                  reason:@"encountered exception"
                                userInfo:userInfo];
}
```

Call Stack

Objective-C's NSException object provides a callStackReturnAddresses property that returns an array of NSNumber objects containing the return addresses of the stack's call chain when the exception was thrown. Unlike Java, Objective-C provides no facility for interpreting these values. An Objective-C program, being compiled machine code, might not even include any symbolic function information, making interpretation impossible.

The *Introduction to Exception Programming Topics for Cocoa*[2] guide includes sample code that uses the atos development tool to translate these numeric stack addresses into program symbols—if possible. If you maintain a copy of your compiled application with debugging symbols, you can manually use the atos tool to perform the same translation for post-mortem analysis of exceptions.

---

[2] Apple, Inc., *Introduction to Exception Programming Topics for Cocoa*, http://developer.apple.com/documentation/Cocoa/Conceptual/Exceptions/, 2007.

Performance

Another reason that exceptions are used less frequently in Objective-C is performance. Setting up and throwing exceptions costs more in Objective-C than in Java. Alternatives to using exceptions are outlined in the "Alternatives to Exceptions" section later in this chapter.

Don't let the above dissuade you from using exceptions in Objective-C. I use exceptions a lot—probably because of my experience programming in Java. I've never seen Objective-C exception handling become a performance liability. My advice is to program using the coding style you are most comfortable with, and if that includes exceptions then by all means use exceptions. If, and only if, a performance analysis shows exception handling to be a performance problem, would I advise considering an alternative error-handling solution.

Uncaught Exceptions

An uncaught exception is one that is allowed to pass outside your application code to the runtime framework. Exceptions can also be generated in response to system events and runtime errors. Uncaught exception processing can be broadly divided into four categories:

- Exceptions thrown on the main thread of a GUI application
- Exceptions thrown in all other situations
- Exceptions generated by system events, such as an invalid memory access
- Exceptions generated by runtime events, like sending a message to a freed object

By default, exceptions thrown in the main thread of an application are absorbed by the NSApplication framework and ignored. For example, an action invoked by the user choosing a menu command throws an uncaught exception. The application's main run loop will discard the exception and continue running. There will be no indication that a problem occurred, with the possible exception of a message logged to the system console. You may have encountered this behavior in an application.

In almost all other circumstances, an uncaught exception terminates the thread, or the process if the exception is thrown in the main thread. System and runtime events immediately terminate the process.

You can intercept these events using the optional ExceptionHandling framework. Using the exception handling framework you can:

- Log or post-process uncaught exceptions thrown on the main thread of a GUI application
- Log or post-process uncaught exceptions thrown any other time
- Cause system events to be converted into uncaught exceptions for logging or post-processing
- Cause runtime events to be converted into uncaught exceptions for logging or post-processing
- Cause the process to hang instead of terminate, allowing you to attach a debugger or other development tool for post-mortem analysis

To change how uncaught exceptions are handled, follow these steps:

1. Link your application to the ExceptionHandling framework.

2. `#import <ExceptionHandling/NSExceptionHandler.h>`

3. Use `[NSExceptionHandler defaultExceptionHandler]` to obtain the singleton NSExceptionHandler object for your process.

4. To cause special handling of uncaught exceptions, system, or runtime events, logically OR together any combination of constants in Table 14-1 and pass the value to `-[NSExceptionHandler setExceptionHandlingMask:]`. See Listing 14-5.

5. As an alternate to step 4, the exception handling flags can be set in the user defaults property NSExceptionHandlingMask. See the "User Defaults" section of Chapter 26 for more details about user defaults and how a process acquires them.

6. To individually filter the exception handling enabled in step 4 or 5, create an object that implements `-exceptionHandler:shouldHandleException:mask:` and `-exceptionHandler: shouldLogException:mask:` and make it the NSExceptionHandler's delegate object. All exceptions are first passed to the delegate for inspection. The delegate can process the exception, let the NSExceptionHandler perform its default processing, neither, or both.

7. To cause the process to hang—rather than terminate—for debugging purposes, logically OR together any of the constants in Table 14-2 and pass the value to `-[NSExceptionHandler setExceptionHangingMask:]`.

The best place to set the exception handling behavior is in your application's initialization code.

Here, the term "handling" means that NSExceptionHandler will pass the exception to its delegate for post-processing and optionally log its details before continuing. NSExceptionHandler doesn't really *do* anything significant with the exceptions, although your delegate object could.

Logging or handling top-level exceptions and low-level exceptions in an NSApplication—the last four options in Table 14-1—should be used only during development. These options can cause a tremendous amount of debug output to be sent to the system console, which would not be appropriate for a shipping application. Furthermore, intercepting, modifying, or ignoring these exceptions can change how the application frameworks normally function.

Your NSExceptionHandler delegate object will only be sent the exceptions whose logging or handling has been enabled in steps 4 or 5. If you enable the flags, but don't set a delegate object, exceptions are only logged.

■**Note** NSExceptionHandler will process an exception *before* the `finally` block of your code executes.

If system and runtime event handling is not set in step 4 or 5, these events are not translated into exceptions. They are processed normally, as they would be in the absence of an NSExceptionHandler.

Table 14-1. *Exception Handling Flags*

Constant	Effect
NSLogUncaughtExceptionMask	Logs uncaught exceptions.
NSHandleUncaughtExceptionMask	Handles uncaught exceptions.
NSLogUncaughtSystemExceptionMask	Turns system events into exceptions and logs them.
NSHandleUncaughtSystemExceptionMask	Turns system events into exceptions and handles them.
NSLogUncaughtRuntimeErrorMask	Turns runtime events into exceptions and logs them.
NSHandleUncaughtRuntimeErrorMask	Turns runtime events into exceptions and handles them.
NSLogTopLevelExceptionMask	Logs uncaught exceptions thrown in the main run loop of the application.
NSHandleTopLevelExceptionMask	Handles uncaught exceptions thrown in the main run loop of the application.
NSLogOtherExceptionMask	Logs all other exceptions thrown in the main run loop of the application, which includes caught exceptions.
NSHandleOtherExceptionMask	Handles all other exceptions thrown in the main run loop of the application, which includes caught exceptions.

You can also cause the NSExceptionHandler to "hang" instead of terminate the process for certain kinds of exceptions. Set the desired hang conditions by logically ORing together any of the constants in Table 14-2 and passing the value to -[NSExceptionHandler setExceptionHangingMask:]. This is strictly for debugging and allows you to launch your application normally. If an uncaught exception causes the application to hang, you can still attach a debugger to the process to investigate the cause, since the process is (technically) still running.

Table 14-2. *Process Hang Condition Flags*

Constant	Effect
NSHangOnUncaughtExceptionMask	Hangs the process if an uncaught exception is encountered.
NSHangOnUncaughtSystemExceptionMask	Hangs the process if a system event occurs.
NSHangOnUncaughtRuntimeErrorMask	Hangs the process if a runtime event occurs.
NSHangOnTopLevelExceptionMask	Hangs the process if the main run loop encounters an uncaught exception.
NSHangOnOtherExceptionMask	Hangs the process if any other kind of exception is thrown.

Listing 14-5 shows the initialization code for an application that wants to have all uncaught exceptions, system events, and runtime events logged.

Listing 14-5. *Initializing Uncaught Exception Handling*

```
#import <ExceptionHandling/NSExceptionHandler.h>

@implementation MyApplicationDelegate

- (void)applicationWillFinishLaunching:(NSNotification*)notification
{
    // Log all uncaught exceptions, but not low-level exceptions
    [[NSExceptionHandler defaultExceptionHandler] setExceptionHandlingMask:
        NSLogUncaughtExceptionMask
        |NSLogUncaughtSystemExceptionMask
        |NSLogUncaughtRuntimeErrorMask
        |NSLogTopLevelExceptionMask
        /*|NSLogOtherExceptionMask*/
        ];
}

@end
```

Legacy Exceptions

The exception syntax in Objective-C is relatively recent. Before it was added, the Objective-C language had no direct support for exceptions. Instead, exception handling was provided by a set of classes and some clever preprocessor macros. Listing 14-6 shows what legacy exception handling looked like.

Listing 14-6. *Legacy Exception Handling*

```
NS_DURING
    NSLog(@"%s trying",__func__);
    [self thrower];
NS_HANDLER
    NSLog(@"caught NSException: %@",localException);
    [localException raise];
NS_ENDHANDLER
```

The legacy NS_DURING, NS_HANDLER, and NS_ENDHANDLER preprocessor macros expanded to C code that used the C longjmp(…) functions to create the necessary execution flow control. There was only one handler block, which caught all exceptions. The variable localException contained the caught exception. There was no finally block. Exceptions were thrown by sending the -raise messages to an NSException object.

Table 14-3 shows the legacy exception syntax and its modern equivalent.

Table 14-3. *Legacy and Modern Exception Syntax*

Legacy Syntax	Equivalent Modern Syntax
NS_DURING	@try {
NS_HANDLER	} @catch (NSException *localException) {
NS_ENDHANDLER	}
[exception raise]	@throw exception
NS_VALUERETURN(value,type)	return (value)
NS_VOIDRETURN	return

You were required to use the NS_...RETURN macros if you wanted to return from the block of code between NS_DURING and NS_HANDLER.

If your Objective-C compiler has modern exception handling enabled—which it probably does—the preprocessor macros in Table 14-3 will expand into the modern syntax instead. Thus, there's no penalty or incompatibility with code written for legacy exceptions, and you can freely mix the two. The one minor difference is that the -raise method performs a @throw, but the modern @throw directive does not send a -raise message to the object being thrown. This could have implications for subclasses that have overridden -raise.

Assertions

Assertions is a programming technique that lets you define your own runtime exceptions. An assertion is a statement that confirms (asserts) that a condition the programmer expects to be true is true. If the statement is found to be false, an NSInternalInconsistencyException exception is thrown. The assertion in Listing 14-7 ensures that the class of the object obtained from the collection is of the expected type.

Listing 14-7. Confirming Class Membership with an Assertion

```
NSDictionary *dictionary = …
NSNumber *value = [dictionary objectForKey:@"Value"];
NSAssert([value isKindOfClass:[NSNumber class]],@"wrong class");


Failed Assertion Output:
*** Assertion failure in -[Tosser catcher], Tosser.m:45
*** Terminating app due to uncaught exception 'NSInternalInconsistencyException',
    reason: 'wrong class'
```

Assertions are a practical way of introducing some of Java's sanity to Objective-C. Objective-C does not test the class of an object during assignment, but an assertion can. Objective-C doesn't test the index in C array statements to ensure they are within bounds, but an assertion can. In short, almost any runtime check that you would expect Java to perform for you can be stated as an assertion.

Assertions can be stated for any expected program condition. If a parameter is assumed to be non-nil, assert it. If an integer value should be positive, assert it.

■**Caution** Assertions are exceptions, like any other. Most Java runtime exceptions are unchecked, and are usually left uncaught. If you want your application to terminate when an exception is encountered, be careful not to swallow the exception in your catch block. See the RethrowAssertion macro in the Listing 14-8.

One particularly attractive feature of assertions is they can be turned off, en masse. The assertion macros provided by the Cocoa framework, listed in Table 14-4, are all conditionally defined based on the NS_BLOCK_ASSERTIONS preprocessor macro. If that macro is defined—the value is immaterial—all of the NSAssert… macros get redefined to nothing. This means your assertion statements effectively disappear, as if they never existed. You can fill your application with thousands of assertion statements that are active during development, then turn them all off when compiling your release version. This is usually accomplished by defining the NS_BLOCK_ASSERTIONS macro in the Preprocessor Macros build settings of the Release configuration. During development, your application checks for any unexpected conditions, but the release version is free of the excess code and performance penalty of each assertion.

Table 14-4. Standard Assertion Macros

Macro	Description
NSAssert(condition,description)	Tests a condition, throwing an exception with the description if false.
NSAssert1(condition,format,arg1)	If condition is false, throws an exception with the description created by formatting a string with one argument.
NSAssert2(condition,format,arg1,arg2)	If condition is false, throws an exception with the description created by formatting a string with two arguments.
NSParameterAssert(condition)	If condition is false, throws an exception with the description that the given condition was not true.

There are actually six NSAssert macros: NSAssert, NSAssert1, NSAssert2, NSAssert3, NSAssert4, and NSAssert5. They differ only in the number of arguments following the format string. (Preprocessor macros are not capable of variables arguments.) These assertions can only be used in the body of an Objective-C method. A parallel set of NSCAssert… macros can be used in C functions.

I highly recommend defining your own assertion macros. Concise, specific assertion statements are more likely to be used. Listing 14-8 shares a few of my favorites, along with some code that uses them.

Listing 14-8. *Custom Assertion Macros*

```
#if !defined(NS_BLOCK_ASSERTIONS)
#define RethrowAssertion(EXCEPTION) \
        if ([[EXCEPTION name] isEqualToString:NSInternalInconsistencyException]) \
            [EXCEPTION raise]
#define AssertObjectIsClass(OBJECT,CLASS) \
        do { \
            if (![OBJECT isKindOfClass:[CLASS class]]) { \
                [[NSAssertionHandler currentHandler] handleFailureInMethod:_cmd \
                    object:self \
                    file:[NSString stringWithUTF8String:__FILE__] \
                    lineNumber:__LINE__ \
                    description:@"object isa %@@%p; expected %s", \
                        [OBJECT className],OBJECT,#CLASS]; \
            } \
        } while(NO)
#define AssertObjectIsNilOrClass(OBJECT,CLASS) \
        do { \
            if ((OBJECT!=nil) && ![OBJECT isKindOfClass:[CLASS class]]) { \
                [[NSAssertionHandler currentHandler] handleFailureInMethod:_cmd \
                    object:self \
                    file:[NSString stringWithUTF8String:__FILE__] \
                    lineNumber:__LINE__ \
                    description:@"object isa %@@%p; expected %s", \
                        [OBJECT className],OBJECT,#CLASS]; \
            } \
        } while(NO)
#define AssertObjectRespondsTo(OBJECT,MESSAGE) \
        do { \
            if (![OBJECT respondsToSelector:@selector(MESSAGE)]) { \
                [[NSAssertionHandler currentHandler] handleFailureInMethod:_cmd \
                    object:self \
                    file:[NSString stringWithUTF8String:__FILE__] \
                    lineNumber:__LINE__ \
                    description:@"object %@@%p does not respond to %s", \
                        [OBJECT className],OBJECT,#MESSAGE]; \
            } \
        } while(NO)
```

```
#define AssertNotNil(OBJ) NSAssert1(OBJ!=nil,@"%s is nil",#OBJ)
#define ParameterAssert NSParameterAssert
#else
#define RethrowAssertion(EXCEPTION)
#define AssertObjectIsClass(OBJECT,CLASS)
#define AssertObjectIsNilOrClass(OBJECT,CLASS)
#define AssertObjectRespondsTo(OBJECT,MESSAGE)
#define AssertNotNil(OBJ)
#define ParameterAssert NSParameterAssert
#endif
```

...

```
// make sure the delegate is set and implements to informal protocol
AssertNotNil(delegate);
AssertObjectRespondsTo(delegate,lookupPartNumber:);

PartNumber part = [delegate lookupPartNumber:inventoryCode];
NSAssert(part>=100000&&part<=999999,@"invalid part number");

Record *partRecord = [PartsDatabase recordForPartNumber:part];
AssertObjectIsClass(partRecord,Record);
```

You can define the macros in terms of other macros—like the AssertNotNil and ParameterAssert macros—or you can define them to invoke the singleton NSAssertionHandler that should be used to throw assertion exceptions. Always design your macros so they act like a single C statement when expanded.

These macros use a number of advanced preprocessor features:

- The single \ at the end of a line continues the #define statement to the next line, as if it had been written as a single line.

- A macro can take the form of a C function with parameters. The parameters create temporary macro definitions that exist during the expansion of the macro's body. The statement #define DO(THIS) [self THIS] will replace the code DO(something) with [self something].

- Macro expansion is recursive. Given #define A B and #define B(X) return X, the statement A(3) will be replaced with B(3), which will be replaced with return 3. Definition order isn't important.

- The special syntax #TOKEN in the macro's text will be replaced with a C string constant containing the text of TOKEN. #define RETURN_STR(S) return (#S) will replace the source code RETURN_STR(100-1) with return ("100-1"). It's particularly handy for converting things like a condition statement into a string that describes the condition.

- The special macros __FILE__ and __LINE__ are generated by the compiler and evaluate to the file name and line number of the source file being compiled. __func__, __DATE__, and __TIME__ are also very useful. __func__ is replaced with the current Objective-C method name as a C string. __DATE__ and __TIME__ expand to the date and time the compile was performed.

I usually take the macros in Listing 14-8 one step further, defining a set of macros that are only compiled during development (DevAssert, DevAssertObjectIsClass, …), a set that are compiled during development and beta testing (BetaAssert, BetaAssertObjectIsClass, …) and a set that are always compiled (RelAssert, RelAssertObjectIsClass, …). This allows me to graduate my use of assertions, producing progressively smaller and faster versions of my application, at the expense of safety.

Alternatives to Exceptions

Some Objective-C APIs, and many programmers, adhere to the traditional C error-handling pattern; the return value of a function or method is tested to determine success or failure. Some prototypical examples are shown in Listing 14-9. The programming philosophy at work here is that exceptions should be reserved for runtime errors (index out of bounds, invalid object, missing application resource, out of memory) and other programming mistakes that should ideally be eliminated from the application during development. Anticipatable failures that could reasonably be expected to occur (file not found, empty database, duplicate name) should be handled using error codes or error objects. This section describes the most commonly used techniques for dealing with errors without using exceptions, and later explains how to combine the two.

Listing 14-9. Examples of Error Handling

```
// Simple Error
NSString *imagePath = [[NSBundle mainBundle] pathForImageResource:@"picture.png"];
if (imagePath==nil) {
    NSLog(@"missing image resource");
    return;
}


// POSIX Error
int fd = open("filename",O_RDONLY);
if (fd<0) {
    NSLog(@"open() failed with error %d",errno);
    return;
}


// Core Foundation Error
QTUUID quickTimeUUID;
OSErr err = QTCreateUUID(&quickTimeUUID,0);
if (err!=noErr) {
    NSLog(@"could not create UUID, error %d",err);
    return;
}


// Cocoa Error
NSError *error = nil;
NSDictionary *attributes;
attributes = [[NSFileManager defaultManager] attributesOfItemAtPath:@"filename"
```

```
                                                              error:&error];
if (error!=nil) {
    NSLog(@"could not get attributes of file: %@",[error localizedDescription]);
    [self presentError:error];
    return;
}
```

Simple Errors

Simple errors occur when any function or method fails to achieve its objective and returns an empty value. The -pathForImageResource: message in Listing 14-9 is a good example. This method returns the path of the desired image file, or nil if no such file could be located. Your code should probably test the results—unless you've designed your code to use absent behavior, described in Chapter 7—and either provide a default, return an NSError, throw an exception, or raise an assertion.

POSIX Error Codes

Most BSD and POSIX functions return a value that will indicate the success or failure of the function. In Listing 14-9, the open(…) function returns a file descriptor integer if successful, or a negative value if it fails. The code that describes the reason for the failure is read from the per-thread errno variable. Note that errno isn't actually a variable, but a preprocessor macro that expands to a function call that obtains the error code. This variable is only guaranteed to contain the error code until the next POSIX function is called, so fetch the code and save it immediately after the failure.

Core Foundation Error Codes

Many Core Foundation functions return a result code directly to the caller. Result codes have the type OSError or OSStatus, and are usually negative numbers. The success of the function is indicated by the value noErr, as demonstrated in Listing 14-9. Because functions like this return the error code, pointers to variables are used to return any additional values.

Cocoa Errors

Modern Cocoa classes and functions prefer to return NSError objects when the operation could not be completed successfully. Invariably, the sender of the message includes a pointer to a nil NSError pointer variable, as shown in Listing 14-9. If the operation fails, the method creates a new NSError object and stores its address in the sender's variable. The sender can examine its variable to see if the receiver returned an NSError.

Use of NSErrors is encouraged whenever the details of the failure will be presented to the user. The NSError class incorporates a number of design features that makes it integral to a well-designed and flexible error handling system. Integrating NSError objects into your application is not a trivial task, but it is highly recommended if your goal is to provide consistent, localizable, modular, and flexible error display and recovery.

This book is too short to go into all the details of NSError objects, but the following sections will give you enough of an overview to appreciate their utility. Before designing NSError management in your application, take a good look at the *Error Handling Programming Guide For Cocoa*.[3]

Error Domains

Each NSError object has a domain. The domain influences how its properties, particularly numeric error codes, are interpreted. For example, both the POSIX and Foundation functions return an integer error value describing the failure. The domain determines which set of constants should be used to interpret the value. The principle domains are listed in Table 14-5. You are encouraged to define your own domain for application-specific errors.

Table 14-5. Cocoa Error Domains

Domain	Description
NSMachErrorDomain	Error codes returned by the kernel.
NSPOSIXErrorDomain	Error codes returned by POSIX and BSD functions
NSOSStatusErrorDomain	Error codes returned by Core Foundation functions
WebKitErrorDomain	Errors generated by WebKit
NSURLErrorDomain	URL-related errors
NSXMLParserErrorDomain	XML parser errors
NSCocoaErrorDomain	All Cocoa framework errors not belonging to one of the more specific domains

Customization and Display

One of the chief roles of NSError objects is not simply to handle an error—exceptions do that nicely—but to display the error to the user and take action based on the user's input. The first two steps in the process are performed through the responder chain. The responder chain is the chain of components in the visual hierarchy that leads to the currently active interface element. It is described fully in Chapter 20.

To display an error to the user, pass the NSError to any object in the responder chain—preferably the leaf-most component—by sending it a -presentError: message. The responder will pass the NSError to each object in the responder chain via the -willPresentError: message. This gives each layer of your application a chance to intercept the error and replace it with something more specific. For example, an "Add Soundtrack" button could replace a generic "File not found" NSError with a "Soundtrack not available. Would you like to choose another song or use the default soundtrack?" error

---

[3] Apple, Inc., *Error Handling Programming Guide For Cocoa*, http://developer.apple.com/documentation/Cocoa/Conceptual/ErrorHandlingCocoa/, 2009.

object. After all responder objects have had a go at the error, the final one is presented to the user in a modal dialog. If the error occurs in the context of a window, the preferred message is -presentError:modalForWindow:delegate:didPresentSelector:contextInfo:, which presents the error in a modal sheet attached to the window.

Localization

The NSError class provides a mechanism for localizing error messages. The localized messages can be stored in the NSError's userInfo dictionary using predefined keys or it can be generated dynamically by overriding its methods. Which you use will depend on your needs. Table 14-6 lists the four messages that will be shown to the user, and the method that returns them. The default implementation of each property accessor is to retrieve the value in the third column from the error's userInfo dictionary.

Table 14-6. NSError Localization Methods and userInfo Keys

Dialog Text	NSError Property	NSError userInfo Key	Description
Error Description	-localized⏎ Description	NSLocalized⏎ DescriptionKey	The primary error message presented to the user.
Failure Reason	-localized⏎ FailureReason	NSLocalized⏎ FailureReasonErrorKey	A brief sentence explaining the reason for the failure. Optional. Not all error dialogs display this property.
Recovery Suggestion	-localized⏎ RecoverySuggestion	NSLocalized⏎ RecoverySuggestionErrorKey	A sentence describing what actions the user can take to recover from the error. Optional.
Recovery Options	-localized⏎ RecoveryOptions	NSLocalized⏎ RecoveryOptionsErrorKey	An array of button names that correspond to the user's options described in the recovery suggestion. If nil, the only option will be "OK."

Recovery

An NSError object can provide a recovery attempter object, and should if the error includes recovery options. The -presentError: message will pass the user's recovery choice to the recovery attempter object, which is expected to carry out the user's wishes. The recovery attempter object must implement one of the methods in the informal NSErrorRecoveryAttempting protocol.

Combining Errors and Exceptions

Academic arguments about the superiority of exceptions and traditional error handling will continue to rage on. In the meantime, I'm a big fan of combining the two. NSError objects have clear advantages in complex applications that must be localized. Java-style exception handling has clear advantages for simplifying code and execution flow. Listing 14-10 shows one way in which traditional C error handling, NSError objects, and exceptions can be combined.

Listing 14-10. Mixing Error Handling

```
@try {
    const char *path = …
    int fd = open(path,O_RDONLY);
    if (fd<0) {
        NSString *errorPath = [NSString stringWithCString:path];
        NSDictionary *info = [NSDictionary dictionaryWithObject:errorPath
                                                         forKey:@"Path"];
        NSError *error = [NSError errorWithDomain:NSPOSIXErrorDomain
                                             code:errno
                                         userInfo:info];
        @throw error;
    }

    …

    close(fd);

} @catch (NSError *error) {
    [self presentError:error];
}
```

Summary

Objective-C exception handling is robust, simple, and on a par with that provided by Java. Much of Objective-C's permissiveness can be reined in with the liberal use of assertions. POSIX, BSD, Core Foundation, and most Cocoa methods only use exceptions for (what are considered to be) runtime errors or programming mistakes. You can embrace this philosophy, or continue to program using exceptions by combining them with traditional design patterns.

CHAPTER 15

■■■

Threads

Java was one of the first programming languages to support threads and thread synchronization directly. It was a very forward-looking decision. Multicore, multiprocessor computer systems have become the norm, rather than the exception. Efficient multi-threaded programming is now essential to effective program development, and it's a trend that continues to accelerate.

Threads and semaphores are conceptually simple, and the high-level differences between Java and Objective-C are trivial. Objective-C also makes extensive use of run loops, which transform a thread into an event processor. Beyond the basic @synchronize directive built into the language, the Cocoa framework provides a number of additional synchronization tools, each tailored to a specific need. And finally, there are classes that perform deferred actions, manage independent threads for you, and perform timed tasks relieving you of the burden of creating and managing your own threads.

This chapter begins by describing how threads are created, run, and destroyed in Objective-C. It also explains run loops and tells you why you would need to create one, and how. After that, it details various ways to synchronize multiple threads and make your code thread safe. Finally, it presents a few useful classes that can make thread management simpler, or possibly unnecessary.

Thread API

Thread management and control is centered on the NSThread Objective-C class, and closely resembles Java's java.lang.Thread class. The equivalent methods are listed in Table 15-1.

Table 15-1. *Equivalent Thread Methods*

java.lang.Thread	NSThread	Description
currentThread()	+currentThread	The thread object for the currently executing thread
start()	-start	Starts a thread
run()	-main	The code to execute
isAlive()	-isExecuting, -isFinished	Determines if the thread has started or finished
sleep(long)	+sleepUntilDate:, +sleepForTimeInterval:	Suspends the thread for a period of time
getPriority()	+threadPriority	The thread's priority

setPriority(int)	+setThreadPriority	Changes a thread's priority
getName()	-name	The name of the thread
setName(String)	-setName:	Sets the name of the thread
getStackTrace()	+callStackReturnAddresses	Gets the array of return addresses on the stack

Here are the key differences between threads in Objective-C and Java:

- There are no thread groups in Objective-C.
- The Objective-C interface does not provide a method for obtaining the list of existing threads.
- There is no security model. Some operations—like setting a thread's priority—can only be performed from the currently running thread, whereas in Java they can be performed on arbitrary threads.
- You cannot interrupt a thread. NSThread does provide a canceled property that can be set and tested, but canceling a thread will not unblock it.
- There are no daemon threads. An Objective-C process runs as long as the main thread is running, and all threads terminate when the process terminates.
- There is no join() function, but the same functionality can be easily accomplished using NSConditionLock, as explained later in this chapter.
- There is no yield() method or any equivalent.

The life cycle of an Objective-C thread is broadly the same as it is in Java. You create a thread that will execute a method of an object. When the method returns, the thread is terminated and destroyed. Any interaction with objects shared with other threads must be coordinated using semaphores.

If that's all you need from threads, read the sections "Starting a Thread" and "Thread Synchronization." If you want to consider ready-made classes that will manage threads for you, check out the "Operations" section. The rest of this chapter explores mostly esoteric details of threads that are less relevant to most programmers.

Starting a Thread

Starting a new thread in Objective-C is even easier than it is in Java—which is saying something, since thread creation in Java is already pretty simple. There are three ways of creating a thread in Objective-C:

- Create and immediately start a thread executing by sending the message +detachNewThreadSelector:toTarget:withObject:. The message identifies the object and method that contains the thread's code and an optional parameter that will be passed to the thread when it begins execution.
- Create a new NSThread object using -initWithTarget:selector:object:. This is identical to the first technique, except that the thread is not started. You can customize the thread object before starting it with the -start message.
- Define your own subclass of NSThread, override the -main method, and create your instance using -init. This is equivalent to subclassing java.lang.Thread and overriding run(). When the object receives the -start message, it creates a new thread and executes its -main method in the new thread.

■**Note** The constructors that create and return an NSThread object are fairly recent additions to the operating system. In versions of Mac OS X prior to 10.5, only +detachNewThreadSelector:toTarget:withObject: could create new threads. You could not subclass NSThread or customize a thread before starting it.

Objective-C threads are easy to create because the thread's code can be any method of any object. In Java, the object containing the code must implement the Runnable interface and implement that code in its run() method. Objective-C's only modest requirement is that the method containing the thread's code accept a single object parameter (which it can ignore) and return void. Listing 15-1 shows how to start a thread.

Listing 15-1. Starting a Thread

Java
```java
public class Runner implements Runnable
{
    public void run()
    {
        System.out.println("Running with threads.");
    }
}
```

...

```java
Runner runner = new Runner();
Thread thread = new Thread(runner);
thread.start();
```

Objective-C
```objc
@implementation Runner

- (void)runMe:(id)ignored
{
    NSLog(@"Running with threads.");
}

@end
```

...

```
Runner *runner = [Runner new];
[NSThread detachNewThreadSelector:@selector(runMe:)
                         toTarget:runner
                       withObject:nil];
```

THE MAIN THREAD

The main thread is the first thread started when the process is created, and is special. All user input and events are sent to the run loop running on the main thread. All changes to the user interface *must* occur on the main thread; the user interface frameworks are not thread safe. Your application's process is, for all intents and purposes, the main thread. When the main thread finishes, the process terminates—instantly killing all other threads.

There are numerous methods that reference, target, test for, or return the main thread. These allow you to easily target the main thread, or its run loop, when necessary.

Managing Threads

The best advice for managing threads is "don't." Threads do not respond well to being micro-managed, and it makes your code fragile and less portable. Above all, do not try to second guess the kernel's thread scheduler or try to coerce it into a particular behavior. As kernel thread scheduling has become more sophisticated, the number of application programmer interfaces for manipulating running threads has decreased. For example, Objective-C has no yield() equivalent, and the java.lang.Thread methods stop(), suspend(), and resume() have all been deprecated.

Threads should be organized around clearly defined, antonymous tasks. They should communicate minimally and coordinate their work with other threads using semaphores. Beyond that, you should simply let threads run when they have work to do, and let them suspend when they don't. If you find yourself interjecting sleep statements or creating semaphores just to force the kernel to switch tasks, then you should revisit the design of your tasks.

Having said that, there are some special circumstances where you may need to alter the task's properties or put it to sleep. Putting a thread to sleep is explained next. Thread properties are discussed in the sections that follow.

Putting a Thread to Sleep

Putting a thread to sleep for a period of time is one of the few thread state manipulations remaining. Putting a thread to sleep suspends the thread until the time interval has elapsed. Afterward, the thread is made "runnable" again, and the kernel will add the thread back into its rotation of running threads. Said another way, the thread isn't guaranteed to start running again immediately after the time interval has elapsed; it just won't run again before the time interval has elapsed.

The NSThread methods +sleepUntilDate: and +sleepForTimeInterval: will cause the current thread to sleep, unconditionally, for the given period of time. This can be an NSDate object in the future or an NSTimeInterval value expressed in seconds. Dates and time intervals use double floating-point values to express seconds, so time intervals down to the nanosecond range can be specified. The kernel doesn't guarantee the accuracy of the time, only that the thread won't execute again until that amount of time has elapsed.

There are also many methods—most of which are described in later sections—that will conditionally put a thread to sleep for a period of time. These messages accept an NSDate object that specifies a time in the future to abandon waiting for the condition and resume. The simplest example are the methods -[NSLock lock] and -[NSLock lockBeforeDate:(NSDate*)limit]. Both attempt to obtain a lock on an NSLock semaphore. The -lock method will wait forever to obtain the lock. In contrast, -lockBeforeDate: will return when either the lock is obtained or the time specified by the NSDate is reached.

■Tip To create an NSDate object with a time two and a half seconds in the future, use [NSDate dateWithTimeIntervalSinceNow:2.5]. To get an NSDate object with a time that will never be reached (in your lifetime), use [NSDate distantFuture].

Put threads to sleep when they need to perform actions at timed intervals. Listing 15-2 demonstrates a simple class that runs a "heartbeat" thread which updates a progress indicator no more than twice per second.

Listing 15-2. Heartbeat Thread

```
@interface Process : NSObject
@property double progress;
@end

@interface Heartbeat : NSObject {
    NSThread            *thread;
    Process             *monitor;
    NSProgressIndicator *indicator;
}

+ (Heartbeat*)startHeartbeatProcess:(id)process
                    withIndicator:(NSProgressIndicator*)progress;

- (void)stop;
- (void)heartbeatThread:(id)ignored;
- (void)updateIndicator;

@end

…

@implementation Heartbeat

+ (Heartbeat*)startHeartbeatProcess:(id)process
                    withIndicator:(NSProgressIndicator*)progress
```

```
{
    Heartbeat *heartbeat = [Heartbeat new];
    heartbeat->monitor = process;
    heartbeat->indicator = progress;
    heartbeat->thread = [[NSThread alloc] initWithTarget:heartbeat
                                        selector:@selector(heartbeatThread:)
                                           object:nil];

    [heartbeat->thread start];

    return heartbeat;
}

- (void)stop
{
    [thread cancel];
}

- (void)heartbeatThread:(id)ignored
{
    while (![thread isCancelled]) {
        [self performSelectorOnMainThread:@selector(updateIndicator)
                               withObject:nil
                            waitUntilDone:YES];
        [NSThread sleepForTimeInterval:0.5];
    }
}

- (void)updateIndicator
{
    [indicator setDoubleValue:monitor.progress];
}

@end

…

Process *process = …
NSProgressIndicator *indicator = …
Heartbeat *heartbeat = [Heartbeat startHeartbeatProcess:process
                                          withIndicator:indicator];

…

[heartbeat stop];
```

The message +startHeartbeatProcess:withIndicator: creates a Heartbeat object and starts its -heartbeatThread: method running in a new thread. Approximately every half-second, the thread queues an -updateIndicator message to be executed on the main thread. The thread runs until the Heartbeat object receives a -stop message.

Note that the example in Listing 15-2 is far from the most effective use of a thread. While it would work, a much more sensible solution is provided in the Timer section at the end of this chapter.

Thread Properties

Thread objects have a number of properties that relate pertinent information. The caveats about superfluous thread management withstanding, there are also a few thread properties that you might need to alter. Some can only be set before the thread is started, while others can only be set after.

Information

The thread informational properties are listed in Table 15-2. You can use them to obtain relevant NSThread objects or inspect the state of a thread. The class methods return global values or information about the currently executing thread. Instance methods can be sent to any NSThread object, from any thread.

Table 15-2. Informational Thread Properties

NSThread Method	Description
+currentThread	The NSThread object of the currently executing thread
+mainThread	The NSThread object of the main thread
+isMainThread	Returns YES if the current thread is the main thread
+isMultiThreaded	Returns YES if another thread, beyond the main thread, has ever been started by NSThread
-isMainThread	Returns YES if the thread object represents the main thread
-isExecuting	Returns YES if the thread has been started and has not finished
-isFinished	Returns YES if the thread has executed and exited
-isCancelled	Returns YES if the thread has ever received a -cancel message

Thread-Specific Values

Sometimes you need a global variable, but only within the context of a specific thread. Each NSThread object has a threadDictionary property exactly for this purpose. The property is a mutable dictionary that your application can use to store whatever values it needs. The example in Listing 15-3 creates an NSNotificationCenter object for a single thread.

Listing 15-3. *Storing a Thread Specific Value*

```
NSMutableDictionary *threadLocal = [[NSThread currentThread] threadDictionary];
[threadLocal setObject:[NSNotificationCenter new]
               forKey:@"NotificationCenter"];
```

The purpose is to create a notification center that will be used to send and observe notification within the thread. Any object can obtain its thread-specific notification center using the statement:
`[[[NSThread currentThread] threadDictionary] objectForKey:@"NotificationCenter"]`

Priority

The priority of the currently running thread can be altered using the +[NSThread setThreadPriority:] message. The priority is a floating point value between 0.0 and 1.0, 1.0 being the highest. You can obtain a thread's current priority with +[NSThread threadPriority]. The typical default priority is 0.5. The actual range of priorities—if they're acknowledged at all—is operating system and kernel dependent.

The kernel makes few guarantees about thread priority other than it will *tend* to give threads with a higher priority more CPU time than those with a lower priority. Use thread priorities judiciously.

Stack Size

Another rarely used property is the thread's stack size, which must be set before the thread is started. This requires that you create an NSThread object, set its stack size, and then start the thread using the -start message. Stack sizes must be set in even multiples of 4K (4096) bytes and currently default to 512K.

The two situations where you would want to change the stack size are:

- A thread is overflowing its stack. In this situation, increase its stack size before starting the thread.

- You create lots of threads that don't use much stack space, and the stack space allocated to each is impacting address space allocation. Reduce the default stack size so that each thread allocates less memory.

Name

Each thread also has a mutable -name property that's an arbitrary NSString value. Thread names are largely ignored by the operating system, so use them for whatever purpose you wish.

Terminating a Thread

A thread stops running when

- The thread's -main method, or the method specified when the thread was created, returns

- The thread's code throws an uncaught exception

- The process terminates

In the first two situations, the thread is destroyed and its resources reclaimed. The uncaught exception handler, described in Chapter 14, handles uncaught exceptions. An NSThread object cannot be restarted. Create a new NSThread object if you want to start another thread.

When the process terminates, all threads are abandoned, regardless of their state. This is not like Java, whose virtual machine will run until all non-daemon threads have finished. If you've created background threads, you do not need to arrange for them to finish for your application to terminate. Conversely, if your background threads need to finish before your application terminates, you will have to coordinate that through semaphores or other means.

Run Loops

Run loops are an integral part of the Cocoa framework. They are the principal event dispatching mechanism for applications, user interface events, distributed objects, timers, deferred object messages, and distributed notifications.

A run loop is an event processing service that synchronously processes events from one or more asynchronous sources. Event sources are referred to as *input sources*, and there are several predefined kinds:

- User interface events (mouse events, keyboard events, etc.)

- Deferred method invocation (-performSelector:withObject:afterDelay:, etc.)

- Distributed object messages

- Timer events

There are other input sources and it's possible to develop your own, although that's exceptional.

There is one (optional) run loop object associated with every thread. The code +[NSRunLoop currentRunLoop] will return the single run loop object associated with the current thread, and +[NSRunLoop mainRunLoop] returns the run loop for the main thread. Run loops are created lazily; if no run loop object exists for the thread, one is created when you send the message. The run loop associated with the main thread is called the *main run loop*.

■**Caution** NSRunLoop is not thread safe. Manipulations of a run loop object should be done from the thread it belongs to.

Run loops are very efficient. They block the thread until an event appears on one of their input sources. The run loop then immediately processes the event, taking whatever action is appropriate, and then "loops" around to wait for the next event. Run loops also take care of periodic housecleaning, like managed memory and stack object garbage collection. You can hand off control of your thread entirely to the run loop, or write your own loop to keep the run loop working.

Starting a Run Loop

You normally don't need to start a run loop. If you are writing a standard application, the NSApplication object will start the main run loop automatically. The main run loop will process all of the significant events of your application. Modal dialogs and NSConnections will also start run loops.

You would need to start your own run loop under the following circumstances:

- You have created a new thread that needs to fire timers or send deferred messages to objects.
- You are vending a distributed object in its own thread, or have passed objects by reference that might receive asynchronous messages from a remote process.
- You are writing a command-line tool or daemon that does not use the application framework and needs to process deferred method invocations, timer events, or distributed objects on the main thread.

The third case is just a special instance of the first two, since the main thread of a command-line tool does not automatically start a run loop.

A run loop requires input sources, and runs only as long as it has input sources. To start a run loop, you must first provide it with one or more input sources. Otherwise, the run loop will do nothing and end immediately.

- Creating and scheduling a timer, described later in this chapter, will create a timer input source for the current run loop.
- Queuing a deferred method invocation will add a message dispatch source to the run loop.
- An NSConnection will add its communication ports to the current run loop.
- The main thread has several input sources already created by the Objective-C framework. A run loop started on the main thread will always start and run forever.

By starting a run loop, you essentially relinquish control of the thread to the run loop. The thread will block until it receives an event from its input sources. To start a run loop and let it run forever—or at least while it has input sources—execute the following:

```
[[NSRunLoop currentRunLoop] run];
```

The message -runUntilDate: is a slight variation that runs the run loop for a period of time. You can use this to perform periodic actions, but using timers is preferable.

To be a little more involved, use something like the code shown in Listing 15-4. This second example "drives" the run loop using your own loop. The -runMode:beforeDate: message suspends the thread until a single event is processed or the beforeDate time has occurred. This allows your code to perform actions between each event or at periodic times, and you can also test any global condition that might be used to halt the run loop or thread.

Listing 15-4. Starting a Run Loop

```
static BOOL keepRunning = YES;

…


while (keepRunning
       && [[NSRunLoop currentRunLoop] runMode:NSDefaultRunLoopMode
                                  beforeDate:[NSDate distantFuture]]) {
    …
}
```

Finally, the -[NSConnection runInNewThread] convenience function does everything needed to start a distributed object server: it creates and starts a new thread, adds the NSConnection's ports to the run loop of the new thread, and sends the run loop a -run message.

Run Loop Modes

Run loops run in modes. Run loop input sources have modes. A run loop only processes the events from the input sources consistent with its current mode. Normally you don't need to know anything about run loop modes, other than that they exist. The basic run loop modes are listed in Table 15-3.

Table 15-3. Run Loop Modes

Mode	Description
NSDefaultRunLoopMode	This is the default mode, and the mode used by any run loop method that doesn't accept a mode parameter.
NSModalPanelRunLoopMode	Processes only events relevant to a modal dialog.
NSEventTrackingRunLoopMode	Processes only events relevant to active mouse tracking.
NSConnectionReplyMode	Processes only distributed object reply events.

Run loop modes are used to defer those events that aren't appropriate to the circumstances. The top-level run loop invariably runs in the NSDefaultRunLoopMode mode, processing all events. If the user interface causes a modal dialog to be displayed, the AppKit framework will start a nested run loop running in NSModalPanelRunLoopMode. This ignores all events that don't pertain to the modal dialog, essentially freezing the rest of the application. Similarly, when a mouse click/drag begins its progress it is tracked using NSEventTrackingRunLoopMode. The NSConnectionReplyMode is used when you've sent a message to a distant object. The distant object starts a nested run loop, ignoring all queued events save the reply from the remote object.

Stopping a Run Loop

Stopping a run loop is actually a little problematic. Earlier, I stated that run loops run as long as they have input sources. That's correct, except that all manner of obscure features will add custom input sources to your run loop. Many of those sources persist for very long periods, if not forever, keeping the run loop alive indefinitely. The most direct solution is to design your thread so the run loop does not need to be stopped. Let the thread sit idle when not doing anything useful, and disappear when the application terminates. For distributed objects, close the NSConnection object when you want to stop sharing your root distributed object. You can always reregister the connection or set a new root object to resurrect the service.

If you must stop a run loop, there are three basic techniques:

- Use code like that in Listing 15-4 to periodically check to see if the run loop should stop. The problem is that the loop will only execute once per event or after the time out. You don't want to make the time out short—this constitutes polling—because it wastes resources.

- Call the Core Foundation function CFRunLoopStop(), passing it the CFRunLoopRef value obtained via -[NSRunLoop getCFRunLoop].

- Create a custom run loop input source and combine it with the technique in Listing 15-4. Your custom input source's event handler can set a flag indicating that the run loop should stop, which will immediately cause -runUntilDate: to return, where your outer loop can exit.

Customizing Run Loops

The NSRunLoop class is a simplistic wrapper around the Core Foundation run loop functions and types. If you want to get involved with run loops at a deeper level, possibly developing your own input sources, read the "Run Loop Management" section of the *Threading Programming Guide*.[1]

Thread Notifications

NSThread sends two notifications, listed in Table 15-4. See Chapter 18 for more about notifications.

Table 15-4. Thread Notifications

Notification	Description
NSThreadWillExitNotification	Sent after a thread's code has returned, but before the thread is destroyed. This notification is sent to all observers on the thread about to be destroyed.
NSWillBecomeMultiThreadedNotification	Sent to all observers before the first new (non-main) thread in the process is created. The notification is sent on the main thread, and is only sent once.

Back in Chapter 7, I presented a FIFO class that could optionally operate in a thread-safe environment. Let's modify that class a little—making it truly automatic—by rewriting its -init method and adding a notification observer, as shown in Listing 15-5.

---

[1] *Apple, Inc., Threading Programming Guide,* http://developer.apple.com/documentation/Cocoa/Conceptual/ Multithreading/, *2008.*

Listing 15-5. Additions to an Automatic Thread-Safe FIFO Class

```objc
@implementation AutoSafeFIFO

- (id) init
{
    self = [super init];
    if (self != nil) {
        stack = [NSMutableArray new];
        if ([NSThread isMultiThreaded]) {
            [self makeThreadSafe];
        } else {
            NSNotificationCenter *center = [NSNotificationCenter defaultCenter];
            [center addObserver:self
                        selector:@selector(willBecomeMultiThreadedNotification)
                            name:NSWillBecomeMultiThreadedNotification
                          object:nil];
        }
    }
    return self;
}

- (void)willBecomeMultiThreadedNotification:(NSNotification*)notification
{
    [self makeThreadSafe];
}

…

@end
```

The object's constructor determines if the application is already running with multiple threads. If it is, it makes itself thread safe. If not, it subscribes to NSWillBecomeMultiThreadedNotification. If a second thread is created any time after the FIFO is created, the FIFO object automatically switches to thread-safe mode.

Thread Synchronization

Concurrent access to objects from two or more independent threads presents a consistent set of problems across almost all programming languages. Java and Objective-C both provide language support in the form of a @synchronized (synchronized) directive. Any block of code marked as @synchronized is protected against being executed by more than one thread at a time.

This section will review the synchronization support in Objective-C. In addition to the @synchronized directive, the Cocoa frameworks provide several utility classes that implement different kinds of mutual exclusion semaphores, a set of classes for organizing concurrent tasks, and timers.

The @synchronize Directive

Objective-C's @synchronized directive is almost identical to Java's synchronized keyword, with only one minor exception: @synchronized can't be used as a method modifier. To accomplish the equivalent, use @synchronized(self) as the outermost block of your method, as shown in Listing 15-6.

Listing 15-6. Synchronized Method

Java
```
public class Timing
{
    public synchronized void safe( )
    {
        // thread safe code
    }
}
```

Objective-C
```
@interface Timing : NSObject

- (void)safe;

@end


@implementation Timing

- (void)safe
{
    @synchronized(self) {
        // thread safe code
    }
}

@end
```

Beyond that minor limitation, you can use @synchronized exactly as you would use synchronized in Java.

Mutual Exclusion Semaphore Objects

Java 5.0 has introduced a wealth of new concurrent process control classes, including various mutual exclusion semaphores, queues, resource counters, and so on. Objective-C has always had the NSLock, NSRecursiveLock, and NSConditionLock classes. Recent versions of the operating system added NSOperation for managing complex sets of tasks. NSOperation is discussed in the next section.

Each of the three NS…Lock classes offers a different kind of mutual exclusion semaphore, or mutex for short. They all work by obtaining a lock, approximately equivalent to entering a @synchronized block of code. All other threads attempting to acquire a lock on the same object will be suspended until the original lock is released. Once the semaphore is unlocked, one of the other threads will be granted the lock and resume execution.

All of the mutex semaphore classes have several things in common:

- They all conform to the NSLocking protocol, which defines the fundamental -lock and -unlock methods.
- They all implement -lockBeforeDate: and -tryLock methods.
- They all implement -name and -setName: methods.

The -tryLock and -lockBeforeDate: messages attempt to acquire the lock and return YES if successful. -tryLock returns immediately, while -lockBeforeDate: will suspend until either the lock is acquired or the time in the NSDate object occurs. This is one of the significant advantages of using NS…Lock objects over @synchronized directives.

Finally, you can name your locks for whatever reason.

NSRecursiveLock

NSRecursiveLock objects behave pretty much like @synchronized blocks. An NSRecursiveLock is a mutual exclusion semaphore between threads, but within a single thread it can be locked as many times as desired. The lock is acquired once during the initial -lock message, equivalent to entering a @synchronized block. Subsequent -lock messages sent on the same thread increment a counter. Once the lock has received one -unlock message for every -lock message, the lock is released.

The one significant difference is that a @synchronized block will automatically catch an exception and release the lock before rethrowing the exception. If you use NSRecursiveLock objects around code that could throw an exception, make sure you catch the exception and clean up your locks.

NSLock

NSLock is the simplest mutex semaphore and only implements the basic -lock, -tryLock, -lockBeforeDate:, and -unlock methods. Objective-C code written before the @synchronized directive was added would most likely use NSLock objects instead of @synchronized blocks, even though the behavior of @synchronized is closer to NSRecursiveLock.

■**Caution** An NSLock must *always* be unlocked from the same thread that locked it. Some programmers, in a misguided attempt to implement cross-thread synchronization, will lock an NSLock object twice on the same thread—causing a deadlock—then release it by unlocking the object from another thread. This is not guaranteed to work and may cause fatal program errors. The correct solution is to use an NSConditionLock, described later.

The primary advantages of NSLock are speed and simplicity. Unlike an NSRecursiveLock, an NSLock can only be acquired once before being unlocked again. Consider the code in Listing 15-7.

Listing 15-7. Recursive Mutex Semaphore

```objc
@interface ZombieController : NSObject {
    NSMutableArray  *nearbyZombies;
    double          totalDamage;
    NSLock          *lock;
}

- (void)inflictDamage:(double)damage onZombieAtIndex:(NSUInteger)index;
- (void)detonateFlashBomb;

@end

@implementation ZombieController

- (id)init
{
    self = [super init];
    if (self!=nil) {
        lock = [NSLock new];
        …
    }
    return self;
}

- (void)inflictDamage:(double)damage onZombieAtIndex:(NSUInteger)index
{
    [lock lock];
    Zombie *zombie = [nearbyZombies objectAtIndex:index];
    [zombie inflictDamage:damage];
    totalDamage += damage;
    [lock unlock];
}

- (void)detonateFlashBomb
{
    // Inflict 10 points of damage on all nearby zombies
    NSUInteger i;
    [lock lock];
    for (i=0; i<[nearbyZombies count]; i++) {
        [self inflictDamage:10.0 onZombieAtIndex:i];
    }
    [lock unlock];
}

@end
```

The code in Listing 15-7 will deadlock (i.e., seize, never to run again) when the detonateFlashBomb message is received. The [lock lock] statement in detonateFlashBomb will acquire the NSLock, preventing other threads from executing the method until it is done. When the object sends itself the inflictDamage:onZombieAtIndex: method, the attempt to acquire the lock a second time will permanently suspend the thread while it waits for itself to release the original lock—which will never happen.

This code could be fixed by replacing the NSLock with an NSRecursiveLock, or by rewriting it to use @synchronized directives.

NSConditionLock

The NSConditionLock class acts like an NSLock with an added condition property. The condition is an arbitrary integer state value. When you request a lock on the object, you can specify the condition value that must be set before the lock is acquired. This provides a simple, flexible, and efficient means to coordinate state information or synchronize events between threads. For example, NSThread does not have a Java-like join() method, but this is trivial to implement using an NSConditionLock object, as shown in Listing 15-8.

Listing 15-8. *Performing a join()*

Java
```java
public class Party implements Runnable {

    public static void main(String[] args) {
        Party party = new Party();
        Thread thread = new Thread(party);


        try {
                System.out.println("Party starting");
                thread.start();
                thread.join();
                System.out.println("Party is over");
        } catch (InterruptedException e) {
            e.printStackTrace();
        }
    }

    public void run() {
        System.out.println("partying...");
    }
}
```

Objective-C
```objc
@interface Party : NSObject {
    NSConditionLock *joinLock;
}
```

```
+ (void)main;

- (id)init;
- (void)party:(id)ignored;

@end

implementation Party

+ (void)main
{
    Party *party = [Party new];

    NSLog(@"Party starting");
    [NSThread detachNewThreadSelector:@selector(party:)
                             toTarget:party
                           withObject:nil];
    [party->joinLock lockWhenCondition:YES];
    [party->joinLock unlock];
    NSLog(@"Party is over");
}

- (id) init
{
    self = [super init];
    if (self != nil) {
        joinLock = [[NSConditionLock alloc] initWithCondition:NO];
    }
    return self;
}

- (void)party:(id)ignored
{
    NSLog(@"partying...");

    [joinLock lock];
    [joinLock unlockWithCondition:YES];
}

@end
```

The agreed-upon condition is a BOOL value. The NSConditionLock is initially created with a condition of NO. The main thread starts the Party thread, then attempts to acquire a lock on the joinLock object, but only when its condition is YES. The main thread blocks until the mutex semaphore is both available *and* in the desired state. This happens only after the -party method is finished, which ends by acquiring the lock and releasing it with a new condition. The lock is now free and the condition is satisfied, so the lock in the main thread can be acquired.

You can conditionally (-lockWhenCondition:) or unconditionally (-lock) acquire a lock. You can examine the state of the condition at any time using -condition—just be aware that if you don't own the lock on the object the condition could change at any time. You can only change the condition when unlocking the mutex by sending -unlockWithCondition:.

NSConditionLock is a powerful way to coordinate states between threads. The fanciful example in Listing 15-9 presents an object that manages a background thread. The background thread produces a single result and then suspends. The result is collected on the main thread. As soon as it is, the background thread immediately goes back to work generating the next result.

Listing 15-9. Thread State Management Using NSConditionLock

```
enum {
    BusyBeeStateNone,
    BusyBeeStateIdle,
    BusyBeeStateBuzzing
};

@interface BusyBee : NSObject {
    NSConditionLock *state;
    BOOL            stopGathering;
    id              pollen;
}
- (id)init;

// Sent on main thread
- (id)collectPollen;
- (void)start;
- (void)stop;

// Background thread
- (void)gatherPollenThread:(id)ignored;

@end

@implementation BusyBee

- (id) init
{
    self = [super init];
    if (self != nil) {
        state = [[NSConditionLock alloc] initWithCondition:BusyBeeStateNone];
    }
    return self;
}
```

```objc
- (id)collectPollen
{
    [self start];

    // Collect one object of pollen
    [state lockWhenCondition:BusyBeeStateIdle];
    id returnPollen = pollen;
    pollen = nil;
    // Start thread looking for more pollen
    [state unlockWithCondition:BusyBeeStateBuzzing];

    return returnPollen;
}

- (void)start
{
    [state lock];
    NSInteger condition = [state condition];
    if (condition==BusyBeeStateNone) {
        [NSThread detachNewThreadSelector:@selector(gatherPollenThread:)
                                 toTarget:self
                               withObject:nil];
        condition = BusyBeeStateBuzzing;
    }
    [state unlockWithCondition:condition];
}

- (void)stop
{
    [state lock];
    NSInteger condition = [state condition];
    if (condition!=BusyBeeStateNone) {
        stopGathering = YES;
        if (condition==BusyBeeStateIdle)
            condition = BusyBeeStateBuzzing;       // wake up to stop
        // wait until thread stops, i.e. join()
        [state unlockWithCondition:condition];
        [state lockWhenCondition:BusyBeeStateNone];
        stopGathering = NO;                        // reset for next start
    }
    [state unlock];
}
```

```
- (void)gatherPollenThread:(id)ignored
{
    [state lock];

    while (!stopGathering) {
        id foundPollen = pollen;
        [state unlock];

        if (foundPollen==nil) {
            // search for pollen...
            foundPollen = …
        }

        [state lock];
        // make pollen available, transition to idle
        pollen = foundPollen;
        if (stopGathering) // could have been set while searching
            break;
        [state unlockWithCondition:BusyBeeStateIdle];

        // wait to begin gathering again
        [state lockWhenCondition:BusyBeeStateBuzzing];
    }

    [state unlockWithCondition:BusyBeeStateNone];
}

@end
```

The NSConditionLock object provides both the mutual exclusion semaphore needed to make this code thread safe, as well as communicating and controlling the state of the -gatherPollenThread. The initial state transition from BusyBeeStateNone to BusyBeeStateBuzzing is performed by -start. After the thread is running, the thread starts working whenever its state is changed to BusyBeeStateBuzzing, and transitions back to BusyBeeStateIdle when it's done.

NSDistributedLock

NSDistributedLock is a special kind of mutex semaphore that uses file system objects to coordinate actions between processes, or even other computer systems via a shared file system. It does not conform to NSLocking protocol and has no -lock method. You initialize it by specifying a path to a file on a writeable file system. The -tryLock method will test the object and attempt to acquire the lock. If unsuccessful, your code must try again later at whatever interval makes sense for your application. Listing 15-10 shows NSDistributedLock used to prevent a group of database files from being modified during a backup.

Listing 15-10. Using Distributed Locks

```
NSString *dbPath = …
NSString *lockPath = [dbPath stringByAppendingPathComponent:@".dblock"];
NSFileManager *fileManager = [NSFileManager defaultManager];

// lock the database directory
NSDistributedLock *lock = [NSDistributedLock lockWithPath:lockPath];
while (![lock tryLock])
    [NSThread sleepForTimeInterval:1.0];

// Copy all .index files to .backup
NSArray *dbFiles = [fileManager contentsOfDirectoryAtPath:dbPath
                                                    error:NULL];
for ( NSString *file in dbFiles ) {
    if ([[file pathExtension] isEqualToString:@"index"]) {
        NSString *srcPath = [dbPath stringByAppendingPathComponent:file];
        NSString *dstPath = [[srcPath stringByDeletingPathExtension]
                            stringByAppendingPathExtension:@"backup"];
        [fileManager removeItemAtPath:dstPath
                                error:NULL];
        [fileManager copyItemAtPath:srcPath
                             toPath:dstPath
                              error:NULL];
    }
}
[lock unlock];
```

Spin Locks

Both the @synchronized directive and the family of NSLock classes are easy to use and efficient, but being really fast is not one of their benefits. The operating system provides a very special kind of mutex semaphore for high-performance thread synchronization called a *spin lock*. All of the mutex semaphores discussed so far suspend the thread if the lock can't be acquired. Suspending, switching, and resuming a thread is an expensive operation. If a heavily used method is acquiring and releasing a lock to accomplish some trivial task, the overheard of the semaphore and any associated thread switching can become a significant performance drain.

When a spin lock can't be acquired (because some other thread has locked it), the thread "spins"—continuously polling the status of the semaphore until it is unlocked. The thread is not suspended and continues to run at full speed, using CPU resources at the expense of other threads. If this sounds like a horrific waste of resources, it is. The advantage of spin locks is that time required to acquire and release an *uncontested* lock is minuscule compared to the high-level mutex semaphores. So the nominal, uncontested case runs much faster and the performance gain ultimately exceeds the performance loss of the occasional contest.

Spin locks are effective when

- The chance that two threads will attempt to acquire the same semaphore at the same time is very small.

- Locks are acquired and released with a high frequency.

- The time between acquiring a lock and releasing it is always very short—less than a few hundred nanoseconds.

Spin locks are used by the operating system wherever contention probability is low, blocking time is minimal, and performance is paramount. For example, the operating system's low-level memory allocation routines all use spin locks to coordinate memory requests from multiple threads.

Listing 15-11 rewrites the FIFO class—yet again—this time using spin locks instead of semaphore objects. To use spin locks, your code must first #include <libkern/OSAtomic.h>.

Listing 15-11. *Fast FIFO Class*

```
#include <libkern/OSAtomic.h>
#import <Cocoa/Cocoa.h>

@interface FastFIFO : NSObject {
    NSMutableArray  *stack;
    OSSpinLock      spinLock;
}

@end

@implementation FastFIFO

- (id) init
{
    self = [super init];
    if (self != nil) {
        stack = [NSMutableArray new];
    }
    return self;
}

- (void)push:(id)object
{
    OSSpinLockLock(&spinLock);
    [stack addObject:object];
    OSSpinLockUnlock(&spinLock);
}
```

```
- (id)pop
{
    id object = nil;

    OSSpinLockLock(&spinLock);
    if ([stack count]!=0) {
        object = [stack objectAtIndex:0];
        [stack removeObjectAtIndex:0];
    }
    OSSpinLockUnlock(&spinLock);

    return object;
}

- (BOOL)hasObjects
{
    OSSpinLockLock(&spinLock);
    BOOL answer = ([stack count]!=0);
    OSSpinLockUnlock(&spinLock);

    return answer;
}

@end
```

The OSSpinLock structure is opaque, but should be initialized to zero before being used. The functions OSSpinLockLock(), OSSpinLockUnlock(), and OSSpinLockTry() perform the same function as -[NSLock lock], -[NSLock unlock], and -[NSLock tryLock], respectively. Each spin lock function is passed the address of the spin lock semaphore structure.

Operations

As you can see from the BusyBee example in Listing 15-9, managing even a "simple" background worker thread is not a trivial undertaking. Mac OS X 10.5 and Java 5.0 both recognize this and have added classes that provide management of antonymous background processes for you.

Java 5.0 added a dizzying array of new classes and interfaces to manage tasks. The principal interface is the ExecutorService, of which there are several implementations. The executor services manage a set of tasks to be executed at some future time. Concrete subclasses like ThreadPoolExecutor execute the tasks asynchronously in separate threads.

In Objective-C, the picture is considerably simpler. The NSOperationQueue class manages a set of NSOperation objects. Each NSOperation object defines one task to be performed. An NSOperation object has state properties that indicate when it is has started, is executing, or has finished.

Using NSOperationQueue can be very simple, or quite complex, depending on your needs. The minimum steps to use NSOperationQueue are as follows:

1. Create an instance of NSOperationQueue.

2. Create an instance of NSInvocationOperation (a concrete subclass of NSOperation) specifying the object and method to invoke. Or, create a subclass of NSOperation and override its -main method.

3. Send -addOperation: to the NSOperationQueue, passing the operation object created in step 2.

Without doing anything else, the NSOperationQueue will create new threads and use them to execute the code in your NSOperation objects. The sample project used in Chapter 4 demonstrates how simple NSOperationQueue is to use. Using NSOperationQueue has several advantages:

• NSOperationQueue will automatically maintain an efficient pool of threads, creating and destroying threads for you.

• NSOperationQueue scales automatically based on the system resources—like the number of CPU cores—and will perform load balancing.

• Operations can be made dependent on other operations, allowing you to define complex trees of operations that must be performed in the correct order.

• You can limit the number of concurrent operations, or let the operation queue determine an optimal number automatically.

• Operations can be prioritized.

• By subclassing NSOperation, you have extensive control over your operation's behavior. You can also implement code that permits your operation to be prematurely canceled.

See the "Creating and Managing Operation Objects" section in the *Threading Programming Guide* for more details.[2]

Timers

Timers are objects that post method invocations to a run loop at specific time intervals. They are incredibly simple to use, and can often replace much more elaborate solutions based on threads or other mechanisms.

Timers run on run loops. They come in two flavors: repeating timers and one-shot (non-repeating) timers. A repeating timer fires an Objective-C message at regular intervals until stopped. A one-shot timer sends one message, and then invalidates itself. When a timer is invalidated, it stops sending messages and removes itself from the run loop.

To use a timer:

1. Create a timer object.

2. Schedule it to run on the current run loop.

3. To stop the timer, send it an -invalidate message.

---

[2] *Apple Inc., Threading Programming Guide, Managing Operation Objects,* http://developer.apple.com/documentation/Cocoa/Conceptual/Multithreading/OperationObjects/, *2008*

When creating a timer object, you specify the time interval in seconds, an optional context object, and a flag that determines if the timer repeats. The target of the timer is either an NSInvocation object or a receiving object pointer and method identifier pair. The method must expect to receive the NSTimer object pointer as its only parameter and return void. The receiver can use the timer object's userInfo property to retrieve the supplementary context object.

NSTimer objects can be created using any of the +timerWithTimeInterval:… messages and later scheduled to run on a run loop using -[NSRunLoop addTimer:forMode:]. However, it is simpler to create and schedule the timer to run using a single +scheduledTimerWithTimeInterval:… message.

Listing 15-2 used a separate thread to invoke a heartbeat message on the main thread approximately every half-second. Listing 15-12 provides an equivalent, and far more frugal, solution using a timer.

Listing 15-12. Heartbeat Timer

```
@interface Process : NSObject
@property double progress;
@end

@interface Heartbeat : NSObject {
    NSTimer             *timer;
    Process             *monitor;
    NSProgressIndicator *indicator;
}

+ (Heartbeat*)startHeartbeatProcess:(id)process
                      withIndicator:(NSProgressIndicator*)progress;

- (void)stop;
- (void)heartbeatTime:(NSTimer*)timer;

@end

@implementation Heartbeat

+ (Heartbeat*)startHeartbeatProcess:(id)process
                      withIndicator:(NSProgressIndicator*)progress
{
    Heartbeat *heartbeat = [Heartbeat new];
    heartbeat->monitor = process;
    heartbeat->indicator = progress;
    heartbeat->timer = [NSTimer scheduledTimerWithTimeInterval:0.5
                                    target:heartbeat
                                  selector:@selector(heartbeatTime:)
                                  userInfo:nil
                                   repeats:YES];

    return heartbeat;
}
```

```
- (void)stop
{
    [timer invalidate];
}

- (void)heartbeatTime:(NSTimer*)timer
{
    [indicator setDoubleValue:monitor.progress];
}

@end
```

Timers are not exceedingly accurate, and their accuracy decreases as the time interval increases. Timers can fire before, or after, their scheduled time depending on a number of factors. Since timers are essentially deferred messages, they are inherently thread safe.

Summary

Basic thread creation and synchronization is very similar to Java. You can create threads and control their access to critical code using @synchronized directives. If you need finer-grained control over thread synchronization, the Objective-C frameworks provide a variety of mutually exclusion semaphores, each with unique capabilities.

Like Java, the modern Objective-C frameworks now provide utility classes for simplifying the complex job of creating and controlling operations in multiple threads. Finally, don't forget the extremely useful NSTimer class. Simple tasks that need to be performed at some future time, or at regular intervals, can be easily scheduled using timers.

PART 3

■■■

Programming Patterns

CHAPTER 16

■■■

Collection Patterns

Organizing collections of objects is a fundamental part of everyday programming. The class frameworks provide several classes for organizing objects into arrays, dictionaries (maps), and sets. Objects in an array have a specific order, addressed by a numeric index. Dictionaries (maps) organize objects into unordered pairs, each pair being a unique key object and a value object. The key object is used to identify and address the value object. Finally, sets are amorphous collections that are neither ordered nor addressable; an object is simply in a set or it's not. The Cocoa framework doesn't provide any tree, linked list, or stack collections.

Collection patterns in Objective-C will present Java programmers with a number of challenges. The biggest will be a false sense of familiarity—*faux amis*, as the French would say. So much of the collection classes resemble Java that it's easy to forget the subtle differences: the base classes of collections are immutable, keys in a dictionary (map) are always copied, collections can't be modified during enumeration, and so on. Many of these behaviors are only footnotes in the regular documentation. This chapter will highlight these differences so that you'll be acutely aware of them. Some differences are blessings, most require slight changes to your programming habits, and a few can profoundly affect your design.

This chapter will explain the collection classes, listed in Table 16-1. It will describe how Objective-C collections are alike and different from their Java siblings, the equality and hash contracts, and how collections are enumerated, sorted, and filtered. The later sections cover enumeration concurrency and thread safety considerations.

Table 16-1. Java and Objective-C Collection Classes

Java	Objective-C
ArrayList	NSArray, NSMutableArray
	NSPointerArray
HashMap	NSDictionary, NSMutableDictionary
WeakHashMap	NSMapTable
HashSet	NSSet, NSMutableSet, NSHashTable
	NSCountedSet
BitSet	NSIndexSet

Immutable Collections

In Java, all collection classes are mutable. It's possible to create an immutable collection using a special method like java.util.Collections.unmodifiableCollection(Collection), but that's rare. For the most part, you design your code with the assumption that all collections are mutable, paying special attention to when collections are passed by reference to other methods.

Most Objective-C collection classes adhere to an immutable base class, mutable subclass design pattern. The base classes of the traditional collection classes (NSArray, NSDictionary, NSSet, and NSIndexSet) are truly immutable. They lack any methods that can modify the collection. When a method accepts or returns one of these classes, it is implicitly immutable—removing most pass-by-reference concerns that Java programmers contend with. You might be wondering just how useful an immutable collection class is, but they're quite handy. They use many of the same programming patterns as java.lang.String objects.

To interactively construct or manipulate a collection, you must create one of the mutable subclasses: NSMutableArray, NSMutableDictionary, NSMutableSet, or NSMutableIndexSet. These subclasses define all of the methods used to alter the contents of the collection. Being subclasses, you can pass any mutable collection object as an immutable type. However, you should take some care when doing this. In Objective-C, the receiver of an immutable collection will likely assume it to be immutable, whereas in Java it would rightly assume it to be mutable. If the receiver keeps a reference to the original object, it may behave erratically if its immutable collection is arbitrarily altered. You can safely pass mutable collections as immutable collections as long as nothing else modifies the collection, or the receiver understands that it might actually be a mutable collection. Otherwise, convert the collection into an immutable collection using one of the lightweight collection copy constructors.

To make immutable classes useful and easy to work with, Objective-C provides an extensive set of constructors and methods that create and return an immutable collection. These convenience constructors make it easy to create immutable copies of other collections or make a single change to an immutable collection by creating a new collection. The immutable collection constructors are listed in Table 16-2.

Table 16-2. Immutable Collection Constructors

Method	Description
+[NSArray arrayWithArray:]	Creates an immutable, shallow copy of another array.
-[[NSArray alloc] initWithArray:copyItems:]	Same as [NSArray arrayWithArray:] if the copyItems parameter is NO. If copyItems is YES, it makes a deep copy of the array by sending a -copyWithZone: message to every object in the collection.
+[NSArray arrayWithObject:]	Creates an immutable array containing one object.
+[NSArray arrayWithObjects:]	Creates an immutable array of objects. The objects are passed as a variable argument list, terminated by with a nil value.
+[NSArray arrayWithObjects:count:]	Creates an immutable array from a C array of object pointers. The parameters are the address of the first element in the array and the element count.

`-[NSArray arrayByAddingObject:]`	Creates a new immutable array that's a shallow copy of the receiver's array plus one additional object.
`-[NSArray arrayByAddingObjectsFromArray:]`	Creates a new immutable array by concatenating the receiver's collection with the objects in the parameter.
`-[NSArray subarrayWithRange:]`	Creates a new immutable array that contains a shallow copy of a subset of the receiver's array.
`-[NSArray filteredArrayUsingPredicate:]`	Returns an immutable array containing the objects in the receiver's array that match the predicate expression.
`-[NSArray sortedArrayUsing…:]`	Any of four different methods that create a new immutable array with the sorted contents of the receiver's array.
`+[NSDictionary dictionaryWithDictionary:]`	Creates an immutable, shallow copy of another dictionary.
`-[[NSDictionary alloc] ↩ initWithDictionary:copyItems:]`	Same as [NSDictionary dictionaryWithDictionary:] if copyItems is NO. If copyItems is YES, the new dictionary is a deep copy of the original dictionary, made by sending every value object a -copyWithZone: message. Key objects are always copied.
`+[NSDictionary dictionaryWithObject:forKey:]`	Creates an immutable dictionary containing a single key/value pair.
`+[NSDictionary dictionaryWithObjects:forKeys:]`	Creates an immutable dictionary from two arrays, one containing the keys and the other the values.
`+[NSDictionary ↩ dictionaryWithObjects:forKeys:count:]`	Creates an immutable dictionary from two C arrays, one containing keys and the other values.
`+[NSDictionary dictionaryWithObjectsAndKeys:]`	Creates an immutable dictionary from an arbitrary number of value/key pairs in a variable argument list. The list is terminated by a single nil value.
`+[NSSet setWithSet:]`	Creates an immutable, shallow copy of another set.
`-[[NSSet alloc] initWithSet:copyItems:]`	Same as +[NSSet setWithSet:] if copyItems is NO. If copyItems is YES, the new set is a deep copy made by sending each object in the set a -copyWithZone: message.
`+[NSSet setWithArray:]`	Creates an immutable set from an array.

+[NSSet setWithObject:]	Creates an immutable set containing a single object.
+[NSSet setWithObjects:]	Creates an immutable set containing the objects in the variable argument list. The list is terminated by a nil object value.
+[NSSet setWithObjects:count:]	Creates an immutable set from a C array of object pointers. The parameters are the address of the first element in the array and the element count.
-[NSSet setByAddingObject:]	Creates a new immutable set that's a shallow copy of the receiver plus one additional object.
-[NSSet setByAddingObjectsFromSet:]	Creates a new immutable set that's a union of the receiver's set and the parameter set.
-[NSSet setByAddingObjectsFromArray:]	Creates a new immutable set that's a union of the receiver's set and the objects in the array.
-[NSSet filteredSetUsingPredicate:]	Creates a new immutable set containing the objects in the receiver's set that match the predicate expression.
+[NSIndexSet indexSetWithIndex:]	Creates an immutable index set containing a single index.
+[NSIndexSet indexSetWithIndexesInRange:]	Creates an immutable index set with all of the indexes in the given range.
-[[NSIndexSet alloc] initWithIndexSet:]	Creates an immutable index set that's a copy of another index set.

Collections created from other collections usually make shallow copies of the original collection, by simply copying the object pointers. This is highly optimized and is usually very fast. It is quite common to create a mutable collection to assemble a set of objects, and then return an immutable copy, as shown in Listing 16-1. This is comparable to creating a java.lang.StringBuilder object, building the string, then returning an immutable String via StringBuilder.toString().

Listing 16-1. Returning an Immutable Collection

```
- (NSArray*)guestList
{
    // Assemble array of guests
    NSMutableArray *scratchArray = [NSMutableArray new];
```

```
for ( … ) {
    …
    [scratchArray addObject:…];
}

// Return immutable array of guests
return [NSArray arrayWithArray:scratchArray];
}
```

A few constructors make deep copies. These have a copyItems parameter. When dictionaries are duplicated, the key objects are always copied.

Since the mutable subclasses inherit all of the methods of their superclass, the mutable collection classes can use any of the class methods in Table 16-2 to pre-populate a new, mutable collection. You typically do this when you have an immutable collection that you need to make changes to, as shown in Listing 16-2.

Listing 16-2. *Creating a Mutable Copy of an Immutable Collection*

```
- (void)hardwareNotification:(NSNotification*)notification
{
    NSDictionary *hwInfo = [notification userInfo]; // details of hardware problem
    NSMutableDictionary *adminInfo = nil;

    // If the hardware alert is serious enough to notify the administrators,
    //   post a new notification with the hardware failure and a time stamp.
    int alertLevel = [[hwInfo objectForKey:@"Level"] intValue];
    if (alertLevel>=notifyAlertLevel) {
        // Make a mutable copy of the hardware failure info dictionary
        adminInfo = [NSMutableDictionary dictionaryWithDictionary:hwInfo];
        // Add a time stamp to the hardware info dictionary
        [adminInfo setObject:[NSDate date] forKey:@"Date"];
        [[NSNotificationCenter defaultCenter] postNotificationName:@"AdminAlert"
                                              object:[notification object]
                                              userInfo:adminInfo];
    }
}
```

Objective-C has recently acquired some new collection classes: NSPointerArray, NSMapTable, and NSHashTable. These classes are inherently mutable and are more like the Java collection classes in that respect. They all have the ability to be "programmed" with a particular personality, such as maintaining weak references to objects, allowing memory blocks or primitive integers to be used as values, or permitting nil object pointers to be stored. The differences between these new classes and the old ones are detailed in the sections that discuss them.

Ordered Collections

NSArray, NSMutableArray, and NSPointerArray organize ordered collections of values, equivalent to java.util.ArrayList. Specifically, Objective-C and Java array classes have these common features:

- Values in the collection are object references.

- Values are addressed by index.

- The same value can be stored at more than one index.

- New values can be appended to the end of the array, or inserted at an existing index pushing existing values up one index. Values cannot be inserted beyond the end of the array.

- Removing a value shifts all subsequent values down to occupy the vacated index.

- NSArray collections can be searched to locate the index of a known value.

  There are a number of key differences:

- NSArray objects cannot be used to store nil (null) values. Consequently, operations that would pad the array with nil values, like -setCount:, are not implemented.

- NSPointerArray objects will not search their content for values. Thus, methods like -containsObject, indexOfObject:, and removeObject: are not implemented. You can iterate over its content to find values.

- NSPointerArray can store much more than object pointer values.

- An NSMutableArray can be initialized with a predetermined capacity. But beyond that, the capacity of the array is opaque, save for the single -compact method implemented by NSPointerArray.

Common Methods

Tables 16-3 and 16-4 list the common array methods in Java and Objective-C. The messages in Table 16-3 do not alter the collection and are implemented for both mutable and immutable collections. The messages in Table 16-4 can only be sent to mutable arrays.

Table 16-3. *Common Array Collection Methods*

java.lang.ArrayList	NSArray	NSPointerArray
size()	count	count
get(int)	objectAtIndex:	pointerAtIndex:
	objectsAtIndexes:	
contains(Object)	containsObject:	
indexOf(Object)	indexOfObject:	
	indexOfObject:inRange:	

	indexOfObjectIdenticalTo:	
	indexOfObjectIdenticalTo:inRange:	
	lastObject:	
lastIndexOf(Object)		
toArray()	getObjects:	allObjects
subList(int,int)	getObjects:range:	

***Table 16-4.** Common Mutable Array Collection Methods*

java.lang.ArrayList	NSMutableArray	NSPointerArray
add(Object)	addObject:	addPointer:
addAll(Collection)	addObjectsFromArray:	
add(int,Object)	insertObject:atIndex:	insertPointer:atIndex:
	insertObjects:atIndexes:	
		setCount:
clear()	removeAllObjects	
	removeLastObject	
remove(Object)	removeObject:	
	removeObject:inRange:	
remove(int)	removeObjectAtIndex:	removePointerAtIndex:
	removeObjectsAtIndexes:	
	removeObjectIdenticalTo:	
	removeObjectIdenticalTo:inRange:	
removeRange(int,int)	removeObjectsFromIndices:numIndices:, removeObjectsInRange:	
	removeObjectsInArray:	

set(int,Object)	replaceObjectAtIndex:withObject:	replacePointerAtIndex:↵ withPointer:
	replaceObjectsAtIndexes:withObjects:	
	replaceObjectsInRange:↵ withObjectsFromArray:range:	
	replaceObjectsInRange:↵ withObjectsFromArray:	
	exchangeObjectAtIndex:↵ withObjectAtIndex:	
	setArray:	
trimToSize()		compact

A few of the methods in Tables 16-3 and 16-4 aren't one-to-one replacements for Java methods, although most are. For example, toArray() returns an array object whereas -getObjects: populates a C array with the collection values. Trivial expressions like arrayList.isEmpty() are easily replaced with [array count]==0. Most methods are self-explanatory.

NSArray, NSMutableArray

Except for not allowing nil (null) values, NSMutableArray is probably as close to java.lang.ArrayList as you're going to get. As you can see from the earlier tables, there are far more convenience methods, so look for an array method before writing your own code to, say, exchange two elements in the collection.

NSArray makes the distinction between two objects that are equal (-indexOfObject:) and two objects that are identical (-indexOfObjectIdenticalTo:). The latter compares object pointers for equality, while the former compares the object's value for equality. See the "Collection Equality Contracts" section later in this chapter.

A number of methods, like -removeObjectsAtIndexes:, operate on an arbitrary list of indexes defined by an NSIndexSet object—another collection class discussed later in the Unordered Collections section. Methods like -objectsAtIndexes: are particularly powerful; it will return a new NSArray object that's an arbitrary subset of the receiver's collection, chosen using the indexes in an NSIndexSet.

COCOA COLLECTION CLASS ORGANIZATION

Java collection classes are neatly organized into inheritance trees. The base Collection interface has List, Map, and Set sub-interfaces, which are embodied in AbstractCollection, AbstractList, AbstractMap, and AbstractSet classes that are eventually implemented as the concrete collection classes we use every day.

Objective-C classes have almost no hierarchy. Most are direct subclasses of NSObject. The fact that they all implement a -count method is by convention, not formal design. Most of the time this makes little or no difference. Objective-C does lack methods like Java's addAll(Collection) because it has no base class that encompasses all collection classes.

One of the reasons for this is that many of the Objective-C collection classes are actually implemented in C. For example the Core Foundation CFArray type implements NSArray, and the two are interchangeable. See the "Toll-Free Bridge" section of Chapter 25 for more details.

NSPointerArray

NSPointerArray is a newer collection class. It has no immutable base class, so in that respect it is more like Java's ArrayList class. What sets NSPointerArray and its siblings NSMapTable and NSHashSet apart from other collection classes is the ability to "program" the collections. The collection is initialized with a set of delegate functions that define its personality. NSPointerArray objects are constructed using an NSPointerFunctions object that contains a set of callback functions that will be used to manipulate the values in the collection. The callback functions are: hash, isEqual, size, description, acquire, and relinquish. When you add a value to the array, the value is passed to the acquire function. When the value is removed, it is processed through relinquish. When comparing values in the collection, the candidate values are passed to the isEqual function for comparison.

■**Note** You might be wondering why the function pointer set includes delegate functions that perform hash and comparisons when NSPointerArray provides no means for searching the collection. This is for consistency with the map and set collections. The latter classes use the same pointer function objects and *do* use the hash and comparison functions extensively.

By employing a set of delegate functions, the collection can tailor itself to a wide variety of solutions. To make the new collection easy to use, the Cocoa framework includes predefined pointer function sets that can be selected by mixing *pointer function option* constants, some of which are listed in Table 16-5. These predefined functions sets implement most of the collection behaviors that you're ever likely to need. The two most common NSPointerArray personalities have convenience constructors: [NSPointerArray pointerArrayWithStrongObjects] creates a regular object array and [NSPointerArray pointerArrayWithWeakObjects] creates an object array that uses weak references.

Table 16-5. *Common NSPointerFunctionsOptions*

Option Identifier	Description
NSPointerFunctionsStrongMemory	Values are pointers, stored using strong references. This is the default memory option if no memory option is specified.
NSPointerFunctionsZeroingWeakMemory	Values are pointers, stored using weak references.
NSPointerFunctionsObjectPersonality	Values are object pointers. Objects are compared using an -isEqual: message. The -description message is used to generate object descriptions. This is the default personality if no personality is specified.
NSPointerFunctionsObjectPointerPersonality	Values are object pointers. Objects are compared by testing their pointers for equality. The -description message is used for object descriptions.
NSPointerFunctionsCStringPersonality	Values are pointers to C strings. Values are compared using the strcmp() function, and descriptions are generated by converting the C string into an NSString object.
NSPointerFunctionsIntegerPersonality	Values are integers.
NSPointerFunctionsCopyIn	Values are copied when added to the collection. If the values are object pointers, they must conform to NSCopying.

You can also create an NSPointerArray by combining one memory storage option, one personality option, and the optional "copy in" option from the list in Table 16-5. The code in Listing 16-3 creates an NSPointerArray collection that makes copies of objects added to the collection, and keeps strong references to those copies.

Listing 16-3. Custom NSPointerArray

```
NSPointerArray *array = [NSPointerArray pointerArrayWithOptions:
                            (NSPointerFunctionsObjectPersonality
                            |NSPointerFunctionsStrongMemory
                            |NSPointerFunctionsCopyIn) ];
```

There are even more progressively esoteric options that allow NSPointerArray to store pointers to C structures, contain copies of whole C structures, use memory managed with C's calloc() and free() functions, and so on. See the documentation for NSPointerFunctionsOptions for a complete list. For the ultimate control, you can create your own NSPointerFunctions objects if the predefined functions don't meet your needs.

Dictionary Collections

NSDictionary, NSMutableDictionary, and NSMapTable organize unordered pairs of objects, equivalent to java.util.HashMap. Each pair consists of a key object and a value object. Values are addressed using objects equal to their keys. Keys in the collection are unique, but values can be duplicated. Specifically, Objective-C and Java dictionary classes have these common features:

- Keys and values in the collection are object references.
- Key objects should not change value.
- Keys must adhere to the equality and hash contracts.
- Keys are unique. Storing a new value for an existing key replaces the exiting key/value pair with the new one.
- A single value can be stored more than once with different keys.
- NSMapTable can use strong or weak references for its key and/or value objects, making it a flexible replacement to java.util.WeakHashMap.

    There are two key differences:
- Value objects cannot be nil (null). A nil value indicates the absence of a key. To store a nil value, remove the key from the collection.

- Key objects are always copied and must conform to NSCopying. The collection retains the copy of the Key object, not the instance used to add the key/value pair.

Common Methods

Tables 16-6 and 16-7 list the common dictionary (map) methods in Java and Objective-C. The messages in Table 16-6 do not alter the collection and are implemented for both mutable and immutable collections. The messages in Table 16-7 can only be sent to mutable dictionaries.

Table 16-6. Common Dictionary Collection Methods

java.lang.HashMap	NSDictionary	NSMapTable
size()	count	count
keySet()	allKeys	
	allKeysForObject:	
values()	allValues	
		dictionaryRepresentation
	getObjects:andKeys:	
	keysSortedByValueUsingSelector:	
get(Object)	objectForKey:	objectForKey:
	objectsForKeys:notFoundMarker:	

Table 16-7. *Common Mutable Dictionary Collection Methods*

java.lang.HashMap	NSMutableDictionary	NSMapTable
put(Object,Object)	setObject:forKey:	setObject:forKey:
putAll(Map)	addEntriesFromDictionary:	
	setDictionary:	
remove(Object)	removeObjectForKey:	removeObjectForKey:
clear()	removeAllObjects	removeAllObjects
	removeObjectsForKeys:	

Dictionary collections will not store nil values; a nil value is used to indicate the absence of a key. The Java statement dictionary.contains(key) can be written as [dictionary objectForKey:key]!=nil. If you must store a key without a value, use NSNull.

-allKeysForObject: returns an array containing all of the keys that map to a given value. The Java statement dictionary.containsValue(object) can be written as [[dictionary allKeysForObject:object] count]!=0.

-keysSortedByValueUsingSelector: returns the keys of an NSDictionary as an array sorted into a particular order, allowing you to iterate through the collection in a well-defined order. See the "Iterator Pattern" and "Sorting" sections.

NSDictionary, NSMutableDictionary

Except for not allowing nil (null) values, NSMutableDictionary is almost identical to java.lang.HashMap. The biggest differences are the handling of nil values and the copying of keys.

You can use any object as a key as long as it can be copied—that is, conforms to NSCopying—and the copy retained by the collection is never modified. When a dictionary is copied, all of the keys are copied.

Like NSArray, NSDictionary has a few methods that operate on groups of entries. For example, -objectsForKeys:notFoundMarker: takes an array of key objects, performs a batch search, and returns an array of value objects. Each entry in the new array corresponds to the value for that key, or the "not found marker" object. Before writing code to iteratively look up, add, or remove sets of objects, check to see if there's a collection method that might do the work for you. Consider the statement:

```
[dictionary removeObjectsForKeys:[dictionary allKeysForObject:value]];
```

NSMapTable

NSMapTable is a newer collection class. Like NSPointerArray, it has no immutable base class, just like Java's HashMap class. Also like NSPointerArray, an NSMapTable is constructed with a set of delegate functions that defines its behavior.

An NSMapTable instance is created using an NSPointerFunction object, or the NSPointerFunctionOptions listed in Table 16-5. Refer to the NSPointerArray section for a description of the NSPointerFunctions class and pointer function options. There are two significant differences between initializing an NSMapTable and an NSPointerArray.

First, NSMapTable only accepts a narrow subset of the function pointer options supported by NSPointerArray. The options in Table 16-8 are the only ones supported by NSMapTable, along with a synonymous symbol for use with NSMapTable constructors. Basically, map tables only support object values, with either strong or weak references, and you have the option of storing a reference or copy of the object. If you restrict yourself to using the NSMapTable option synonyms, you won't accidentally choose an NSPointerFunctions option that isn't supported.

Table 16-8. *NSMapTable Options*

NSMapTable Synonym	NSPointerArray
NSMapTableStrongMemory	NSPointerFunctionsStrongMemory
NSMapTableZeroingWeakMemory	NSPointerFunctionsZeroingWeakMemory
NSMapTableCopyIn	NSPointerFunctionsCopyIn
NSMapTableObjectPointerPersonality	NSPointerFunctionsObjectPointerPersonality

The second difference is that NSMapTable objects are initialized with two sets of function pointers: one set for the keys and one set for the values. This allows you to define a map that stores copies of keys using strong references and weak references to values, references to key and copies of values, weak keys and weak values, or any other combination that makes sense to your application. There are four convenience constructors for the most common configurations: +mapTableWithStrongToStrongObjects, +mapTableWithWeakToStrongObjects, +mapTableWithStrongToWeakObjects, and +mapTableWithWeakToWeakObjects.

Set Collections

NSSet, NSMutableSet, NSCountedSet, NSIndexSet, and NSHashTable organize sets of unordered objects, broadly equivalent to java.util.HashSet and java.util.BitSet. The set collections adhere to the mathematical concept of a set: an object is a member of a set or it's not. The objects aren't organized in any particular order, nor are they addressable. You can add an object to the set, test for its presence, and remove it. NSIndexSet applies the same concepts to integer values, and NSCountedSet is a special set that allows an object to occur more than once in a collection. Specifically, Objective-C and Java set classes have these common features:

- Values in the collection are object references or integers.

- A value can be stored in a set only once. Adding a duplicate value does nothing. (NSCountedSet is an exception to this rule.)

Common Methods

Tables 16-9 and 16-10 list the common set methods in Java and Objective-C that apply to collections of objects. The messages in Table 16-9 do not alter the collection and are implemented for both mutable and immutable collections. The messages in Table 16-10 can only be sent to mutable sets.

Table 16-9. Common Set Collection Methods

java.lang.HashSet	NSSet	NSHashTable
size()	count	count
toArray()	allObjects	allObjects
	anyObject	anyObject
contains(Object)	containsObject:	containsObject:
containsAll(Collection)	isSubsetOfSet:	isSubsetOfHashTable:
	intersectsSet:	intersectsHashTable:
		setRepresentation

Table 16-10. Common Mutable Set Collection Methods

java.lang.HashSet	NSMutableSet	NSHashTable
add(Object)	addObject:	addObject:
remove(Object)	removeObject:	removeObject:
clear()	removeAllObjects	removeAllObjects
addAll(Collection)	addObjectsFromArray:	
addAll(Collection)	unionSet:	unionHashTable:
removeAll(Collection)	minusSet:	minusHashTable:
	intersectSet:	intersectHashTable:
	setSet:	

The Objective-C classes include some high-level methods, like -intersectSet:, that make it easy to perform set operations. They also include the amusing -anyObject message that returns an arbitrary member of the set.

NSSet, NSMutableSet

The NSSet classes are virtually identical in behavior to java.util.HashSet. The statement set.isEmpty() can be replaced by [set count]==0.

Mutable set objects can be initialized with an initial capacity, which can help optimize its performance. An accurate initial capacity is most helpful when creating large sets.

NSCountedSet

NSCountedSet is a subclass of NSMutableSet that allows a single object to be added to the set multiple times. In essence, it treats every object added to the set as a distinct, although indistinguishable, entity. Internally, the set maintains a single reference to the object and a count of the number of times it has been added to the set. To remove an object, the set must receive one -removeObject: message for each -addObject: message previously received. The method -countForObject: will return the number of -addObject: messages, less the number of -removeObject: messages, received for that object.

NSIndexSet

NSIndexSet is a special collection class that maintains a set of integer values, much like java.util.BitSet. Tables 16-11 and 16-12 list the common methods in Java and Objective-C.

Table 16-11. *Common Index Set Collection Methods*

java.util.BitSet	NSIndexSet
cardinality()	count
	countOfIndexesInRange:
get(int)	containsIndex:
	containsIndexes:
	containsIndexesInRange:
intersects(BitSet)	
	intersectsIndexesInRange:
	firstIndex
length()	lastIndex
	indexLessThanIndex:
	indexLessThanOrEqualToIndex:
nextBitSet(int)	indexGreaterThanOrEqualToIndex:
	indexGreaterThanIndex:
get(int,int)	getIndexes:maxCount:inIndexRange:

Table 16-12. Common Mutable Index Set Collection Methods

java.util.BitSet	NSMutableIndexSet
set(int)	addIndex:
or(BitSet)	addIndexes:
set(int,int,true)	addIndexesInRange:
clear(int)	removeIndex:
andNot(BitSet)	removeIndexes:
clear()	removeAllIndexes
clear(int,int)	removeIndexesInRange:
	shiftIndexesStartingAtIndex:by:

The common functionality of NSIndexSet and java.util.BitSet is smaller than most of the other collection classes. The Java class has a number of methods for flipping bits and performing Boolean operations that the Objective-C class lacks.

The primary use of NSIndexSet is to efficiently encapsulate an arbitrary subset of an ordered collection. The NSArray classes and user interface display classes use them extensively. For example, a table view returns the user's current selection as an NSIndexSet that identifies the selected rows. The interface has a number of methods, such as -indexLessThanIndex:, that make it easy to iterate through the collection in any direction.

NSHashTable

NSHashTable is the sister class to NSMapTable. Like NSMapTable, it is constructed using a set of delegate functions that define its behavior. Also like NSMapTable, it only accepts a limited number of function pointer options, listed in Table 16-13. See the sections NSMapTable and NSPointerArray for an explanation of these function pointer options.

Table 16-13. NSMapTable Options

NSHashTable Synonym	NSPointerArray
NSHashTableStrongMemory	NSPointerFunctionsStrongMemory
NSHashTableZeroingWeakMemory	NSPointerFunctionsZeroingWeakMemory
NSHashTableCopyIn	NSPointerFunctionsCopyIn
NSHashTableObjectPointerPersonality	NSPointerFunctionsObjectPointerPersonality

The only significant difference between NSHashTable and NSMapTable is that NSHashTable is a set and only needs a single set of function pointers to define its behavior.

Note Don't confuse NSHashTable (the class) with NSHashTable (the C type). The latter belongs to an older C API that implements low-level hash tables. The Objective-C NSHashTable class subsumes much of its functionality.

Composite Pattern

One aspect of the Composite Pattern is the ability to interact with groups of objects through a single object. The NSArray and NSSet classes each provide two methods that let you send a single messages to all of the objects in a collection:

- `(void)makeObjectsPerformSelector:(SEL)aSelector`

- `(void)makeObjectsPerformSelector:(SEL)aSelector withObject:(id)anObject`

The code in Listing 16-4 demonstrates how to send a message to every object in a collection.

Listing 16-4. Composite Message

Java
```java
ArrayList<Example> array = …
for ( Example example : array ) {
    example.setDelegate(this);
}
```

Objective-C
```objc
NSArray *array = …
[array makeObjectsPerformSelector:@selector(setDelegate:) withObject:self];
```

Collection Equality Contracts

Collection search and sorting features depend on objects responding to the `-isEqual:` message in a consistent and reasonable manner. This is called the *equality contract*. The set and dictionary collections locate objects through the use of a hash table. This depends on an object's `-hash` message returning a consistent value that has a predictable relationship to the `-isEqual:` response. This is called the *hash contract*.

The equality and hash contracts are identical to those in Java. The equality contract is as follows:

1. Two objects with equivalent values must return YES from `-isEqual:`, and NO otherwise.

2. Two object pointers that are equal are always considered equal, and identical. Thus, `[self isEqual:self]` always returns YES.

3. A valid object pointer and a nil object pointer are always considered not equal. The statement `[self isEqual:nil]` must always return NO.

4. [a isEqual:b] must always return the same value as [b isEqual:a].

      The equality contract rules must be considered in order. For example, rule 2 supersedes rules 3 and 4 in the special case where both object pointers are nil; nil is always equal to nil.

      The hash contract is simple and also consistent with Java's:

1. Two objects that are equal ([a isEqual:b]==YES) must return the same hash value ([a hash]==[b hash]).

2. Ideally, objects that are different ([a isEqual:b]==NO) should return hash values that are significantly different and evenly distributed across a large integer range.

      The -isEqual: and -hash methods are defined in NSObject, so every object inherits them. The default implementation of -hash is not, however, suitable for use in sets and dictionaries. If you create a subclass of NSObject that you plan to use in a collection, you should override -isEqual: and implement the equality contract. If the object will be stored in a set or used as a key in a dictionary, you must also override -hash to implement the hash contract. Listing 16-5 shows correctly implemented equality and hash methods.

Listing 16-5. *Equality and Hash Methods*

```
@interface AircraftIdentifier : NSObject {
    NSString        *registrationNumber;
    unsigned int    transponderCode;
}

@property (readonly) NSString *registrationNumber;
@property unsigned int transponderCode;

- (id)initWithRegistrationNumber:(NSString*)registration;

@end

@implementation AircraftIdentifier

@synthesize registrationNumber, transponderCode;

- (id)initWithRegistrationNumber:(NSString*)registration
{
    self = [super init];
    if (self != nil) {
        registrationNumber = registration;
        transponderCode = 1200;     // default for VFR
    }
    return self;
}
- (BOOL)isEqual:(id)object
{
    if (self==object)   // identity rule
```

```
        return YES;
    if (object==nil)      // nil rule
        return NO;
    if (![object isKindOfClass:[AircraftIdentifier class]])
        return NO;        // unrecognized class

    // Aircraft identifiers are the same if their registration numbers are equal
    AircraftIdentifier *r = (AircraftIdentifier*)object;
    return [registrationNumber isEqualToString:r->registrationNumber];
}

- (NSUInteger)hash
{
    // Return a hash of the properties used to determine equality
    return [registrationNumber hash];
}

@end
```

In the AircraftIdentifier class, the value assigned to the transponderCode is not considered to be significant when comparing two identifier objects for equality. That's because this value can change, but doesn't materially change the identity of the aircraft. How you determine equality for your classes will vary; just remember that the -hash method must *always* return a value consistent with -isEqual:.

Comparing Collections

Collections themselves can be compared to like collections. The methods in Table 16-14 list the collection comparison methods.

Table 16-14. *Collection Comparison Methods*

Classes	Method
NSArray, NSMutableArray	-isEqualToArray:
NSDictionary, NSMutableDictionary	isEqualToDictionary:
NSSet, NSMutableSet, NSCountedSet	isEqualToSet:
NSIndexSet, NSMutableIndexSet	isEqualToIndexSet:
NSHashTable	isEqualToHashTable:

Two object collections are considered equal if they contain the same number of objects and every object in the collection return YES when sent an -isEqual: message with the corresponding object in the other collection.

Some set collections have inequality comparisons that determine if a set is a subset or superset of another set. These are -[NSSet isSubsetOfSet:], -[NSHashTable isSubsetOfHashTable:], and -[NSIndexSet containsIndexes:].

Iterator Pattern

Probably the most common programming task of all time is to iterate through the elements of a collection, performing some test or action on each member. Both Java and Objective-C have recognized this and have made significant language changes designed to simplify this tedious and repetitive (no pun intended) programming pattern. You can iterate through the collection using the new syntax, with a legacy enumeration class, or by addressing each member object directly. This section will explain how each is done, and what it takes to add enumeration support to your classes.

The major differences between Objective-C enumeration and Java iterators are

- Objective-C collections are not typed.

- An Objective-C collection must not be modified during enumeration.

Java added parameterized types to collections, removing much of the tedium required to use the collection classes. A parameterized collection ensures that all objects added to the collection are of the correct type, and automatically casts objects extracted from the collection to a base type. Objective-C does not need any such constructs because it doesn't verify the class of an object during assignment. All collection classes accept and return the anonymous id object identifier, which the compiler assumes to be freely interchangeable with any class. If you want to ensure that an object added to, or obtained from, a collection is the correct class, add an assertion. See Chapter 14 for more about assertions.

The section "Collection Concurrency" describes how to deal with the limitation of not being able to modify a collection during enumeration. This also means that the Objective-C enumeration classes have no methods to modify the collection.

Using Fast Enumeration

Fast enumeration was added in Objective-C 2.0. It is a shorthand for(…) loop syntax for enumerating through the objects in a collection. Java has something very similar, called For-Each Loop syntax. Examples of both are shown in Listing 16-6. The use, syntax, and behavior of the two are practically identical.

Listing 16-6. Fast Enumeration Syntax

Java
```
for ( Object object : collection ) {
    …
}
```

Objective-C
```
for ( id object in collection ) {
    …
}
```

The "fast" in fast enumeration is more than a euphemistic reference to the time saved typing code. Fast enumeration is actually fast. The fast enumeration interface allows collections to fetch objects in batches, reducing overhead and improving performance. In all but a few cases, fast enumeration is the fastest way to iterate through the objects in a collection.

This makes fast enumeration far and away the preferred method of iterating arrays, since it is the easiest to write, most readable, and most efficient solution.

Using Enumerators

Before fast enumeration, Objective-C collections were enumerated via the NSEnumerator class. NSEnumerator is very similar in function to java.util.Iterator. Instead of Iterator's two methods, next() and hasNext(), NSEnumerator has a single -nextObject method. The -nextObject message returns a non-nil pointer until the enumeration is exhausted. This is possible because the collection classes that support NSEnumerator do not allow nil values. The collections that do allow nil values, like NSPointerArray, do not support NSEnumerator. The code in Listing 16-7 demonstrates using enumerator objects.

Listing 16-7. *Enumerating Through a Collection with NSEnumerator*

Java
```
ArrayList<Object> array = …
for (Iterator<Object> i = array.iterator(); i.hasNext(); ) {
    Object object = i.next();
    …
}
```

Objective-C
```
NSArray *array = …
NSEnumerator *e = [array objectEnumerator];
id object;
while ( (object=[e nextObject])!=nil ) {
    …
}
```

You obtain an NSEnumerator object just as you obtain an Iterator in Java—by asking the collection to provide you with one. Collections may provide several different kinds of enumerators. NSDictionary will produce a -keyEnumerator and an -objectEnumerator object that will iterate its key or value objects, respectively. The NSArray class provides -objectEnumerator and -reverseObjectEnumerator objects.

There are a few special-purpose subclasses of NSEnumerator, such as NSDirectoryEnumerator. In addition to enumerating through the contents of a directory, it implements additional methods for controlling recursion and obtaining the attributes of the current file. See Chapter 11 for an example of NSDirectoryEnumerator.

The only other method defined by NSEnumerator is -allObjects. This message is somewhat of a misnomer, because it returns an array of the objects the enumerator has *yet* to return. It really should have been named -remainingObjects.

Enumerator objects cannot be reset or restarted. Once they have finished their enumeration they become inert. Enumerator objects retain a reference to the collection that they are enumerating until the enumeration is finished.

Addressing Collection Objects

Collections of addressable objects (arrays and dictionaries) can also be iterated by addressing each member object individually. This gives you the ultimate control, although it might not be as efficient as using one of the earlier enumeration methods.

Array collections are the easiest to process in this way, and are not much less efficient than using an enumerator. Listing 16-8 shows a typical example.

Listing 16-8. *Array Index Loop*

Java
```java
ArrayList<Object> array = …
for (int i=0; i<array.size(); i++) {
    Object object = array.get(i);

    …

}
```

Objective-C
```objc
NSArray *array = …
NSUInteger i;
for (i=0; i<[array count]; i++) {
    id object = [array objectAtIndex:i];

    …

}
```

Dictionary values are addressed by their keys. Iterating through a dictionary via its keys requires a combination of enumeration and collection addressing, as shown in Listing 16-9.

Listing 16-9. *Enumerating a Dictionary by Key*

Java
```java
HashMap<Object,Object> dictionary = …
for (Iterator<Object> i = dictionary.keySet().iterator(); i.hasNext(); ) {
    Object key = i.next();
    Object object = dictionary.get(key);

    …

}
```

Objective-C
```objc
NSDictionary *dictionary = …
NSEnumerator *e = [dictionary keyEnumerator];
id key;
while ( (key=[e nextObject])!=nil ) {
    id object = [dictionary objectForKey:key];

    …

}
```

The code in listing 16-9 becomes particularly interesting if you replace the NSEnumerator assignment statement with the code in Listing 16-10. The -keysSortedByValueUsingSelector: message returns a sorted array of keys, allowing you to iterate the values of the dictionary in a predictable order. See the "Sorting Collections" section about how to control the sorting order.

Listing 16-10. *Ordered Dictionary Enumeration*

```
NSEnumerator *e = [[dictionary keysSortedByValueUsingSelector:@selector(compare:)]
                objectEnumerator];
```

■**Tip** A little known fact is that NSEnumerator also conforms to NSFastEnumeration. This allows any NSEnumerator object to be the collection in a fast enumeration statement. In Listing 16-9, the while(…) statement could be replaced with for (key in e). The enumerator object assumes the role of the collection. This is not optimized—the enumerator simply sends -nextObject messages to itself—so don't expect performance typical of fast enumerations.

There is no Objective-C equivalent to the java.util.Map.Entry object. The closest you can achieve is to use -[NSDictionary getObjects:andKeys:] to populate two C arrays, one with the keys and the other with the values, as shown in Listing 16-11.

Listing 16-11. *Enumerating Dictionary Key/Value Pairs*

```
NSDictionary *dictionary = …
NSUInteger count = dictionary.count;
__strong id *keys = NSAllocateCollectable(sizeof(id)*count,NSScannedOption);
__strong id *values = NSAllocateCollectable(sizeof(id)*count,NSScannedOption);
[dictionary getObjects:values andKeys:keys];
NSUInteger i;
for (i=0; i<count; i++) {
    id key = keys[i];
    id object = values[i];
    // ...
}
```

Adding Enumeration Support

You can easily subclass NSEnumerator to implement your own enumerators. It really only has to implement a -nextObject method. Implement the rarely used -allObjects method only if you find it useful, or your enumerator object is meant for a wide audience. See the TicTacToe project in Chapter 20 for an example of custom NSEnumerators. And, as mentioned in the earlier Tip, any NSEnumerator can be used in a fast enumeration statement.

Providing fast enumerator support for a custom object is a little more involved. In concept, it's easy; simply conform to the NSFastEnumeration protocol and implement the -countByEnumeratingWithState: objects:count: method.

The fast enumeration code sends this message to your object repeatedly until it returns 0. Each time your collection receives the message, it must assemble the next batch of objects to be processed in a C array and return the number prepared. Fast enumeration is most efficient when your class assembles batches of objects, but a simple non-optimized implementation can be achieved by returning one object at a time.

The progress of an individual iteration is maintained in an NSFastEnumerationState structure. This structure is empty when first passed to your method, and the same structure is passed again with each subsequent message. Your collection must update the structure to keep track of the enumeration's progress and protect against the collection changing during the enumeration. Fast enumerations are expected to throw an exception if the collection is modified during the course of the enumeration.

See the documentation for the NSFastEnumeration protocol for a complete description of the -countByEnumeratingWithState:objects:count: method and NSFastEnumerationState structures.

Sorting Collections

Ordered collections provide three basic techniques for sorting member objects into order: sort using an Objective-C message, sort using a C callback function to compare objects, and sort using sort descriptors. The methods that sort collections are listed in Table 16-15.

Table 16-15. Sort Methods

Method	Description
-[NSArray sortedArrayUsingDescriptors:]	Returns a copy of the array sorted using the sort descriptors.
-[NSArray sortedArrayUsingSelector:]	Returns a copy of the array, sorted using an Objective-C message.
-[NSArray sortedArrayUsingFunction:context:]	Returns a copy of the array, sorted using a C function to compare objects.
-[NSArray ↵ sortedArrayUsingFunction:context:hint:]	Same as -sortedArrayUsingFunction:context: except that it accepts an optimization hint obtained with -sortedArrayHint.
-[NSMutableArray sortUsingDescriptors:]	Sorts the array in situ using the sort descriptors.
-[NSMutableArray sortUsingFunction:context:]	Sorts the array in situ using a C function to compare objects.
-[NSMutableArray sortUsingSelector:]	Sorts the array in situ using an Objective-C message.
-[NSDictionary ↵ keysSortedByValueUsingSelector:]	Returns a copy of the keys in a dictionary as an array, sorted using an Objective-C message.

Objective-C Message Sorting

The methods -sortedArrayUsingSelector:, -sortUsingSelector:, and -keysSortedByValueUsingSelector: sort an array of objects using an Objective-C message to compare objects. You can use any message you want, as long as it's compatible with the following prototype and all of the objects in the collection respond to it:

```
-(NSComparisionResult)comparisonMethod:(id)object
```

The left hand object receives the message along with a pointer to the right hand object. It compares itself to the other object and returns an NSComparisionResult value. The return value must be one of NSOrderedAscending, NSOrderedSame, or NSOrderedDescending. The receiver returns NSOrderedAscending if it considers itself to be before the other object, NSOrderedSame if equal, and NSOrderedDescending otherwise. The canonical example of a suitable sort message is the -compare: method implemented by NSString, NSNumber, and NSDate. A mutable array of NSString objects can be sorted using [array sortArrayUsingSelector:@selector(compare:)], [array sortArrayUsingSelector:@selector (caseInsensitiveCompare:)], [array sortArrayUsingSelector:@selector (localizedCompare:)], and so on.

C Function Sorting

A sorting technique that doesn't require the object to implement its own comparison method is to supply a C function that accepts two Objective-C object pointers, compares them, and returns the results. The function must have a prototype compatible with

```
NSInteger comparisonFunction( id leftObject, id rightObject, void *context )
```

The function performs the same comparison that the comparison message does; it compares the left hand object to the right hand object and returns NSOrderedAscending, NSOrderedSame, or NSOrderedDescending. The optional context pointer passed to the sort method is passed along to the comparison function, allowing your function to tailor its behavior or implement different sorting schemes using a single function. Listing 16-12 sorts an array of strings by order of length.

Listing 16-12. String Sort Function

```
static NSInteger sortStringsByLength( id left, id right, void *ignored )
{
    // Order objects first by length, then by content
    NSUInteger lLength = [left length];
    NSUInteger rLength = [right length];
    if (lLength<rLength)
        return NSOrderedAscending;
    else if (lLength>rLength)
        return NSOrderedDescending;
    return [left compare:right];
}

…

NSMutableArray *array = …
[array sortUsingFunction:sortStringsByLength context:NULL];
```

Sort Descriptors

Finally, the collection classes provide a more object-oriented sorting alternative to the C function method that uses sort descriptors. Sort descriptors are instances of NSSortDescriptor, and are essentially a property comparison encapsulated in an object. An NSSortDescriptor identifies a property of an object, whether it should be sorted in ascending or descending order, and an optional Objective-C message that will be used to compare the two properties. If you don't specify a comparison method, the sort descriptor will use -compare: to compare objects. Unlike the -sortUsingSelector: message discussed earlier, a sort descriptor compares a common property of the two objects obtained using Key-Value coding—not the objects themselves (unless the property is @"self"). The code in Listing 16-13 is equivalent to the sort implemented in Listing 16-12, although not as fast.

Listing 16-13. Sorting Strings Using NSSortDescriptor

```
NSSortDescriptor *lengthSort = [[NSSortDescriptor alloc] initWithKey:@"length"
                                                    ascending:YES];
NSSortDescriptor *selfSort = [[NSSortDescriptor alloc] initWithKey:@"self"
                                                    ascending:YES];
NSArray *sortDescriptors = [NSArray arrayWithObjects:lengthSort,selfSort,nil];

NSMutableArray *array = …
[array sortUsingDescriptors:sortDescriptors];
```

The collection's -sortUsingDescriptors: method takes an array of NSSortDescriptor objects to form a comparison hierarchy. The objects in the collection are compared using the first descriptor in the array. If the first descriptor determines that the objects are equal, the second descriptor is used, and so on.

NSSortDescriptors are very useful in user interfaces. Various views that display collections of objects in columns and rows typically have an interface in which the user can click on a column and have the items in the display sorted using that property. What happens behind the scene is that each column is associated with an object property and will produce an NSSortDescriptor object for that property. Collecting all of the active sort descriptors into an array produces a sorting definition suitable for use with -sortUsingDescriptors:.

Filtering Collections

The NSArray and NSSet collections support a sophisticated filtering mechanism using predicates. A predicate is a tree of expression objects that describe an abstract evaluation, like timeRemaining==0 AND projectStatus!='finished'. Predicates can be obtained from the user through a graphical interface, created by interpreting a predicate statement string like the example just given, or (rarely) constructed programmatically.

The immutable collections implement methods that return a new collection with only those objects that cause the predicate to evaluate to YES. The mutable collections have additional methods that will remove all objects that cause the predicate to evaluate to NO.

See the *Predicate Programming Guide*[1] for a complete description of predicate objects and predicate expression syntax.

---

[1] Apple, Inc., *Predicate Programming Guide*, http://developer.apple.com/documentation/Cocoa/Conceptual/Predicates/, 2008.

Collection Concurrency

Collections should not be modified during an enumeration or modified concurrently from another thread. This section describes a couple of techniques for avoiding changes in a collection until after an enumeration is complete. After that, the thread-safety issues are addressed.

Enumerate a Copy of the Collection

The first technique to avoid modifying a collection while it is being iterated is to simply copy the collection and iterate through the copy, leaving the original free to be altered. The code in Listing 16-14 demonstrates this technique.

Listing 16-14. Enumerating a Collection Copy

```
NSMutableDictionary *zombies = …
for ( NSString *key in [zombies allKeys] ) {
    Zombie *zombie = [zombies objectForKey:key];
    if ([zombie hasExpired])
        [zombies removeObjectForKey:key];
}
```

The expression [zombies allKeys] returns a new, immutable array containing a copy of all the keys in the dictionary. The fast enumeration then occurs over the keys in the array, not the keys in the dictionary, so you are free to modify the contents of the dictionary during the enumeration.

The technique works equally well for arrays and sets.

Defer Changes to the Collection

The other technique is to defer the changes by collecting them and performing the changes after the enumeration is complete. Listing 16-15 demonstrates this technique using an array and an NSIndexSet.

Listing 16-15. Deferring Collection Changes

```
NSMutableArray *zombies = …
NSMutableIndexSet *deadZombies = [NSMutableIndexSet indexSet];
NSUInteger i;
for (i=0; i<[zombies count]; i++) {
    Zombie *zombie = [zombies objectAtIndex:i];
    if ([zombie hasExpired])
        [deadZombies addIndex:i];
}
[zombies removeObjectsAtIndexes:deadZombies];
```

The NSMutableIndexSet collects the indexes of the objects we intend to delete from the collection. At the end of the enumeration, all of the identified objects are deleted en masse using a single -removeObjectsAtIndexes: message.

Thread Safety

Like Java, none of the mutable collection classes are thread safe. Unlike Java, Objective-C doesn't provide any thread-safe mutable collections. However, the immutable collections are all inherently thread safe.

All of the immutable collections (NSArray, NSDictionary, NSSet) are thread safe, since it's impossible to change their content. Collections are also thread safe if you simply avoid making any changes to them. You could safely share an NSMutableArray with another thread as an NSArray object, as long as you could guarantee that the underlying mutable array would never be modified in the future. If you can't guarantee that, then make an immutable copy of the collection and return that instead.

■**Caution** A thread-safe collection does not automatically protect the objects within that collection. Any object used from more than one thread must be thread safe.

If you need to share a mutable collection between threads, protect the changes to the collection with @synchronized accessor functions or semaphores. The AutoSafeFIFO and FastFIFO classes shown in Chapter 15 are good examples.

Garbage Collection and Weak Collections

Tangentially related to thread safety are the potential problems with collections that maintain weak references to objects. Garbage collection runs concurrently and can collect weakly referenced objects at any time. Collections that maintain weak references can spontaneously lose objects or return nil values. This can affect their count and enumerations. Specifically, be mindful of these potential problems:

- The collection -count can change at any time.
- Any previously stored value in an array may return nil. Any member of a dictionary or set may spontaneously disappear.
- A fast enumeration may iterate over nil values anywhere during the enumeration.
- NSEnumerator objects should not be used when the collection uses weak references. The -nextObject message could return nil for any value, which would be interpreted as the end of the enumeration. Use fast enumeration or programmatic iteration.

If these effects are problematic, you can eliminate them by making a temporary copy of the collection using a collection object that uses strong references. Enumerate the values of the copy, and then forget the temporary collection.

Summary

Collections in Objective-C fulfill very similar roles to those in Java. You need to be cognizant of some of the subtle differences, like not modifying a collection during enumeration. But with those in mind, the familiar programming patterns and uses for arrays, dictionaries (maps), and sets remain largely the same.

■ ■ ■

CHAPTER 17

Delegation Pattern

The delegation pattern is an alternative to inheritance that allows an object's behavior to be customized or overridden without subclassing. The delegation pattern is *enthusiastically* embraced in Objective-C. Understanding the role of delegate objects in the Cocoa framework is crucial to effective use of the frameworks, especially the application and user interface classes. This chapter will explain the delegation pattern, the role and use of delegate objects, how to define your own delegates, and how to incorporate the delegation pattern in your own designs.

Understanding Delegates

The delegation pattern externalizes, or delegates, selected decisions or actions to another object, termed the delegate object. It embodies a design principle known as *inversion of responsibility*. The delegate can customize or influence the normal behavior of the object with code that is not contained within the object's class hierarchy. Delegates can be queried to make decisions, filter data, define conditional behavior, or inject additional processing at key times. Delegate objects are invariably optional. The class implements a default strategy in the absence of a delegate object or method.

The traditional way to customize a class is to subclass it and override specific methods. To redefine how your object gets copied, you override -copyWithZone:. To redefine how it compares itself with other objects, you override -isEqual:, and so forth. However, the inheritance pattern is not as effective when trying to customize the behavior of a tree of existing classes. Take the example in Figure 17-1.

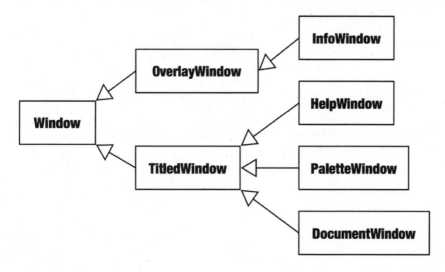

Figure 17-1. *Window class model*

Figure 17-1 shows a set of window classes. At the base is the abstract Window class that defines common properties like position, dimensions, and order, along with common behavior such as dragging, resizing, minimizing, and reordering. The TitledWindow class defines additional attributes, like the window's title, and behavior such as inserting the window's title into the application's Window menu. There are non-titled subclasses of the Window class along with specialized subclasses of the titled window class. In short, it's a succinct and logical class hierarchy.

Now the application developer—that's you—would like to enhance the user experience by implementing windows that "snap" to optimal positions as the user drags them around. Using inheritance, your only customization strategy is to subclass DocumentWindow and override its -dragWindow method. But that only redefines the behavior for the DocumentWindow. To implement the same customization for the palette, help, and info windows, additional subclasses must be defined, each duplicating the same customization. The modified class tree is shown in Figure 17-2.

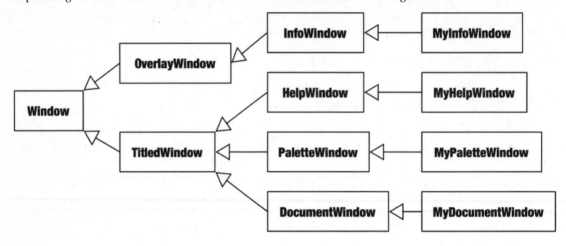

Figure 17-2. Customization using inheritance

Not only is this a lot of work and duplicate code, but the poor programmer—that's you—now discovers that the application doesn't work on systems with more than one monitor. Apparently, Window's -dragWindow method handles some special cases when dragging between monitors that only the original designer is privy to. Not knowing what that solution is, it's impossible to effectively duplicate the behavior of -dragWindow in the subclasses. The feature is a disaster and must be abandoned, or you risk additional development and the potential for future incompatibility.

Had the original developers of the Window class foreseen this situation, they could have easily avoided the problem by adopting the delegation pattern. The solution is to define a delegate object in the Window base class, as shown in Figure 17-3.

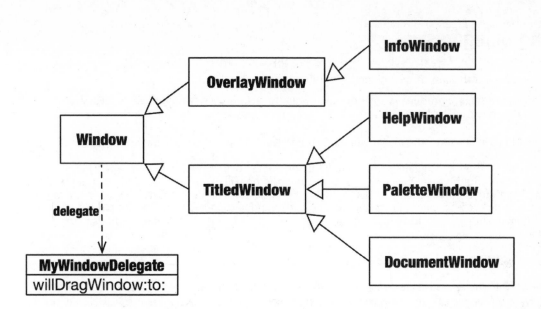

Figure 17-3. *Customization using delegation*

In its -dragWindow method, the Window class repeatedly sends the delegate object a -willDragWindow:to: message as the user drags the window. The message includes the window and the user's latest drag position. The delegate is expected to return the same or a modified position that the Window class will actually use when positioning the window.

It's a trivial but powerful interface. The delegate object is free to implement whatever drag position scheme it desires. It can "snap" the window's position to nearby edges, prevent the window from being dragged to certain regions, or use the information to move other windows out of the way. More importantly:

- All of the subclasses (InfoWindow, HelpWindow, PaletteWindow, and DocumentWindow) can be customized using a single delegate.

- Different delegate objects can be created to define different customizations.

- Customization can be applied per window instance, rather than per class.

- The new feature will be compatible with future versions of the Window class and all of its subclasses.

- Existing classes and interfaces that create DocumentWindow objects do not have to be modified.

- Any Window object that does not have a delegate object will use the standard window drag behavior.

Using Delegates

Using a delegate object is very simple, which is one of the features that makes them so useful.

1. Implement the appropriate delegate methods in your class.

2. Set the delegate property of the object you want to customize to your delegate object, typically by sending -setDelegate:.

That's it. Once set, the object will send your delegate object the delegate messages that class has defined.

The methods a delegate is expected to implement are usually defined informally. Their use, however, is so common that Objective-C class documentation will explicitly identify them as a "delegate method" or group them together in a "Delegate Methods" section. Remember that these document the methods the delegate property object should, or could, respond to, not the methods implemented by the class. When looking to customize the behavior of any object, first look for delegate methods in its documentation.

■**Note** Some methods listed in the delegate methods section of the documentation are actually notifications sent to observers, not messages sent to the delegate object. The documentation should make this distinction clear, but the biggest clue is that notification methods always receive an NSNotification object as their only parameter. See Chapter 18 for more about notifications.

The delegation pattern is widely used in the Cocoa framework. So much so that it catches Java and C++ developers off guard at first. For example, most customization of the single NSApplication object is not accomplished by subclassing NSApplication, but by attaching a delegate object to NSApplication during initialization. Here's a sample of the tasks that NSApplication defers to its delegate object:

- Open one or more document files.

- Open a temporary document file.

- Automatically reopen documents.

- Open an untitled document window.

- Print a document.

- Present an error message to the user.

- Determine if the application should quit when the last window is closed.

- Determine if the application is ready to quit.

In other object-oriented programming languages, customizations like these would typically be accomplished by subclassing the Application class and overriding its methods. Because of the power of delegates to augment the behavior of the NSApplication object, subclassing NSApplication is actually quite rare.

Listing 17-1 shows a simple delegate object that performs validation for an NSControl view object. The NSControl object sends its delegate a -control:isValidObject: message whenever it needs to validate its input value.

Listing 17-1. Input Value Validation Delegate

```
@interface PositiveIntValidationDelegate : NSObject

- (BOOL)control:(NSControl*)control isValidObject:(id)object;

@end

@implementation PositiveIntValidationDelegate

- (BOOL)control:(NSControl*)control isValidObject:(id)object
{
    return ([object intValue]>0);
}

@end

…

NSTextField *inputTextField = …
[inputTextField setDelegate:[PositiveIntValidationDelegate new]];
```

Once the delegate object is set for the input view, the NSTexField (a subclass of NSControl) will only accept text values that are interpreted as a positive integer value.

Usually, classes are designed so that delegates are optional. The object will adopt some default behavior if there is no delegate, or if the delegate doesn't implement an optional delegate method. In a few cases, the delegate is critical to the object's operation. For example, an NSURLConnection object sends all of the connection's events to its delegate. Without a delegate object to receive those messages, the object won't accomplish much.

Delegate Methods

Some delegate methods are expected while others are optional. The delegate must implement any expected delegate methods. The object using the delegate will send expected delegate messages to the delegate object unconditionally. If the delegate fails to implement them, an unrecognized selector exception will be thrown at runtime.

Optional delegate methods are more common, and make the delegation pattern exceptionally flexible. The object sending the delegate message will first test to see if the delegate object responds to it. If it does, the delegate is sent the message. If not, the object falls back to using its baseline behavior.

The delegate object is free to implement just those optional delegate methods that it requires. Optional delegate methods are particularly flexible because the delegate object only needs to implement those methods it wants, or needs, to affect. If a class defines 4 delegate methods, the delegate object has 15 different combinations of customizations available to it. Optional delegate methods also avoid the common Java practice of creating so-called "Simple" classes that implement default behavior for a set of interface methods, expecting you to subclass the "Simple" class and override only those methods you want to alter. This both simplifies the class hierarchy and localizes the default delegate behavior in the object's class rather than in the "Simple" class.

Delegate objects are often "real" objects, not classes specifically designed to be delegates. For example, a document object may also implement the delegate methods for NSToolbar. The toolbar delegate defines which toolbar controls are shown and appropriate, derived from information specific to the document object. The document object can transparently influence the toolbar user interface without any complicated inter-object dependencies.

A delegate object could also implement multiple sets of delegate methods and set itself as the delegate for a wide variety of objects. This is common in the case of the application delegate object. An application delegate will make itself the delegate object of the single NSApplication object, but may also assign itself as the delegate to other objects like windows, the file manager, and so on. The single application delegate object can then influence a wide range of behaviors using information localized in a single object. If the application delegate class becomes unwieldy, its individual roles can be subdivided into categories for improved modularity. See Chapter 5 for more about categories.

Delegate Protocols

The methods implemented by a delegate are typically defined as informal protocols in the Cocoa framework. (See Chapter 5 if you need a refresher on informal and formal protocols.) Delegate object properties are of type id, allowing them to be set to any object. The methods the delegate object is expected to implement are defined in the documentation.

You're free to do the same in your design, or you can adopt a more formal approach, as shown in Listing 17-2. You can't do this in Java, because Java has no concept of optional interface methods. If you're curious, the code to implement an informal protocol in Java—by testing for the presence of a method—was demonstrated in Chapter 10.

Listing 17-2. Automatic Defense Gun with Formal Delegate

```
@interface Gun : NSObject
…
@end

@protocol Targeting

@required
- (BOOL)gun:(Gun*)gun shouldShootAt:(id)target;

@optional
- (NSArray*)gun:(Gun*)gun prioritizeTargets:(NSArray*)targets;
- (BOOL)gunShouldStopFiring:(Gun*)gun;

@end

@interface AutomaticPerimeterDefenseGun : Gun {
    id<Targeting>    delegate;
}
```

```objc
@property (assign) id<Targeting> delegate;

- (void)engage;
- (void)disengage;

- (float)ammunitionRemaining;
- (void)reload;

@end

…

@interface AutomaticPerimeterDefenseGun () // private methods
- (void)defendPerimeter;
- (NSArray*)acquireTargets;
- (NSArray*)targetsFromSensor;
- (void)fireAtTarget:(id)target;
@end

@implementation AutomaticPerimeterDefenseGun

@synthesize delegate;

- (void)defendPerimeter
{
    // Check with the delegate to see if the gun should stop
    if ([(id)delegate respondsToSelector:@selector(gunShouldStopFiring:)]) {
        if ([delegate gunShouldStopFiring:self]) {
            [self disengage];
            return;
        }
    }

    // Gather the potential targets
    NSArray *targets = [self aquireTargets];
    // Fire at the ones the delegate identifies as enemies
    for ( id target in targets ) {
        if ([delegate gun:self shouldShootAt:target]) {
            [self fireAtTarget:target];
        }
    }
}
```

```objc
- (NSArray*)acquireTargets
{
    NSArray *targets = [self targetsFromSensor];

    // Pass the targets through the delegate for prioritization, filtering, ...
    if ([(id)delegate respondsToSelector:@selector(gun:prioritizeTargets:)])
        targets = [delegate gun:self prioritizeTargets:targets];

    return targets;
}

- (NSArray*)targetsFromSensor
{
    …
}

- (void)fireAtTarget:(id)target
{
    …
}

…

@end
```

The code implements an automatic perimeter defense gun for our mythical adventure game that, once engaged, acquires and shoots at targets autonomously. It defers several targeting and gun control decisions to a delegate object. The single most important is the identification of which targets it should shoot at.

The delegate property is formally declared to be an object that adopts the Targeting protocol. Using the Objective-C 2.0 @required and @optional directives, the delegate's requirements are spelled out to the compiler. The delegate *must* implement the -gun:shouldShootAt: message, and *may* implement -gun:prioritizeTargets: or -gunShouldStopFiring:.

If you don't generate documentation for your classes, this is an effective way of communicating the delegate requirements to the compiler and other programmers.

■**Tip** The delegate is cast to (id) when sending it the -respondsToSelector: message. The reason is because the type id<Targeting> defines an object pointer that is assumed to *only* respond to methods defined in the Targeting protocol. This doesn't include any methods defined in NSObject, so the compiler complains that the delegate might not respond to -respondsToSelector:. An alternative would be to declare the delegate object's pointer as id<Targeting,NSObject>. The NSObject protocol (not class) is a convenience protocol that declares the core set of methods defined by NSObject and its subclasses.

The single disadvantage to this approach emerges if you later subclass AutomaticPerimeterDefenseGun and want to define additional delegate methods. The delegate property is already defined as id<Targeting> and subclasses can't change the type of an inherited property. The subclasses have few options but to document the additional delegate methods they use and adopt them as informal protocols.

Incorporating the Delegation Pattern

The delegation pattern simplifies a number of thorny inheritance and domain design problems. When incorporating the delegation pattern in your application, consider these principles:

- Use the delegation pattern when the behavior of an object should be open to customization and the nature or knowledge needed to implement that customization is outside the domain of the class. In the AutomaticPerimeterDefenseGun example, the class encapsulates a weapon that shoots at targets, but deciding on which targets are friendly is outside its domain.

- Delegates are particularly effective when implemented in the base class with multiple subclasses. Each subclass can consistently employ the delegate without complicating the number or organization of subclasses.

- An object should have a well-defined behavior in the absence of a delegate object (delegate==nil). In the -defendPerimeter method, the delegate is unconditionally sent the -gun:shouldShootAt: message. If the delegate is nil, the message returns nil, and the gun shoots at nothing—a desirable trait in the absence of any targeting information. See the "absent behavior" and "consistency with nothing" design patterns in Chapter 7.

- Similarly, an object should provide some natural baseline functionality when optional delegate methods are absent. The -acquireTargets method in Listing 17-2 tests the delegate to see if it responds to -gun:prioritizeTargets:. If it does, it passes the known target list to the delegate that will prioritize, filter, or possibly supply its own targets. If the delegate doesn't implement the method, the gun uses the targets it obtained from its sensors. Note that this is also consistent with the previous principle, as -responsesToSelector: will return NO if the delegate is nil.

- An object should always provide context in the delegate message. The delegate methods in Listing 17-2 all include the Gun object that's sending the message to the receiver. This allows the delegate to include the sender in its decision process, like telling the gun to stop firing if its ammunition gets too low. Remember that a single delegate object might be set as the delegate for two, or a hundred, different objects. Some delegates act as reusable traits, like the validation routine in Listing 17-1, that can be shared by arbitrary groups of similar objects.

Summary

The delegation pattern is pervasive in Objective-C. It simplifies class structures and opens a broad range of customizations to you. Objective-C programmers and the Cocoa framework embrace this pattern enthusiastically, and you are encouraged to do the same. The delegation pattern is equally applicable to Java development, but the formal nature of Java interfaces, and the lack of a simple "is method implemented" test, make it more cumbersome to employ.

CHAPTER 18

■ ■ ■

Provider/Subscriber Pattern

The provider/subscriber pattern defines a one-to-many, unidirectional flow of information from a provider object to any number of subscriber objects. The concept is that the provider has useful information or events that need to be communicated to other objects, its subscribers, which will use that information to perform additional actions or stay in synchronization with the provider. In Java parlance, the provider *fires* notifications to its *listeners*. In Objective-C terminology, the provider *posts* notifications to its *observers*.

The provider/subscriber pattern is used heavily in Java, but Java doesn't provide any intrinsic service for helping objects manage their subscribers or coordinate messages. Consequently, most Java objects implement their own subscriber management. This isn't terribly difficult, but it does impose an important limitation: the provider and subscribers must have references to each other. Objective-C strongly encourages the provider/subscriber pattern by providing systemwide services for managing a provider's subscribers and delivering notifications to them. By providing intermediate management, providers and observers (subscribers) might know everything about each other, or nearly nothing at all.

The chapter begins by showing how a typical Java listener interface is duplicated using Cocoa's notification services. It will then describe other possible provider/subscriber relationships and how you can use them in your design. Finally, distributed notifications—notifications that travel between processes—are described along with thread safety and other considerations. You'll also want to read about the observer pattern in the next chapter, as the two patterns are very similar.

Notifications

In Objective-C, a notification sent to an observer is encapsulated in an NSNotification instance. The provider determines the contents of the NSNotification object. The receiver determines the Objective-C message that it will receive.

Listings 18-1 and 18-2 contrast the differences between a Java listener and an Objective-C observer. Listing 18-1 defines a Thermometer class that monitors a temperature. Whenever the temperature changes, it notifies its observers.

Listing 18-1. *Thermometer, Temperature Provider*

Java
```
public interface TemperatureListener
{
    public void temperatureChanged( Thermometer thermometer, float temperature );
}
```

```java
public class Thermometer
{
    private float temperature;
    private HashSet<TemperatureListener> listeners =
                new HashSet<TemperatureListener>();

    public float getTemperature( )
    {
        return temperature;
    }

    public void setTemperature( float newTemp )
    {
        if (temperature!=newTemp) {
            temperature = newTemp;
            fireTemperatureChange();
        }
    }

    public void addListener( TemperatureListener listener )
    {
        listeners.add(listener);
    }

    public void removeListener( TemperatureListener listener )
    {
        listeners.remove(listener);
    }

    public void fireTemperatureChange( )
    {
        for ( TemperatureListener listener : listeners ) {
            listener.temperatureChanged(this,temperature);
        }
    }

}
```

Objective-C
```objc
#define TempDidChange    @"TemperatureDidChange"

@interface Thermometer : NSObject {
    float    temperature;
}
```

```
@property float temperature;

@end

@implementation Thermometer

- (float)temperature
{
    return temperature;
}

- (void)setTemperature:(float)newTemp
{
    if (temperature!=newTemp) {
        temperature = newTemp;
        NSNumber *tempValue = [NSNumber numberWithFloat:temperature];
        NSDictionary *info = [NSDictionary dictionaryWithObject:tempValue
                                                    forKey:@"Temperature"];
        [[NSNotificationCenter defaultCenter] postNotificationName:TempDidChange
                                                    object:self
                                                    userInfo:info];
    }
}

@end
```

Listing 18-2 shows a temperature observer that receives temperature change notifications from a Thermometer object. It is initialized with the Thermometer object it will observe, and logs any changes to the temperature value.

Listing 18-2. TemperatureMonitor, Temperature Observer

Java
```
public class TemperatureMonitor implements TemperatureListener
{
    public TemperatureMonitor( Thermometer thermometer )
    {
        thermometer.addListener(this);
    }

    public void temperatureChanged( Thermometer thermometer, float temperature )
    {
        System.out.println("Temperature is now "+temperature);
    }
}
```

Objective-C
```objc
#import "Thermometer.h"

@interface TemperatureMonitor : NSObject

- (id)initWithThermometer:(Thermometer*)thermometer;
- (void)tempChanged:(NSNotification*)notification;

@end

@implementation TemperatureMonitor

- (id)initWithThermometer:(Thermometer*)thermometer
{
    self = [super init];
    if (self != nil) {
        [[NSNotificationCenter defaultCenter] addObserver:self
                                          selector:@selector(tempChanged:)
                                              name:TempDidChange
                                            object:thermometer];

    }
    return self;
}


- (void)tempChanged:(NSNotification*)notification
{
    id tempValue = [[notification userInfo] objectForKey:@"Temperature"];
    NSLog(@"Temperature is now %@",tempValue);
}

@end
```

The Java and Objective-C solutions in Listings 18-1 and 18-2 are functionally equivalent. Specifically:

- The Thermometer class defines the notifications it will send.

- The Thermometer class notifies its observers whenever the temperature changes.

- A TemperatureMonitor object receives only temperature change notifications from the one Thermometer object it is observing.

- A notification includes the new temperature value and a reference to the Thermometer object that posted the notification.

- Notifications are delivered as synchronous method invocations. That is, all of the notification methods execute before setTemperature returns.

The significant differences are as follows:

- The Java Thermometer class must maintain its own set of listener objects. The observers of the Objective-C Thermometer object are maintained by its NSNotificationCenter.

- The Java solution defines the method it will invoke via a TemperatureListener interface, and the listener object must implement this interface. In Objective-C, notifications are always delivered as NSNotification objects.

- The sender defines the Java method that receives the notification. In Objective-C, the observer determines the notification message it will receive.

Objective-C objects can register to observe notifications using flexible criteria. In addition to the simple case illustrated in the code, an observer can choose to receive multiple notifications from a single object, or similar notifications from multiple objects. In fact, the observer doesn't have to have a reference to the provider or even know what class it is. In the case of distributed notifications, the provider object might not even be in the same process.

An NSNotificationCenter object organizes and manages observers and dynamically pairs notifications to observers. NSNotificationCenter relieves the providers of implementing their own observer management; a provider only needs to concern itself with sending notifications. Since NSNotificationCenters are the nexus of notifications, they will be discussed next, followed by how notifications are posted and how observers register to receive them.

Notification Centers

An NSNotificationCenter manages a set of observers. Providers can post a notification to a notification center, which will distribute it to all of the interested observers registered with that center.

Normally, your objects interact with the single default NSNotificationCenter created by the Cocoa framework for the process. This per-process instance is obtained with the class message [NSNotificationCenter defaultCenter]. This is the Grand Central Station of notifications, and the notification center used by the bulk of the Cocoa framework. Consequently, if you intend to receive any of those notifications, you must register your object with [NSNotificationCenter defaultCenter].

There are a few other specialized notification centers and you can create your own. Each notification center is completely self-contained. A notification posted to a center will only be delivered to the objects registered with that notification center. The NSWorkspace object defines its own notification center that can be obtained with [[NSWorkspace sharedWorkspace] notificationCenter]. If you want to receive an NSWorkspace notification, your object must register with that notification center.

Note An NSNotificationCenter distributes all notifications synchronously. You can, however, attach an NSNotificationQueue, as described in the "Notification Queuing" section later in this chapter, to a notification center to deliver notifications asynchronously.

You may also want to define your own notification centers. Chapter 15 showed code for creating a per-thread notification center. Since notifications are always delivered in the thread that posted them, a per-thread notification center would allow you to organize your observers by thread.

Posting Synchronous Notifications

Posting a synchronous notification is simple, deftly demonstrated by the Thermometer class in Listing 18-1. There are three pieces of information that make up a notification:

- The notification name
- The sender
- A dictionary of supplementary information

The notification name is a string object. It can be any value you choose, as long as it doesn't conflict with the notification names used by other objects. Generally, a descriptive title like @"TemperatureDidChange" is sufficient to be unique. Notification name constants defined by frameworks tend to use class naming conventions. For example, all of the Cocoa framework notification names begin with "NS."

The object property of a notification contains a reference to the sender. Thus, every notification includes an implicit reference to the object that sent it. In the example in Listings 18-1 and 18-2, it wasn't strictly necessary to include the temperature value in the userInfo dictionary. The notification receiver could have obtained the value with ((Thermometer*)[notification object]).temperature.

The optional userInfo dictionary is an immutable dictionary containing whatever supplementary objects the provider wants to include. As mentioned, it wasn't strictly necessary to include the temperature value in the userInfo dictionary, but it's often a good idea. Having the temperature included in the dictionary relieves the observer of having to make too many assumptions about the sender (such as, "is the new temperature value still valid when the notification is received?"). The userInfo dictionary is a great place to include other useful or transient information, such as the previous temperature value, the rate the temperature is changing, and so on. Then again, in many notifications the only interesting bit of information *is* the sender.

The notification name and sender are required. The userInfo dictionary is optional, or can be empty. There are three methods for posting notifications:

- `- (void)postNotificationName:(NSString*)name object:(id)sender`

- `- (void)postNotificationName:(NSString*)name object:(id)sender userInfo:(NSDictionary*)info`

- `- (void)postNotification:(NSNotification*)notification`

The first two messages construct a new NSNotification object from the name, sender, and optional dictionary. The last message accepts a pre-assembled NSNotification object and posts it. Note that while the object parameter is required, there's no rule that says it *must* be the object sending the notification. You're welcome to post notifications on behalf of other objects.

Notifications are delivered synchronously to all observers in the same thread before the `-postNotification…` message returns. It's possible to send notifications asynchronously using an NSNotificationQueue, described in the "Notification Queuing" section later in the chapter.

Being a Discriminating Observer

The real power of notifications is in the flexible ways an observer can register to receive them. To register to receive notifications, send the NSNotificationCenter an `-addObserver:selector:name:object:` message. The four parameters define what notifications it will receive and how it will receive them:

- The `observer` and `selector` parameters define the object that will receive the notifications and the Objective-C message that will be sent to it. The method must be compatible with `-(void)notificationMessage:(NSNotification*)notification`. While the observer parameter is typically `self`, you are free to register other objects.

- The `name` parameter is the name of the desired notification.

- The `object` parameter is the desired provider.

The selector parameter allows the observer to choose the message it will receive when the notification is sent. Your observer can send multiple notifications to a single method, or route the same notification from different sources to different methods.

One or both of the name and object parameters can be nil. When omitted, they act as wildcards, accepting any notification that matches the other criteria. Table 18-1 lists the combinations of name and object values that can be specified by the observer.

Table 18-1. *Observer Notification Criteria*

Name	Object	Notifications
@"name"	object	Receive notifications posted by object with the name @"name".
@"name"	nil	Receive all notifications with the name @"name" from *any* object.
nil	object	Receive *all* notifications posted by object.
nil	nil	Receive all notifications posted to this notification center.

The second form is the most common. The observer will receive all notifications with the given name posted by any object. The observer doesn't have to know what that object is, nor does it need a reference to the object to register. It only needs to know the name of the notification.

Here are two practical examples, both using notifications to manage an auxiliary window.

- Your application implements a persistent "inspector" palette window that always displays information about the front document window. The palette window object will register to receive NSWindowDidBecomeMainNotification notifications from any object (nil). Whenever a document window becomes active, it receives a notification and updates its display. The window that became active is included in the notification.

- Your application implements an "inspector" palette window that's attached to a specific window. The palette window object will register to receive NSWindowDidBecomeMainNotification and NSWindowDidResignMainNotification notifications from the specific document window object. The palette will be notified whenever that specific window becomes, or ceases to be, active. The palette window uses these events to automatically show or hide itself.

An observer can register to receive notifications as many times as it wants for multiple notification names, different providers, or some combination of the two. If the observer registers for the same notification in different ways, it may receive a single notification multiple times. The order is unpredictable.

Removing an Observer

Observers can cancel a previous registration by sending a -removeObserver: or -removeObserver: name:object: message to the notification center. The observer parameter is required, but the name and object parameters are both optional and either may be nil. The notification center revokes the subscription for all notifications that match the criteria, as listed in Table 18-2.

Table 18-2. Remove Observer Criteria

Name	Object	Registration Effect
nil	nil	Cancels all registrations for the observer. Same as -removeObserver:
@"name"	nil	Cancels all registrations for notifications with the name @"name"
nil	object	Cancels all registrations for notifications posted by object
@"name"	object	Cancels the registration for notifications with the name @"name" sent by object

In the second palette window example above, the observer has registered to receive two specific notifications, both from a specific provider. The message [notificationCenter -removeObserver:self name:nil object:paletteWindow] will remove both registrations, since both specify the same provider. However, the message [notificationCenter -removeObserver:self name:NSWindowDidBecome↩ MainNotification object:nil] will remove only one registration.

In a garbage-collected memory environment, notification centers hold weak references to observers. Once your observer is forgotten and collected, it is effectively removed from its notification center. So you aren't required to send [[NSNotificationCenter defaultCenter] removeObserver:self] before your object can be collected. However, if there's an obvious point at which your object should stop receiving notifications, removing it from the notification center is appropriate and desirable.

Notification Queuing

An NSNotificationQueue object manages a queue of yet-to-be delivered notifications. An NSNotificationQueue object, or just a *notification queue*, allows you to turn a synchronous notification center into an asynchronous notification service. Notifications are posted to a notification queue that will, at some future time, pass them on to its notification center for delivery.

Each notification queue is attached to an existing notification center. It does not change the behavior of the notification center. A notification queue places notifications in a buffer, then uses the current run loop to later dequeue and post them to its notification center. There is a default notification queue for each thread, and you can create additional ones if you like. You can create multiple queues that share a single notification center; remember that from the perspective of a notification center, a queue is just another source of notifications.

Notification queues have several useful features:

- Notifications in a queue can be delivered with varying degrees of urgency.
- Similar notifications can be coalesced, so that observers only receive a single notification if several were generated before they could be delivered.
- Undelivered notifications can be removed from the queue.

The process of queuing, coalescing, and removing notifications from a queue is described in the following sections.

■**Caution** Notification queues require a running run loop to function. If your thread isn't using a run loop, you can't use that thread's notification queue.

Queuing a Notification

Queuing a notification isn't that much different than posting a notification directly to a notification center. First, you must provide the queue with an NSNotification object—there are no convenience methods that create one for you. Second, you must specify its urgency, called its *posting style*, and optionally how it should be coalesced with similar notifications already in the queue. Coalescing is described in the next section.

To change the Thermometer class in Listing 18-1 to use a notification queue instead of a notification center, replace the -setTemperature: method with the code in Listing 18-3.

Listing 18-3. *Queued Temperature Notifications*

```
- (void)setTemperature:(float)newTemp
{
    if (temperature!=newTemp) {
        temperature = newTemp;
        NSNumber *tempValue = [NSNumber numberWithFloat:temperature];
        NSDictionary *info = [NSDictionary dictionaryWithObject:tempValue
                                                forKey:@"Temperature"];
        NSNotification *n = [NSNotification notificationWithName:TempDidChange
                                                object:self
                                                userInfo:info];
        [[NSNotificationQueue defaultQueue] enqueueNotification:n
                                                postingStyle:NSPostASAP];
    }
}
```

A notification object is created and placed in the queue. It will be pulled off the queue by the run loop at the next opportunity and posted to the default notification center. There are three possible posting styles, listed in Table 18-3.

Table 18-3. *Notification Queue Posting Styles*

Style	Description
NSPostASAP	The notification will be delivered by the run loop at its next opportunity, along with other regular run loop events. This is the typical posting style.
NSPostWhenIdle	The notification will be left in the queue until the run loop is idle. That is, the run loop has no other events waiting to be dispatched immediately.
NSPostNow	Delivers the notification synchronously. This is identical to posting the notification directly to the notification center, except that the queue may perform notification coalescing first.

The Thermometer class now queues the notification to be delivered asynchronously at some point in the future. In an asynchronous design, it is even more important that the provider include relevant information—like the current temperature value—in the userInfo dictionary of the notification. When the notification arrives, the Thermometer's state may be different than it was when it sent the notification.

Multiple notifications pushed with the same posting style will be delivered in the order they were queued.

Coalescing Notifications

When you queue a notification, you can optionally specify a coalescing mask and a run loop mode. The coalescing mask determines how the notification is matched against similar notifications already in the queue. The matching criteria are the same used to request notifications: the notification must match the name, the sender, or both, of any currently queued notifications. The criteria selection is formed by logically ORing one or both NSNotificationCoalescingOnName or NSNotificationCoalescingOnSender. If the notification matches other notifications in the queue, those notifications are removed and the new notification replaces them. Again, we modify the Thermometer class by replacing the -enqueueNotification:postingStyle: message with the code in Listing 18-4.

Listing 18-4. Coalesced Temperature Notifications

```
[[NSNotificationQueue defaultQueue] enqueueNotification:n
    postingStyle:NSPostWhenIdle
    coalesceMask:(NSNotificationCoalescingOnName|NSNotificationCoalescingOnSender)
        forModes:nil];
```

Now temperature change events are pushed onto the queue, only to be delivered to their observers when the run loop is idle. If a second or third temperature change notification from the same Thermometer object is posted before the first is delivered, the earlier ones are discarded. Eventually, only the last posted notification is sent to the observers.

The forModes: parameter lets you specify the run loop modes that the notification will be delivered in. Normally this is nil or NSDefaultRunLoopMode. Use this if you want notifications to be delivered in a particular mode, like only when the run loop is processing events for a modal dialog. See the "Run Loops" section of the Chapter 15 for more about run loop modes. You can pass the NSNotificationNoCoalescing constant if you want to specify a run loop mode, but no coalescing.

Dequeuing Notifications

If you should later change your mind about a notification, it can be removed form the queue if it hasn't yet been delivered. Send the notification queue a -dequeueNotificationsMatching:coalesceMask: message with the notification you want to remove and the constant NSNotificationNoCoalescing. If instead you pass a combination of the coalescing masks described in the "Coalescing Notifications" section, any other notifications that would be coalesced with that notification will also be removed.

Distributed Notifications

Distributed notifications have the ability to send notifications to objects in other processes. They are very similar to regular notifications, with three important differences:

- The notifications are sent to all processes.
- Notifications can only include property-list values.
- Notifications are posted and received asynchronously.

The first feature is what makes distributed notifications so powerful. A single -postNotification… message is all that's required to communicate between objects in separate processes, making distributed notifications by far the easiest inter-process communications service available. While the objects can be in different processes, they don't have to be; distributed notifications will be delivered to any local observers as well.

The program in Listing 18-5 can be entertaining. It registers to receive all distributed notifications and logs them. Build it as a command-line tool, run it, and then go about using your system. Or use it to test sending notifications from your application. Kill the process to stop it.

Listing 18-5. *Distributed Notifications Monitor*

```
#import <Foundation/Foundation.h>
#import <AppKit/NSWorkspace.h>

@interface DistributedNotificationListener : NSObject

- (void)dumpNotification:(NSNotification*)notification;

@end

@implementation DistributedNotificationListener

- (void)dumpNotification:(NSNotification*)notification
{
    NSString*       message = [notification name];
    id              object = [notification object];
    NSDictionary*   info = [notification userInfo];
    if (info!=nil) {
        NSLog(@"%@ from %@ with %@",message,object,info);
    }
    else {
        if (object!=nil)
            NSLog(@"%@ from %@",message,object);
        else
            NSLog(@"%@",message);
    }
}

@end

int main (int argc, const char * argv[])
{
    DistributedNotificationListener *listener;
    NSDistributedNotificationCenter *center;
```

```
    listener = [DistributedNotificationListener new];
    center = [NSDistributedNotificationCenter defaultCenter];
    [center addObserver:listener
                selector:@selector(dumpNotification:)
                    name:nil
                  object:nil];

    [[NSRunLoop currentRunLoop] run];
    // This never returns: kill the process to stop the program

    return 0;
}
```

To use distributed notifications, you need to be aware of some of its limitations and complications, described in the next few sections.

Distributed Notifications Center

To post or observe distributed notifications, your objects must interact with the singleton NSDistributedNotificationCenter created for each process. You obtain it with [NSDistributed⏎ NotificationCenter defaultCenter]. The framework may define other distributed notification centers in the future, but for now there's only one. You cannot create your own distributed notification centers. If you need a more sophisticated inter-process communications path, consider distributed objects, described in Chapter 13.

Distributed notification centers exchange messages using Mach (kernel) ports. The security model of Mac OS X organizes Mach ports into a hierarchy of bootstrap namespaces. Posted notifications will be broadcast to all of the processes in your account's local and parent namespaces, but not to sister namespaces created by other users.

Property List Values

The information in a distributed notification is serialized (see the "Objective-C Serialization" section of Chapter 12). This restricts the objects passed in the object and userInfo parameters to property-list values—basically array, dictionary, string, number, and date objects. The object parameter in a distributed notification center is used exactly the same way it is in a regular notification center, except it's just a string instead of a pointer to the provider object. Use a descriptive value like @"com.apress.learnobjc.DemoProvider" to identify the sender or group notifications.

Asynchronous Notification Delivery

Similar to NSNotificationQueue, distributed notifications are queued, optionally coalesced, and delivered asynchronously. Distributed notifications are (as of Mac OS X 10.3) always delivered on the main run loop. The primary difference between notification queues and distributed notifications is that the observer, not the provider, determines how notifications are queued and coalesced.

An NSDistributedNotificationCenter operates in one of two modes: suspended or not. When not suspended, notifications are delivered as they are posted. When suspended, notifications are discarded, coalesced, buffered, or delivered depending on the suspensionBehavior: mode requested by the observer. The four possible modes are listed in Table 18-4.

Table 18-4. *Suspended Notification Center Observer Modes*

Mode	Description
NSNotificationSuspensionBehaviorDrop	Notifications are discarded.
NSNotificationSuspensionBehaviorCoalesce	Similar notifications are coalesced and saved. This is the default.
NSNotificationSuspensionBehaviorHold	Notifications are saved, up to the buffer limit of the notification center.
NSNotificationSuspensionBehaviorDeliverImmediately	Notifications are delivered anyway, ignoring the suspended state of the distributed notification center.

The observer requests a suspension mode using the `-addObserver:selector:name:↵object:suspensionBehavior:` message. The regular `-addObserver:selector:name:object:` message registers the observer in the NSNotificationSuspensionBehaviorCoalesce mode.

A provider can force a notification to be delivered by posting it with the `-postNotificationName:object:userInfo:deliverImmediately:` message, passing `YES` in the `deliverImmediately:` parameter. This ignores the suspended state and behavior modes and delivers the notification to all observers.

Suspending a Distributed Notification Center

A distributed notification center is suspended or reactivated with the `-setSuspended:` message. When it's reactivated, any buffered notifications are delivered immediately.

The distributed notification center in an AppKit (GUI framework) application is automatically suspended whenever the application becomes inactive—that is, when it is no longer the front application. When the application becomes active again, it is automatically unsuspended. You should not interfere with this; use the `NSNotificationSuspensionBehaviorDeliverImmediately` or `deliverImmediately:` options to deliver notifications to observers in suspended applications. Daemons or command-line tools may suspend or activate their distributed notification centers as they see fit.

Summary

Notifications provide a flexible way for disparate objects to communicate with one another. Observers can register to receive specific notifications or a broad range of notifications. Observers can register to receive notifications from objects they know nothing about. Provider and observer management is handled for your objects by the notification center.

Notifications can also be pushed onto queues to be delivered asynchronously, or posted to a distributed notification center to be exchanged between processes. Simple load balancing can be accomplished by coalescing redundant notifications.

CHAPTER 19

■ ■ ■

Observer Pattern

The observer pattern creates a one-to-many, unidirectional relationship between a source object and a set of observers. The observers receive a notification message whenever a property of the source object changes. The observers can use this information to stay in synchronization with the observed object or perform additional tasks.

Is it just me, or does that sound exactly like the provider/subscriber pattern from the last chapter? At this level of abstraction, the provider/subscriber and observer patterns are extremely similar. In Java, both would be implemented using listener interfaces, objects, and management as was illustrated in Chapter 18. But the observer and provider/subscriber patterns are different, as outlined in Table 19-1.

Table 19-1. Differences Between Provider/Subscriber and Observer Patterns

Provider/Subscriber Pattern	Observer Pattern
The provider/subscriber pattern is centered on notifications. Notification objects can contain arbitrary information and be defined for any purpose.	The observer pattern concerns itself with *specific* properties of an object. An observer observes *a* property of another object and is notified when *that* property changes. The only information contained in the notification is the object and the details of the change.
A provider object actively participates in the provider/subscriber design pattern. It explicitly defines the notifications that it will send and when.	An observed object is typically passive. It doesn't define what properties can be observed nor is it required to perform any action when they change; the framework generates notifications on its behalf.
A provider must implement code to post notifications.	An observed object doesn't have to implement any code to be observed. You may choose to implement custom notification code if the class expects to be observed and has non-trivial properties or relationships.
Notifications are posted to notification centers.	Observed property notifications are sent directly from the source object to its observers.

Objective-C provides a very specific technology for implementing the observer pattern called Key-Value Observing (KVO). It's an important technology to understand, because it's an integral component in the Model-View-Controller pattern that permeates the user interface framework. Because of the very unique capabilities of Key-Value Observing, there are no Java examples in this chapter. They would, essentially, be identical in nature to the Java examples in Chapter 18.

This chapter describes the basic principles of the observer pattern and the Key-Value Observing technology. You should read at least that much to gain an appreciation for KVO. Later sections explain how to use KVO and add KVO support for non-trivial properties. Key-Value Observing uses Key-Value Coding (KVC). If that doesn't sound familiar, you may want to peek at the "Key-Value Coding" section of Chapter 10 for a quick refresher.

Key-Value Observing at Work

Key-Value Observing works by notifying an object, the observer, whenever a specific property of another object, the observed object, changes. The relationship is created using a single -addObserver:… message sent to the object that will be observed. Once established, the observer object will receive a notification message every time that property of the observed object changes. Listing 19-1 shows a simple example of Key-Value Observing at work. The classes are first, followed by the executed code, and finally the program's output.

Listing 19-1. *Example of Key-Value Observing*

```
@interface Chameleon : NSObject {
    NSColor *color;
}

@property (assign) NSColor *color;

@end


@implementation Chameleon

- (NSColor*)color
{
    return color;
}

- (void)setColor:(NSColor*)newColor
{
    color = newColor;
}

@end



@interface Watcher : NSObject

@end

@implementation Watcher
```

```
- (void)observeValueForKeyPath:(NSString*)keyPath
                      ofObject:(id)object
                        change:(NSDictionary*)change
                       context:(void*)context
{
    NSLog(@"Property '%@' of object '%@' changed: %@",keyPath,object,change);
}

@end

...

Chameleon *chameleon = [Chameleon new];
Watcher *watcher = [Watcher new];

[chameleon addObserver:watcher
           forKeyPath:@"color"
               options:NSKeyValueObservingOptionNew
               context:NULL];

chameleon.color = [NSColor greenColor];

Output:
Property 'color' of object '<Chameleon: 0x139330>' changed: {
    kind = 1;
    new = NSCalibratedRGBColorSpace 0 1 0 1;
}
```

Here's what happens in Listing 19-1:

1. The Chameleon class implements a property. There's nothing special about the property, other than it conforms to the Key-Value Coding guidelines.

2. The Watcher class implements an -observeValueForKeyPath:ofObject:change:context: method. This makes it eligible to be a key-value observer.

3. The watcher object registers to be an observer of the chameleon object's color property.

4. When the chameleon object's color property changes, the watcher object receives a notification that tells it the property (key path) that changed and the new value.

That's Key-Value Observing in a nutshell. Any object that implements an -observeValueForKeyPath:ofObject:change:context: method can register to observe almost any property of another object. Whenever the property changes, the observer receives a notification.

KEY-VALUE OBSERVING MAGIC

If you're scratching your head wondering how the Key-Value Observing framework knew that the Chameleon object received a -setColor: message, it was done with a little bit of magic called *isa swizzling*. It's described in a bit more detail in Chapter 26.

KVO exploits the dynamic nature of Objective-C objects. When the watcher requests to observe the Chameleon object, the KVO framework spontaneously creates a new Objective-C subclass of Chameleon, overrides its -setColor: method, and changes the class of the object to the new subclass. When the Chameleon object later receives a -setColor: message, the method of the synthetic subclass gets invoked. The subclass method calls [super setColor:newColor] and then sends the requested property change notifications to its observers. It's fast, effective, and completely transparent to the observed object.

KVO only overrides the setter methods of the properties being observed, so there is no performance penalty for other methods. If you later remove all the observers of an object, KVO will change the object back to its original class.

Continuing the comparison between the provider/subscriber and observer patterns, the Thermometer and TemperatureMonitor examples presented in Chapter 18 could have easily been implemented using Key-Value Observing, with these caveats:

- The Thermometer object could not choose its audience of observers based on what notification center it posts to.
- A temperature change notification wouldn't contain any additional information about the change beyond the new, and possibly old, temperature values.
- An observer couldn't register to receive notifications from an unknown object.
- Temperature change notifications could not be queued for asynchronous delivery or coalesced.
- Change notifications could only be sent to objects in the same process.

The most important feature of Key-Value Observing is that it doesn't (typically) require any programming support on the part of the observed object. For example, the NSProgressIndicator class defines a KVC-compliant indeterminate property. It's a simple, read-only, BOOL property value that is either set or not. If you had a user interface object that needed to change its appearance based on whether the progress indicator was indeterminate, your object could observe the indeterminate property of the view object and update itself whenever it changed. The beautiful part is that NSProgressIndicator was never designed to notify observers when its indeterminate property changes, but with KVO it can still participate in the observer design pattern.

■**Note** Key-Value Observing will also notice property changes made using Key-Value Coding, as in [chameleon setValue:[NSColor greenColor] forKey:@"color"], as described in the Key-Value Coding section of Chapter 10. KVO cannot, however, observe changes made to properties through direct assignment, as in chameleon->color=[NSColor greenColor]. If you use direct assignment and want your class to be compatible with Key-Value Observing, you will need to implement manual KVO notifications, explained later in this chapter.

That's the basics of Key-Value Observing. The rest of this chapter delves into some of the options available to observers, and then gets into the more complex issues of manually implementing KVO and supporting interrelated and non-trivial properties.

Registering a Key-Value Observer

When an observer object registers to observe another object's property, five pieces of information are required:

- The source object
- The observer
- The key-value path of the source object's property
- A set of observer options.
- An optional context value.

The key-value path of the property to observe is more flexible than might be obvious at first. The key path parameter accepts a Key-Value Coding path, as described in the "Key-Value Coding" section of Chapter 10. The path can describe properties of properties, which subtly affords KVO a great deal of flexibility and power. Consider the code in Listing 19-2, which extends the code in Listing 19-1.

Listing 19-2. *Observing Complex Key-Value Coding Paths*

```
#import "Chameleon.h"

@interface ReptileZoo : NSObject {
    Chameleon *chameleon;
}

@property (assign) Chameleon *chameleon;

@end

@implementation ReptileZoo

@synthesize chameleon;

@end

…

ReptileZoo *zoo = [ReptileZoo new];
Chameleon *chameleon1 = [Chameleon new];
Chameleon *chameleon2 = [Chameleon new];
Watcher *watcher = [Watcher new];

chameleon1.color = [NSColor blueColor];
chameleon2.color = [NSColor redColor];
```

```
zoo.chameleon = chameleon1;
[zoo addObserver:watcher
     forKeyPath:@"chameleon.color"
        options:NSKeyValueObservingOptionNew
        context:NULL];

chameleon1.color = [NSColor greenColor];
zoo.chameleon = chameleon2;

Output:
Property 'chameleon.color' of object '<ReptileZoo: 0x13a0c0>' changed: {
    kind = 1;
    new = NSCalibratedRGBColorSpace 0 1 0 1;
}
Property 'chameleon.color' of object '<ReptileZoo: 0x13a0c0>' changed: {
    kind = 1;
    new = NSCalibratedRGBColorSpace 1 0 0 1;
}
```

The watcher object in Listing 19-2 is set to watch the color property of the chameleon property of the zoo object. It received two property change notifications. The first was because the color property of zoo's current chameleon property was set directly. The second notification occurred because the chameleon property was replaced with a different object, indirectly changing the color of zoo's chameleon property. In both cases, the observer is notified of the complete path that was affected and its new value.

When registering to receive property change notifications, the notification includes some information about the change in a *change dictionary*. There are four options, chosen by logically ORing any of the constants in Table 19-2 together, that control what information is included in the change dictionary and the order notifications that are sent. If your observer isn't interested in any of these options, pass 0 in the options: parameter.

Table 19-2. *Key-Value Observer Options*

KVO Option	Effect
NSKeyValueObservingOptionNew	Notification change dictionary includes the new value.
NSKeyValueObservingOptionOld	Notification change dictionary includes the previous value.
NSKeyValueObservingOptionInitial	A notification is sent immediately with the current value (before -addObserver:… returns).
NSKeyValueObservingOptionPrior	Each change sends two notifications: a pre-change notification, sent before the value is changed, and a regular notification afterwards. The pre-change notification will contain an NSKeyValueChangeNotificationIsPriorKey key in its change dictionary.

The final parameter is an optional context value. It's a C pointer that isn't managed by the garbage collection system, so if you use it to pass an object pointer, make sure the object isn't collected prematurely. Beyond that restriction, it can contain any compatible value and will be passed back to the observer's `-observeValueForKeyPath:ofObject:change:context:` method in all notifications triggered by that registration.

Processing Key-Value Change Notifications

Once registered, your object will begin to receive key-value observer change notifications in the form of `-observeValueForKeyPath:ofObject:change:context:` messages. The message includes four parameters:

- The key-value path of the property being observed

- The source object

- A `change:` parameter containing an immutable dictionary that describes the change

- A `context:` parameter containing the `context:` value passed to `-addObserver:forKeyPath:options:context:` when the observer registered

If your object has registered to observe more than one property, use the key-value path parameter, the source object pointer, or the context value to case out the property and deal with each appropriately.

The change dictionary contains information about the change. Its contents depend on the type of the property, the nature of the change, and what information you requested to be included, as determined by the options in Table 19-2. The possible dictionary keys and a description of each value are listed in Table 19-3.

Table 19-3. *Change Notification Dictionary Keys*

Key	Value	Description
NSKeyValueChange↵ KindKey	NSKeyValueChangeSetting, NSKeyValueChangeInsertion, NSKeyValueChangeRemoval, or NSKeyValueChangeReplacement	Describes how the property changed. If the property is a simple property, like an integer or an object, this value will be NSKeyValueChangeSetting. The other three values describe changes to a collection property.
NSKeyValueChange↵ NewKey	Value object	Contains the new property value, or an array of inserted or replaced values. Only included if the NSKeyValueObservingOptionNew option was requested.
NSKeyValueChange↵ OldKey	Value object	The previous property value, or an array of removed or replaced values. Only included if the NSKeyValueObservingOptionOld option was requested.

| NSKeyValueChange↵ NotificationIsPriorKey | YES | Included if this is a pre-change notification requested with the NSKeyValueObservingOptionPrior observing option. |
| NSKeyValueChange↵ IndexesKey | NSIndexSet | For changes to an array collection property, this NSIndexSet value contains the indexes that were affected by the insert, removal, or replacement. |

When observing changes to a property that's a primitive value or object pointer, the change kind is always NSKeyValueChangeSetting and the dictionary may optionally include the old and new values.

When the observed property is a to-many object property, the change information is a little more complex. A change is described as either an insertion, a removal, or a replacement of one or more objects in the collection. The NSKeyValueChangeIndexesKey value lists the indexes in the collection that were affected by the change. The NSKeyValueChangeNewKey and NSKeyValueChangeOldKey values contain a compact array of the objects inserted, removed, or replaced (as appropriate) at the corresponding indexes in the NSKeyValueChangeIndexesKey set. For example, if two objects were removed from a property at indexes 3 and 5, the NSKeyValueChangeIndexesKey would contain the set { 3, 5 }, the NSKeyValueChangeOldKey would contain the object removed at index 3 at index 0 and the object removed at index 5 at index 1, and the NSKeyValueChangeNewKey value would be empty, since no new objects were added.

■**Note** Observing a to-many property requires that the observed object implement the mutable array property accessory methods described in the "Designing KVC-Compliant Classes" section of Chapter 10. The regular NSMutableArray class does *not* implement these methods. If your object has an NSMutableArray *array property, and you observe the @"array" property of that object, your observer will be notified when the array object is set, but not when objects are added or removed from that array. Classes like NSArrayController do implement this protocol and are designed to be observable.

Unregistering an Observer

When your observer wants to stop receiving property change notifications, send the observed object a -removeObserver:forKeyPath: message with the same key-value path used when the observer was added.

Objects maintain weak references to their observers, so it isn't necessary to remove the observer before the observer can be collected. However, if there's a logical point in which an observer no longer needs to receive property change notifications, it should remove itself. On the other hand, just being an observer of an object will not keep the observer from being collected; the observer will need to have at least one strong reference.

Making Your Classes KVO Compliant

When an object property is *Key-Value Observing compliant*, it means the property can be reliably observed using Key-Value Observing. To be KVO compliant, the property of an object must

- Be Key-Value Coding compliant

- Send Key-Value Observing notifications when it is set

If you implement standard getter and setter methods for your property and change the property by sending setter messages, your property will be 100 percent KVO compliant.

There are, however, some circumstances where your property won't be KVO compliant. These situations require that you add KVO support code directly to your class—assuming that you want to make the property observable. Don't worry; the code isn't complex. What code you add, where, and under what circumstances is described in the next few sections. Here are the primary reasons why a property would *not* be KVO compliant:

- The property is set using direct assignment (i.e., `object->property=1`) outside its setter method.

- The property is a combination of other properties. A read-only `fullName` property that's generated by concatenating the `firstName` and `lastName` properties is the canonical example.

- The property changes as a consequence of some other state change. For example, an `isFinished` property that's defined as `return ([lock condition]!=RUNNING)`.

Direct assignment circumvents KVO's ability to intercept the setter methods of the object and inject the prerequisite notifications. To fix this, send KVO notifications manually or rewrite the code to use the property's setter method when changing its value.

Dependent properties can be made KVO compliant by communicating the dependencies to the Key-Value Observing framework. KVO provides special methods so you can describe the dependent keys in your class. Once implemented, KVO will know that changing either of the `firstName` or `lastName` properties also changes the `fullName` property, and it will send all of the expected notifications.

Properties that spontaneously change as a result of some other state change will usually require a solution that is some combination of manual KVO notifications or dependent properties.

In addition to simply being a well-behaved KVO participant, there are other reasons why you might want to add KVO support code directly to your class. One reason is performance. Key-Value Observing notifications are a bit "dumb." Whenever the setter method is called, KVO notifies its observers—even if the new value is the same as the old one. If this causes performance or recursion problems, you can implement your own KVO notifications that are only sent when you deem appropriate.

And there will also, undoubtedly, arise a situation not described above that can only be resolved by implementing your own KVO support. These special cases involve not only adding manual KVO notification code to your class, but you may also need to tell the KVO framework *not* to perform its normal services, or else one will end up stepping on the other. Finally, it should be noted that these solutions frequently overlap; there's often more than one way to solve a particular KVO problem. Read through the next few sections before deciding on the solution that's best for your situation.

Sending Manual KVO Notifications

Whenever an observable property is changed, you need to ensure that the correct KVO notification messages are sent. In a KVC-compliant setter method, this happens automatically. You may need to manually send KVO notifications when

- The property is read-only and has no setter method.

- The property is set using a direct assignment, outside the property's setter method.

- The property is a synthesized value, calculated from other property values.

The most direct approach is to trigger the required notifications manually by sending -[NSObject willChangeValueForKey:] and -[NSObject didChangeValueForKey:] messages before and after the code that might modify the property. These messages inform the KVO framework that something is about to happen which may cause the property to change. The KVO framework takes care of sending the appropriate notifications to any observers. Listing 19-3 demonstrates this in a simple Budget class.

Listing 19-3. *Triggering KVO Notifications Manually*

```
@interface Budget : NSObject {
    double budget;
    double plannedExpense;
}

@property double budget;
@property (readonly) double plannedExpense;

- (void)addExpenditure:(double)amount;

@end

@implementation Budget

@synthesize budget, plannedExpense;

- (void)addExpenditure:(double)amount
{
    [self willChangeValueForKey:@"plannedExpense"];
    plannedExpense += amount;
    [self didChangeValueForKey:@"plannedExpense"];
}

@end
```

The Budget class has a plannedExpense property that's stored in a variable. It's a readonly property with no setter method. The -addExpenditure: method changes the property when it adds an amount to it. The -willChangeValueForKey: and -didChangeValueForKey: messages that bracket the change inform the Key-Value Observing framework of the change, and allow it to send the property notifications to the observers.

■**Caution** Each -willChangeValueForKey: message for a given key must be balanced with a corresponding -didChangeValueForKey: message for that same key.

If the -addExpenditure: method modified multiple properties, it would send one pair of -willChangeValueForKey:/-didChangeValueForKey: messages for each property. These can be nested: the code could send three -willChange… messages, change three properties, and then send three -didChange… messages.

If the property being modified is a to-many array property, use the -willChange:valuesAtIndexes:forKey: and -didChange:valuesAtIndexes:forKey: messages instead.

Creating Property Dependencies

Another common problem is a property that implicitly changes when another property changes. This is called a *dependent property*. Adding a remainingBudget property to the Budget class creates a dependent property that would be affected by a change to either the budget or plannedExpense properties. The Key-Value Observing framework defines an informal protocol that lets your class describe its dependent properties. The modified Budget class is shown in Listing 19-4.

Listing 19-4. *Defining Dependent Properties*

```
@interface Budget : NSObject {
    double budget;
    double plannedExpense;
}

@property double budget;
@property (readonly) double plannedExpense;
@property (readonly) double remainingBudget;

- (void)addExpenditure:(double)amount;

@end

@implementation Budget

@synthesize budget, plannedExpense;

- (void)addExpenditure:(double)amount
{
    [self willChangeValueForKey:@"plannedExpense"];
    plannedExpense += amount;
    [self didChangeValueForKey:@"plannedExpense"];
}
```

```
+ (NSSet*)keyPathsForValuesAffectingRemainingBudget
{
    return [NSSet setWithObjects:@"budget", @"plannedExpense", nil];
}

- (double)remainingBudget
{
    // amount remaining or 0.0
    return MAX(0,budget-plannedExpense);
}

@end
```

For each observed property, the Key-Value Observing framework looks for a class method named +keyPathsForValuesAffecting*Property*; replace the "Property" part of the method name with the name of the dependent property. The method returns a set of property names that the property is dependent on. Whenever one of those other properties changes, KVO sends a change notification for the dependent property as well. Implement one class method for each dependent property.

Note It would be possible to accomplish the same solution using manual KVO notifications, as demonstrated in the previous section. You would modify -addExpenditure: to send an additional -willChangeValueForKey: and -didChangeValueForKey: messages for the @"remainingBudget" path, and then do the same in a handwritten -setBudget: method. The advantage of the dependent property protocol is that it doesn't require modifying the other property setters or adding more manual KVO notifications. This is particularly convenient in subclasses that define properties that are dependent on properties of its superclass. It also keeps the KVO code from cluttering up the implementation.

There are actually three ways of communicating dependent properties to the Key-Value Observing framework:

- Implement a per-property +keyPathsForValuesAffecting*Property* class method as demonstrated in Listing 19-4.

- Override the single +keyPathsForValuesAffectingValueForKey: class method and return the dependent set for the requested key. The base class implementation of this method uses the key-path to look for and invoke the method name implemented in option 1.

- At some point before any object of your class is observed—typically in your class's +initialization method—send a +setKeys:triggerChangeNotificationsForDependentKey: message for each dependent key implemented in your class.

Implement exactly one of these solutions for each dependent property. When implementing either of the first two solutions, don't forget to include any dependent keys defined by the superclass in the returned set.

The first two solutions are only applicable to simple (to-one) properties that are running on Mac OS X 10.5 or later. If you need to establish a to-many dependent property, or are targeting Mac OS X 10.4 or earlier, use the last solution. If you have a to-many dependent property and are targeting

Mac OS X 10.5 or later (where the +setKey:… method is deprecated), refer to the "Registering Dependent Keys" section of the *Key-Value Observing Programming Guide*[1] for a number of possible solutions.

Overriding Key-Value Observing

To implement manual KVO notifications in a KVC-compliant setter method, you must disable the normal change notifications that the Key-Value Observing framework will perform. Otherwise KVO and your code will both be sending notifications, resulting in either duplicate or out-of-order notifications.

One very prudent reason to do this is to optimize the setter method so it only notifies observers when the value actually changes. This can have performance advantages and solve recursive or circular update problems. In Listing 19-5, the budget property setter of the class is reimplemented so it only sends KVO notifications when the budget value actually changes.

Listing 19-5. Optimizing KVO Notifications

```
@implementation Budget

+ (BOOL)automaticallyNotifiesObserversForKey:(NSString*)key
{
    if ([key isEqualToString:@"budget"])
        return NO;

    return [super automaticallyNotifiesObserversForKey:key];
}

- (double)budget
{
    return budget;
}

- (void)setBudget:(double)value
{
    if (budget!=value) {
        [self willChangeValueForKey:@"budget"];
        budget = value;
        [self didChangeValueForKey:@"budget"];
    }
}

...
```

To prevent the KVO framework from overriding the -setBudget: method and sending its own notifications, the +automaticallyNotifiesObserversForKey: class method is overridden. This method

---

[1] Apple, Inc., *Key-Value Observing Programming Guide*, http://developer.apple.com/documentation/ Cocoa/Conceptual/KeyValueObserving/, 2009.

should return NO for observable properties that generate their own notifications. The base class implementation returns YES for all keys.

The -setBudget: method is then rewritten to send KVO notifications only when the new budget value is different than the previous value. This kind of optimization can ripple out. For example, now that the remainingBudget property is dependent on the budget property, not sending a superfluous budget notification actually avoids two superfluous notifications.

Optimizing Key-Value Observing

In addition to eliminating redundant notifications, as described in the previous section, there's another way that your object can help the Key-Value Observing framework. For objects that are heavily observed, you can optimize KVO performance by providing a place to store observation information about your object. While KVO can mutate the class of your object using isa swizzling, it can't change its structure or store any new values in it. Instead, KVO keeps an object's observation information in a global collection that must be consulted every time a property is changed.

You can reduce this overhead by providing KVO a void *observationInfo property, as shown in Listing 19-6. The Key-Value Observing framework will use this property to store your object's observation information directly in the object.

Listing 19-6. Providing Local Key-Value Observing Information Storage

```
@interface KVOFriendly : NSObject {
    @private
    void* observationInfo;
}

@property (assign) void *observationInfo;

@end

@implementation KVOFriendly

@synthesize observationInfo;

@end
```

Summary

Although similar in concept to the provider/subscriber pattern, the observer pattern provides a significantly different solution set. Its primary advantage is that observation and notifications are largely transparent to the observed object, and it typically doesn't need to be designed in advance to provide the desired notifications. While basic properties are Key-Value Observing compliant automatically, some properties may require some additional code to fully support KVO.

CHAPTER 20

■ ■ ■

Model-View-Controller Pattern

The Model-View-Controller design pattern is one of the most important design patterns in computer science. Whereas most patterns address specific problems, Model-View-Controller (MVC) describes the architecture of a system of objects. It can be applied to isolated subsystems or entire applications. The Model-View-Controller design pattern is also less clearly defined than many other patterns, leaving a lot of latitude for alternate implementations. It's more a philosophy than a recipe.

A clear understanding of MVC is critical to using Cocoa, because the entire Cocoa framework is designed around the Model-View-Controller design pattern (where applicable). Where Java adopts MVC for many tasks, Cocoa passionately embraces it. MVC is the soul of Cocoa. Designing with MVC will smooth your development, since so many of the framework objects are designed to integrate effortlessly with an MVC design.

Befitting a broad design pattern, this is an expansive chapter that touches on a wide range of classes and technologies. (It wouldn't be very useful if it merely described the MVC design pattern—something you're probably already familiar with, anyway). To be practical, each section not only describes design concepts but goes on to explore the classes, protocols, frameworks, and development tools that you'll use to implement those concepts. For example, this chapter begins with the basic MVC design principles, and then goes on to describe bindings (a technology used to implement MVC communications) and Interface Builder (a development tool used to connect MVC objects). The section on view objects explains the role of view objects, and then goes on to explain how to use pre-built view objects, how to create your own view objects, how those view objects draw themselves, and the basics of the Cocoa graphics environment. The sections on data model objects describe not only the conceptual role of data model objects, but some of the classes and development tools that can be used to create complex data models. In short, this is a really long chapter, so settle in and take your time. You should be comfortable with each concept before moving on to the next.

To help you put each piece into perspective, I've created a simple Cocoa application that plays Tic Tac Toe. It's a relatively small project that touches on most of the topics in this chapter, and will be used to illustrate many of them. I recommend that you download the project from the Source Code/Downloads section of http://www.apress.com so you can see how each concept fits into the whole. There is also a section on Interface Builder, a key Cocoa development tool, and how it supports the MVC design pattern. At the end of this chapter is a brief section that describes some noteworthy aspects of the project that aren't covered elsewhere.

Model-View-Controller sits atop a broad base of supporting technologies, at the apex of the design pyramid. To master MVC, you need a firm grasp of the technologies that support it. You should be familiar with, or review, the following before attempting to tackle MVC in Cocoa:

- Objective-C Messages (Chapter 6)

- Informal Protocols (Chapter 5)

- Delegates (Chapter 17)

- Key-Value Coding (Chapter 10)

- Key-Value Observing (Chapter 19)

Understanding Model-View-Controller

The Model-View-Controller design pattern is simply stated:

- Data model objects encapsulate information.

- View objects display information to the user.

- Controller objects implement actions.

- View objects observe data model objects and update their display whenever it changes.

- View objects gather user input and pass it to a controller object that performs the action.

The key to successfully implementing an MVC design is to pay close attention to the *role* of objects and the *communications* between those objects. The first three rules define the role of your objects.

- Data model objects store, encapsulate, and abstract your data. They should not contain methods or logic specific to making your application function. For example, a data model class should implement a method that serializes its data, but it should not implement the "Save As…" command. Even if the two functions are nearly identical, the code that deals with the abstract data transformation should be implemented in the data model object and the code that implements the user command should be implemented in the controller object.

- View objects display the information in the data model to the user. View class design runs from the extremely generic to the very specific; generic view classes are provided by the framework to display almost any kind of string, number, or image, while you are more likely to implement very specific view objects designed for your application. View objects also interact with the user and initiate actions by interpreting user-initiated events, such as mouse movement and keystrokes. It converts those events into actions that are passed to the controller object for execution. The event and resulting action are often very simple; clicking the mouse over a button object will send an action message to a controller. Complex gestures, like drag-and-drop, are more involved.

- Controller objects implement your application's actions. Actions are usually initiated by view objects in response to user events.

The other aspect of the Model-View-Controller design is the communication between the data model, controller, and view objects. The fundamental communication paths are illustrated in Figure 20-1.

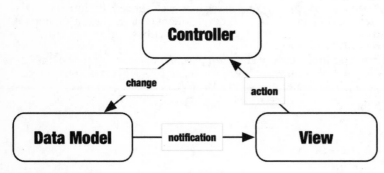

Figure 20-1. Fundamental MVC communications

When the user does something, like typing a keyboard shortcut, a view object interprets it and sends an action message to the controller object. The controller object performs the action, which often involves sending messages to the data model object. When the data model changes, it notifies its observers by sending messages to the view object, which updates the display.

MVC Variations

There's a lot of latitude to the basic MVC model. Roles can blend or use alternate communication paths. The next few sections describe the significant variants.

Combined Controller and Data Model

The controller and data model may be the same object, as shown in Figure 20-2. This is often the case when the data model is trivial. Technically, a single integer is a data model, but it would be a waste of your programming talent to create a data model class *just* to encapsulate one number. Instead, the value is stored in the controller and attached to a view object for display.

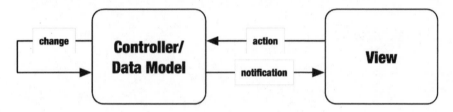

Figure 20-2. *Combined controller and data model*

This limits the modularity of your design, as described later in the chapter. But unless the data model and controller are inappropriately entangled, it should be easy to refactor your application into separate controller and data model classes in the future, without disrupting your design. The key is to keep the *concept* of the data model independent of your controller, even while they occupy the same object.

Mediating Controller

A popular variation of the Model-View-Controller design pattern is the mediated MVC pattern, as shown in Figure 20-3. This pattern appears repeatedly in the Cocoa framework; it's the pattern adopted by the NSController classes, described towards the end of this chapter.

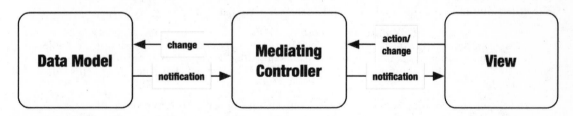

Figure 20-3. *Mediated Model-View-Controller design pattern*

In a mediated MVC design, the controller also acts as the data model for the view. It is a data model proxy. The mediating controller passes data model messages to the actual data model, and forwards any change notifications from the data model on to its observers.

This design is particularly well suited to database applications. The data model object encapsulates the raw data. It takes responsibility for fetching the data from a persistent store, caching it, and performing any alterations to it. The controller object performs it normal role, but also presents the data, *as it will appear in the application*, to the view objects. This might involve filtering, sorting, and transforming the data. How the data is sorted, the user's current selection in the table, and so on, are specific to the application, not the data. From the view object's perspective, the controller *is* the data model. The view displays the sorted, filtered, and transformed data presented to it by the controller, and has no direct knowledge of the underlying data model.

Direct View and Data Model Binding

Often, there's no "action" per se associated with a change to a displayed value. If the view object is displaying a simple value (a number, string, or Boolean), it can communicate changes directly to the data model object, as shown in Figure 20-4.

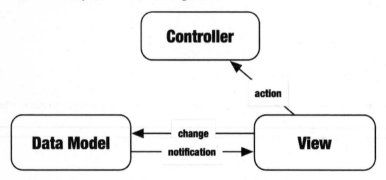

Figure 20-4. *Direct data model and view binding*

The relationship between the data model property and the view is described as a *binding*. The view object displays the value and updates its display whenever the value changes (via observing). If the user edits the displayed value, the view object communicates that to the data model by setting the new value directly. Bindings are described in more detail later in this chapter.

Other Variations

Some other common variations to the basic MVC design pattern are as follows:

- *View objects bound to controller properties*: It is often the case that view objects will be bound to property values of the controller object. For example, a controller might define data objects to hold a temporary transaction or the results of search. This isn't an appropriate property for the data model; it is appropriate for the controller, but from the view's perspective it's a data model.

- *Combined view and data model object*: A check box button maintains its current value (checked or unchecked) and is, in effect, its own data model. The controller may choose *not* to store the state of the check box, electing instead to query the state of the view object to learn its value. This isn't a recommended pattern, but it is quite commonly used.

The Advantages of MVC

So what's all the fuss about MVC? At first blush, it seems like MVC creates a lot of additional work for the programmer, taking what could be a single object and breaking it up into multiple objects with complex communications.. To create a custom button using MVC, for example, one would create a new cell subclass (see the Scaling section), override its drawing method, create a controller class, implement an action method, create instances of both classes, and attach them to an NSButton view object. If you think it would be simpler just to subclass NSButton and override its drawing and "mouse clicked" methods, you need to read this section.

In a very small set of circumstances, you'd be right—it would be simpler to just subclass NSButton. But most applications aren't that simple, or don't remain that simple. MVC is, in many respects, like object-oriented programming itself. It's a discipline that occasionally creates more work, but more often allows for the design of large, elegant, flexible, and sophisticated applications that are both comprehensible and well behaved.

The following sections highlight some of the significant advantages of employing the Model-View-Controller design pattern.

Modularity

The Model-View-Controller design pattern is an extension of the computer science principles of *separation of concern* and *encapsulation*. It encourages you to identify the roles that your application plays and compartmentalize those roles into distinct objects.

These principles improve your MVC design for all the same reasons they improve object-oriented programming in general. They localize interrelated functionality into containers with identifiable boundaries. Changes to a class tend to be localized. When the change affects other classes, it's easier to analyze how they will be affected since the interface to the changed class is well defined. They can later be subclassed, replaced, or reused with little or no impact on the rest of your design.

Flexibility

One of the greatest strengths of the Model-View-Controller design pattern is its flexibility. By separating the data model and controller concerns from the display view, the two can be mixed and matched at will.

MVC's most powerful feature is probably the ability to effortlessly replace view objects, or use multiple view objects, without changing the data model or controller. You probably use many applications that exploit this feature every day. Here are two examples.

Apple's iTunes application uses several different view objects to display the contents of your music and video library. There's a table list view, a browser, a thumbnail view, and a Cover Flow view. All four present the same information from the same data model, just in different ways. By separating the data model from the views, new views can be developed without making any changes to the data model or the other views. Even much of the controller logic, such as current song selection, drag and drop, the play song action, and getting info can all be implemented once and used interchangeably with any of the four views.

The Xcode application is a good example of a document-based MVC application with multiple views. A data model object represents the contents of a document (source file). Source code editing panes that appear in the Xcode environment are the view objects. You can open the same source document in multiple windows or panes and they will all display the same content. More amazingly, editing one pane updates all of the other panes instantly. This works because the data model and all of the views conform to the same MVC communication rules. When one of the view objects is edited, it sends those editing requests to its controller, which updates the data modal, which broadcasts the changes to all observers. Without writing any special code, multiple views of a single data model are kept in perfect synchronization.

Programming with well-designed MVC objects is like working with a giant Lego set. Any object (data model, controller, or view) is interchangeable with any functionally equivalent object. Substituting objects, or attaching multiple objects, does not disturb the rest of the design. The mantra of MVC is to create complex applications by interconnecting simple objects.

Reuse

Reuse is closely related to flexibility. By abstracting the functionality of your classes, you can reuse your objects in other applications or for other purposes. The most commonly reused objects are data model and view objects. The core Cocoa view objects (buttons, text fields, image viewers) are reused daily for thousands of different purposes, just by connecting them to different data model and controller objects.

Scaling

The Model-View-Controller design pattern reoccurs at different scales. If you take a close look at a Cocoa view object like NSButton, you'll actually discover a miniature MVC design at work. What you normally treat as a single view object (a button) is actually two or three objects:

- The NSButton object is an NSControl that implements the controller role in the MVC design. NSButton determines how the button behaves.

- The role of the view is handled by an NSButtonCell object, a subclass of NSCell. This object is responsible for drawing the button image and processing mouse and keyboard events.

- The NSButton object can maintain its own state (acting as the data model), or be bound to a separate data model object.

To customize the look of a button, you don't subclass NSButton. Instead, you create your own NSCell subclass that implements the look you want and attach that to a plain-vanilla NSButton instance. Just as iTunes can use alternate views to change the look of your music library without changing any of its functionality, you can change the look of a button without interfering with its behavior. Flexibility and reuse mean that your custom NSCell will be compatible with future versions of NSButton and could potentially be used with other NSControl subclasses as well.

By now, I hope you appreciate the advantages of using the Model-View-Controller design pattern. Now it's time for me to get off my soap box and get down to the details of how MVC is used in application design.

Bindings

So far I've discussed MVC communications in a generic way, but the Cocoa framework defines a very specific form of MVC communications called a *binding*. A binding defines a relationship between two properties in different objects. A binding forms a connection that *binds* one property of an observer object to a property of another object. A binding keeps the two properties synchronized. Cocoa provides a framework and an informal bindings communication protocol that does this for you. These can be any two objects, but the observer is invariably a view object and the observed property will be in a data model or controller object.

■**Note** As of this writing, the iPhone OS does not support the Cocoa bindings technology. If you're targeting the iPhone OS, you'll have to use Objective-C messages, actions, outlets, Key-Value Observing, notifications, or other techniques to implement your MVC communications. Actions are outlets are described in the "Interface Builder" section.

In practice, a view object displays the value of the property. Editing the value in the view sends messages, via the binding, to the data model to alter its value. Any change to the data model's value notifies the view. Bindings have the following attributes:

- Properties are identified using Key-Value paths. Both objects must implement Key-Value Coding–compliant properties.

- The observer object listens for changes to the property value using Key-Value Observing. The bound property must be KVO compliant.

- NSController objects are designed to work with bindings. Specifically, NSController objects can bind compound values such as sets and arrays. NSController also defines the concept of a *selection*, so you can bind a property to the selected value(s) of a compound property.

- A binding can specify when an edited value is committed and when changes to the bound property are updated.

- A binding can provide a default value to use when the bound property is nil.

- A binding can be filtered through a *value transformer* that converts a bound value to a form suitable for use by the observer, and vice versa. For example, a transformer might automatically convert between currencies or change centigrade to Fahrenheit.

Bindings can be created programmatically, but that's rare. Even more unusual is creating your own classes that actively participate in a binding; most of the classes that you'd ever want to bind to (the NSView objects provided by the Cocoa framework) and objects with complex bindable properties (subclasses of NSController) have already been implemented for you. Most of the time you establish a binding in Interface Builder from a library view object property to either a KVO-compliant property of any object or to a subclass of NSController—none of which involves any serious programming. You *might* want to create your own subclass of NSController or NSObjectController, but the base class is already a Cocoa bindings–compatible class, so you still won't get too involved in the mechanics of bindings. If you find you need explore these options, refer to the *Cocoa Bindings Programming Topics* guide.[1]

The vast majority of the time, you bind views to properties of your own objects and the only prerequisite is that they be Key-Value Observing compliant—which most properties are, or else they can easily be made KVO compliant with a small amount of work. See Chapter 19 if you need to make sure.

So far I've focused on viewing the value of a property, but bindings are useful for many other kinds of properties. A view object, like a check box control, has many properties: the button's title, the font of the title, the state of the check box, whether it's enabled, whether it's visible, and so on. Any of these properties can be bound to a property of another object. Take the TicTacToe project as an example. The interface has a Reset button that clears the board and starts a new game. The enabled

---

[1] Apple Inc., *Cocoa Bindings Programming Topics*, http://developer.apple.com/documentation/ Cocoa/Conceptual/CocoaBindings/, 2009.

property of this button is bound to the isStarted property of the game object. Before the game begins, while isStarted is NO, the button is disabled. As soon as the game starts, the button becomes enabled. There's no code in the game object to enable or disable the button, and the button doesn't know anything about the Tic Tac Toe game. The enabled property of the view is simply bound to an observable BOOL property of another object; no additional programming is required.

If you need to create a binding programmatically—say, for a view object you created programmatically—send a -bind:toObject:withKeyPath:options: message to a Bindings-compliant observer.

If you are creating custom view objects to display custom data, it's more expedient to create an informal binding between the view and data model objects. This is just a fancy way of saying, "roll your own MVC communications." Your custom view should implement the fundamental MVC communications using Objective-C messages, notifications, and observing. The view should use direct knowledge about the controller and data model, rather than trying to create an abstract, reusable view class that communicates through bindings. In the TicTacToe project, the ChalkboardView object is a good example. It displays a Tic Tac Toe game and sends "move" actions to its controller when the user clicks on the board. The object knows it is connected to a TTTDocument controller and it explicitly observes changes to its game property. The object conforms to the MVC design pattern, but isn't abstracted beyond its purpose.

Interface Builder

Before I get too far into the details of view objects, events, and controllers, I'll take a moment to shed some light on some of the "magic" of Cocoa application development. If you're not used to developing with Cocoa—and I assume that you aren't or you wouldn't be reading this book—you are likely to open the TicTacToe project and start scratching your head. The Objective-C source code clearly implements the functionality of the objects, but you can sift through the code line by line and never find any of the following:

- Code to create a document window, or any of the view objects in that window

- Code that connects the document object to any of its view objects

- Code that binds a view object to a controller or data model property

- Code to connect view objects (like buttons and menu items) with the controller object that implements those actions

All of these tasks are accomplished through Interface Builder, an essential development tool that makes Cocoa application development effortless and simultaneously mystifying.

In a nutshell, Interface Builder edits NIB files. NIB files, which you remember from Chapter 4, contain an archived (serialized) representation of the objects you want to instantiate at runtime. The archived objects include properties and inter-object references. The NIB file is part of the application bundle. When a NIB file is "loaded" at runtime, the objects are unarchived; this instantiates the graph of objects, sets their properties, and connects any inter-object references.

If you read Chapter 12 about archiving, what NIB files accomplish isn't a great mystery. If you come from another development environment, keep in mind that Interface Builder *is not* a code generator. It does nothing but edit a virtual representation of the objects that will be instantiated at runtime via standard archive decoding. There's no "magic" involved, nor is any code generated. The end result is identical to unarchiving a graph of objects that were previously created programmatically.

If you understand that basic concept, Interface Builder's role in development and how the objects in a NIB document get created and initialized ceases to be a mystery. It's one thing to say "a view object sends an action message to its controller when the user clicks on it," and another to actually implement it. In Cocoa development, that connection between those objects and the message that gets sent is (more often than not) defined in Interface Builder. Getting comfortable with Interface Builder is an important step in becoming a productive Cocoa developer.

NIB Documents

As mentioned earlier, Interface Builder (IB) is primarily a NIB document editor. In its modern form, Interface Builder edits an Interface Builder Document, which is the IB equivalent of a source file. The source file is compiled into its final binary form when the application is built. In the old days, Interface Builder would edit the actual binary archive file and there was no separate compilation phase; the NIB file was simply copied into the application bundle.

NIB documents have names, and your application can have as many NIB documents as it needs. A Cocoa application designates one as the *main* NIB document, normally MainMenu.nib. The main NIB document is loaded during program initialization and should contain all of the standard view elements of the application. This invariably includes the menu objects, but might also include shared windows or other objects.

The standard Cocoa document controller assigns a NIB document to every document type your application supports. When you open a document in the application, an instance of NSDocument is created and then its NIB file is loaded; this creates the NSWindow for the document and populates it with whatever additional view objects (buttons, fields, tables, tabs, toolbars, drawers, auxiliary windows, dialog windows, and custom objects) that it needs.

In addition, you can create additional NIB documents and load them programmatically for any purpose you can conceive. For example, you might have a very complex document window that uses many different subviews. You could define that window and container views in the document's NIB document, then define the view objects for each subview in auxiliary NIB documents which you would load programmatically as needed. The only thing you need to establish when loading a NIB document is the owner object, which is described a little later in the Owner Object section.

The NIB Document Window

When you open a NIB document in Interface Builder you see either graphical or symbolic representations of the objects in the NIB. You edit the properties of these objects using the various Inspector palettes. You can create new objects by dragging icons from the Library palette into the document. You can also reorganize and delete them.

View objects (windows, controls, fields, menus) can also appear with a visual representation, much as they will when they're instantiated by your application. A typical NIB document window is shown in Figure 20-5, with the graphical representation of the Window and view objects behind it. In most cases, the symbolic and visual representation of an object is synonymous.

Object Properties

Now that you understand that a NIB document simply contains the archived version of a graph of objects, it's easy to understand Interface Builder properties. In Interface Builder you edit the properties of these objects using the various Inspector palettes. There are inspectors for the basic properties, as shown in Figure 20-5: size, position, resizing behavior, animation effects, connections, bindings, and so on.

Figure 20-5. *Interface Builder properties*

You can edit an object's properties by selecting either its symbolic representation in the main NIB document window or its visual representation. In Figure 20-5, the Reset button properties can be edited by selecting either the Push Button (Reset) object or the Reset button in the window behind it. Overt properties such as an object's title, size, and position can be directly manipulated by clicking, dragging, and resizing the visual representation of a view object.

The properties you set are stored in the object's archive stream and are implicitly restored when the NIB document is unarchived.

Placeholder Objects

There are a few special objects that appear in your NIB document. These are placeholders for objects that will already exist when the NIB is loaded, and are there solely to allow you to make connections with those objects. Some proxy objects you may have in your NIB:

- File's Owner
- First Responder
- Application
- Font Manager
- User Defaults Controller.

For example, you can create a connection between an object in your NIB and the single global NSApplication object, even though the NSApplication object is not part of the NIB.

Connections

In Interface Builder terminology, a relationship between two objects in a NIB document is called a *connection*. There are three types of connections: outlets, actions, and bindings.

Outlets

An outlet is nothing more than an object reference. Outlets allow you to set object references in Interface Builder using graphical design tools. Any object pointer property can be an outlet. If you include the keyword IBOutlet in your instance variable declaration, as shown in Listing 20-1, Interface Builder will automatically recognize it as an outlet and let you set the variable in the NIB. You can also manually declare outlets by editing a class's definition in Interface Builder's Identity Inspector palette, but the IBOutlet method is preferred and has the advantage of documenting your outlets in your source file.

Listing 20-1. *Interface Builder Outlet Declaration*

```
@interface TTTDocument : NSDocument {
    TicTacToeGame           *game;
    NSString                *gameOutcome;
    IBOutlet ChalkboardView *chalkboardView;
}
```

In the TicTacToe project, the TTTDocument object needs a reference to the ChalkboardView object that displays the Tic Tac Toe game. To make the connection in Interface Builder requires two steps: First, declare the outlet variable as an IBOutlet in TTTDocument's @interface, as shown in Listing 20-1. Then open the TTTDocument NIB document, select the TTTDocument object, and in the Connections Inspector drag the outlet's connection dot to the ChalkboardView object, as shown in Figure 20-6.

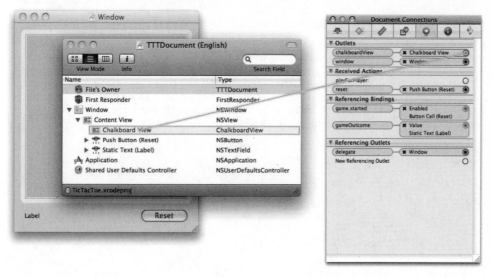

Figure 20-6. *Connecting an outlet in Interface Builder*

When the NIB is loaded, the chalkboardView property of TTTDocument will be set with the pointer to the newly created instance of ChalkboardView. This is functionally identical to writing the following code:

```
document.chalkboardView = [ChalkboardView new];
```

Making connections is such a common task in Interface Builder that there are several shortcuts:

- Right/Control-Click on an object to bring up a pop-up outlet inspector panel. Set or break any connection just as you would with the Inspector palettes.

- Right/Control-Drag *from* the object with the outlet *to* the object you want it connected to. A pop-up outlet completion panel will appear. Click the outlet you want to set.

- When dragging between objects, you can start or finish using either the symbolic object in the NIB document window or its visual representation in any other window.

Actions

The second kind of connection is an action. An action is an Objective-C message sent to an object when some event occurs. An action is defined by a pair of properties that form an informal protocol: an action property of type SEL that determines the Objective-C message to send, and a target property of type id that determines the recipient. Action messages are sent to the recipient, typically a controller object, when "something" happens. What defines "something" is left to the discretion of the view object, but it's typically a mouse click (buttons, check boxes, menu items), editing event (pressing return or tabbing out of an input text field), or a keyboard shortcut (menu items).

The receiver of the action must implement a method to receive the message. The form of the message must look like this:

```
- (IBAction)playForPlayer:(id)sender;
```

An action always receives, as its sole parameter, a pointer to the object that sent the message. The IBAction keyword is synonymous with void, but is used by Interface Builder to automatically recognize action methods. Once Interface Builder knows about an action, you can set it almost exactly as you would an outlet connection. Select the object that sends the action, then drag its Sent Actions connection to the object that will receive the action, as shown in Figure 20-7. Once you drag the action connection to the recipient, Interface Builder will pop up an action completion panel where you complete the connection by choosing which message to send.

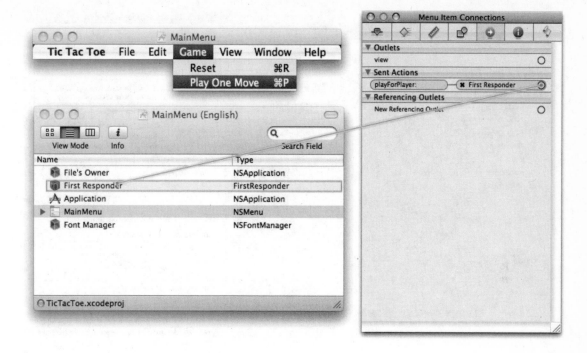

Figure 20-7. *Connecting an action in Interface Builder*

Making an action connection in Interface Builder sets both the action (message identifier) and the target recipient (object pointer). The First Responder target is a special placeholder object that sets an action message and a nil target. The actual target will be determined dynamically, as described later in the Responder Chain section.

Bindings
Use the Bindings palette to set the binding for your objects. In the earlier section on bindings, I described binding the enabled property of the Reset button to the started property of the game object. Figure 20-8 shows how that binding is set in Interface Builder.

Figure 20-8. *Setting a binding in Interface Builder*

To set a binding, select the object to bind and open the Bindings palette. In Figure 20-8, the visual representation of the Reset button is selected. Expand the property to bind, and then choose the object and key path (property name) to bind it to. In this example, the enabled property of the button is bound to the started property of the game property of the NIB's owner. Since this is the document's NIB file, the NIB's owner is the TTTDocument object—owner objects are explained in the next section.

There are lots of settings in a binding, many of which will vary depending on the type of property and the type of value being bound. The settings of most interest are as follows:

The object to bind to: This is the object containing the property you want to bind to.

Model Key Path: The key-value path of the property to bind to. This can be any KVC path relative to the bound object. To bind to the object itself, use the path self.

Controller Key: If you bind to an NSController object, the model key path is in two parts. The controller key describes the property of the controller, and the model key path then specifies the property of the object described by the controller key. For example, binding with a controller key of selection and a model key path of name would bind the property to the name of the currently selected object in the controller's collection—equivalent to a path of selection.name. Here are some common NSController properties:

- content binds to whole content encapsulated by the controller. This might be a single object or an entire collection.

- arrangedContent binds to the content, sorted and filtered by the controller. Bind to this property when displaying contents in a table or other sorted list.

- `selection` is the object currently selected by the controller.

- `selectedObjects` is the collection of objects currently selected by the controller. Use this binding with controllers that allow more than one object to be selected at a time.

- `isEditable`, `canAdd`, and `canRemove` are a few of the many informational properties provided by controllers. For example, you would bind the `enabled` property of an Add Record button to the `canAdd` property of the controller. The button will be enabled only when the controller allows new objects to be added.

Value Transformer: Choose the transformer object you want to use to convert property values between the two objects.

Null Placeholder: Choose the object you want the binding to use when the bound property is nil.

Owner Object

Loading a NIB document differs from unarchiving a graph of objects in one minor respect. When you unarchive a graph of objects you get all new objects, typically connected to a single root object returned to the sender. When you load a NIB document, you pass in a single existing object that becomes the NIB's owner. The owner object is essentially the root of the NIB document's object graph, but it exists *before* the NIB is loaded.

The NIB's owner object is represented in the NIB document as the File's Owner placeholder object. All of the objects in your NIB should connect directly, or indirectly, to the File's Owner in order to be accessible.

When the main NIB file is loaded during program initialization, the owner is the single NSApplication object. When the document controller loads a NIB to create a document window, the owner is the NSDocument object that will own that interface. When you programmatically load a NIB file, you can specify whatever owner object you want, just make sure it agrees with the class of the File's Owner defined in the NIB document.

In the TicTacToe example, shown in Listing 20-1 and Figure 20-6, the NIB contains an instance of ChalkboardView connected to the `chalkboardView` property of the owner. Since this is a document NIB, TTTDocument is the NIB's owner. When loaded, its `chalkboardView` property is set to the newly created ChalkboardView object.

Custom Objects

The NIB document in the TicTacToe project instantiates two classes that I created: TTTDocument and ChalkboardView. This is accomplished by creating or selecting a generic object that Interface Builder already understands, and then altering its class in the Identity Inspector, as shown in Figure 20-9.

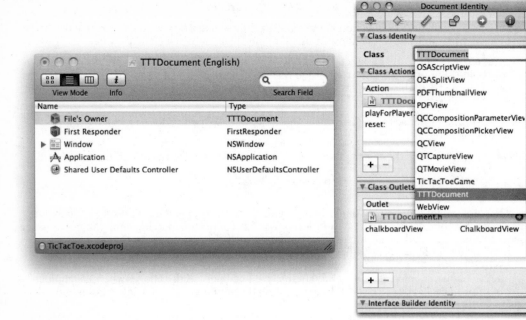

Figure 20-9. *Changing the class of a NIB object*

In the case of TTTDocument, I started in Xcode by subclassing NSDocument to create TTTDocument. In Interface Builder, I chose the existing File's Owner instance in the TTTDocument NIB document and changed its class to TTTDocument. Interface Builder now treats the File's Owner object as an instance of TTTDocument. Interface Builder understands inheritance; TTTDocument inherits all of the attributes, outlets, and behavior of NSDocument.

To create the ChalkboardView object, I first created a ChalkboardView class (a subclass of NSView) in Xcode. In Interface Builder, I dragged a Custom View object from the Library into the window, and then changed its class from NSView to ChalkboardView. The object inherits all of the base class NSView attributes. That is, Interface Builder understands that it's a view object that has a position, size, visibility, subviews, and so on.

You create arbitrary class instances by dragging a generic Object from the Library into the NIB and then changing its class to whatever you want. Object inherits only the basic properties of NSObject—which is to say almost nothing. Once added, the object can be connected to any appropriate outlet.

Interface Builder will not automatically provide editing of your class's custom properties, but it will recognize outlets and actions that you've defined. If you design a custom class that you'd like to have appear in Interface Builder's Library palette, with properties that are editable using the Attributes palette, you can create an Interface Builder plug-in. That's a somewhat involved process, but if you're interested, refer to the Interface Builder Plug-in Programming Guide.[2]

---

[2] Apple Inc., *Interface Builder Plug-in Programming Guide*, http://developer.apple.com/documentation/ DeveloperTools/Conceptual/IBPlugInGuide/, 2007.

Object Instantiation

Although I describe NIB objects as being created through standard unarchiving, the NIB loader makes a few concessions for some objects. Here is how objects in a NIB are created:

- Custom view objects (subclasses of NSView) are initialized with -initWithFrame:. This is to be consistent with programmatic creation of custom view objects.

- Non-view custom objects (subclasses of NSObject) are initialized with an -init message.

- All other objects provided by Interface Builder (i.e., those that appear in the Library palette) are unarchived with the normal -initWithCoder: message. This also applies to any custom objects that you've provide via an Interface Builder Plug-in.

Initializing custom objects via the standard initializer messages, -init and -initWithFrame:, means that custom objects do *not* have to conform to NSCoding to be archived in a NIB document. It also means you can instantiate virtually any object available to your application and connect it to other objects in your NIB. The advantage of decoding objects using -initWithCoder: is that the NIB can include preset property values. But since Interface Builder doesn't allow you to edit the properties of custom objects, it's a moot point.

NIB Object Initialization

You will often want to perform some additional initialization. After all of the objects in a NIB document have been created, each receives a single -awakeFromNib message—if implemented. The -awakeFromNib message is sent after all the NIB objects have been created and all connections and bindings have been set.

Take a moment to absorb what's been covered so far. You've learned the tenets of the Model-View-Controller design pattern, along with some popular variations. You've learned the essential communication responsibilities of the data model, view, and controller objects. You've learned about bindings, which are a very specific implementation of MVC communications. Using Interface Builder, you've learned to instantiate objects in your application and establish the connections they will use to communicate with each other. The only thing remaining is the actual classes that implement those roles.

The next few sections will examine each MVC role and introduce you to the basic set of Objective-C and Cocoa technologies used to implement your own. The views section describes the visual hierarchy of windows and their contents, how view objects work, the graphics coordinate system, and the primitive drawing tools available to you. Later sections will describe data model objects and the data modeling tools for creating them, followed by some of the pre-built controller objects that are useful with bindings. In between is a detailed description of how user events get to view objects, and how view objects pass the resulting actions to their controllers.

Views

The organization of view objects in Cocoa is remarkably similar to that in Java Swing and other GUI class libraries. This isn't surprising, since the logical organization of visual elements and controls in a window-based user interface is fairly consistent across all modern platforms.

Table 20-1 lists the principal Swing classes and their Cocoa counterparts.

Table 20-1. *Fundamental Java and Objective-C View Classes*

javax.swing	Cocoa
JWindow	NSWindow
JComponent	NSView
	NSControl
AbstractButton	
JButton	NSButton (style=NSMomentaryPushInButton)
JComboBox	NSComboBox
JPopupMenu	NSPopUpButton
JCheckBox	NSButton (style=NSSwitchButton)
JRadioButton	NSButton (style=NSRadioButton)
JSpinner.DateEditor	NSDatePicker
JSlider	NSSlider
JLabel	NSTextField
JTextArea	NSTextField
JTextField	NSTextField
JEditorPane	NSTextView
JPasswordField	NSSecureTextField
JProgressBar	NSProgressIndicator
JList	NSTableButton
JTable	NSTableView
JTree	NSOutlineView, NSBrowser
JScrollPane	NSScrollView
JSplitPane	NSSplitView
JTabbedPane	NSTabView
JToolbar	NSToolbar

When working with the Cocoa classes, be aware of these key differences:

NSWindow is not a subclass of NSView and is not, itself, a view object. Instead, NSWindow has a contentView property that's the root of the window's view hierarchy. To add subviews to a window, add them to window.contentView. This is initially a generic NSView object that just acts as a container for the subviews, but you can replace it with any NSView subclass.

The dimensions of an NSView are described by two rectangle properties: its frame and its bounds. The frame property describes the position and size of the view in its superview, and is expressed in the superview's coordinate system. Thus, an NSView's frame is conceptually equivalent to the *bounds* of a JComponent. An NSView's bounds property is the logical dimensions of its content expressed in view-relative coordinates, typically with an origin of (0,0). If you do not set a custom bounds, it will reflect whatever the frame is in local coordinates. If you set the bounds to something different, it defines a local coordinate system independent of the frame (bounds).

Unlike Swing, all Cocoa view classes that send action events (i.e., all view objects that "do something"—push buttons, text fields, sliders, etc.) are subclasses of NSControl. NSControl is conceptually like AbstractButton, but is the base class for *all* Cocoa control objects, not just buttons. NSControl defines four common concepts for all of its subclasses:

- Controls have a cell property that's an NSCell object. The cell performs all of the drawing and user interaction for the control; the NSControl object does not perform any drawing itself. In effect, the NSCell is the control's view object and NSControl is the controller object. There is a default NSCell subclass for every instance of the NSControl subclass: NSButton uses an NSButtonCell, NSSlider uses an NSSliderCell, and so on. To customize the look and feel of any NSControl, replace its NSCell with your own custom subclass.

- Controls send action messages. NSControl defines action and target properties that can be set programmatically or in Interface Builder. Typically, a control sends its action message whenever it is activated or changed.

- Controls have an objectValue property that defines its content. This is not applicable to every NSControl subclass, but for controls that represent or display a value, this is the object that represents its content. For text fields, it's a plain or formatted string, or anything that can be converted into a string. For image views it would an image object. The convenience properties stringValue, integerValue, doubleValue, and floatValue get or set the objectValue property.

- NSControl defines an enabled property, which all subclasses are expected to honor. NSControl also defines a common set of editing, validation, and formatting behavior that is applicable to some subclasses.

To remove an NSView from its superview, send the NSView object a -removeFromSuperview message, or -removeFromSuperviewWithoutNeedingDisplay if you want to suppress an automatic redraw. This differs from Java, where you must tell the superview to remove the particular component.

NSView does not use layout managers. Instead, each NSView object has a set of resizing flags that control how its subviews are repositioned. These flags are easily configured in Interface Builder. You can disable this by setting the autoresizesSubviews property to NO. You can customize autoresizing in one of three ways: override the superview's -resizeSubviewsWithOldSize: to redefine how its subviews are resized, override the subview's -resizeWithOldSuperviewSize: to redefine how it resizes itself, or set the postsBoundsChangedNotifications property to YES and observe the NSViewBoundsDidChangeNotification notification. Also see the section "Animation" later in this chapter. There are also a few view classes that accomplish nearly the same effect as using a layout manager; NSMatrix provides essentially the same functionality as java.awt.GridLayout.

NSView defines a tag property—useful for identifying individual subviews—but the property is immutable and always returns 0 in the base class. NSControl and some other subclasses override tag so that it's a mutable property. If you want to create a custom subclass of NSView and assign it a tag, you must override the tag property, make it mutable, and provide a place to store the value.

NSTextField is a multi-purpose class that is used to display most text in a window. It can be configured to display immutable text (a label), display and edit a single line of text (text field), or display and edit multiline text (text area). It implements a rich set of properties that determine how the text is displayed, aligned, scrolled, and wrapped.

■**Tip** When creating your own NSView subclass, use the Objective-C NSView subclass source file template in Xcode. It creates a subclass with stub implementations of the commonly overridden NSView methods.

Now that you understand the basic organization of the view classes, you'll want to start populating views with subviews, and possibly even create your own custom view classes. To do that, you need to understand the Cocoa drawing environment and how a custom NSView objects works, which are described in the next few sections.

View Geometry

Drawing geometry is a little different in Cocoa than it is in Swing. Cocoa's natural coordinate system is inverted from the one used in Java, but can optionally be flipped so that it's the same. Pen position and drawing bounds are also different.

In Cocoa, all graphic values are floating-point numbers. This includes coordinates, sizes, widths, and color values. Values like red or transparency are typically expressed as a range between 0.0 and 1.0, inclusive. This keeps all of the drawing primitives independent of resolution, display devices, and media.

Coordinate Points

Coordinates in Cocoa are abstract points in a continuous coordinate system. Think of the coordinate grid as infinitely thin lines on a plane. Most of the time, coordinates are mapped 1:1 to pixels that fill the space between the lines (refer to Figures 20-11 and 20-12, later in this section).

Thinking in coordinates helps avoid "enditus"—that anxiety induced by the difference between the drawing coordinates and the pixels that will actually be drawn. Cocoa drawing always occurs *between* the logical coordinates. A line from coordinate 0.0 to 10.0 will draw a line exactly 10 coordinate spaces long. Filling a 10×10 rectangle fills exactly 100 coordinate units' worth of pixels. There are few exceptions to this. One notable exception is Bezier lines that can have non-square line end caps, which can cause it to draw beyond the end point of the line.

All drawing is anti-aliased, so it's easy for drawing to partially affect pixels.

Coordinate System

Cocoa's natural coordinate system is Cartesian, which places the X,Y origin in the lower left-hand corner of view, as shown in Figure 20-10.

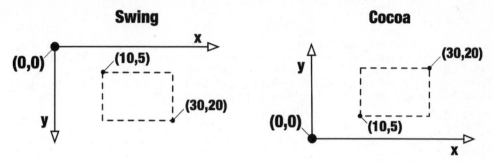

Figure 20-10. *Java and native Cocoa coordinate systems*

This is Cocoa's natural coordinate system, but it's not the only one available. NSView defines a readonly flipped property that's queried by the graphics system. If an NSView subclass returns YES when sent -isFlipped, Cocoa will "flip" the view's Y-axis, creating a coordinate system identical to Java's. The base NSView class, view classes that draw images, and views that are containers (tab view, split view, scroll view) all use natural, Cartesian, coordinates. View objects with content that "flows" from the top down (table, outline, list, browser, and text views) use flipped coordinate systems. When creating your own NSView subclass you're free to override isFlipped and choose the coordinate system that works most naturally with your content. The flipped property is assumed to be an immutable property of the view; changing it spontaneously could have unpredictable results.

■**Caution** A flipped coordinate system changes the meaning of the frame rectangles for its subviews. When working with frame rectangles, your code may have to consider if the coordinate system of the superview is flipped.

In addition to flipping the coordinate system, an NSView's frame or content can be arbitrarily rotated and repositioned. Rotating the frame by setting the frameRotation property rotates the view in its superview, but does not change the local coordinate system of the view's content. Setting the boundsRotation property changes the orientation of its content, but doesn't change its location in the superview. Setting the boundsOrigin property to something other than (0,0) shifts the coordinate system used by the view when drawing.

NSView provides a raft of methods to convert between coordinate systems. The principal ones are -[NSView convertPoint:toView:] and -[NSView convertPoint:fromView:]. These take a coordinate in either the view's local coordinate system or the coordinate system of another view and convert it to the other. The other view can be any view within the window's view hierarchy. If the view object parameter is nil, it converts to or from the window's base coordinate system. There are also methods to convert coordinates between coordinate systems with arbitrary origins and an orthogonal set of methods that convert rectangle and size structures.

■**Tip** If you need to convert coordinates between windows, first convert the point to the window's base coordinate system, and then use the -[NSWindow convertBaseToScreen:] method to convert that to global screen coordinates. Global screen coordinates can be converted to local window coordinates with -[NSWindow convertScreenToBase:], which can then be converted to the local coordinates of any subview.

Like Java, Cocoa maintains a distinction between logical coordinates and physical screen pixels. Most of the time this distinction can be ignored, as a unit in the coordinate space normally corresponds to a single pixel on the screen. However, ever-changing screen resolutions, assistive technologies, and hand-held devices are driving developers to take resolution-independent drawing seriously. Once you're comfortable with the basic drawing tools and techniques, I encourage you to read the *Resolution Independence Guidelines.*[3]

Pen Orientation

Lines in both Swing and Cocoa are drawn using an imaginary pen that changes pixels by "dragging" the pen shape from one set of coordinates to another. In Java, the pen extends down and to the right of coordinates. In Cocoa, the pen is infinitely thin and is centered over the line defined by the logical coordinates. The line shown in Figure 20-11 is drawn from coordinates (0,0) to (0,5) with a 3-pixel pen (a 3×3 pixel pen in Java).

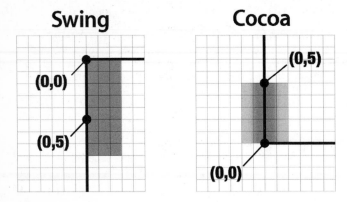

Figure 20-11. *Swing and Cocoa pen orientation*

The illustration shows that the Cocoa pen has drawn an anti-aliased line that straddles four pixel columns. That's because the 3.0-pixel-wide pen is centered over the Y-axis, so the left edge of the pen's "brush" is at X coordinate -1.5 and the right edge is at 1.5. To draw a 3-pixel-wide line that emulates the one drawn in Java, the Cocoa line would need to be drawn from coordinate (1.5,0.0) to (1.5,8.0).

---

[3] Apple Inc., *Resolution Independence Guidelines,* http://developer.apple.com/documentation/ UserExperience/Conceptual/HiDPIOverview/, 2007.

Drawing Bounds

Cocoa rectangles, and any drawing method that draws inside a given bounds, always draws *inside* the coordinate bounds of the rectangle. Figure 20-12 shows filling a 3×5 rectangle.

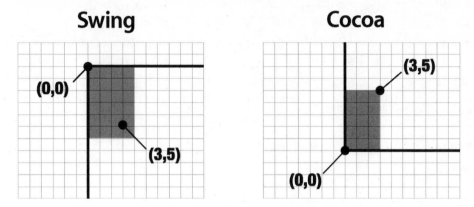

Figure 20-12. *Filling rectangles in Swing and Cocoa*

In Java, the rectangle drawn by Graphics2D.fillRect(Shape) with a 1×1-pixel pen extends 1 pixel beyond the rectangle. In Cocoa, only pixels in the interior of the rectangle are filled. The code to fill the rectangle was NSRectFill(NSMakeRect(0.0,0.0,3.0,5.0)).

Drawing Lines and Shapes

Java provides a number of primitives for immediately drawing lines, rectangles, ovals, and other shapes. Cocoa provides only a collection of C functions that mostly fill rectangles and the versatile NSBezierPath class. NSBezierPath is the catch-all object for drawing any kind of line, geometric shape, or both.

An NSBezierPath can consist of one or more line segments. Line segments can be straight or curved, solid or dashed. Line segments can be connected or unconnected. They can form closed shapes, like a star or an oval, or open shapes, like an arc. Once defined, the Bezier path object can be filled (draw the interior of the shape) or stroked (draw the lines that define the shape). The path has a number of properties that control how the joints and ends of lines are drawn. It also has a "winding rule" that determines what constitutes the interior of a shape when the line segments intersect each other. The line in Figure 20-11 was drawn with the code in Listing 20-2.

Listing 20-2. *Drawing a 5.0-Pixel Line*

```
NSBezierPath *path = [NSBezierPath new];
[path moveToPoint:NSMakePoint(0.0,0.0)];
[path lineToPoint:NSMakePoint(0.0,5.0)];
[path setLineWidth:3.0];
[path stroke];
```

There are convenience constructors that create a Bezier path that form an oval or rounded rectangle.

Custom Views

Custom view objects are created by subclassing NSView, in almost exactly the way you would subclass JComponent in Swing. Your NSView class must provide, at a minimum, the following:

- An `-(id)initWithFrame:(NSRect)frame` initialization method. This is the designated initialization method for all NSView subclasses.

- Optionally override `-(void)drawRect:(NSRect)rect` to provide custom drawing of your view's interior. This method is equivalent to javax.swing.JComponent.paint(Graphics).

The code in Listing 20-3 demonstrates a custom NSView subclass that draws the image stored in the file `Chalkboard.png`. (This was the original version of the ChalkboardView class in the TicTacToe project, before it was reworked to add animation.)

Listing 20-3. *Custom NSView Drawing Method*

```
- (void)drawRect:(NSRect)rect
{
    NSImage *chalkboardImage = [NSImage imageNamed:@"Chalkboard"];
    NSRect imageRect;
    imageRect.origin = NSMakePoint(0.0,0.0);
    imageRect.size = [chalkboardImage size];

    [chalkboardImage drawInRect:[self bounds]
                       fromRect:imageRect
                      operation:NSCompositeSourceOver
                       fraction:1.0];
}
```

Invalidating and Drawing Views

Drawing in Cocoa is almost identical to that in Swing and similar GUI frameworks. When the contents of a view need to be redrawn, the region it occupies is *invalidated*. To invalidate an NSView, set needsDisplay to YES or send a `-setNeedsDisplayInRect:` message. The AppKit framework adds the region, or subregion, of the view to the conglomerate area of the user interface that needs to be redrawn. Eventually, the application framework sends each invalid view object a `-drawRect:` message. The message includes the specific subregion of the view that requires drawing. Unless your view is very complex, this can be ignored; all drawing is automatically clipped to the invalid region.

■**Note** The `-drawRect:` method is only responsible for drawing its content. A view is actually drawn when it receives a `-display` message. This is the high-level message that recursively sends `-drawRect:` messages to itself and all of its subviews. You typically don't override `-display`, and you'd normally never send `-display` to a view object. To redraw a view, set its needsDisplay property and let the framework add it to the queue of view objects that need to be updated, and then wait to receive a `-drawRect:` message.

Graphics Context

In Java, the graphics object used by the component to draw itself is passed to the JComponent.paint(Graphics) method as a parameter. In Cocoa, all drawing occurs in the implied context of the global NSGraphicsContext object. The framework will prepare the context for your view before the -drawRect: method is sent. Your view draws in the local coordinate system defined by its bounds property. You should not make any assumptions about the drawing context after your -drawRect: method has returned.

The NSGraphics Context defines a number of properties that apply to all drawing commands:

- clipping region

- drawing color

- stroke (pen) color

- fill color

- font

- shadow

- affine transform

Quite unlike the organization of java.awt.Graphics, the methods that set these properties are scattered among the classes that define them. Table 20-2 lists where to find the approximate equivalents of java.awt.Graphics2D properties in the Cocoa framework.

Table 20-2. *Graphics Context Property Settings*

java.awt.Graphics2D	Cocoa Function or Method
setClip(int,int,int,int)	NSRectClip(…), NSRectClipList(…)
clipRect(int,int,int,int)	-[NSBezierPath addClip]
setColor(Color)	-[NSColor set], -[NSColor setStroke], -[NSColor setFill]
setBackground(Color)	None: NSEraseRect(…) always paints with white. Fill a rectangle with NSRectFill(…).
setFont(Font)	-[NSFont set]
	-[NSShadow set]
setTransform(AffineTransform)	-[NSAffineTransform set]
setComposite(Composite)	-[NSGraphicsContext setCompositingOperation:]

Setting these properties and using them is identical to Java: set the desired properties, and then invoke a drawing command. The drawing command will use the applicable properties of the current graphics context, as demonstrated in Listing 20-4.

Listing 20-4. *Setting and Using Graphics Context Properties*

```
NSBezierPath *path = …
[[NSColor blueColor] setFill];      // set fill color to blue
[[NSColor greenColor] setStroke];   // set stroke color to green
[path fill];                        // fills a blue shape
[path stroke];                      // draws a green line
```

The graphics context also includes a loose set of esoteric attributes and rendering hints, much like Graphics2D, that influence scaling, anti-aliasing, color space adjustments, and so on.

Some of the properties of Graphics2D are not properties of the graphics context in Cocoa. Instead, they are properties of the definition object. For example, the width and shape of lines drawn by an NSBezierPath are properties of the Bezier path object, not the graphics context.

NSGraphicsContext has a compositingOperation property that is used for drawing commands that do not specify an explicit compositing mode as a parameter.

The Graphics Context State Stack

You may need several graphics contexts, configured differently, to accomplish your drawing tasks. It isn't always easy to undo the changes made to any one graphics context, and all subsequent drawing operations will be affected by any changes, so it's easy for the current context to become "polluted." This is where the graphics context state stack is handy.

The current state of the graphics context can be pushed, preserving all of its properties on a per-thread stack. You can then make whatever changes you want to the graphics context. When the previous state is restored, any changes made since it was saved are discarded. This is particularly useful when setting complex properties, like clipping, shadow, and affine transforms, that only apply to a few drawing commands. Listing 20-5 demonstrates the basic pattern for pushing and restoring a graphics context.

Listing 20-5. *Saving and Restoring a Graphics Context*

```
NSGraphicsContext *currentContext = [NSGraphicsContext currentContext];
NSRect circleRect = NSMakeRect(0.0,0.0,20.0,20.0);
NSBezierPath *path = [NSBezierPath bezierPathWithOvalInRect:circleRect];


// Fill the circle interior (with a drop shadow)
[currentContext saveGraphicsState];       // push context state
NSShadow *shadow = [NSShadow new];         // create a shadow
[shadow setShadowColor:[NSColor blackColor]];
[shadow setShadowOffset:NSMakeSize(3.0,-3.0)];
[shadow setShadowBlurRadius:1.5];
[shadow set];                              // set shadow for all drawing
[[NSColor whiteColor] setFill];            // set fill color to white
[path fill];                               // draw white circle + shadow
[currentContext restoreGraphicsState];     // restore previous context
```

```
// Draw the circle permimeter (without a shadow)
[[NSColor blueColor] setStroke];
[path stroke];
```

You must balance each -saveGraphicsState message with a -restoreGraphicsState message.

Drawing Tools

Like graphics context properties, the methods to draw objects are scattered among the objects themselves. The exceptions are a few C functions that fill rectangles or draw multipart images. The most commonly used C functions are listed in Table 20-3.

Table 20-3. Common Cocoa Drawing Functions

AppKit Draw Function	Description
NSEraseRect(NSRect)	Fills a rectangle with white.
NSRectFill(NSRect)	Fills a rectangle with the current color.
NSRectFillUsingOperation(NSRect,NSCompositingOperation)	Fills a rectangle using a specific compositing mode.
NSRectFillList(NSRect*,NSInteger)	Fills a list of rectangles with the current color.
NSFrameRect(NSRect)	Draws a 1.0 width line inside the bounds of the rectangle in the current color.
NSFrameRectWithWidth(NSRect,CGFloat)	Draws a line inside the rectangle with the given width in the current color.

There are about thirty of these functions. They are mostly utilities that make it easy to draw objects like resizable buttons built from multiple images, embossed edges, drop shadows, dotted outlines (used to indicate selections), and so on. Refer to the *Application Kit Functions Reference*[4] for a complete list.

The rest of the drawing methods are implemented in the objects that define them, sometimes through a category. For example, the AppKit framework defines a category that attaches a -drawAtPoint:WithAttributes: method to the NSString class. Table 20-4 lists common Java drawing methods and where you'll find close approximations in the Cocoa framework.

---

[4] Apple Inc., *Application Kit Functions Reference*, http://developer.apple.com/documentation/Cocoa/ Reference/ApplicationKit/Miscellaneous/AppKit_Functions/Reference/, 2008.

Table 20-4. *Common Drawing Methods*

java.awt.Graphics2D	Cocoa Function or Method
drawImage(Image,int,int,int,int,int,int,int,↵ int,ImageObserver)	-[NSImage ↵ drawAtPoint:fromRect:operation:fraction:]
clearRect(int,int,int,int)	NSEraseRect(…), NSRectFill(…)
drawArc(int,int,int,int,int,int)	-[NSBezierPath stroke]
drawString(AttributedCharacterIterator,int,int)	-[NSString drawAtPoint:withAttributes:]
drawLine(int,int,int,int)	-[NSBezierPath stroke]
drawOval(int,int,int,int)	-[NSBezierPath stroke]
drawPolygon(Polygon)	-[NSBezierPath stroke]
drawPolyline(int[],int[],int)	-[NSBezierPath stroke]
drawRect(int,int,int,int)	NSFrameRect(…)
drawRoundRect(int,int,int,int,int,int)	-[NSBezierPath stroke]
fillArc(int,int,int,int,int,int)	-[NSBezierPath fill]
fillOval(int,int,int,int)	-[NSBezierPath fill]
fillPolygon(Polygon)	-[NSBezierPath fill]
fillRect(int,int,int,int)	NSRectFill(…)
fillRoundRect(int,int,int,int,int,int)	-[NSBezierPath fill]

Animation

Core Animation, a recent addition to Mac OS X, has created an entirely new family of view objects, specifically designed to animate the user interface. The new framework makes it remarkably easy to add very sophisticated animations to your application.

The Core Animation classes are actually modeled a little closer to Swing than the traditional Cocoa view classes. For example, Core Animation views use layout managers. There are a number of important concepts to grasp when adding animation to your view objects:

- The central player in Core Animation is the CALayer class. This is logically equivalent to NSView, but the two are not interchangeable. A layer has a size, position, content, and acts as a container for any number of sublayers.

- CALayer objects are functional view objects, capable of drawing basic data types, like images and text, on their own. To create a custom layer, you can either subclass CALayer (much like NSView) or defer drawing to a delegate object. Much like Java's paint(Graphics) method, the -[CALayer drawInContext:] is passed the graphics context reference that should be used for drawing. The clipping bounds of the context contains the region that needs to be redrawn.

- To add animated objects to your NSView, set the root CALayer object in the NSView's layer property, then send it -setWantsLayer: passing YES. The NSView then becomes the host to a hierarchy of CALayer objects, much the way NSWindow hosts a root contentView object.

- Animations occur by transitioning from one state to another; most animations are created by simply setting a property and letting Core Animation do the rest. For example, setting the size of a layer object spontaneously creates an animation that smoothly transitions the view from its old size to its new one.

- The layer objects you add to a view are collectively called the *layer-tree*. Core Animation creates a parallel set of objects, initially copies of the ones you added, collectively called the *presentation-tree*. Presentation objects hold the properties that are being animated. In the example of changing the size of a layer, the size of the layer-tree object changes immediately. The size of its presentation object changes over time as the animation progresses. You can examine a layer's presentation object—say, to obtain the current position of a moving object—by sending it a -presentationLayer message.

- Setting a new layer object property creates implicit animation. You can take control of this by creating explicit animations. This gives you control of animation attributes, like speed and acceleration. One common use of explicit animations is to suppress the animation altogether, allowing you to change layer properties without animating them.

- Unlike NSView, CALayer employs a layout manager object, conforming to the informal CALayoutManager protocol, to reposition and resize layers. Core Animation provides the CAConstraintLayoutManager, which is very similar to javax.swing.SpringLayout.

- Core Animation uses Quartz and Core Graphics data types, rather than the Cocoa data types discussed so far. Most data types are easy to translate; for example, there are NSRectToCGRect() and NSRectFromCGRect() functions that convert between NSRect and CGRect structures. Other data types, like NSImage and CGImage, are not so easy to translate. This, unfortunately, adds a certain degree of tedium to using animation in a Cocoa application.

The TicTacToe project demonstrates using both implicit and explicit animations. For example, simply removing an object from its view creates an implicit animation that causes the view to fade out smoothly—rather than simply blinking out of existence.

```
[xoLayer removeFromSuperlayer];    // (fade out)
```

Making property changes between the statements [CATransaction begin] and [CATransaction commit] forms an explicit animation. You can set properties of the animation, like speed, or suppress animation altogether before the -commit message groups and queues the animation effects to begin.

If you want to learn more about animation, refer to the *Core Animation Programming Guide*.[5]

---

[5] Apple Inc., *Core Animation Programming Guide*, http://developer.apple.com/documentation/Cocoa/Conceptual/CoreAnimation_guide/, 2008.

iPhone View Classes

If you're targeting the iPhone OS, you'll be using a completely different set of view classes: UIView instead of NSView, UIWindow instead of NSWindows, etc. However, they are conceptually very similar to their Cocoa counterparts:

- UIView is functionally the same as NSView. The main properties, such as frame, bounds, and subviews, are the same.

- Customizing a UIView is almost identical to customizing an NSView except that the drawing context is a Quartz 2D drawing destination. All drawing is done using Core Graphics C functions, like those described in the "Drawing Tools" section. The concepts and capabilities (coordinate systems, clipping, Bezier paths, colors, graphic context stacks, etc.) are nearly identical to those described for NSGraphicsContext—there's just no object-oriented interface.

- UIViews are designed to be animated and come with a permanently installed CALayer object.

- The iPhone OS conforms to the MVC design pattern more rigorously than the Cocoa framework. Almost every iPhone interface requires a UIViewController object. The framework also provides a number of specialized subclasses, like UINavigationController and UITabBarController. These are the classes that control your view objects and are the natural place to add your application's functionality. You can use or subclass these classes as you please.

- Unlike NSCell, UICell is a subclass of UIView. So cell objects in the iPhone OS are fully functional views that can be animated and can contain subviews. You can also design them in Interface Builder.

- Many common user interface elements that you're familiar with in Swing, like menu bars, multiple windows, file chooser dialogs, and so on, simply do not exist in the iPhone OS. Conversely, the iPhone OS provides many unique interface objects. While your knowledge of Objective-C will give you tools to create iPhone applications, you'll want to review Apple's guides that describe how iPhone user-interface design differs from that of traditional desktop applications.

Advanced View Topics

Graphics programming in Cocoa is an expansive subject, worthy of an entire book itself. In addition to the basic NSView classes discussed so far, here are some advanced topics you should be aware of:

- You can perform off-screen drawing into an NSImage. Create an NSImage with the desired properties, and then send it a -lockFocus message. This sets up the current graphics context with the NSImage as its output device. Subsequent drawing commands will be rendered directly in the NSImage. Send -unlockFocus when you're done drawing.

- An NSOpenGLView implements an entire 3D drawing environment in a single view object.

- WebKit embeds a fully functional web page as a view. It uses the shared WebKit framework, the same one used by Safari, iTunes, and other applications. Many slick applications have been delivered that simply present XHTML content in a WebKit view.

- Movies and other multimedia can be embedded using a QTMovieView.

- If you are writing an application that presents collections of images, the Image Kit framework provides ready-made classes for displaying groups of images (think iPhoto), complete with animation.

- PDF Kit is a powerful framework for embedding, displaying, and creating PDF images and documents. If you've ever dragged an icon outside a sidebar or dock and seen the little "poof" animation, that animation is actually a multi-frame PDF document.

- The Quartz Composer is a framework that performs advanced, real-time, image filtering, compositing, and transformations. It supports a plug-in architecture that allows for unlimited effects.

Read more about these, and many other advanced drawing topics, in the *Cocoa Drawing Guide*,[6] *WebKit Objective-C Programming Guide*,[7] and *Quartz Composer Programming Guide*.[8]

You now understand half of what a view object does. View objects are the intermediary between your application and the user. They display the content of your application, but they also translate the user's actions. View objects have to be aware of what the user is doing (pressing keys, moving the mouse), interpret it, and turn it into action messages to be sent to controller objects. The next few sections describe how view objects participate in event handling.

Document Model

As you'll discover in the next few sections, the organization of objects defines how your application responds to events, and influences the design of your classes. It's important to understand the organization of objects in a document-based application. A document-based application is one that opens the content of data files in windows, often allowing you to manipulate its content, and save the results in a new or existing document file. The TicTacToe project is a document-based application. You can save a game as a `tictactoe` document, open old games, and revert to a previously saved game.

The key objects in document-based applications are show in Figure 20-13.

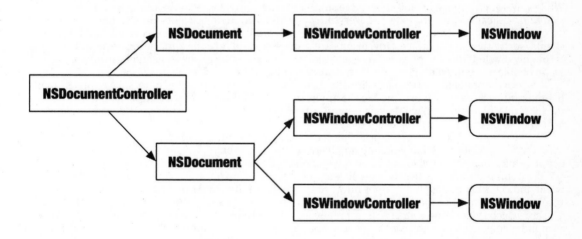

Figure 20-13. *Document-based application objects*

---

[6] Apple Inc., *Cocoa Drawing Guide*, http://developer.apple.com/documentation/Cocoa/Conceptual/CocoaDrawingGuide/, 2009.

[7] Apple Inc., *WebKit Objective-C Programming Guide*, http://developer.apple.com/documentation/Cocoa/Conceptual/DisplayWebContent/, 2008.

[8] Apple Inc., *Quartz Composer Programming Guide*, http://developer.apple.com/documentation/GraphicsImaging/Conceptual/QuartzComposer/, 2008.

A document-based application has a single NSDocumentController object. This is the object responsible for creating new document objects (when you choose New or Open from the menu), associating document types with the document classes that implement them, and keeping track of the documents that are currently open. An application normally only defines a single document type, but NSDocumentController can arbitrarily map multiple file types to multiple document classes. When you choose to open an existing document, the NSDocumentController uses the file's type to determine what subclass of NSDocument to instantiate.

■**Tip** When creating a document-based application project in Xcode, start with the Cocoa Document-based Application template. It will save you a lot of work later.

The data model of a document is an NSDocument object. NSDocument, or your NSDocument subclass, is the object responsible for actually encoding and decoding the data in the document file. Each document object can be viewed in one or more windows, each of which is controlled by an NSWindowController/NSWindow pair. Normally, a document only appears in a single window, but that can be overridden to allow the user to open multiple views to the same data.

Non-document windows are not associated with a document object, and often don't have a window controller, either. Document and non-document windows can be freely mixed.

Events and Responders

While views and drawing in Objective-C are similar to what's in Java, event handling is *completely different*. Basically, you need to forget everything you know about Java events and listeners.

User events—mouse events, keyboard events, scroll-wheel events, tablet events, and track pad events—drive the user interface. How events are processed, and how the applications responds to them, is roughly divided into two phases: The event phase and the response phase. Each phase employs a *chain* of objects, defined dynamically by the current state of the application interface.

An event begins in the hardware drivers of the operating system and enters the application via the main run loop, where it is passed to the application object. From there, it follows a path *down* into the hierarchy of document, window, view, and subview objects until it finds one to interpret it. This sequence of objects is called the *event chain*.

Once an object interprets the event, it becomes an action. Actions travel *up* the hierarchy of subview, view, window, document, and application objects searching for one that will *respond* to that action. This sequence of objects is called the *responder chain*.

This section describes the organization of objects in an application and how that interacts with event and action handling. It describes how events are distributed and how your view objects can receive basic events, but that's probably superfluous; most applications don't work with events directly. The core Cocoa view classes already interpret events and turn them into actions that interact with the responder chain. So enjoy the events section, but pay particular attention to the responder chain section that follows. That's the key to understanding how Cocoa applications work.

The Dynamic Application

One of the important concepts in a Cocoa application is the idea that how an event or action is handled is determined by the chain of objects implied by the current state of the user interface. To understand this, you need to learn some Cocoa terminology. Start with the user interface depicted in Figure 20-14.

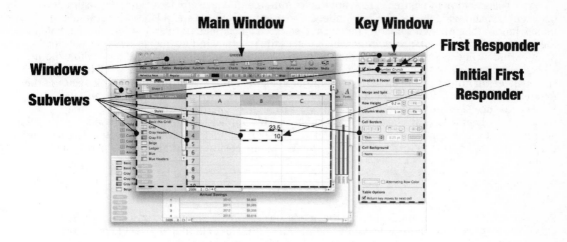

Figure 20-14. *Main and key windows, first responder*

Cocoa applications form a hierarchy of objects that begin with a single NSApplication (non-document applications) or NSWindowController (document-based applications) object at the top. Underneath the application object may be NSDocument objects. Below those are the NSWindow objects, which contain a nested tree of NSView objects. Figure 20-14 shows the visible portion of that hierarchy.

Event and action processing is directed by the windows and views that are active. Cocoa refers to these using specific terms, listed in Table 20-5.

Table 20-5. *Active Window and View Terminology*

Term	Description
Active Application	The currently active, frontmost application.
Main Window	The single, frontmost, active application window. Most menu commands apply to the main window. The main window has a visually distinct title and border, which differentiates it from the inactive windows behind it.
Key Window	The window containing the first responder.
First Responder	The view object that is active or has the current "focus." This is typically the object that responds to keystrokes. A window object can also be the first responder.
Initial First Responder	The view in a non-key window that will become the first responder (by default) when the window becomes the key window. The initial first responder is meaningful in a main window that is not the key window.

The situation in Figure 20-14 is not that common, but it is useful in making the distinction between the main window and the key window. The user has an open spreadsheet document in the main window, then opened a floating palette and selected a text field. In this situation, the text field in the palette becomes the *first responder*, which makes the palette window the *key window*. But the palette window doesn't cause the document window to become inactive, so it's still the *main window*.

A more typical arrangement occurs while the user is editing the content of a cell in the spreadsheet (identified as the initial first responder in Figure 20-14). The spreadsheet cell becomes the first responder. That makes the document window both the *main window* and the *key window*.

As the user switches windows and views, the chain, or "path," of objects from the first responder to the top-level application object changes. This implicitly alters how both events and actions are processed by the application. Objects don't actively participate in these changes—that is, they don't receive "you are now in the responder chain" events. An object simply is, or is not, in the responder chain.

Events

Events are delivered to the application by the operating system in response to mouse movement, mouse clicks, keyboard activity, scroll-wheel movement, and so on. The path that an event takes varies depending on the event type—keyboard events do not follow the same path as mouse events, for example. You may be interested in creating objects that receive and respond to events, but you're unlikely to get involved in the actual dissemination of events. If you have event processing or filtering needs that aren't described in this section, refer to the *Cocoa Event-Handling Guide*.[9]

Event Objects

Events enter an application via one of the event ports attached to the main run loop. The first thing the main run loop does with an event is to encapsulate it in an NSEvent object. An NSEvent object has the properties listed in Table 20-6.

Table 20-6. NSEvent Properties

Property	Description
type	The type of events. Typical events are NSLeftMouseDown, NSLeftMouseDragged, NSLeftMouseUp, NSKeyDown, NSKeyUp, and NSScrollWheel
timestamp	The time the event occurred.
window	The NSWindow associated with the event.
locationInWindow	The mouse position, in window coordinates, when the event occurred.
clickCount	The number of mouse clicks that have occurred in rapid succession. Used to distinguish single clicks from double and triple clicks.

---

[9] Apple Inc., *Cocoa Event-Handling Guide*, http://developer.apple.com/documentation/Cocoa/ Conceptual/EventOverview/, 2009.

modifierFlags	Keyboard modifiers (Shift, Option, Command, Control, Caps Lock) that were being held down when the event occurred.
characters	The string of characters associated with the key event.
charactersIgnoringModifiers	The string associated with the key event, devoid of any key modifiers (Control, Option, …).
isARepeat	YES if the key event was caused by holding down a key until it auto-repeats.
keyCode	The virtual keyboard code of the key.

Not all properties are applicable to all events, and there are many other obscure properties (like pressure) that apply only to drawing tablet or force-feedback input devices. You will almost never need to create NSEvent objects yourself, but every event handling method will receive the event as an NSEvent object.

Key Events

Key events are distributed down the object hierarchy, usually in search of the first responder. The type of event, and several layers of filtering, heavily influence key event dispatching. Key events are passed first to the application object, then to the key window, to the first responders, and in some cases on to the menu bar.

In simplified terms, a key event goes through the following steps:

1. The operating system translates the hardware key codes into the user's current language. The key event is filtered through the system-wide key bindings, and then passed to system components that have registered to intercept global key events. This is how "hot keys" are processed.

2. The key event is pushed onto the event queue of the active application.

3. The main run loop of the application pulls the next key event, wraps it in an NSEvent object, and sends it to the NSApplication object in a -sendEvent: message.

4. If the key might be a key equivalent (typically a command+key combination), the application sends a -performKeyEquivalent: message to the key window, which interprets it or passes it to its first responder. If neither responds to the event, it's sent to the application's menu bar.

5. The message -sendEvent: is sent to the key window.

6. If the key is an interface control key (Tab, Right Arrow, Page Down, Home), as defined by the currently active view, the window and/or control translates that into an action and sends the appropriate key action message (-setNextKeyView:, -forward:, -pageDown:, -moveToBeginningOfDocument:, respectively) to the window or its first responder.

7. If the event is not a key equivalent or interface control, the first responder receives a -keyDown:, -keyUp:, or -flagsChanged: message.

8. If there isn't a first responder and the window doesn't process the key event, it's passed to the menu bar.

Most views need only override -keyDown:, and possibly -keyUp: or -flagsChanged:, to automatically receive regular key events. If you are writing a view that edits text—and I would discourage you from trying—your view object must conform to the NSTextInput protocol.

To be honest, key event processing is significantly more complex than this, but unless you're writing an application that needs to filter keystrokes or create key bindings, you can generally ignore the more esoteric aspects of key-event processing. A complete description can be found in the Cocoa Event-Handling Guide.

Mouse Events

Mouse and touch events are distributed using the geometry of the user interface. A mouse event is always associated with a location and a window, which is used to determine the recipient of the event.

Mouse Down Event

Mouse event processing usually beings with a mouse down event:

1. When the mouse is clicked, the system's WindowServer determines which application should receive the event.

2. The main run loop of the application sends the mouse event to the NSApplication object via a -sendEvent: message.

3. NSApplication uses the location of the event to determine which window the event occurred in, and forwards the event to that window via another -sendEvent: message.

4. The window's -sendEvent: method uses the location to find the subview corresponding to the click and sends that view a -mouseDown: message.

The first mouse down event in a view will attempt to make it the first responder. This makes the view the recipient of key events; its window becomes the key window and inherently redefines the responder chain, described later in this chapter. To be eligible, a view must return YES when sent an -acceptsFirstResponder message. By default, NSView returns NO. If the view accedes, it will be designated the first responder and receives a -becomeFirstResponder message. When the window is deactivated, or another view becomes the first responder, the view receives a matching -resignFirstResponder message.

A view can also control "click through." Normally, a mouse click in an inactive window activates the window, but does nothing else with the event. Clicking a control in an inactive window normally requires two clicks: the first to activate the window and the second to send a -mouseDown: event to the view. The view can change this behavior by overriding -acceptsFirstMouse:. When a window is activated via a mouse click, it queries the view underneath the click coordinate by sending it an -acceptsFirstMouse: message. If the view returns YES, the window will immediately send the view a -mouseDown: message—both activating the window *and* clicking the view with a single event. By default, NSView returns NO for -acceptsFirstMouse:.

Mouse Drag and Mouse Up Events

Once a view receives a -mouseDown: message, it may then receive -mouseDragged: and -mouseUp: messages. These messages are collectively referred to as the mouse tracking messages. The same view object will receive subsequent -mouseDragged: and -mouseUp: messages, even if the mouse is dragged outside the frame of the view. -mouseDragged: is only sent when the mouse is moved while its button is held down. The view may receive many -mouseDragged: messages, or none at all. A view will never receive a -mouseDragged: or -mouseUp: message before a -mouseDown: message.

If you want your view to do something interesting during a mouse drag gesture, you'll probably want to override all three methods. If you're only interested in implementing click behavior, override -mouseUp: and test the location of the event to see that the mouse is still positioned over your object. The -mouseUp: handler in the TicTacToe project is shown in Listing 20-6.

Listing 20-6. -mouseUp: Event Handler

```
- (void)mouseUp:(NSEvent*)theEvent
{
    NSPoint loc = [self convertPoint:[theEvent locationInWindow] fromView:nil];

    SquareIndex index;
    for (index=0; index<9; index++) {
        if (NSPointInRect(loc,[ChalkboardView rectOfSquare:index])) {
            [[self document] playerClickedSquare:index];
            break;
        }
    }
}
```

The method in Listing 20-6 receives the mouse event information via an NSEvent object. Events are always in the window's coordinate system, so the first thing it does is convert the location into the view's local coordinate system. It then searches to see if the user released the mouse inside any of the nine squares on the playing board. If they did, the view sends a -playerClickedSquare: message to its controller object, which will make the move and update the game board.

Another approach to handling mouse drag events is to stay in your -mouseDown: method and start a nested run loop until the drag is complete. This is, essentially, a "modal" mouse drag loop, that blocks the rest of your application from executing until the drag is finished. The *Cocoa Event-Handling Guide* includes an example of a mouse tracking loop.

Mouse Tracking

Mouse movement during a drag gesture is provided automatically. Mouse movement while the mouse buttons are up is normally ignored. Mouse movement is common, computationally expensive, and normally of no interest to the application.

There are, however, instances where you want to be notified of normal mouse movement in your interface. There are two techniques for tracking the mouse while the mouse buttons are up.

The first method is to request mouse-moved events from the window:

1. Set the acceptsMouseMovedEvents property of the window containing the view to YES.

2. Implement -mouseMoved: methods in your subviews.

Once acceptsMouseMovedEvents is set, the window will begin sending -mouseMoved: messages to its views, much the way it distributes other mouse events.

The second method is to define a mouse tracking rectangle. A mouse tracking rectangle defines a discrete area of your view where mouse tracking is desired. It notifies your object when the mouse moves into the region, moves around in the region, and again when it leaves the region. This is much more efficient than fielding every mouse movement, but it is a little more complicated to set up:

1. Implement the methods -mouseEntered:, -mouseExited:, -mouseMoved: and -cursorUpdate: in an object. This could be your view object, or something else.
2. Create an NSTrackingArea object using the rectangle of the area to track (in view coordinates) and the owner object created in step 1. You may also specify additional tracking options or provide a dictionary of context information.
3. Attach the NSTrackingArea object to an NSView object by sending it an -addTrackingArea: message.

Once attached, the owner object will receive mouse entered, moved, exited, and cursor update events.

The Responder Chain

The responder chain is the sequence of objects that starts with the first responder and goes up through the object hierarchy. The responder chain is the principal mechanism for determining how your application responds to commands and other actions.

The complete responder chain is shown in Figure 20-15.

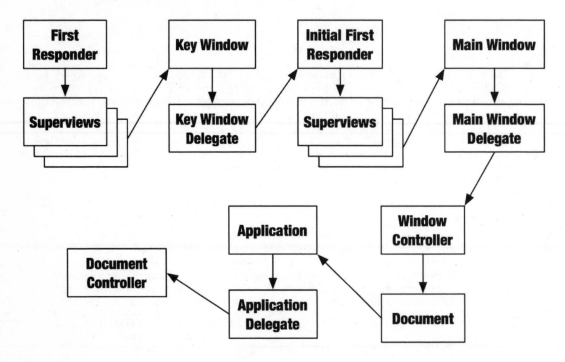

Figure 20-15. *The responder chain*

The responder chain processes action messages, which are Objective-C messages of the form -(IBAction)action:(id)sender, by examining each object in the chain to determine if it *responds to* (implements) the given message. If it does, the object receives the message. If not, the process examines the next object in the chain until an object that responds to the message is found, or there are no more objects.

The two first responders in Figure 20-15 require a little explanation: the first responder is the single object that's the "focus" of the interface. When a window loses key window status, it remembers the object that was formally its first responder. This becomes the window's *initial* first responder. The initial first responder becomes first responder automatically when the window becomes key—assuming some other view doesn't become first responder in the process. When the key and main windows are different, the responder chain starts with the first responder, goes through the key window, and then to the initial first responder of the main window.

Much of the responder chain in Figure 20-15 is optional, and it's unusual to find a situation where the entire chain is traversed. If the key window has no first responder object, the responder chain begins with the key window itself. If the key and main windows are the same, the responder's superview hierarchy is only traversed once. Windows without controllers do not include a window controller in the chain. Non-document windows don't have controllers or document objects and jump directly to the application. Window and application objects might not have delegates. Non-document-based applications do not have a document controller object, so the responder chain in those applications ends with the application or its delegate.

If you're developing an iPhone application, the responder chain principles are the same. The responder chains themselves will tend to be fairly simple. An iPhone application only displays a single UIWindow at a time, so the key and main windows are always one and the same. Actions passed to a UIView are first passed to its UIViewController, if it has one, before going to its enclosing UIView.

Action Messages

Actions, menu status queries, services, and error interpretations are all filtered through the responder chain. The simplest explanation of how the responder chain integrates with your application is to use an example. Take the application depicted in Figure 20-14, and consider the four menu commands Copy, Close, Save, and New. Each of these commands sends an action message (-copy:, -performClose:, -saveDocument:, and -newDocument:, respectively) to the first responder.

- The -copy: action message is sent to the first responder. The first responder in Figure 20-14 is an editable text field that implements clipboard functionality. It responds to the -copy: message by transferring the current selection to the application's pasteboard (clipboard).

- The first responder does not implement the -performClose: method, nor do any of its superviews. The key window does, and it responds to -performClose: method by closing itself.

- The first responder does not implement the -saveDocument: message. Neither do any of its superviews, the key window, its delegate, the views in the main window, the main window, its delegate, or the window controller. The NSDocument object is the object responsible for document management and is the object that implements the Save, and Save As... commands. It responds to the -saveDocument: message by encoding the contents of the active document and writing it to a file.

- The -newDocument: message passes through every object in the responder chain until it reaches the single document controller object, created for document-based applications. The document controller creates a new document and opens an untitled window.

The application's response to commands changes, depending on the state of the responder chain:

- If another view object was the first responder, the application might not respond to the Copy command.

- Other windows in the application ignore the Close action, because they aren't in the responder chain.

- If the main window is not a document window, there would be no NSDocument object in its responder chain, so that window wouldn't respond to a Save action.

- The application always responds to the New command, because the top-level object in the chain consistently responds to it.

Sending Action Messages

An action message sent to a specific object is called a *targeted* action. An action sent to the responder chain is an *untargeted* action. An action consists of an Objective-C message identifier (SEL) and an object identifier (id). If the target identifier points to an object, it's a targeted action. If the target identifier is nil, it's an untargeted action.

Actions are sent by sending the NSApplication object a -sendAction:to:from: message. The target (to:) parameter is either an object (targeted) or nil (untargeted). The application determines if the target responds to the action, or attempts to find a target that responds to the action in the responder chain. If successful, the target object is sent the action message and -sendAction:to:from: returns YES. You can send actions programmatically, but NSControl views, menu items, and keyboard equivalents usually send them for you.

In Interface Builder, an action is defined as a message/object pair. If the action is connected directly to another object in the NIB document, it defines a targeted action. Connecting an action to the First Responder placeholder NIB object creates an untargeted action that will be delivered to the current first responder at runtime.

Menu Actions

The menu items in a Cocoa application are another prominent use of the responder chain. When you drop down an application menu, only those items that are applicable to the current interface state are enabled. Menu items that are inappropriate are disabled.

The Cocoa framework determines this dynamically by examining the objects in the responder chain. Each menu item is associated with an action. When the user drops down a menu, the responder chain is searched to find objects that will respond to each item in the menu. If there's an object in the chain that responds to an action, that menu item is enabled. If not, it's disabled.

▪**Note** You can search the responder chain for objects yourself using -[NSApplication targetForAction: to:from:].

The beauty of this system is that views and controller do not spend any time or effort determining what menu items should be enabled. It's determined empirically, based on the collection of objects in the responder chain.

To implement a menu command in an application that performs some function and is automatically enabled and disabled, do the following:

1. In the object responsible for implementing the command, create an action method:
   -(IBAction)*action*:(id)sender.

2. Create a menu item in Interface Builder and set its action to the message identifier in step 1, connected to the first responder.

That's it. That's all you have to do. The actions sent by the menu item will be automatically connected to the appropriate object in the responder chain, or disabled otherwise.

In the TicTacToe project, the TTTDocument object implements two actions: -reset: and -playForPlayer:. The menu items Reset and Play One Move send these actions. There's also a Reset button that sends the same action. Open and close TicTacToe document windows and see how this affects that state of the menu items.

Disabling Action Menu Items

While the automatic appearance of menu items based on the objects in the responder chain is cool, there are situations where an object in the responder chain implements an action, but the action is still not always appropriate. The Cocoa framework makes this easy to accomplish, again using the responder chain.

I omitted a step about menu items in the previous section. Once the responder to a menu item is located, the menu framework checks to see if it implements a -validateMenuItem: method. If it does, it gives the object a chance to disable the item by sending it that message, passing the menu item to consider. If the object returns YES, the menu item is enabled. Otherwise, it's disabled just as if the object did not respond to the action.

In the TicTacToe project, both the Reset and Play One Move menu items send actions to the responder chain. Without doing anything else, both would be enabled as long as the document object is in the responder chain. But the game's reset command only makes sense once the game has started, and the play command is only applicable when it is the user's move. Listing 20-7 implements a -validateMenuItem: method that accounts for these conditions.

Listing 20-7. Menu Item Validation Method

```
- (BOOL)validateMenuItem:(NSMenuItem*)menuItem
{
    if ([menuItem action]==@selector(reset:)) {
        return game.isStarted;
    } else if ([menuItem action]==@selector(playForPlayer:)) {
        return (game.nextPlayer==USER_PLAYER);
    }
    return [super validateMenuItem:menuItem];
}
```

The code in Listing 20-7 examines the menuItem to determine which command is being validated. It then determines whether the menu item should be enabled or not, based on the state of the game. This implementation identifies the menu item by the action that it sends. Another popular technique is to assign unique tag values to the menu items in Interface Builder, which make them easy to identify (i.e., if ([menuitem tag]==1001) …). You can use any identification method you choose. Your object will only receive -validateMenuItem: messages for the actions it responds to.

Designing with the Responder Chain

The responder chain is also used for some other miscellaneous purposes. It's used to translate error objects (see Chapter 14) and to determine what services are available (services is a plug-in architecture that lets other applications interact with yours).

The responder chain will deeply influence how, and specifically where, you implement the functionality of your applications. When designing Cocoa applications, keep these guidelines in mind:

Implement a menu item action in the object that's in the responder chain when the menu command is applicable, and not in the chain when it isn't.

In general, actions should be implemented in the root object that encompasses the domain of the action:

- A command that reads or writes the document should be implemented in the document object, not the window.

- Actions that change the state of the data model should be implemented in the controller or data model object, not the view.

- Views should implement editing actions directly, but the final change should be sent as a discrete action to a controller or data model.

Implement your target action in the logically correct object in the hierarchy, even if it duplicates a function elsewhere and does nothing but send a single message to another object. It's easier than trying to fight the organization of the responder chain.

That finally brings us to the end of view objects. Your application's entire look and feel is implemented by view objects, so they have a lot to do. The next couple of sections will explore data model objects and, finally, controller objects.

Data Models

A data model is essentially any object that holds the data of your application. The form the data takes, how it gets used, and how it's presented to the user is as varied as there are applications. There are four general types of data model objects in a Cocoa application: legacy table and tree data sources, collection controllers, Core Data objects, and custom classes.

Legacy Table and Tree Models

Like Swing, Cocoa provides views that display a collection of objects as tables and trees. These can interface with a legacy data model provider, very similar to that in Swing, or be bound to an NSObjectController object. The equivalent view and data source classes are listed in Table 20-7.

Table 20-7. *Collection View Classes*

Swing	Cocoa
javax.swing.JTable	NSTableView
javax.swing.table.TableModel	NSTableDataSource
javax.swing.table.TableCellRenderer	NSCell
javax.swing.table.JTableHeader	NSTableHeaderView
javax.swing.table.TableColumn	NSTableColumn
javax.swing.JTree	NSOutlineView, NSBrowserView
javax.swing.tree.TreeModel	NSOutlineViewDataSource
javax.swing.tree.TreeCellRenderer	NSCell

If you're used to working with Swing tables and trees, you'll be very comfortable with the Cocoa classes. The architecture of each is remarkably similar:

- NSTableView implements a tabular view of a collection of data.

- The data for a table is supplied by a dataSource object that conforms to the NSTableDataSource informal protocol.

- Cell renderers are subclasses of NSCell.

- An NSTableView has a collection of NSTableColumn objects that define the title and cell renderer for each column in the table.

- NSOutlineView displays a tree of data in a hierarchical view where parent nodes can be expanded and collapsed, and subnodes are indented.

- The data for an outline is supplied by a dataSource object that conforms to the NSOutlineViewDataSource informal protocol.

- Unlike Java, NSOutlineView is a subclass of NSTableView, where it inherits its column and cell behavior. The equivalent of a tree view in Swing is a single column NSOutlineView. One column is designated as the tree; the rest of the view can display other tabular data associated with each node. The List view in the Finder is an example of an outline view.

- NSBrowserView is an alternate tree viewer that displays each level of tree in separate columns. The data is obtained from the view's delegate object. The Column view in the Finder is an example of a browser.

Your data source object must conform to an informal protocol, either NSTableDataSource or NSOutlineViewDataSource. The protocol defines a number of required methods that supply cell and node data to the view. There are also a number of optional methods, many of which define whether the cells in the view are editable or not. If you omit these methods, the collection is immutable and the view is display only.

■**Caution** A common mistake is to overlook the fact that NSCell conforms to NSCopying. NSCell objects get copied—a lot. If you subclass NSCell, you *must* make sure it still conforms to the NSCoping protocol. You may have to override -`copyWithZone:`.

---

iPhone developers will find a similar, but vastly simplified, set of view classes for displaying tables and lists. The principal class is UITableView. It communicates with objects that conform to UITableViewDelegate and UITableViewDataSource in much the same way that NSTableView uses an NSTableDataSource object. UITableView splits it queries between its delegate, which provides display and behavior properties, and its data source, which provides individual cell values. In practice, the two sources are often the same object—usually the view's controller. These are the only data sources for iPhone table views, since the iPhone OS does not support the Cocoa bindings technology that allows collection controllers, described in the next section, to work.

While the traditional data source objects are considered "legacy" interfaces, they still afford a few advantages. They are particularly well suited to data that's generated dynamically. They can provide better performance than the modern data model interfaces. And they're similar in organization to other frameworks, like Swing, which might make porting easier.

Collection Controllers

The "modern" way of populating an NSTableView, NSOutlineView, NSBrowser, or any other collection view is by binding the content property of the view to an NSArrayController or NSTreeController. The advantage is that you don't have to create your own data model or data source class, just bind your existing compatible data model—typically an NSArray—to the controller and the controller to the view; the framework takes care of the rest. How to create the bindings is not entirely intuitive. Unlike the traditional data source method, which is connected to the table view object, table bindings are set for each column:

- Bind the individual columns of a table to an array controller, specifying the model key path of the object's property to display in that cell. To display the object itself, set the model key path to "self."

- Bind the individual columns of an outline to a tree controller, specifying the model key path of the object's property to display in that cell. To display the object itself, set the model key path to "self."

The controller's key—that is, the whole collection of objects being bound to—will typically be the same for all of the columns, ensuring that the cells in a row all reflect the same object. However, your data can be organized into multiple arrays or trees—just make sure that the collections agree.

While the mechanics of supplying the data is done for you, you are still free to customize the look and feel of the view by supplying your own cell renderers, specifying column properties, and customizing the header view, just as you would with the traditional data models.

NSCollectionView is a modern view that largely replaces NSMatrix and works with bindings.

Core Data

Core Data is a data modeling and persistence framework that delivers soup-to-nuts data modeling and storage. It handles many of the "tasks associated with object life-cycle and object graph management, including persistence."[10] If you want to use Core Data objects as a (or the) data model of your applications, you will generally follow these steps:

1. Create your Xcode project using one of the Core Data or Core Data Document–based project templates. These templates include generic support for encoding your Core Data objects as an XML document, or documents. This isn't difficult to set up, but starting with the templates saves you the effort.
2. The default persistence store (i.e., the place where Core Data encodes and saves your data model) will be an XML document. You can override this to store your objects in an SQLite database or some other format; just note that creating a custom storage format can be rather involved.
3. Design your data model in Xcode using the Data Modeling tool. You define entities (objects) that have attributes (properties) and relationships (connections). When you build your application, the model is compiled into a Managed Object Model (mom) file that's loaded at runtime. This model is used to create your data model objects.
4. If you are creating a document-based Core Data application, make sure you use or subclass NSPersistentDocument. It handles much of the document-level management of your document data model for you.
5. Use NSManagedObject instances created by Core Data pretty much as you would use your own custom data model objects. You can get and set their properties, add them to collections, bind views to them, observe them, and so on. The Core Data framework takes care of the fetching, caching, and encoding of your objects automatically.

One initially confusing aspect, particularly for Java developers, is the dynamic nature of the NSManagedObject class. Each entity in your data model instantiates an NSManagedObject at runtime; every object managed by Core Data must be an instance of NSManagedObject, or a subclass. While it's *possible* to subclass NSManagedObject in special cases, most of the time you don't. The attributes that you assign the entity in the data modeling tool become Objective-C properties at runtime—and it's done without subclassing. NSManagedObject uses Objective-C's ability to respond to messages and properties that it doesn't implement and "synthesize" those properties at runtime. So, if you define an entity with an integer property named tag, you can treat that object at runtime as though it was a subclass of NSManagedObject with an `int` tag property: `if (entity.tag>0) entity.tag -= 1`. See Chapters 6 and 10 for more details.

The Core Data tools and frameworks make it really easy to start using Core Data in your application. But Core Data is actually a deep and complex architecture that's highly customizable and extensible. For a complete explanation, consult the *Core Data Programming Guide*.[11]

Custom Data Model Objects

Often the best data model solution is to simply define a class and populate it with data. The TicTacToeGame class in the TicTacToe project is a custom data model.

When designing an application, first look at the ready-made classes like NSArray, NSArrayController, and Core Data to see if they can effectively model your data. If they can, then by all means use the solution that's already solved. If not, then create your own classes or subclass existing ones, like NSManagedObject and NSObjectController.

---

[10] Apple Inc., *Core Data Programming Guide*, http://developer.apple.com/documentation/Cocoa/Conceptual/CoreData/, 2009.
[11] Ibid.

Controllers

The Cocoa framework provides a few basic controller objects, like NSApplication and NSDocument. It also provides mediating controller objects that are subclasses of NSController.

Custom Controllers

Most controller objects are going to be custom classes or subclasses of NSApplication and NSDocument. Controllers implement the actions of your application; providing custom actions will eventually involve implementing your own methods.

One consideration is to decide whether to implement your application's actions in a subclass of a controller or in a delegate.

- If you need to override the methods of a controller, create a subclass.

- If it makes sense to extend the controller class with new instance variables, create a subclass.

- If you are only implementing custom action methods, implement them in the delegate.

- If you need sets of actions that can be "plugged-in" to different controllers to create customized behavior, implement them in a delegate.

- If your solution has a mixture of needs, you can implement both: subclass the controller and attach a delegate.

There are a couple of steps to creating subclasses of NSApplication and NSDocument, because these objects are created by the framework—by the NSApplicationMain() function and the NSDocumentController, respectively. If you subclass them, you have to tell the framework which class to instantiate.

Creating a Custom NSApplication

To create a subclass of NSApplication, do the following:

1. Define a subclass of NSApplication.

2. Set the Principal Class (NSPrincipalClass) value in the application's Info.plist file to the name of the class created in step 1.

The NSApplicationMain() function reads the Info.plist property file at startup and uses that value to create the single application object. You can obtain a reference to the application object using +[NSApplication sharedApplication] or through the global NSApp variable.

If you create a subclass of NSApplication, you can directly access its outlets and actions in Interface Builder by changing the class of the Application placeholder object in your NIB documents to your custom class.

To create an NSApplication delegate:

1. Define your class. Populate it with your application delegate methods and actions.

2. In Interface Builder, open the MainMenu NIB document and create an instance of your custom object. Do this by dragging in a generic Object from the library and changing its class to the one created in step 1.

3. Connect the delegate outlet of the Application placeholder object to your delegate object.

When the MainMenu NIB document is loaded during application startup, the NIB connection will cause an instance of your delegate object to be created and set as the application object's delegate.

Your delegate object can elect to receive many notifications, which are especially handy for doing additional initialization and housekeeping at startup and before shutdown. The most commonly implemented delegate methods are -applicationWillFinishLaunching:, -applicationDidFinish↵ Launching:, and -applicationWillTerminate:.

Creating a Custom NSDocument

To use a subclass of NSDocument, follow these steps:

1. Define a subclass of NSDocument.

2. In the application's Info.plist file, locate the entry in the Document Types (CFBundleDocumentTypes) collection that corresponds to the document type associated with your custom class. Most applications only edit one document type. Change the Cocoa NSDocument Class (NSDocumentClass) value to the name of the class created in step 1.

The NSDocumentController will use the class name it finds in the DocumentType record to instantiate the correct subclass of NSDocument whenever it creates a new NSDocument object. It's also possible to do this programmatically by subclassing NSDocumentController and overriding its -documentClassForType: method, but that's exceptional.

To create a document delegate, follow these steps:

1. Define your class. Populate it with your document delegate methods and actions.

2. In Interface Builder, open the NIB document associated with your document (the name is defined by your document's windowNibName property). Create an instance of your custom object. Do this by dragging in a generic Object from the library and changing its class to the one created in step 1.

3. Connect the delegate outlet of the File's Owner placeholder object to your delegate object. The NSDocument object is the owner of the NIB when it is loaded. If you also created a custom subclass of NSDocument, you may want to change the class of the File's Owner placeholder to your custom document subclass.

When NSDocumentController creates a new document window, it begins by creating an instance of NSDocument or your custom subclass of NSDocument. It then queries the object to obtain the name of the NIB document it should load to create the user interface. Loading the NIB also creates your delegate instance and connects it to the document object.

Alternatively, you could override the initialization of your custom NSDocument class and programmatically create and attach your delegate object. But that would only be advantageous if you needed your delegate object before the NIB was loaded.

NSController Controllers

The Cocoa framework provides several concrete subclasses of NSController: NSObjectController, NSArrayController, NSTreeController, and NSDictionaryController. Each implements everything you need to bind an existing collection of objects to a view, manage selection, edit individual values, insert new objects, remove objects, and sort the objects in the collection.

There's just one rule you need to remember when working with NSController objects: most NSControllers *do not* observe their collections. The core collection classes, like NSArray, are not Key-Value Observing compliant. If you make a change to a managed collection, do it *through* the controller. The controller provides methods to insert, remove, and change objects in the collection. Those methods also perform all necessary notifications and housekeeping.

It's really unlikely that you ever need to create your own subclass of NSController. If you do, the process is explained in the *Cocoa Bindings Programming Topics* guide.

About TicTacToe

This chapter has used the TicTacToe application, shown in Figure 20-16, to illustrate many aspects of designing and implementing a Model-View-Controller design. There are, however, still a few odds and ends that might be confusing to someone new to Cocoa application development, which could bear some elucidation.

Figure 20-16. TicTacToe application

Info.plist

An application's `Info.plist` document is critical to its function and to customization. The `Info.plist` file is a property file that contains a number of key values:

- *The class of the program's application object*: Always a subclass of NSApplication, this is the object that gets created during program startup.

- *The name of the main NIB file*: This is the NIB file that's loaded during program initialization. It usually contains all of the core user interface elements, like the menu bar, and often contains instances of global objects, like the application delegate.

- *The application's identifier*: This uniquely identifies the application to the world. TicTacToe's application identifier is com.apress.learnobjc.TicTacToe.

- *The name of the file that contains the application's icon.*

- *A list of Document Type records*: Each record maps a file type (extension) to the NSDocument class that implements it. It also supplies a user-readable description of the document and its icon to Launch Services.

An `Info.plist` can also contain default preferences, a version number, and a user-readable copyright message, among other things. Basically, `Info.plist` contains all of the application's public metadata.

Undo

The TicTacToe application uses the Undo manager. Adding basic undo to your application is extremely easy:

1. When a change is made in your document, obtain the document's undo manager and "push" the following triplet: a target object, an Objective-C message identifier, and an object containing the previous value. If you were implementing a drawing program, resizing a shape might push a -setShapeSize: message along with the previous size of the shape.

2. It's also polite to name the action that was pushed. Using the drawing program again, setting "Resize Shape" as the name of the action will display "Undo Resize Shape" in the Edit menu to the user. This makes it easier for the user to understand what will be undone.

3. When the user selects the Undo command, the undo manager gets the last action pushed onto the stack and sends the object the message with the value. In this example, the drawing object would be sent a -setShapeSize: message with its old size.

4. The undo action handler should also push the (now) previous size as a "redo" action. The messages are exactly the same for pushing an action onto the undo stack—when undoing an action, the undo manager switches into a temporary mode that pushes actions onto a "redo" stack. This allows your single -setShapeSize: method to act as a "do," "undo," and "redo" method.

TicTacToe's data model is trivially simple, so it just pushes the entire state of the document (game and message) on the undo stack after each move. A more complex data model would push specific changes, but the principle is the same.

To simplify both the undo and open/save commands, the TTTDocument implements a `contents` property that returns the entire document state as a single, immutable object.

There is a hidden advantage to implementing undo: the undo manager also maintains the document's `isDocumentEdited` property for you. This tells the document controller when your document contains unsaved changes. If you don't use the undo manager, you must manage the isDocumentEdited property yourself.

Resources

Resources are data files that are copied into your application's bundle. The framework defines many resource files, such as NIB documents, managed object model files, and the executable. You are free to add whatever additional files you want. Typically these are image, sound, and help files, but there are no limitations. A program can include frameworks, even another application, as part of its resources.

You can get a resource using the NSBundle class. Classes like NSImage often have convenience methods, like +[NSImage imageNamed:], that will locate a resource file and load it into an object.

Localized Resources

Almost any resource in an application bundle can be organized by language. These are referred to as *localizations*. A localized version of a file is stored inside a variant subfolder. NSBundle will first look in the variant folder for the user's preferred languages. If it can't find a suitable file (or variant) it will use the file that's not in any variant. This allows you to create alternate language-specific versions for any resource. This includes NIB documents, images, sounds, lists of strings that are shown to the user, and so on.

In Xcode, localized versions of resources are shown as sub-documents to the main document. To create a localized version, open the Info window for the file and choose Add Localization. Every localization is a completely separate file that you must maintain.

Summary

This chapter covered a lot of ground. The Model-View-Controller design pattern permeates the Cocoa frameworks. It influences many different aspects of an application, and brings together the user interface, business logic, and data organization. It involves a dizzying number of classes and employs almost every communications technique discussed so far.

Understanding, and embracing, MVC is a critical step in understanding Cocoa applications. You also learned about key development tools, like Interface Builder, that leverage many Objective-C technologies to create complex user interfaces with almost no code.

CHAPTER 21

■ ■ ■

Lazy Initialization Pattern

The lazy initialization pattern embodies the just-in-time philosophy of data delivery. It delays the construction of values or data structures until that data is actually needed. Lazy initialization is a popular design pattern in both Java and Objective-C. Objective-C adds another level by implementing its own lazy initialization of class structures, which you can integrate into your own classes.

Implementing the Pattern

Here's how to implement the lazy initialization pattern:

1. Create a private instance or private static variable that will eventually contain the data, but is initialized with a placeholder value (typically nil).

2. Wrap the variable in a property that provides a public getter method.

3. In the getter method, test the variable for its placeholder value. If it has not been initialized, construct it and save the results. Return the newly, or previously, constructed data to the sender.

Lazy initialization is usually applied when

- The memory or resources required to create or calculate the data is excessive and can be deferred.

- There is a significant possibility that the data will never be needed.

- The prerequisites of the data do not exist, or are not available, when an object is instantiated.

Deferring the calculation of a value, or assembling a large or complex data structure, preserves memory and CPU resources until the data is actually needed. In some cases, the data may never be needed, resulting in a substantial performance improvement. Perceived performance can be improved by deferring operations to a later time, allowing the application to immediately update a display or respond to a user event, while more complex and time-consuming work is done later. The canonical example is a photo browsing application that immediately presents placeholder or thumbnail images to the user while the actual images are loaded in the background. The user perceives the application as performing faster, because it's more responsive, even if the actual amount of time it takes to load and display the final images is slower.

An object constructor that creates an object, quickly and with minimal memory demands, is called a *lightweight* constructor. The constructor can be lightweight even if the object is *heavyweight*. Using the example above, an image view object could be initialized almost instantly with nothing more than the dimensions of the image and a URL where the image data can be obtained. The constructor, and the properties needed to update a window or lay out a multipage document, is lightweight and available immediately—even if the actual image takes megabytes of memory and several seconds to obtain.

Lazy Initialization of Global Variables

Lazy initialization is often applied to global variables. An advantage that Java has over Objective-C is its ability to declare object initializers for static variables. The Java runtime evaluates the initialization statements when the class is loaded.

```
public final static String[] ColorNames = new String[] { "White", "Black" };
```

A truly global variable in Objective-C is a static C variable. Static C variables can only be initialized with constants or static addresses, and this initialization occurs before the Objective-C runtime starts. To achieve the same effect requires some form of automatic initialization that occurs after the Objective-C runtime has started.

The ChessPiece class, shown in Listings 21-1 and 21-2, accomplishes this by defining two class properties: +[ChessPiece colorNames] and +[ChessPiece pieceNames]. These return an immutable collection of strings that can be used to convert a color or piece enum (int) into a string. They use lazy initialization to create, and save, the immutable arrays the first time they are requested.

Listing 21-1. *ChessPiece.h*

```
#import <Cocoa/Cocoa.h>

typedef enum {
    White=0,
    Black
} Color;

typedef enum {
    Pawn=0,
    Rook,
    Bishop,
    Knight,
    Queen,
    King
} Piece;

@interface ChessPiece : NSObject {
    Color   color;
    Piece   piece;
}

+ (NSArray*)colorNames;
+ (NSArray*)pieceNames;
+ (NSDictionary*)images;

+ (NSString*)nameOfPiece:(Piece)piece color:(Color)color;

- (id)initWithPiece:(Piece)thePiece color:(Color)theColor;
```

```objc
@property (readonly) Color color;
@property (readonly) Piece piece;
@property (readonly) NSString *name;
@property (readonly) NSImage *image;

@end
```

Listing 21-2. *ChessPiece.m*

```objc
#import "ChessPiece.h"

static NSArray *ColorNames;
static NSArray *PieceNames;
static NSDictionary *PieceImages;

@implementation ChessPiece

+ (NSArray*)colorNames
{
    if (ColorNames==nil) {
        ColorNames = [NSArray arrayWithObjects:
                        @"White",
                        @"Black",
                        nil];
    }
    return ColorNames;
}

+ (NSArray*)pieceNames
{
    if (PieceNames==nil) {
        PieceNames = [NSArray arrayWithObjects:
                        @"Pawn",
                        @"Rook",
                        @"Bishop",
                        @"Knight",
                        @"Queen",
                        @"King",
                        nil];
    }
    return PieceNames;
}

+ (NSDictionary*)images
```

```objc
{
    if (PieceImages==nil) {
        // Load the entire set of playing piece images
        NSMutableDictionary *images = [NSMutableDictionary new];
        Color color;
        Piece piece;
        for (color=White; color<=Black; color++) {
            for (piece=Pawn; piece<=King; piece++) {
                NSString *name = [ChessPiece nameOfPiece:piece color:color];
                [images setObject:[NSImage imageNamed:name] forKey:name];
            }
        }
        PieceImages = [NSDictionary dictionaryWithDictionary:images];
    }
    return PieceImages;
}

+ (NSString*)nameOfPiece:(Piece)piece color:(Color)color
{
    return [NSString stringWithFormat:@"%@ %@",
            [[ChessPiece colorNames] objectAtIndex:color],
            [[ChessPiece pieceNames] objectAtIndex:piece]];
}

- (id)initWithPiece:(Piece)thePiece color:(Color)theColor
{
    self = [super init];
    if (self != nil) {
        piece = thePiece;
        color = theColor;
    }
    return self;
}

@synthesize color, piece;

- (NSString*)name
{
    return [ChessPiece nameOfPiece:piece color:color];
}

- (NSImage*)image
{
    return [[ChessPiece images] objectForKey:[self name]];
}

@end
```

It also defines a +[ChessPiece images] class property that contains the images of all the chess pieces. This is lazily initialized the first time a ChessPiece object attempts to acquire its graphic representation. It's a time-consuming and resource-intensive initialization, and it requires that the application be fully initialized and running since it depends on locating image resource files in its application bundle.

The Class +initialize Method

Objective-C classes are themselves initialized lazily. The structure that defines a class is not constructed until the first message is sent to the class. This keeps the runtime nimble, allowing it to start up with the minimum amount of initialization required. But Objective-C goes one step further; after initializing the Class object, and before any other messages are sent, the runtime sends a single +initialize message to the newly created Class object. You can override this method to perform additional class-level initialization.

By exploiting the +initialize message, the ChessPiece class can be significantly simplified, as shown in Listings 21-3 and 21-4.

Listing 21-3. ChessPiece.h Using +initialize

```
#import <Cocoa/Cocoa.h>

typedef enum {
    White=0,
    Black
} Color;

typedef enum {
    Pawn=0,
    Rook,
    Bishop,
    Knight,
    Queen,
    King
} Piece;

@interface ChessPiece : NSObject {
    Color   color;
    Piece   piece;
}

+ (NSString*)nameOfPiece:(Piece)piece color:(Color)color;

- (id)initWithPiece:(Piece)thePiece color:(Color)theColor;
```

```objc
@property (readonly) Color color;
@property (readonly) Piece piece;
@property (readonly) NSString *name;
@property (readonly) NSImage *image;

@end
```

Listing 21-4. *ChessPiece.m Using +initialize*

```objc
#import "ChessPiece.h"

static NSArray *ColorNames;
static NSArray *PieceNames;
static NSDictionary *PieceImages;

@implementation ChessPiece

+ (void)initialize
{
    if (PieceImages==nil) {
        ColorNames = [NSArray arrayWithObjects:
                        @"White",
                        @"Black",
                        nil];
        PieceNames = [NSArray arrayWithObjects:
                        @"Pawn",
                        @"Rook",
                        @"Bishop",
                        @"Knight",
                        @"Queen",
                        @"King",
                        nil];
        // Load the entire set of playing piece images
        NSMutableDictionary *images = [NSMutableDictionary dictionary];
        Color color;
        Piece piece;
        for (color=White; color<=Black; color++) {
            for (piece=Pawn; piece<=King; piece++) {
                NSString *name = [ChessPiece nameOfPiece:piece color:color];
                [images setObject:[NSImage imageNamed:name] forKey:name];
            }
        }
        PieceImages = [NSDictionary dictionaryWithDictionary:images];
    }
}
```

```
+ (NSString*)nameOfPiece:(Piece)piece color:(Color)color
{
    return [NSString stringWithFormat:@"%@ %@",
            [ColorNames objectAtIndex:color],
            [PieceNames objectAtIndex:piece]];
}

- (id)initWithPiece:(Piece)thePiece color:(Color)theColor
{
    self = [super init];
    if (self != nil) {
        piece = thePiece;
        color = theColor;
    }
    return self;
}

@synthesize color, piece;

- (NSString*)name
{
    return [ChessPiece nameOfPiece:piece color:color];
}

- (NSImage*)image
{
    return [PieceImages objectForKey:[self name]];
}

@end
```

In this updated version, all of the global initialization is performed once in the +initialize method. All tests to check if the static variables have been initialized can be removed. All code can safely assume that +initialize has executed before any other method (class or instance) is executed. As an added bonus, the name and image cache collections are now completely private, accessible only to the code in ChessPiece.m.

Externally, the implementations shown in Listings 21-2 and 21-4 behave the same: a -name message returns the name of the chess piece, and an -image message returns its image. Internally the only significant difference is the timing. In Listing 21-2, the array of images will be loaded the first time an -image message requests it. In Listing 21-4, the array of images will be created the first time the ChessPiece class is used, regardless of whether any code ever requests an image.

When using the +initialize method to perform class-level lazy initialization, keep these points in mind:

- The first message sent to a class, or the first attempt to create an instance of a class, creates the Class object for that class and sends it an +initialize message.

- The +initialize method is only sent once per class. That can be deceiving, however, because Objective-C subclasses inherit the class methods of their superclass. So a class may receive additional +initialize messages for its subclasses. This is why the +initialize method in Listing 21-4 tests to see if PieceImages has already been initialized. This test could be omitted if it was known that ChessPiece had no subclasses.

- The Class object is completely initialized before the +initialize message is sent, so it's safe to call other class methods or create instances of itself from within the +initialize method.

Summary

Lazy initialization is a useful design pattern for both global and instance variables. It optimizes performance by constructing only the information that's actually needed, and defers optional and ancillary calculations to a more appropriate time. Objective-C's lack of static initialization statements can be largely overcome by employing the +initialize class method to programmatically construct any global variables the class needs to function.

■ ■ ■

CHAPTER 22

Factory Pattern

The factory pattern consigns the task of creating objects to another class, called the factory. Factories take many forms. Factories can implement convenience constructors that simplify the construction of common objects by encapsulating repetitive or tedious preparations. They can be used to implement singletons and reusable pools of objects. But the most significant use is deciding the class of the new object on behalf of the client—the pattern we'll explore in this chapter. (A singleton factory pattern is described in Chapter 23).

The factory pattern is employed when the client—the code creating the object—cannot easily determine the class of the new object because it cannot know, or should not know, what class to create. There is often a choice between several closely related subclasses, where the correct choice depends on decisions or implementation details that are hidden from the client. In Java, this is usually implemented using static methods or abstract factory objects. Objective-C has a powerful pattern called a *class cluster* that implement the factory pattern right in the object's initializer.

URL Factory

A good example of the factory pattern would be a URL object factory. URL objects can be created from URI strings (i.e., `"http://www.apress.com/"`). The URL class library might define several URL classes: a base URL class, along with specialized subclasses like FileURL, HTTPURL, SecureURL, and so on. Requiring the client of the URL class to decide which subclass to instantiate by examining the string would be a really poor design. Instead, the base URL class would declare a URL object factory, something like this:

```
public static URL makeURL( String uri );
```

The static `URL.makeURL(String)` method would parse the string, determine its protocol, and then create and return an object of the appropriate class. The string `"file://users/home/file.data"` might return an instance of FileURL, while the string `"https://secure.apress.com/"` might return an instance of SecureURL. The actual subclass, and the logic used to determine what class is created, is of little concern to the client.

Matrix Class

The characteristic evolution of a class will be used to explore this genre of the factory pattern. The example used is a Matrix class that encapsulates the concept of a mathematical matrix and performs simple matrix operations. Listing 22-1 shows the initial version of the class in Java and Listing 22-2 shows an equivalent implementation in Objective-C.

The listing omits much of the minutiae of the actual implementation, so that you can concentrate on the factory pattern. The complete implementation is available for download at `http://www.apress.com/` in the Source Code/Downloads section.

Listing 22-1. *Initial Matrix Class in Java*

```java
public class Matrix
{
    protected int rows;
    protected int columns;
    double[] values;

    public Matrix( double[] values, int rows, int columns )
    {
        this(values,true,rows,columns);
    }

    protected Matrix( double[] values, boolean copyValues, int rows, int columns )
    {
        this.rows = rows;
        this.columns = columns;
        if (copyValues) {
            this.values = new double[values.length];
            System.arraycopy(values,0,this.values,0,rows*columns);
        } else {
            this.values = values;
        }
    }

    public int getRows()
    {
        return rows;
    }

    public int getColumns()
    {
        return columns;
    }

    public double getValue( int row, int column )
    {
        return values[row*columns+column];
    }
```

```java
    public boolean isIdentity( )
    {
        if (rows!=columns)
            return false;

        ...

        return true;
    }

    public Matrix add( Matrix matrix )
    {
        double[] sumArray = new double[rows*columns];
        ...
        return new Matrix(sumArray,false,rows,columns);
    }

    public Matrix multiply( Matrix right )
    {
        double[] productArray = new double[rows*right.columns];

        ...

        return new Matrix(productArray,false,rows,right.columns);
    }

    public Matrix multiply( double scalar )
    {
        double[] productArray = new double[rows*columns];

        ...

        return new Matrix(productArray,false,rows,columns);
    }

    public Matrix transpose( )
    {
        double[] transArray = new double[rows*columns];

        ...

        return new Matrix(transArray,false,columns,rows);
    }
}
```

The basic design of the Java Matrix class, shown in Listing 22-1, is straightforward. It encapsulates a two-dimensional matrix of floating-point numbers. A new Matrix object is created from a one-dimensional array of numbers and is immutable. The dimensions of the matrix are obtained through the row and column properties. Matrix operations are performed by the add(Matrix), multiply(Matrix), multiply(double), and transpose() methods. An identity property returns true if the object represents an identity matrix.

Listing 22-2. *Initial Matrix Class in Objective-C*

```
@interface Matrix : NSObject {
    @protected
    NSUInteger       rows;
    NSUInteger       columns;
    __strong double *values;
}

- (id)initIdentityWithDimensions:(NSUInteger)dimensions;
- (id)initWithValues:(const double*)valueArray
                rows:(NSUInteger)rowCount
             columns:(NSUInteger)colCount;

@property (readonly) NSUInteger rows;
@property (readonly) NSUInteger columns;
@property (readonly,getter=isIdentity) BOOL identity;

- (double)valueAtRow:(NSUInteger)row column:(NSUInteger)column;

- (Matrix*)addMatrix:(Matrix*)matrix;
- (Matrix*)multiplyMatrix:(Matrix*)matrix;
- (Matrix*)multiplyScalar:(double)scalar;
- (Matrix*)transpose;

@end

@interface Matrix () // private methods

- (id)initWithAllocatedArray:(__strong double*)array
                        rows:(NSUInteger)rowCount
                     columns:(NSUInteger)colCount;

@end

#define VALUE(ARRAY,COLUMNS,ROW,COLUMN)    ARRAY[((ROW)*(COLUMNS))+(COLUMN)]
#define IVALUE(ROW,COLUMN)                 VALUE(values,columns,ROW,COLUMN)
#define SIZEOFARRAY(ROWS,COLUMNS)          (sizeof(double)*(ROWS)*(COLUMNS))
```

```objc
@implementation Matrix

- (id)initIdentityWithDimensions:(NSUInteger)dimensions
{
    self = [super init];
    if (self != nil) {
        values = MatrixAllocateEmptyArray(dimensions,dimensions);
        NSUInteger i;
        for (i=0; i<dimensions; i++)
            IVALUE(i,i) = 1.0;
    }
    return self;
}

- (id)initWithValues:(const double*)valueArray
                rows:(NSUInteger)rowCount
             columns:(NSUInteger)colCount
{
    __strong double *dupArray = MatrixCopyArray(valueArray,rowCount,colCount);
    return [self initWithAllocatedArray:dupArray rows:rowCount columns:colCount];
}

- (id)initWithAllocatedArray:(__strong double*)array
                        rows:(NSUInteger)rowCount
                     columns:(NSUInteger)colCount
{
    self = [super init];
    if (self!=nil) {
        rows = rowCount;
        columns = colCount;
        values = array;
    }
    return self;
}

@synthesize rows, columns;

- (BOOL)isIdentity
{
    if (rows!=columns)
        return NO;
    …
    return YES;
}
```

```objc
- (double)valueAtRow:(NSUInteger)row column:(NSUInteger)column
{
    return IVALUE(row,column);
}


- (Matrix*)addMatrix:(Matrix*)matrix
{
    __strong double *sumArray = MatrixAllocateArray(rows,columns);
    ...
    return [[Matrix alloc] initWithAllocatedArray:sumArray
                                             rows:rows
                                          columns:columns];
}


- (Matrix*)multiplyMatrix:(Matrix*)matrix
{
    __strong double *productArray = MatrixAllocateArray(leftMatrix.rows,columns);
    ...
    return [[Matrix alloc] initWithAllocatedArray:productArray
                                             rows:leftMatrix.rows
                                          columns:columns];
}


- (Matrix*)multiplyScalar:(double)scalar
{
    __strong double *productArray = MatrixAllocateArray(rows,columns);
    ...
    return [[Matrix alloc] initWithAllocatedArray:productArray
                                             rows:rows
                                          columns:columns];
}


- (Matrix*)transpose
{
    __strong double *transArray = MatrixAllocateArray(columns,rows);
    ...
    return [[Matrix alloc] initWithAllocatedArray:transArray
                                             rows:columns
                                          columns:rows];
}

@end
```

```
double *MatrixCopyArray( const __strong double *srcArray,
                         NSUInteger rows,
                         NSUInteger columns )
{
    __strong double *duplicateArray = MatrixAllocateArray(rows,columns);
    NSCopyMemoryPages(srcArray,duplicateArray,SIZEOFARRAY(rows,columns));
    return duplicateArray;
}


double *MatrixAllocateEmptyArray( NSUInteger rows, NSUInteger columns )
{
    __strong double *emptyArray = MatrixAllocateArray(rows,columns);
    bzero(emptyArray,SIZEOFARRAY(rows,columns));
    return emptyArray;
}


double *MatrixAllocateArray( NSUInteger rows, NSUInteger columns )
{
    __strong double *array = NSAllocateCollectable(SIZEOFARRAY(rows,columns),0);
    return array;
}
```

The Objective-C implementation, shown in Listing 22-2, is very similar in functionality to the Java version, although there are some notable implementation differences. It defines some utility C functions (MatrixCopyArray, MatrixAllocateEmptyArray, and MatrixAllocateArray) to make it easier to create and manipulate arrays of primitive floating-point values. It also declares some convenience macros (VALUE, IVALUE, and SIZEOFARRAY) for efficiently accessing the value array. But beyond that, it has essentially the same constructors, properties, and operations as its Java cousin.

Finally, Listing 22-3 shows some code that illustrates how Matrix classes are created and used to perform matrix operations in both Java and Objective-C.

Listing 22-3. *Matrix Class Demonstration Code*

Java
```
double[] a_values = {
      1.0, 0.0, 2.0,
      -1.0, 3.0, 1.0
      };
double[] b_values = {
      3.0, 1.0,
      2.0, 1.0,
      1.0, 0.0
      };
```

417

```
double[] i_values = {
        1.0, 0.0, 0.0,
        0.0, 1.0, 0.0,
        0.0, 0.0, 1.0
        };
Matrix A = new Matrix(a_values,2,3);
Matrix B = new Matrix(b_values,3,2);
Matrix I = new Matrix(i_values,3,3);
System.out.println("A="+A);
System.out.println("B="+B);
System.out.println("I="+I);
System.out.println("B+B="+B.add(B));
System.out.println("A*3="+A.multiply(3.0));
System.out.println("A*B="+A.multiply(B));
System.out.println("A*I="+A.multiply(I));
System.out.println("Atr="+A.transpose());
```

Objective-C
```
double a_values[] = {
     1.0, 0.0, 2.0,
    -1.0, 3.0, 1.0
    };
double b_values[] = {
    3.0, 1.0,
    2.0, 1.0,
    1.0, 0.0
    };
double i_values[] = {
    1.0, 0.0, 0.0,
    0.0, 1.0, 0.0,
    0.0, 0.0, 1.0,
    };
Matrix *A = [[Matrix alloc] initWithValues:a_values rows:2 columns:3];
Matrix *B = [[Matrix alloc] initWithValues:b_values rows:3 columns:2];
Matrix *I = [[Matrix alloc] initWithValues:i_values rows:3 columns:3];
NSLog(@"A=%@",A);
NSLog(@"B=%@",B);
NSLog(@"I=%@",I);
NSLog(@"B+B=%@",[B addMatrix:B]);
NSLog(@"A*3=%@",[A multiplyScalar:3.0]);
NSLog(@"A*B=%@",[A multiplyMatrix:B]);
NSLog(@"A*I=%@",[A multiplyMatrix:I]);
NSLog(@"Atr=%@",[A transpose]);
```

The Matrix objects in both Java and Objective-C are simple, clean, and compact. There's only one problem: as the dimensions of a matrix grow, the computations required to add and multiply two matrices increases exponentially. In this particular application, it's discovered that a significant number of matrices are the identity matrix. Multiplication can be optimized if it's known that at least one of the two matrices is an identity matrix.

One solution is to first test the two matrices of an operation to determine if either is the identity matrix. This could significantly reduce the computations to multiply two matrices when one of them is an identity matrix. However, it adds additional overhead to all multiplications and only manages to replace exponential growth with linear growth.

You decide that the most efficient solution is to create a subclass of Matrix that represents identity matrices. The subclass will override the math methods with optimized versions. The next two sections will contrast a solution in Java, using class factory methods, with an equivalent solution in Objective-C, using class clusters.

Java Matrix Factory

Listings 22-4 and 22-5 show the updated portions of the Matrix classes in Java, with the significant changes highlighted. The new version uses a factory method to create Matrix objects.

Listing 22-4. *Modified Java Matrix Class*

```
public class Matrix {
    protected int rows;
    protected int columns;
    double[] values;

    public static Matrix makeMatrix( double[] values, int rows, int columns )
    {
        return Matrix.makeMatrix(values,false,rows,columns);
    }

    protected static Matrix makeMatrix( double[] values,
                                        boolean copyValues,
                                        int rows,
                                        int columns )
    {
        if (isIdentityMatrix(values,rows,columns)) {
            return new IdentityMatrix(values,copyValues,rows);
        }
        return new Matrix(values,copyValues,rows,columns);
    }

    protected static boolean isIdentityMatrix( double[] values,
                                               int rows,
                                               int columns )
```

```
    {
        if (rows!=columns)
            return false;
        …
        return true;
    }

    protected Matrix( double[] values, int rows, int columns )
    {
        this(values,true,rows,columns);
    }

    protected Matrix( double[] values, boolean copyValues, int rows, int columns )
    {
        this.rows = rows;
        this.columns = columns;
        if (copyValues) {
            this.values = new double[values.length];
            System.arraycopy(values,0,this.values,0,rows*columns);
        } else {
            this.values = values;
        }
    }

    …

    public boolean isIdentity( )
    {
        return false;
    }

    public Matrix add( Matrix matrix )
    {
        double[] sumArray = new double[rows*columns];
        …
        return Matrix.makeMatrix(sumArray,false,rows,columns);
    }

    public Matrix multiply( Matrix right )
    {
        return right.leftMultiply(this);
    }
```

```
protected Matrix leftMultiply( Matrix leftMatrix )
    {
        double[] productArray = new double[leftMatrix.rows*columns];
        ...
        return Matrix.makeMatrix(productArray,false,leftMatrix.rows,columns);
    }

    public Matrix multiply( double scalar )
    {
        double[] productArray = new double[rows*columns];
        ...
        return Matrix.makeMatrix(productArray,false,rows,columns);
    }

    public Matrix transpose( )
    {
        double[] transArray = new double[rows*columns];
        ...
        return Matrix.makeMatrix(transArray,false,columns,rows);
    }
}
```

Here's what changed in the Matrix:

- The public Matrix(…) constructor was made protected and replaced with a public static makeMatrix(…) factory method. Any client that needs to create a Matrix object must be rewritten to call Matrix.makeMatrix(…) instead of new Matrix(…).

- The makeMatrix(…) factory determines if the values in the matrix describe an identity matrix, using a static version of the old isIdentity() test. If the values do, the factory creates and returns an instance of IdentityMatrix; otherwise, it creates a Matrix object.

- The multiply(Matrix) method was reengineered to call the protected leftMultiply(Matrix) method of the right operand object. This allows a subclass of Matrix to intercept the multiplication operation regardless of whether it's the left or right matrix in the equation.

Now an IdentityMatrix subclass, shown in Listing 22-5, is created.

Listing 22-5. *Java IdentityMatrix Class*

```
class IdentityMatrix extends Matrix
{

    protected IdentityMatrix( double[] values, boolean copyValues, int dimensions )
    {
        super(values,copyValues,dimensions,dimensions);
    }
```

```java
    public boolean isIdentity()
    {
        return true;
    }

    public Matrix multiply(Matrix right)
    {
        return right;
    }

    protected Matrix leftMultiply(Matrix leftMatrix)
    {
        return leftMatrix;
    }

    public Matrix transpose()
    {
        return this;
    }
}
```

The IdentityMatrix subclass only represents identity matrices. It overrides the math methods of Matrix with optimized versions. It can intercept multiplications whether it's the left or right operand by overriding both `multiply(Matrix)` and `leftMultiply(Matrix)`.

Now, whenever a Matrix object is created for an identity matrix, the `makeMatrix(…)` method creates an instance of IdentityMatrix instead. This is completely transparent to the client; the client treats all objects as if they were Matrix objects. Operations between Matrix and IdentityMatrix objects are optimized by the overridden IdentityMatrix methods.

Finally, the code that uses the Matrix class is modified to use the new Matrix factory method, shown in Listing 22-6.

Listing 22-6. *Modified Java Matrix Class Usage*

```java
double[] a_values = {
        1.0, 0.0, 2.0,
        -1.0, 3.0, 1.0
        };
double[] b_values = {
        3.0, 1.0,
        2.0, 1.0,
        1.0, 0.0
        };
double[] i_values = {
        1.0, 0.0, 0.0,
        0.0, 1.0, 0.0,
        0.0, 0.0, 1.0
        };
```

```java
Matrix A = Matrix.makeMatrix(a_values,2,3);
Matrix B = Matrix.makeMatrix(b_values,3,2);
Matrix I = Matrix.makeMatrix(i_values,3,3);
System.out.println("A="+A);
System.out.println("B="+B);
System.out.println("I="+I);
```

Objective-C Matrix Class Cluster

Now consider the same solution in Objective-C. The updated versions of the Objective-C Matrix classes are shown in Listings 22-7 through 22-9. The significant changes are highlighted.

Listing 22-7. *Matrix.h and Matrix+Private.h*

```objc
@interface Matrix : NSObject {
    @protected
    NSUInteger      rows;
    NSUInteger      columns;
    __strong double *values;
}

- (id)initWithValues:(const double*)valueArray
                rows:(NSUInteger)rowCount
             columns:(NSUInteger)colCount;

@property (readonly) NSUInteger rows;
@property (readonly) NSUInteger columns;
@property (readonly,getter=isIdentity) BOOL identity;

- (double)valueAtRow:(NSUInteger)row column:(NSUInteger)column;

- (Matrix*)addMatrix:(Matrix*)matrix;
- (Matrix*)multiplyMatrix:(Matrix*)matrix;
- (Matrix*)multiplyScalar:(double)scalar;
- (Matrix*)transpose;

@end

#define VALUE(ARRAY,COLUMNS,ROW,COLUMN)    ARRAY[((ROW)*(COLUMNS))+(COLUMN)]
#define IVALUE(ROW,COLUMN)                 VALUE(values,columns,ROW,COLUMN)
#define SIZEOFARRAY(ROWS,COLUMNS)          (sizeof(double)*(ROWS)*(COLUMNS))
```

```
@interface Matrix () // private methods

- (id)initWithAllocatedArray:(__strong double*)array
                        rows:(NSUInteger)rowCount
                     columns:(NSUInteger)colCount;


- (Matrix*)leftMultiplyMatrix:(Matrix*)leftMatrix;

@end
```

There is no change in the @interface for the Matrix class. In the private @interface extension, a -leftMultiplyMatrix: method is declared, just as it was in Java.

Listing 22-8. Matrix.m

```
@implementation Matrix

- (id)initWithValues:(const double*)valueArray
                rows:(NSUInteger)rowCount
             columns:(NSUInteger)colCount
{
    __strong double *dupArray = MatrixCopyArray(valueArray,rowCount,colCount);
    return [self initWithAllocatedArray:dupArray rows:rowCount columns:colCount];
}


- (id)initWithAllocatedArray:(__strong double*)array
                        rows:(NSUInteger)rowCount
                     columns:(NSUInteger)colCount
{
    self = [super init];
    if (self!=nil) {
        if ([self isMemberOfClass:[Matrix class]]) {
            if (MatrixIsIdentity(array,rowCount,colCount)) {
                return [[IdentityMatrix alloc] initWithAllocatedArray:array
                                                                 rows:rowCount
                                                              columns:colCount];
            }
        }
        rows = rowCount;
        columns = colCount;
        values = array;
    }
    return self;
}
```

…

```
- (BOOL)isIdentity
{
    return NO;
}
```

…

```
- (Matrix*)multiplyMatrix:(Matrix*)matrix
{
    return [matrix leftMultiplyMatrix:self];
}

- (Matrix*)leftMultiplyMatrix:(Matrix*)leftMatrix
{
    __strong double *productArray = MatrixAllocateArray(leftMatrix.rows,columns);
    …
    return [[Matrix alloc] initWithAllocatedArray:productArray
                                    rows:leftMatrix.rows
                                 columns:columns];
}
```

…

```
@end
```

…

```
BOOL MatrixIsIdentity( const __strong double *array,
                       NSUInteger rows,
                       NSUInteger columns )
{
    if (rows!=columns)
        return NO;
    …
    return YES;
}
```

The most striking difference between the two solutions is that there is *no factory method* in the Objective-C implementation. Instead, the modified -[Matrix initWithAllocatedArray:rows:columns:] method spontaneously replaces the instance of the Matrix object being created with an instance of IdentityMatrix whenever appropriate. It does this by discarding the originally created object, creating a new object of the desired class, and returning the substitute object to the sender.

Objective-C refers to this as a *class cluster*, so named because the base Matrix class is the access point to a cluster of subclasses. Creating a Matrix class object may return an instance of Matrix or one of its subclasses.

The rest of the changes to the Matrix class mimic those in the Java implementation. A local MatrixIsIdentity() C function is used to determine which value arrays form identity matrices, and the multiplication logic is relocated to -leftMultiplyMatrix:. Before the updated Matrix class will function, an IdentityMatrix subclass must be defined, as shown in Listing 22-9.

Listing 22-9. *IdentityMatrix.m*

```
@implementation IdentityMatrix

- (BOOL)isIdentity
{
    return YES;
}

- (Matrix*)multiplyMatrix:(Matrix*)matrix
{
    return matrix;
}

- (Matrix*)leftMultiplyMatrix:(Matrix*)leftMatrix
{
    return leftMatrix;
}

- (Matrix*)transpose
{
    return self;
}

@end
```

The real power of class clusters will become evident when you review the code, shown in Listing 22-10, that uses the modified Matrix objects in Objective-C.

Listing 22-10. *Modified Objective-C Matrix Class Usage*

```
double a_values[] = {
    1.0, 0.0, 2.0,
    -1.0, 3.0, 1.0
};
```

```
double b_values[] = {
    3.0, 1.0,
    2.0, 1.0,
    1.0, 0.0
};
double i_values[] = {
    1.0, 0.0, 0.0,
    0.0, 1.0, 0.0,
    0.0, 0.0, 1.0,
};
Matrix *A = [[Matrix alloc] initWithValues:a_values rows:2 columns:3];
Matrix *B = [[Matrix alloc] initWithValues:b_values rows:3 columns:2];
Matrix *I = [[Matrix alloc] initWithValues:i_values rows:3 columns:3];
NSLog(@"A=%@",A);
NSLog(@"B=%@",B);
NSLog(@"I=%@",I);
…
```

What you should immediately notice in Listing 22-10 is that it is identical to the Objective-C code in Listing 22-3. The real power of class clusters is the ability to implement a factory method in the constructor of a class—without changing its external interface.

Class clusters have some important ramifications:

- Class clusters can be implemented without changing the code that creates objects.

- Class clusters are the reason it's so important to adhere to the init contract.

- It is often difficult to subclass a class cluster.

The first feature is what makes class clusters so powerful: any initializer can be turned into a class cluster. The change is largely transparent to existing code that creates objects. This is extremely helpful in an evolving design. A simple base class can be defined and then later replaced with a class cluster without requiring global changes to your existing code.

One side effect of class clusters it that they may make it difficult, or impossible, to create your own subclass of the class cluster's base class. The base class initializer is usually where the class decides what class of object to create. Since a subclass must call its superclass initializer during initialization, your subclass intializer runs the risk that it will be replaced with a different object at the whim of the base class. Class clusters that are designed to be subclassed will usually have a designated initializer for use by non-cluster subclasses, or be written so they will act reasonably when invoked by a subclass. If you have a class cluster that you'd like to subclass, refer to the Subclassing Notes section of the class's documentation.

■**Caution** A common programming pitfall is to invoke a subclass initializer from the base class cluster initializer that recursively invokes the base class initializer. If the base class initializer blindly creates a new subclass object, it will result in an infinite recursion loop. The Matrix class avoids this by having the `-initWithAllocatedArray:rows:columns:` method examine the class of the object being initialized (i.e., `if ([self isMemberOfClass: [Matrix class]]) …`). Only if it's the base class does it consider replacing the object with a subclass. When a subclass invokes the base class initializer, the base class initializer behaves normally. Another approach is to strategically organize your subclass initialization methods so that they don't recursively invoke the base class initializer that implements the class cluster.

Class clusters also solve the mystery of why the *init contract* should be followed so carefully. See the "Writing an init Method" section of Chapter 3. Class clusters reinforce the maxim that your code should *never* assume that the object returned from an initializer is the same one that was originally created.

Summary

Objective-C class clusters add a new dimension to the factory pattern. They make it possible to implement object factories that are completely transparent to the client. This means that subclassing must be approached with a bit more caution; class clusters may make it difficult, or even impossible, for you to define subclasses of some classes.

CHAPTER 23

■ ■ ■

Singleton Pattern

Singletons are classes with a single instance. They are usually objects that provide an object-oriented interface to a single, often global, facility or resource. A class that manages a cache of database objects would want to create a single per-process instance of itself so that it could coordinate all of the object caching for the entire application. A class that provides file management methods could create a singleton object that all other classes would use to interact with the file system. The latter could also be implemented by defining a class that consists of nothing but class methods, but that pattern is unusual in Objective-C.

Singleton objects are typically created by an idempotent class method or C function that's responsible for creating and maintaining the single instance of the class. This is essentially a specialized factory method, described in Chapter 22. Like factory methods, singletons can be implemented using class methods or a degenerate variation of a class cluster.

Implementing Singletons

The following are examples of singleton objects in the Cocoa framework:

- NSApplication
- NSFileManager
- NSDistributedNotificationCenter
- NSWorkspace

Singletons are sometimes created during startup, but are usually provided through an idempotent method that returns the reference to the singleton, creating it for the first time if necessary. In the Cocoa framework, the following class methods return the singletons for the classes listed above:

- [NSApplication sharedApplication]
- [NSFileManager defaultManager]
- [NSDistributedNotificationCenter defaultCenter]
- [NSWorkspace sharedWorkspace]

A typical implementation of the singleton pattern is shown in Listing 23-1.

Listing 23-1. Singleton Pattern

Java
```java
public class CommandCenter {
    private static CommandCenter sharedCommandCenter;

    public static CommandCenter getCommandCenter( )
    {
        if (sharedCommandCenter==null) {
            sharedCommandCenter = new CommandCenter();
        }
        return sharedCommandCenter;
    }
}
```

Objective-C
```objc
@interface CommandCenter : NSObject

+ (CommandCenter*)sharedCommandCenter;

@end

static CommandCenter *SharedCommandCenter;

@implementation CommandCenter

+ (CommandCenter*)sharedCommandCenter
{
    if (SharedCommandCenter==nil) {
        SharedCommandCenter = [CommandCenter new];
        }
    return SharedCommandCenter;
}

@end
```

The exact same pattern can be implemented in Java or Objective-C. However, Objective-C presents two alternatives to the typical singleton design pattern. The first is to use the class's +initialize method, and the second is a variation on class clusters. Both are explored in the next sections.

Lazy Singletons

Most singletons are lazy; they are spontaneously constructed the first time they are requested. An alternative to implementing this yourself is to exploit the lazy initialization of the class itself, as demonstrated in Chapter 21. Basically, the singleton object is created the first time the class receives a message by overriding its +initialize class method. A rewriting of the CommandCenter class is shown in Listing 23-2.

Listing 23-2. *Lazy Singleton Pattern*

```
@interface CommandCenter : NSObject

+ (CommandCenter*)sharedCommandCenter;

@end

static CommandCenter *SharedCommandCenter;

@implementation CommandCenter

+ (void)initialize
{
    SharedCommandCenter = [CommandCenter new];
}

+ (CommandCenter*)sharedCommandCenter
{
    return SharedCommandCenter;
}

@end
```

The class's +initialize method is always the first message a class receives. It's a convenient location to create a singleton. It also simplifies the code in the class; any class method can reference the SharedCommandCenter variable directly (i.e., instead of using [CommandCenter sharedCommandCenter] each time), with the assurance that it has already been initialized.

Be mindful of the fact that +initialize is not called during application startup or when the class is loaded, like Java initialization statements are. The +initialize message is sent the first time the class receives a message. If the class is never used, the +initialize message will never be sent.

Singleton Factory

The factory pattern can be repurposed to turn a class cluster into a singleton factory. In Chapter 22, you saw how a class's initializer can substitute a different class for the one being requested. This same technique can be used to return an existing object as well. To implement the singleton pattern, cripple the initializer so that it returns the same object every time. The code in Listing 23-3 implements a singleton using the class's initializer.

Listing 23-3. *Singleton Factory Pattern*

```
@interface CommandCenter : NSObject

@end

static CommandCenter* SharedCommandCenter;
```

```
@implementation CommandCenter

- (id)init
{
    self = [super init];
    if (self!=nil) {
        if (SharedCommandCenter!=nil)
            return SharedCommandCenter;

        ...
        SharedCommandCenter = self;
    }
    return self;
}

@end
```

The initializer method for the CommandCenter class implements the singleton pattern. The first instance of CommandCenter created (using [[CommandCenter alloc] init]) is saved in the global variable. Any subsequent attempt to create another instance of CommandCenter returns the original instance.

This implementation of the singleton pattern has all of the advantages, and disadvantages, of a class cluster. The principal advantage is that the client code does not have to use a special message to obtain the singleton, or even be aware that the class is a singleton. It simply creates the object and uses it. Another advantage is that the class author doesn't have to take any extraordinary measures to discourage clients from attempting to create additional instances of the class.

■**Note** For obvious reasons, your singleton class would probably *not* conform to the NSCopying protocol. If it needs to—say, to be used as a key in an NSDictionary—override the -copyWithZone: method and have it return self.

A variation of this pattern returns objects from a pool of immutable objects. A Letter class that encapsulates the properties of a letter in the alphabet might implement a singleton factory for each letter. Every invocation of [[Letter alloc] initWithLetter:'a'] would return a singleton 'a' object, while every [[Letter alloc] initWithLetter:'b'] would return a singleton 'b' object, and so forth. This is one alternative to implementing the flyweight design pattern.

Summary

The singleton pattern is extremely common in both Java and Objective-C. Objective-C presents some intriguing alternatives that can simplify its implementation. It's also possible to transform a class cluster into a singleton factory, hiding its singleton nature.

■ ■ ■

PART 4

Advanced Objective-C

CHAPTER 24

■■■

Memory Management

Garbage collection is a recent feature in Objective-C and, while this is a huge step in the right direction, it's not universally available. The alternative is traditional Objective-C managed memory, wherein your code takes responsibility for destroying objects.

The principal reasons you'd choose to use managed memory instead of garbage collection are as follows:

- The operating system or compiler doesn't support garbage collection (specifically, this is the case with the iPhone OS and older versions of Mac OS X).

- You're working on a project that's already using managed memory.

- The code must function in a managed memory environment (for example, a plug-in).

In the first case, your only choice is to embrace managed memory. This chapter will show you the basics of traditional memory management. Objective-C provides an object management model that's very sensible and easy to learn. If you're thinking this will be like C or C++ memory management, you can relax.

In the second case, it may be more trouble than its worth to convert an existing project from managed memory to garbage collection. Managed memory in Objective-C is not radically different from garbage collection, so adoption might be the most expedient solution.

■**Note** When compiling code that will run in a managed memory environment, the compiler's support for garbage collection should be turned off. In Xcode, this is accomplished by setting the Objective-C Garbage Collection build setting to Unsupported. This turns off all garbage collection support, producing code that is compatible with operating systems that lack garbage collection.

Specialized components, like plug-ins, frameworks, and services, which are loaded into another application's runtime environment, must coexist with the memory management scheme employed by its host. It may even be necessary to write your code so that it can function in both a garbage-collected and managed memory environment. There are some notes about doing that towards the end of the chapter.

This chapter explains the basics of memory allocation and deallocation. It then describes Objective-C's reference counting scheme and autorelease pools. As each concept is examined, simple programming rules are introduced. Taken together, they define the programming practices that you should adopt to use managed memory. Later sections touch on some of the situations where reference counting can get tricky and what to do about them.

C Memory Allocation

At the core of all memory management are the POSIX memory allocation functions. They are used by all higher APIs and you're welcome to use them yourself. They are extremely simple, fast, and efficient. The basic use pattern is shown in Listing 24-1.

Listing 24-1. C Memory Allocation

```
void *memory = malloc(100);
…
free(memory);
```

The `malloc()` function in Listing 24-1 allocates 100 consecutive bytes of memory and returns the address of the first byte. You are free to use those 100 bytes in any way you see fit. When you're done with that block of memory, the `free()` function releases and recycles it, after which you should not access that range of memory again.

There are also variations to `malloc()`. The two most common are `calloc()`, which allocates memory and fills it with zeros, and `realloc()`, which changes the size of a previously allocated block of memory. Regardless of what POSIX function you used to allocate the memory, `free()` will release it.

Although it is simple, POSIX memory allocation is also brutally awkward: it is up to your application to release the memory once you're done with it, it can only be released once, and the pointer must not be used again afterwards. This presents the following difficulties:

- If you fail to release the memory, but "forget" the pointer to it, that block of memory becomes permanently unusable. This is called a memory leak.

- Sharing the pointer with other code creates an ambiguity over what code should take responsibility for releasing the memory, and when.

- Using a pointer to a block of memory that has been released can be disastrous.

These three issues have been the driving force for finding better ways of managing blocks of memory, and by extension objects, for the past half century of computer science.

Objective-C Reference Counting

While garbage collection is a far more elegant solution—neatly solving all three problems at once—it's a complex system, requiring significant resources, and has only recently matured. Pre-garbage collection Objective-C employed a simple alternative: reference counting.

Reference counting introduces the concept of *owners*: code or objects that hold a pointer to another object are said to *own* that object. When an object or block of code wants to hold a reference to an object, it first *retains* it. When it's done with the object, it *releases* it.

The goal of reference counting is to apply the same logic to object management that garbage collection does: an object is kept alive as long as it has owners (references). The primary difference between reference counting and garbage collection is that in reference counting, it's up to the programmer to inform the object when a reference to it has been established or forgotten.

Here's how reference counting works:

1. When an object is initially allocated, it has a reference count of 1.

2. Any code that wants to use the object first increases its reference count by 1. This is called a *retain*.

3. When the code that holds the pointer in steps 1 or 2 no longer uses it, it decreases the object's reference count by 1 and it forgets the pointer. This is called a *release*.

4. When an object's reference count decreases to 0, the object is immediately destroyed and its memory freed.

An example of reference counting is shown in Listing 24-2.

Listing 24-2. *Fundamental Reference Counting Pattern*

```
id myObject = [[MyClass alloc] init];
…
[myObject doSomething];
…
[myObject release];
```

In Listing 24-2, the reference points to an object that was just created. Newly created objects have an implicit reference count of 1 (or they wouldn't exist). The program uses the object, and then sends it a -release message to indicate that it will never use that object again. The -release message decrements the object's retain count and immediately destroys the object. This assumes that no other object or code -retained the object in the interim. If so, the object would continue to exist because it still had at least one owner.

In practice, managing release counts manually isn't as onerous as it might seem. The next few sections will explain the role of autorelease pools and describe the common programming patterns for using reference counting with objects. Autorelease pools are brilliant, and the patterns are easy to apply. If consistently applied—and that's a big "if"—reference counting provides an experience that's equivalent to using garbage collection about 80 percent of the time. In fact the biggest problem you're likely to encounter, coming from a garbage collection environment, is forgetting to apply the required patterns the remaining 20 percent of the time.

Autorelease Pools

Autorelease pools add the very garbage collection–like concept of deferring the destruction of an unreferenced object until some unspecified time in the future. Autorelease pools seem to mystify many new Objective-C programmers, but they are stunningly simple:

• An autorelease pool is a collection of objects that will eventually receive a -*release* message.

That's it. To use an autorelease pool, send an object an -autorelease message instead of a -release message. The receiver is not immediately released; it is simply added to the autorelease pool. Later—usually long after your code has finished—the pool is drained and each object in the pool receives its -release message.

The cardinal rule to remember is this: release an object by sending it *either* a -release or an -autorelease message, but never both. The two messages are logically equivalent and differ only in timing. The former releases the object immediately. The latter adds it to the autorelease pool, to be released at some future time.

To illustrate what autorelease pools do for you, the next few sections describe some fundamental problems with reference counting and how autorelease pools avoid them.

Autorelease Pool Lifetime

Normally, you don't create autorelease pools yourself. (A later section in this chapter explains why, and how, you would.) For the most part, always assume that there's an active autorelease pool and the -autorelease message will add the receiver to the current pool. Despite their vague assurances of "eventually" releasing objects, autorelease pools have a very definite lifespan. Most autorelease pools are created by the working run loop at the beginning of each event dispatch. The pool is drained after the code that handled the event has returned. This mechanism defines an important rule about the lifespan of autorelease pools:

- The current autorelease pool will *never* be drained before your method or function returns.

The importance of this rule probably isn't immediately obvious, but it will be as you work through the next few sections.

Returned References

The reference counting rules laid out in the previous section appear simple and sound, but they actually contain one huge flaw: how do you release an object (decrease its reference count) *after* the code no longer has a pointer to it? You could avoid this situation in many cases with careful coding, but there's one inescapable case where you can't—returning an object reference to the sender. Using the reference counting rules learned so far, you'd probably be tempted to write something like the code shown in Listing 24-3.

Listing 24-3. *Retain and Return Problem*

```
@implementation Zombie

- (void)recitePoetry
{
    NSString *myName = [[self zombieName] retain];
    [self speakFormat:@"Hello, my name is %@. This is my poem.",myName];
    ...
    [myName release];
}

- (NSString*)zombieName
{
    NSMutableString *z = [[NSMutableString alloc] init];
    [z appendString:@"Zombie "];
    [z appendString:[self humanName]]; // e.g. "Zombie Bob"
    return z;
    // [z release] ? ? ? ? ?
}

...

@end
```

In the -recitePoetry method, the NSString object returned by -zombieName is retained, used in the body of the method, and then released. In the -zombieName method, the string object is implicitly retained when it is created, used in the body of the method, and returned to the sender. But wait! It also needs to be released, since -zombieNames will never use it again. Yet there's no way to do that *after* the method has returned to its sender.

Autorelease pools solve this by deferring the needed release to some later time. The -zombieName method is rewritten in Listing 24-4 to use the autorelease pool.

Listing 24-4. *Autoreleasing a Returned Object*

```
- (NSString*)zombieName
{
    NSMutableString *z = [[NSMutableString alloc] init];
    [z appendString:@"Zombie "];
    [z appendString:[self humanName]];
    return [z autorelease];
}
```

The string object is added to the autorelease pool before being returned to the sender. This correctly balances the implied retain that occurred when the object was created, and ensures that it will eventually be destroyed.

■**Note** The -retain and -autorelease messages returns the receiver to the sender, allowing it to be chained into expressions like return [obj autorelease] and property = [obj retain]. This avoids having to write [obj autorelease] and return obj as separate statements.

When an object reference is returned to the sender, it has already received the correct number of -release or -autorelease messages. In Objective-C parlance, this is called an *autoreleased object*. This creates another rule for Objective-C objects:

• Every object returned from a method is either owned or autoreleased.

What it means to you is that you do not have to worry about the ownership of objects you receive from other objects. Either they are still owned, they have been autoreleased, or maybe both. The point is, your code is only responsible for its ownership of the object. Never worry about an object's ownership by other objects (except in a few rare cases that are covered later in the chapter).

The exception to the above rule are the messages that create new objects: +alloc, +new, -copy, and -mutableCopy. Theses are just about the only methods that return a retained object. That is, the object has an unbalanced retain and the receiver is implicitly its new owner. You may encounter other methods that return retained objects. By convention, these methods have names that begin with *new*, as in -[NSObjectController newObject].

Autoreleased Objects

The code in Listing 24-4 works because of the lifespan rule of autorelease pools; the autorelease pool that's being used when -recitePoetry begins won't be drained until it returns. That means that any objects added to the autorelease pool will exist until the method is finished.

Knowing that, the code in Listings 24-2 and 24-4 can be further simplified, as shown in Listing 24-5.

Listing 24-5. Simplified Release Management

```
- (void)recitePoetry
{
    NSString *myName = [self zombieName];
    [self speakFormat:@"Hello, my name is %@. This is my poem.",myName];
    …
}

- (NSString*)zombieName
{
    NSMutableString *z = [[[NSMutableString alloc] init] autorelease];
    [z appendString:@"Zombie "];
    [z appendString:[self humanName]];
    return z;
}
```

Listing 24-5 is starting to look a lot like code written for a garbage collection environment. The only difference is the single -autorelease message when the NSMutableString is initially created.

The reason is the string object has been autoreleased, and all references to the object are contained within the scope of the executing methods. Remember that an autorelease pool will never be drained before a method returns, and objects returned by other methods are always retained or autoreleased objects. This creates a new, and important, rule for managing object retain counts:

• An autoreleased object only needs to be retained if it will be referenced beyond the lifetime of the current autorelease pool.

This aspect of autorelease pools is what makes them so useful, and why I wrote that managed memory and garbage collection are indistinguishable 80 percent of the time. Most object references are fleeting—defined and forgotten within a single method. These references, as long as they are to autoreleased objects, don't require any memory management.

Because of this convenience, most objects are created and autoreleased immediately, exactly as shown in Listing 24-5, rather than the pattern shown in Listing 24-4. Once autoreleased, the object requires almost no management unless some other code needs to retain it—and that would be the responsibility of that other code. The exception is the obvious case where an object is created by code that intends to retain it. It would be silly to write [[[[MyClass alloc] init] autorelease] retain] when [[MyClass alloc] init] would accomplish the same thing.

So what about references that persist beyond the lifespan of the current autorelease pool? The programming patterns in the next few sections address those very cases.

Managed Memory Patterns

The following sections show the basic programming patterns used when working in a managed memory environment. Some of these patterns have already been shown, but are included again for completeness and future reference.

New Object Patterns

When a new object is created it begins with a retain count of 1, implicitly making its creator the first owner. The principal messages that return new objects are: +alloc, +new, and -copy. This implied ownership must be balanced by a -release message when the object is no longer used, as shown in Listing 24-6, or an -autorelease message, as shown in Listing 24-7.

Listing 24-6. *Retained New Object Pattern*

```
id object = [[NSObject alloc] init];
…
[object release];
```

Listing 24-7. *Autoreleased New Object Pattern*

```
id object = [[[NSObject alloc] init] autorelease];
…
```

Autoreleased Object Pattern

Objects returned by most messages are returned as *autoreleased objects*. That is, the object has already received a correctly balanced series of -retain, -release, or -autorelease messages and does not demand any additional management. Specifically, class convenience constructors, like +[NSMutableArray arrayWithCapacity:], return autoreleased objects. Even though the convenience constructors exist to create new objects, the objects are not "new" from the perspective of memory management. Common examples are shown in Listing 24-8.

Listing 24-8. *Autoreleased Objects*

```
NSNumber *number = [NSNumber numberWithInt:10];
NSString *path = [NSString stringWithFormat:@"Folder %@",number];
NSFileManager *fileManager = [NSFileManager defaultManager];
NSDictionary *attrs = [fileManager attributesOfItemAtPath:path error:NULL];
NSArray *attrKeys = [attrs keysSortedByValueUsingSelector:@selector(compare:)];
```

Every object returned by a class or instance method in Listing 24-8 is autoreleased and requires no additional management. If you store the reference in a persistent location, like an instance variable, then you should retain the object like this:

```
myArray = [[NSMutableArray arrayWithCapacity:100] retain];
```

See the "Setter Patterns" section below for more about retaining references in properties.

Returning Autoreleased Objects

So that your code is consistent with the rest of Objective-C, your methods should always return autoreleased objects, as shown in Listing 24-9.

Listing 24-9. *Returning an Autoreleased Object*

```
- (id)someObject
{
    id object = [[[NSObject alloc] init] autorelease];
    ...
    return object; // autoreleased
}
```

Setter Patterns

When setting a property of your object, you should retain the referenced object until you replace the reference with something else. The reference being replaced should be released or autoreleased. There are four popular patterns for writing setter methods, as shown in Listing 24-10.

Listing 24-10. *Setter Patterns*

```
@interface MyClass : NSObject {
    id one;
    id two;
    id three;
    id four;
}

@property (retain,nonatomic) id one;
@property (retain,nonatomic) id two;
@property (retain,nonatomic) id three;
@property (copy,nonatomic) id four;

@end

@implementation MyClass

- (id)one
{
    return one;
}

- (void)setOne:(id)object
{
    [one autorelease];
    one = [object retain];
}

- (id)two
```

```
{
    return two;
}

- (void)setTwo:(id)object
{
    id oldTwo = two;
    two = [object retain];
    [oldTwo release];
}

- (id)three
{
    return three;
}

- (void)setThree:(id)object
{
    if (three!=object) {
        [three release];
        three = [object retain];
    }
}

- (id)four
{
    return four;
}

- (void)setFour:(id)object
{
    [four autorelease];
    four = [object copy];
}

@end
```

All of the setter patterns in Listing 24-10 accomplish three important tasks:

- The object being stored is sent a -retain message.

- The object being forgotten is sent a -release or -autorelease message.

- The -retain message is sent before the -release message.

The last point is the tricky one. If the object being set is the same as the object already stored in the property, sending it a -release message before the -retain message could prematurely destroy the object. The third pattern, shown in -setThree:, avoids this problem by explicitly testing for that condition.

The final property stores a copy of the original. It can adopt any of the first three patterns; just replace [object retain] with [object copy]. It should be noted that all of these patterns are compatible with nil values.

■**Note** The behavior of your property setter method must be consistent with your @property directive. The first three patterns are consistent with the retain property attribute, and the last one is consistent with the copy attribute. If you let the Objective-C compiler @synthesize the setter methods for you, it will generate code equivalent to what's shown.

The setter pattern code examples are presented as guides for writing well-behaved property accessors, but the principles apply to *any* object reference that you store in a persistent variable. If you were setting an instance or static variable directly, your code must follow the same pattern—retaining the new reference and releasing the old one.

init Patterns

This is really a corollary to the rule that an object should retain the objects it has references to, but it's still worth highlighting. Most object -init methods create new objects, and those objects must be retained as shown in Listing 24-11.

Listing 24-11. -init Pattern

```
@interface ZombiePoetryGroup : NSObject {
    NSMutableSet    *zombies;
}

@end


@implementation ZombiePoetryGroup

- (id) init
{
    self = [super init];
    if (self != nil) {
        zombies = [[NSMutableSet set] retain];
    }
    return self;
}

@end
```

Remember that new objects created with +new, +alloc and -init, or -copy are already retained. A statement equivalent to the one highlighted in Listing 24-11 would be

```
zombies = [NSMutableSet new];
```

dealloc Patterns

When an object with a reference count of 1 receives a -release message, it is immediately destroyed. This is accomplished by sending the object a single -dealloc message. An object's -dealloc method performs much the same role as a -finalize method, but is also responsible for releasing any retained objects, allocated memory, and any other resource that it owns, and for ultimately freeing the memory it occupies. If your object retains any object references, it *must* have a -dealloc method. Listings 24-12 and 24-13 present two common patterns for writing -dealloc methods.

Listing 24-12. *-dealloc Using -release*

```
- (void)dealloc
{
    [one release];
    [two release];
    [three release];
    [four release];

    [super dealloc];
}
```

Listing 24-13. *-dealloc Using Property Setters*

```
- (void)dealloc
{
    [self setOne:nil];
    [self setTwo:nil];
    [self setThree:nil];
    [self setFour:nil];

    [super dealloc];
}
```

A -dealloc method must do the following:

- Close any open files, release any resources, free any non-object memory, and any other actions that would be appropriate in a -finalize method.

- Release all retained objects with a -release or -autorelease message.

- Send [super dealloc] as its last statement.

The pattern in Listing 24-12 is the fastest and most efficient, avoids side-effects of property setters, and is the most commonly used pattern.

The pattern in Listing 24-13 is less efficient, but has a couple of advantages. It clears the references using the property setters. If the setters need to notify observers or perform other housekeeping, this pattern permits them to do so. In addition to releasing the held property, it sets the property value to nil. This could be important if any code later in the -dealloc method attempts to use the property for any purpose—which would be very bad if the property was still pointing to a deallocated instance. The first pattern, as coded, tries to avoid this problem by not sending any other messages to itself during deallocation. But as object relationships become more complex, it's harder to ensure that will always work. For example, a retained object might have a pointer back to the object that owns it (self), and during its deallocation might attempt to use one of the properties of its owner.

■Caution -dealloc is sent to an object by -release. You should never send a -dealloc message to another object.

Sending -dealloc to the superclass is an absolute requirement. So much so that modern Objective-C compilers now emit a warning if you fail to do so. The base class -dealloc method is the one that actually deallocates (frees) the memory occupied by the instance. Failing to send -dealloc will cause memory leaks. After the superclass's -dealloc message returns, the object no longer exists and self is invalid. You *cannot* access any of the object's instance variables nor send it a message.

Implicitly Retained Objects

Objects retained by other objects your object retains are referred to as *implicitly retained objects*. An object should only retain objects it maintains a direct reference to; objects retained by other objects are managed by those objects. An example of implicitly retained Zombie objects is shown in Listing 24-14.

Listing 24-14. Implicitly Retained Objects

```
@class Zombie;

@interface ZombiePoetryGroup : NSObject {
    NSMutableDictionary *members;
}

- (BOOL)hasMemberNamed:(NSString*)zombieName;
- (void)addMember:(Zombie*)newZombie;
- (void)removeMember:(Zombie*)zombieZombie;

@end

@implementation ZombiePoetryGroup
```

```
- (id) init
{
    self = [super init];
    if (self != nil) {
        members = [NSMutableDictionary new];
    }
    return self;
}

- (void) dealloc
{
    [members release];
    [super dealloc];
}

- (BOOL)hasMemberNamed:(NSString*)zombieName
{
    return ([members objectForKey:zombieName]!=nil);
}

- (void)addMember:(Zombie*)newZombie
{
    [members setObject:newZombie forKey:[newZombie zombieName]];
}

- (void)removeMember:(Zombie*)zombie
{
    [members removeObjectForKey:[zombie zombieName]];
}

@end
```

The ZombiePoetryGroup object creates and retains an NSMutableDictionary object. All Cocoa collection classes retain the objects added to the collection and release them again when they are removed. The ZombiePoetryGroup object retains its direct reference to the NSMutableDictionary object, and lets the dictionary object retain and release its objects.

Managed Memory Problems

There are some unique coding difficulties when using managed memory. The next few sections describe the most common, and what you can do about them.

Overretained or Underreleased Objects

Overretained (or underreleased) objects are ones that have received more -retain messages than is appropriate, or fail to receive a balanced number of -release messages. The object is never deallocated, resulting in a memory leak. This can often be a subtle problem to detect, as the incidence of even a few thousand leaked objects won't be obvious.

The best solution to this problem is judicious use of developer tools. The Xcode developer tools include several memory leak detection tools, but the preeminent tool for Objective-C developers is ObjectAlloc, shown in Figure 24-1.

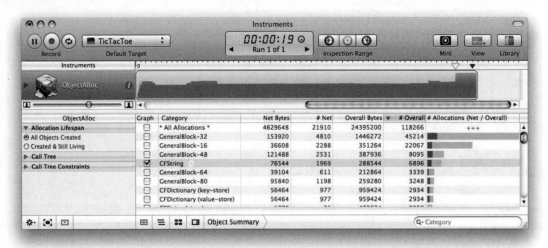

Figure 24-1. *ObjectAlloc*

ObjectAlloc tracks the lifetime of all of the Objective-C objects in your application. It records when each was allocated, retained, released, and deallocated. It presents the total instances of each class graphically, allowing you to quickly identify a group of objects that are being allocated but never deallocated. You should occasionally run your application under the gaze of ObjectAlloc to look for object leaks.

Once you find a leak, use ObjectAlloc again to examine the history of +alloc, -retain, -release, and -dealloc messages sent to those objects. An instance's history should expose where the imbalance is occurring.

Overreleased or Underretained Objects

Overreleased or underretained objects are ones that receive one too many -release messages. The object is destroyed while still being retained by other objects. The orphaned object pointer then points to invalid memory. The effects of using an invalid object pointer can range from the inconsistent to the catastrophic.

The best debugging tool for finding overreleased objects is NSZombies, not to be confused with any of the zombie examples in this book. There are several debugging facilities built into the Objective-C runtime that can be enabled through environment variables. The two most commonly used to find overreleased objects are listed in Table 24-1.

Table 24-1. *NSZombie Environment Variables*

Environment Variable	Description
NSZombieEnabled	If set to YES, destroyed objects are replaced with zombie objects that throw an exception if they receive any message.
NSAutoreleaseFreedObjectCheckEnabled	If set to YES, the autorelease pool will print a warning if it attempts to release an already destroyed object.

To use these facilities, set up the desired environment variables and pass that environment to the application when it's launched. Some of these features can also be enabled programmatically in your application.

A zombie object is created when the object is deallocated. Instead of being freed, the class of the object is changed to a special zombie class. It's still an object, and any message sent to the object will throw an exception, helping you identify the object that was overreleased. Once identified, you can use ObjectAlloc tool to examine the history of the object and locate the code that prematurely released it.

Figure 24-2 shows how environment variables can be set for an executable in Xcode.

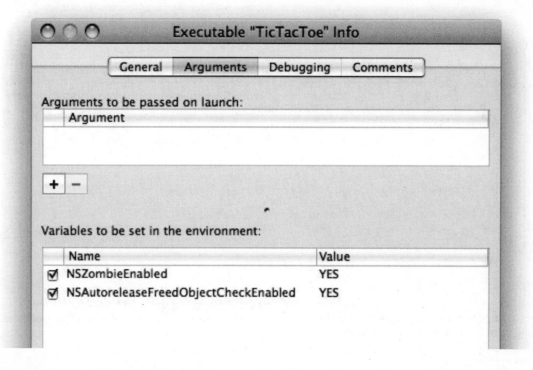

Figure 24-2. *Setting NSZombie Debug Environment Variables*

A complete description of tools used to detect memory leaks and overrelease bugs is described in Apple's "Technical Note 2124: Mac OS X Debugging Magic."[1]

Prematurely Released Objects

A problem closely related to overreleased objects is objects that are simply released prematurely—while there are still working references to it. The most common cause is releasing the object as a side-effect of setting a property or removing it from a collection. Listings 24-15 and 24-17 show two very common scenarios where objects are prematurely destroyed.

Listing 24-15. *Object Destroyed By Collection*

```
@implementation FIFO

…

- (id)pop
{
    id object = [stack objectAtIndex:0];
    [stack removeObjectAtIndex:0];
    return object; // |object| does not exist!
}

@end
```

In Listing 24-15, the objects in the FIFO are implicitly retained by the collection. To pop an object off the stack, the object is removed from the collection and returned to the sender. The problem is that the collection might be the object's only owner. Removing it releases it, destroying the object. The -pop method then returns a pointer to a destroyed object. The solution is to *re-autorelease* the object, as shown in Listing 24-16.

Listing 24-16. *Re-autoreleasing an Object*

```
- (id)pop
{
    id object = [[[stack objectAtIndex:0] retain] autorelease];
    [stack removeObjectAtIndex:0];

    return object;
}
```

The solution is to send -retain and -autorelease messages to the object before removing it from the collection. The additional -retain prevents the object from being immediately destroyed, and the -autorelease creates an autoreleased object suitable for return to the sender.

---

[1] Apple Inc., "Technical Note TN2124: Mac OS X Debugging Magic," http://developer.apple.com/technotes/tn2004/tn2124.html, 2006.

In Listing 24-17, an autoreleased object is returned from a property getter. The property is changed, releasing the previous object, while the object is still being referenced.

Listing 24-17. Object Destroyed By Setter

```
id two = [self two];
[self setTwo:nil];
// |two| does not exist!
```

There are three solutions to this problem:

- Use the setter pattern demonstrated in -setOne: found in Listing 24-10. That setter autoreleases the previous object instead of releasing it immediately.

- Explicitly retain the property object in the assignment (i.e., id two = [[[self two] retain] autorelease]), which will protect it from being released by the -setTwo: message.

- Write the property getter to re-autorelease the object every time it is returned (i.e., return [[two retain] autorelease]).

Of these solutions, the first is the preferred. It requires no involvement from the sender, preserves the autoreleased contract for returned property values, and is efficient. The second alternative should be used if you don't have control over the class's implementation. The last solution is inefficient, and is used incessantly by inexperienced programmers.

Circular References

One major problem with reference counting, for which there is no universal solution, is the problem of circular references. If two objects both retain references to the other, the objects will never be released.

How you solve this will depend on your circumstances. One common solution is to store unretained or so-called *weak references*. This should not be confused with the term *weak reference* as it applies to garbage collection, so I'll use the term *unretained reference*. Unretained references are typically used for delegate, observer, and parent object references. Listing 24-18 shows the interface for a node in an object tree that holds an unretained reference to its parent node.

Listing 24-18. Unretained Object Property

```
@interface TreeNode : NSObject {
    TreeNode        *parent;
    NSMutableArray  *children;
}
```

```
@property (assign) TreeNode *parent;

…

@end
```

By using the `assign` property attribute, the parent property is not retained when set. The hazard is that the node could be removed from the tree, and later attempt to send a message to its parent object, which might not exist anymore. This approach is workable if you carefully engineer the object so that there's no possibility that it will attempt to use any unretained references in a situation where those objects might have been released.

The best solution to this type of problem is to add code that explicitly clears the parent reference before the node is removed from the tree. In the case where the reference is retained, this breaks the circular reference and allows the nodes to be destroyed. In the case where the reference is not retained, it ensures that the node won't attempt to use a stale reference.

Creating Autorelease Pools

Normally, you don't create autorelease pools yourself, but there are a few times where you must, and times where you might want to.

All Objective-C objects assume that they are operating within the scope of an active autorelease pool. If no autorelease pool exists, sending an object an `-autorelease` message will print a warning message to the console that your application is leaking objects.

The run loop and the AppKit framework create and drain autorelease pools for you. The two cases where you must create your own autorelease pools are at the beginning of a command-line tool or when creating a new thread. Autorelease pools belong to the thread, so any new thread should begin by immediately creating an autorelease pool, as shown in Listing 24-19.

Listing 24-19. Creating a Thread's Autorelease Pool

```
@implementation Threader

- (void)myThread:(id)ignored
{
    NSAutoreleasePool *pool = [NSAutoreleasePool new];

    …

    [pool drain];
}

@end
```

The -myThread: method in Listing 24-19 is started in its own thread. Its first task is to create a top-level autorelease pool that will be used by all objects until the thread ends, where the pool must be drained.

■**Note** The -[NSAutoreleasePool drain] message is fairly new. Older code sends a -release message instead. In a managed memory environment the two are identical. When mixing managed memory with garbage collection (see the next section), -drain sends a hint to the garbage collector to start collecting. Both are correct.

If the thread in Listing 24-19 performed some action in a loop, it should create nested autorelease pools to periodically release transient objects. This also applies to any method that produces a large number of transient objects before returning. Listing 24-20 shows a loop that periodically creates and releases autorelease pools as it works.

Listing 24-20. Creating Nested Autorelease Pools

```
NSAutoreleasePool *wadingPool = nil;
int poolCount = 0;
NSUInteger i;
for (i=0; i<1000000; i++) {
    if (wadingPool==nil)
        wadingPool = [NSAutoreleasePool new];


    ...


    if (++poolCount>2000) {
        poolCount = 0;
        [wadingPool drain];
        wadingPool = nil;
    }
}
```

The loop in Listing 24-20 periodically creates a nested autorelease pool that is drained to release transient objects created in the body of the loop. This, of course, breaks the rule that autoreleased objects won't be released until the current method returns, but that's because you're draining the pool yourself—so you should know that.

New autorelease pools are inherently nested inside the previously active autorelease pool. Draining a pool implicitly drains any autorelease pools that were created inside it. It's not necessary for the code in Listing 24-20 to ensure that wadingPool is drained before exiting the loop. The autorelease pool that contains wadingPool will drain it when it gets drained. For example, an exception handler does *not* need to drain any nested autorelease pools. The only thing that's important is that the top-level autorelease pool is drained before the thread terminates.

Mixing Managed Memory and Garbage Collection

You may find yourself in a situation where you need to write Objective-C code that must function in both a managed memory and a garbage collection environment. It's possible to do this because the managed memory methods and garbage collection techniques have very little overlap. In a garbage collection environment, the messages that manage reference counting (-retain, -release, -autorelease) are ignored. In a managed memory environment, the compiler's support for garbage collection (__strong and __weak pointer types) is ignored. The end result is code that will operate correctly in either environment.

When compiling code that will run in a mixed memory environment, the compiler's support for garbage collection should be made inclusive. In Xcode, set the Objective-C Garbage Collection build setting to Supported. This causes the compiler to include support for garbage collection, but also includes the code needed to support managed memory. When the Objective-C Garbage Collection build setting is set to Required (garbage collection only), the compiler actively strips out code that's only useful to managed memory. This makes the code more efficient, but sacrifices backward compatibility.

Writing the code that will function in both environments is fairly straightforward. In general, code that correctly implements managed memory will also work in a garbage collection environment. For example, all of the code samples in this chapter would function correctly with garbage collection turned on. Table 24-2 lists the effects of each environment on your code.

Table 24-2. *Effects of Managed Memory vs. Garbage Collection*

Code	Managed Memory	Garbage Collection
-retain	Retains an object	Ignored
-release	Releases an object	Ignored
-autorelease	Adds object to autorelease pool	Ignored
-retainCount	Returns the current retain count	Meaningless
-dealloc	Sent to an object to destroy it	Runtime blocks this message from being sent
-finalize	Never sent	Sent when an object is about to be collected
__strong	Ignored	Indicates a strong reference
__weak	Ignored	Indicates a weak reference
-drain	Drains the autorelease pool	Triggers garbage collection
@property (assign)	Unretained property	Strong reference
@property (retain)	Retained property	Strong reference

NSAutoreleasePool's -drain method is about the only method that's functional in both environments. With garbage collection turned on, it hints to the garbage collector that it might want to start a garbage collection cycle.

Summary

Managed memory requires some additional effort, but it isn't onerous. Just remember these basic rules:

- When storing an object reference in a persistent variable, retain it.
- Release or autorelease any retained reference before discarding it.
- Write a `-dealloc` method to release all retained objects.
- Always return retained or autoreleased objects.
- Autoreleased objects won't be released until after the current method has returned.

CHAPTER 25

■ ■ ■

Mixing C and Objective-C

One of the great strengths of Objective-C is that it allows seamless integration with C functions and variables. This gives you direct access to the vast wealth of existing C APIs. This chapter discusses the basic ways to mix C and Objective-C code in the same application, and covers Core Foundation, a C library that includes data structures that are interchangeable with Objective-C objects. Mixing languages creates some interesting memory management issues, which are explained toward the end of the chapter.

Using C in Objective-C

"Using C in Objective-C" is somewhat misleading, because Objective-C is a strict superset of the C language. You really can't *use* C in Objective-C, since Objective-C *is* C. The term is usually applied when you write code that uses C structures and calls C functions directly, instead of using Objective-C objects and messages.

Calling C Functions from Objective-C

There have been a number of code examples presented in the book that implement C functions and use them in Objective-C classes. These are standard C functions that can be called from C or Objective-C code. A C function with a `static` type limits its scope to the code in the module being compiled. Non-static functions are global and can be called from any module. (Remember that in this context, "static" means `private`, not `static` in the Java sense.) An example of a static C function is shown in Listing 25-1.

Listing 25-1. C Function and Objective-C Method

```
static NSInteger compareZombieBrains( id l, id r, void *ignored )
{
    float lSize = [l brainSize];
    float rSize = [r brainSize];
    if (lSize<rSize)
        return NSOrderedAscending;
    else if (lSize>rSize)
        return NSOrderedDescending;
    return NSOrderedSame;
}
```

```
- (NSArray*)zombiesSortedByIntelligence
{
    return [zombieArray sortedArrayUsingFunction:compareZombieBrains
context:NULL];
}
```

C functions can be defined anywhere outside of an Objective-C directive, or anywhere an Objective-C method can be defined. This means that you can mix C functions and Objective-C methods in an @implementation directive, but some programmers will group their C functions outside the @implementation. It's a matter of style.

Your Objective-C application can call C APIs provided by the operating system, it can link to standard C libraries, and you can include C source modules in your project. This makes it easy to interface with the wide universe of POSIX functions, C frameworks, shared libraries, and open-source code.

Using Objective-C Objects in C

C functions in an Objective-C module (.m) are compiled as Objective-C code, not just C. The C function in Listing 25-1 sends Objective-C messages to objects just as if it were an Objective-C method. The only difference is that there is no object context (self). In this respect, a C function is the equivalent of a static class method in Java.

When you add a C source file (.c) to your Xcode project, it will be compiled as plain C. The source file cannot include any Objective-C syntax. If you need to use Objective-C objects in a C module, you have two choices:

- Isolate the functions that use Objective-C objects and move them to an Objective-C (.m) source file. The file can consist entirely of C functions, but it will be compiled as Objective-C and can use Objective-C syntax to reference objects and send messages.
- Send Objective-C messages directly using one of the Objective-C runtime functions, such as objc_msgSend(id,SEL,…).

The latter solution is awkward, but technically you can do anything in C that you can do in Objective-C. The entire Objective-C runtime is, after all, written in C. See the *Objective-C 2.0 Runtime Reference*[1] for specific details.

Core Foundation

Core Foundation is a large library of C functions that are engineered around the concept of objects, which it terms *opaque types* or just *types*. These opaque types have an internal structure that is compatible with Objective-C objects, and a respectable number of Core Foundation types are interchangeable with Objective-C classes. This reciprocity is called the *toll-free bridge*. The goal of Core Foundation is to seamlessly provide a large number of operating system and framework services to *both* C and Objective-C programmers. C programmers use CFTypeRef values, which are pointers to opaque data structures, and pass them to Core Foundation functions. Objective-C programmers store object pointers and send them messages. The code executed is the same in both cases.

Most Core Foundation types do not have a toll-free bridge to Objective-C. If you need their functionality, you'll need to use the Core Foundation data types and functions directly. Core Foundation employs many of the same concepts as Objective-C, it just implements them with its own types,

---

[1] Apple Inc., *Objective-C 2.0 Runtime Reference*, http://developer.apple.com/documentation/Cocoa/Reference/ObjCRuntimeRef/, 2008.

functions, and terminology. A comparison of common Core Foundation types and functions along with their Objective-C equivalents are listed in Table 25-1.

Table 25-1. *Core Foundation Terminology*

Objective-C	Core Foundation
Class	CFTypeID
id or NSObject*	CFTypeRef
NSString*	CFStringRef
[t class]	CFGetTypeID(t)
[t1 isEqual:t2]	CFEqual(t1,t2)
[t description]	CFCopyDescription(t)
[t retain]	CFRetain(t)
[t release]	CFRelease(t)

A Core Foundation *type* is an identifier that is conceptually equivalent to an Objective-C class. A Core Foundation *reference*, or ref for short, is an instance of a type, functionally identical to an identifier (id) or object pointer.

Types are organized in an inheritance hierarchy just like classes. CFStringRef is a subtype of CFTypeRef, just as NSString is a subclass of NSObject. A CFStringRef can be passed to any function that accepts a CFStringRef or a CFTypeRef parameter, just as an NSString object will respond to any message defined for NSString or NSObject.

The Toll-Free Bridge

Core Foundation and the Objective-C class frameworks are engineered so that select Core Foundation types are interchangeable with equivalent Objective-C classes. The types and classes that form the toll-free bridge are listed in Table 25-2.

Table 25-2. *Core Foundation Toll-Free Bridge*

Cocoa Class	Core Foundation Type
NSArray	CFArrayRef
NSAttributedString	CFAttributedStringRef
NSCalendar	CFCalendarRef
NSCharacterSet	CFCharacterSetRef
NSData	CFDataRef
NSDate	CFDateRef
NSDictionary	CFDictionaryRef
NSError	CFErrorRef
NSInputStream	CFReadStreamRef
NSLocale	CFLocaleRef
NSMutableArray	CFMutableArrayRef
NSMutableAttributedString	CFMutableAttributedStringRef
NSMutableCharacterSet	CFMutableCharacterSetRef
NSMutableData	CFMutableDataRef
NSMutableDictionary	CFMutableDictionaryRef
NSMutableSet	CFMutableSetRef
NSMutableString	CFMutableStringRef
NSNumber	CFNumberRef
NSOutputStream	CFWriteStreamRef
NSSet	CFSetRef
NSString	CFStringRef
NSTimer	CFRunLoopTimerRef
NSTimeZone	CFTimeZoneRef
NSURL	CFURLRef

Put simply, an object pointer to one of the classes in Table 25-2 is functionally identical to its matching Core Foundation type reference. The single value can be transparently treated as either type. The code in Listing 25-2 demonstrates this with an Objective-C class that incorporates a Core Foundation UUID type.

Listing 25-2. *Using Core Foundation Types in an Objective-C Class*

```objc
#include <CoreFoundation/CoreFoundation.h>

@interface Unique : NSObject <NSCoding> {
    @private
    __strong CFUUIDRef  uuid;
}

@property (readonly) NSString *uuid;

@end

@implementation Unique

- (id)init
{
    self = [super init];
    if (self != nil) {
        CFUUIDRef newUUID = CFUUIDCreate(kCFAllocatorDefault);
        uuid = CFMakeCollectable(newUUID);
    }
    return self;
}

- (id)initWithCoder:(NSCoder*)decoder
{
    self = [super init];
    if (self != nil) {
        NSString *uuidString = [decoder decodeObjectForKey:@"UUID"];
        CFUUIDRef savedUUID = CFUUIDCreateFromString(kCFAllocatorDefault,

    (CFStringRef)uuidString);
        uuid = CFMakeCollectable(savedUUID);
    }
    return self;
}

- (void)encodeWithCoder:(NSCoder*)encoder
{
    [encoder encodeObject:self.uuid forKey:@"UUID"];
}

- (NSString*)uuid
{
```

```
    CFStringRef cfString = CFUUIDCreateString(kCFAllocatorDefault,uuid);
    NSString *objcString = (NSString*)CFMakeCollectable(cfString);
    return objcString;
}
```

@end

The standard Objective-C class frameworks do not include a class that encapsulates Universally Unique Identifiers (UUIDs). The Core Foundation framework, however, has the very handy CFUUIDRef type along with a set of functions for creating and encoding UUIDs. The Unique class in Listing 25-2 stores a CFUUIDRef value, equivalent to an object pointer, to a Core Foundation type as it would any other C pointer. The -init method creates a universally unique ID type and stores a reference to it.

The Core Foundation function CFUUIDCreateString(…) creates a textual representation of the UUID from a CFUUIDRef and returns it as a new CFStringRef. Looking at Table 25-2, CFStringRef and NSString are a toll-free bridge. So the reference to the Core Foundation string type can be treated as if it were an NSString object pointer and returned to the caller.

Similarly, the -initWithCoder: method begins by decoding an NSString object from the serialized data stream. It passes the NSString object pointer to CFUUIDCreateFromString(…) just as if it were a CFStringRef. The CFUUIDCreateFromString(…) function uses the CFStringRef to reconstruct the UUID opaque type.

The toll-free bridge means that you can seamlessly work with many common Core Foundation types exactly as if they were Objective-C objects, and vice versa. The only significant difference between Core Foundation types and their doppelganger Objective-C classes is their memory management. This is discussed in the next section.

Tip There are other Objective-C bridges that you might find interesting. For example, there are bridges from Objective-C to both the Ruby and Python programming languages. Apple once developed a bridge between Objective-C and Java, which has since been deprecated.

The Objective-C classes listed in Table 25-2 are the only ones that have toll-free bridges to Core Foundation types. For example, NSRunLoop is *not* interchangeable with CFRunLoopRef. To use Core Foundation functions on an NSRunLoop, send the object a -getCFRunLoop message, which will return its underlying CFRunLoopRef.

C Memory Management

C memory management, or lack thereof, was described in Chapter 24. Core Foundation memory management either works with, or is layered over, the memory management used by Objective-C. When using Core Foundation types you must either adopt the Core Foundation memory management patterns, or transition the references to the memory management scheme being employed by Objective-C.

Core Foundation types use simple reference counting. If you skipped Chapter 24, you might want to review it so you understand the basic principles. Here are the key concepts about Core Foundation memory management you need to know:

- Core Foundation uses reference counting.
- Every Core Foundation type is allocated using an *allocator*. The allocator equivalent to `+alloc` is either `kCFAllocatorDefault` or `NULL`.
- The Core Foundation functions `CFRetain(o)` and `CFRelease(o)` are equivalent to `[o retain]` and `[o release]` (in a managed memory environment).
- Core Foundation does not use autorelease pools. Refs returned by functions are either new (just created and implicitly owned by the caller) or owned (retained at least once by some other owner).

Using Core Foundation Memory Management Patterns

Unless you need to keep or return a reference to a Core Foundation type, the simplest approach is to adhere to the Core Foundation memory management patterns. Core Foundation does not use autorelease pools, so all refs returned are either new or owned. To use Core Foundation memory management, your code should do the following:

Use a new ref exactly as you would a new object in a managed memory environment.

- Use the ref for as long as you need.
- Call `CFRelease(ref)` when finished with it.

Treat owned references much as you would autoreleased objects in a managed memory environment.

- Owned refs can (typically) be used freely before returning from the current method or function.
- Alternatively, call `CFRetain(ref)` to retain the type, use it as long as you need, and then call `CFRelease(ref)` to release it.

A complete description of Core Foundation memory management conventions and rules can be found in the *Memory Management Programming Guide for Core Foundation*.[2]

Using Core Foundation with Garbage Collection

Even when using garbage collection in Objective-C, Core Foundation continues to use reference counting. The garbage collector is aware of Core Foundation reference counts and incorporates them into its collection logic. Specifically, a Core Foundation type is destroyed (collected) only when there are no `__strong` references to it *and* it has a Core Foundation reference count of 0. This allows Core Foundation and Objective-C garbage collection to coexist peacefully, but does require some attention when treating CFTypeRefs like Objective-C objects. Unlike Objective-C, you can't simply ignore reference counts when using garbage collection.

When storing a Core Foundation type in an Objective-C object pointer (or any `__strong` or `__weak` pointer type), transition it to garbage collection by passing it through the `CFMakeCollectable(CFTypeRef)` function, as was shown in Listing 25-2. This function performs a `CFRelease()`—decrementing its reference count to 0, but without destroying the type—and returns a `__strong` reference to it. The type/object now becomes the responsibility of the garbage collector.

---

[2] Apple Inc., *Memory Management Programming Guide for Core Foundation*, http://developer.apple.com/documentation/CoreFoundation/Conceptual/CFMemoryMgmt/, 2007.

Caution Garbage collection can only be used with Core Foundation types allocated using the standard or default allocator function (kCFAllocatorDefault or NULL). Fortunately, this will be true for virtually all Core Foundation types you work with. Core Foundation types allocated using a different allocator, specifically kCFAllocatorMalloc, will be allocated in another memory zone and will *not* be scanned by the garbage collector. Any such types must be managed using Core Foundation memory management.

Although CFRetain() and CFRelease() are functionally identical to -[NSObject retain] and -[NSObject release], you can't use the Objective-C messages to retain and release Core Foundation types in a garbage collection environment. Remember that the Objective-C messages -retain and -release are disabled when the garbage collector is started. So while CFRetain() and CFRelease() continue to function, -retain and -release do nothing.

Using Core Foundation with Managed Memory

In a managed memory environment, Core Foundation and Objective-C share the same reference counting mechanism. In this environment, CFRetain() and CFRelease() are synonymous with -[NSObject retain] and -[NSObject release].

The simplest way of dealing with a retained Core Foundation type is to immediately add it to the autorelease pool. If the -uuid method in Listing 25-2 were written for a managed memory environment, it would look something like the code in Listing 25-3.

Listing 25-3. Returning an Autoreleased Core Foundation Reference

```
- (NSString*)uuid
{
    CFStringRef cfString = CFUUIDCreateString(kCFAllocatorDefault,uuid);
    return [(NSString*)cfString autorelease];
}
```

The object returned by -uuid in Listing 25-3 is autoreleased and behaves like any other autoreleased string object. Most managed memory patterns described in Chapter 24 apply equally to Core Foundation types.

Summary

Invoking C functions from Objective-C is effortless, giving your code direct access to a universe of C-based solutions. Working with Core Foundation types is made easier by the toll-free bridge, allowing you to interact with many Core Foundation types as though they were Objective-C objects. The most common programming issue to deal with is matching, or rectifying, the memory management styles of the two languages.

CHAPTER 26

Runtime

The runtime environment of an Objective-C application has some traits that you should be aware of. These include the information about the Mac OS X process that comprises your running application, its environment variables, the connections with its parent process, and so on. Some are inherited from the operating system, while others are features of Objective-C and the Cocoa framework. Many have already been described in other chapters. We will briefly review them here along with other important aspects of the runtime environment.

Process

In Mac OS X, every Objective-C program executes as a process. Technically, Java bytecode executes in an abstract virtual machine; but most virtual machines run in a process and embody almost identical attributes. Every process includes

- A memory address space

- One or more executing threads

- A set of environment variables in a map of key/value pairs

- An array of command-line arguments

In Java, the virtual machine has access to the process's local address space, but you (the programmer) don't. In Objective-C, you have direct access to the logical address space assigned to the process. The hardware physically prohibits direct access to memory addresses outside your process's local address space. Any access attempt will result in a memory address violation, which usually results in the termination of your process. Access to any resources outside of your process is accomplished by sending messages to the kernel. You'll almost never do this directly, but you should know that all APIs that interact with the hardware or operating system ultimately end up sending messages to the kernel.

In Mac OS X, the process is synonymous with the main thread. The process exists as long as the main thread exists, and terminates when the main thread terminates—or the process is intentionally terminated using a function like exit(). You can create or destroy other threads, as described in Chapter 15.

Not all Objective-C code will run in its own process. Objective-C can also be used to develop frameworks and plug-ins. These are bundles of code and resources that can be loaded by another application and execute within that application's environment. For example, you can provide custom indexing of your documents by providing the operating system with a Spotlight Plug-In bundle. The bundle contains code that's executed when the Spotlight search engine wants to index the contents of your document type. The code in your Spotlight Plug-In runs inside the metadata importer process, not your application.

In addition to its environment variables, command-line arguments, and process attributes, there is also an odd collection of per-process properties, such as the current working directory. All of these are discussed in the following sections.

Environment

Every process inherits the *environment* defined by its parent process (the process that created your process). An environment is a set of key/value string pairs that allow settings and other information to be passed from one process to another. In Java, you can obtain the environment variables using java.lang.System.getenv() or java.lang.System.getenv(String). In Objective-C, send the -environment message to the singleton NSProcessInfo object, obtained using [NSProcessInfo processInfo].

Command-Line Arguments

Java processes launched from the command line include an array of command-line arguments, which are passed to its main(String[]) method. Objective-C programs are hosted in a C application, which is started when main(int,char**) is invoked. You can intercept and interpret the command-line arguments in main(…), or refer to them later by sending -arguments to the singleton NSProcessInfo object.

Process Attributes

Java provides an interface to get *properties*. These are like environment variables, but can be supplied by classes, the virtual machine, and property list files among other sources. Most dynamic Java properties, like the current working directory, are obtained through function calls or object messages in Objective-C. Properties used to store default values and user preferences are called *user defaults* in Objective-C, and there's a specific interface for working with them described later in the chapter.

Table 25-1 lists a few of the more interesting process properties supplied by Java, and where to find them in Objective-C.

Table 25-1. *Process Attributes*

Java Property	Objective-C
os.name	-[NSProcessInfo operatingSystemName]
os.arch	N/A
os.version	-[NSProcessInfo operatingSystemVersionString]
user.name	NSUserName()
user.home	NSHomeDirectory()
user.dir	-[NSFileManager currentDirectoryPath]

The "os.arch" property is not applicable in Objective-C, because it's a compiled language. The code that executes on a particular processor must be compiled for that architecture. The binary file that stores an executable program often contains multiple versions of the application, one for each supported architecture. Xcode automatically recompiles your application for each architecture, and then combines them into a single executable. Architecture-specific traits, like pointer size and byte order, can be determined at compile time. You can use the preprocessor #if directive to compile code that's specific to a particular processor or architecture.

NSProcessInfo has other useful information about the process, operating system, and hardware. It will report, among other things, the amount of physical RAM and the number of CPU cores. Finer-level detail can be obtained from POSIX functions like sysctl(…).

Version

Creating applications that are compatible with multiple versions of a framework or operating system can be a tricky endeavor. The Cocoa frameworks provide a number of version control and compatibility features that make this easier, or at least manageable.

Controlling Development and Deployment Versions

The Xcode build settings for your application project contain two important settings:

- Base SDK (SDKROOT) defines the version of headers and frameworks used to compile the program.

- Deployment Target (MACOSX_DEPLOYMENT_TARGET) defines the earliest version of the operating system your application is allowed to run on.

The base SDK selects the set of source header files and libraries that your application will be compiled and linked with. Each version of the operating system defines a new set of classes, constants, and data types. By specifying a particular base SDK, you limit your code to the APIs that were available when that SDK was produced. Your application can't use new classes, methods, or functions because (at least as far as the compiler is concerned) those functions don't exist and your code will fail to compile.

The deployment target applies only to GUI applications. It determines the earliest (oldest) version of the operating system your application is allowed to launch in. The value of this build setting is stored in the application's bundle and tested by the OS when launched.

Testing for Classes, Methods, and Functions

Taken together, the above two build settings define a range of operating system versions that your application can function in. This is called *cross-development.* Within that range, later operating systems will have certain functions, classes, and methods implemented that earlier ones do not. To use any of those, your code will have to test for their existence at runtime:

- Test for the existence of a class by calling NSClassFromString() and checking the results for Nil.

- Test for the existence of a method using -respondsToSelector:.

- Test for the existence of a function by comparing its pointer to NULL.

The first two techniques use Objective-C introspection. The last test applies to C functions and works through a feature called *weak linking.* A weak link is a reference to a symbol that is assumed to be defined by the operating system. If that symbol does not actually exist when the application is loaded, the reference is set to NULL. In contrast to strong linking, a weakly linked reference won't prevent your application from loading. You can test for the existence of the symbol at runtime, like this:

```
if (NSDisableScreenUpdates!=NULL) { NSDisableScreenUpdates(); }
```

Remember that the name of C function by itself (without any parentheses) evaluates to the address of the function's entry point. A complete description of cross-development settings and techniques can be found in the *Cross-Development Programming Guide*.[1]

Packages and Bundles

A *package* is a collection of related files. From the user's perspective, a package acts like a single filesystem object: an application, a document, or a plug-in component. In reality, a package is a directory that can contain any number of files or subdirectories. Packages are used in much the way JAR files are—to organize a group of related files and keep them together—except that in Mac OS X the content of the package is not compressed or archived.

■**Tip** You can explore the contents of a package directly from the Finder. Select a package and Control/right-click on the item. In the contextual pop-up menu, choose Show Package Contents.

A *bundle* is a package with a predefined structure. Cocoa applications, browser plug-ins, Automator Actions, frameworks, and Core Image filters are just a few of the bundle types that are defined by the operating system. Any of these bundle types can include an arbitrary number of support files: NIB files, string properties, images, sounds, movies, HTML documents, scripts, executable utilities, even other bundles. What additional files you include in your bundle is entirely up to you.

You access and interact with bundles using the NSBundle class. Basic bundle functions and their organization were discussed in Chapter 20. To learn more about bundles, refer to the NSBundle class documentation and the *Bundle Programming Guide*.[2]

Not all program types are contained within bundles. A command-line tool, for example, produces a single executable file. Additional resource files can't be bundled in a command-line tool.

Frameworks

One type of bundle is a framework. A framework contains a deployment of programming resources that can be shared by multiple applications. A framework can include shared libraries, Objective-C classes, images, sounds, NIB files, and other resources. In this respect, frameworks are roughly equivalent to JAR files used to deploy a library of Java class files, property files, and other resources. They can include any or all of the following:

- Shared libraries of compiled functions and classes

- Header files that define the interface to the framework API

- Documentation

- Arbitrary resources: NIB files, images, localized strings, scripts, help files, etc.

---

[1] Apple Inc., *Cross-Development Programming Guide*, http://developer.apple.com/documentation/DeveloperTools/ Conceptual/cross_development/, 2006.
[2] Apple Inc., *Bundle Programming Guide*, http://developer.apple.com/documentation/CoreFoundation/ Conceptual/CFBundles/, 2005.

All of these components are optional, allowing for flexible deployment solutions. A framework with shared libraries but no header files is suitable for distribution to a wide audience. A framework with code, headers, and documentation is a self-contained deployment vehicle, useable by both programmers and end users alike. The frameworks included in the Xcode SDK are special frameworks that contain header files and documentation, but no actual code—so-called *stub libraries*. These allow you to develop applications that use the system's frameworks, without actually including a copy of the entire OS.

Frameworks have some very useful features:

- A single copy of a framework's code is loaded into memory and is shared by all applications that use the framework.

- A framework can contain multiple versions of itself.

- Frameworks make it easy to deploy complex collections of code, resources, and documentation as a single entity.

- Frameworks can be loaded automatically or programmatically.

Most projects link to frameworks directly during development. You add the frameworks your application needs to an Xcode project, as shown in Figure 26-1. The header and documentation files in the framework define its interface for the programmer, and its library files are used to link the application.

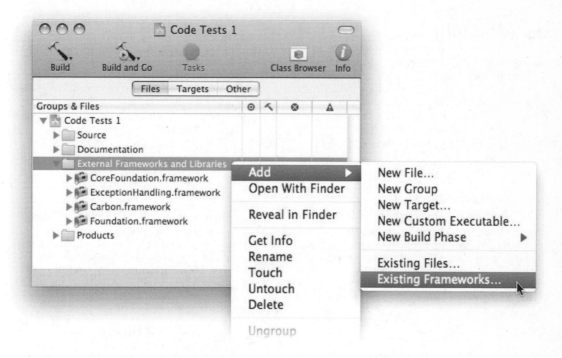

Figure 26-1. Frameworks in an Xcode Project

At runtime, frameworks are automatically loaded from a number of predefined locations (most notably /System/Library/Frameworks and /Library/Frameworks), very similarly to how Java finds classes using its classpath variable. Alternatively, you can embed a framework in an application's bundle, or locate and load a framework programmatically. To load a framework directly, create an NSBundle object for the framework's package directory and send it a -load message. This is approximately equivalent to creating a java.lang.ClassLoader. Unlike Java, framework code is not garbage collected. Send the bundle an -unload message if you need to release it.

■**Note** Although frameworks usually contain shared libraries, loading a framework is more like using java.lang.ClassLoader than the java.lang.Runtime.loadLibrary(String) method. The latter is equivalent to the POSIX function dlopen(…).

Most of the time you use frameworks developed by others, but you can also develop and deploy your own frameworks. Frameworks make it easy to develop reusable solutions that become the building blocks for new applications, which are deployed with those applications. If you are considering developing your own framework, refer to the *Framework Programming Guide*.[3]

User Defaults

User defaults consist of several layered sets of property values, much like Java properties. User defaults are stored as property list dictionaries, so they can only contain property value objects (NSString, NSNumber, NSDate, NSData, NSArray, or NSDictionary). You employ user defaults much as you would Java property values. User defaults also incorporate your application's editable preferences. Preferences are saved automatically and are available the next time your application executes.

User default values are stored by name (key) in one or more domains. Following are the major domains (in descending search order):

1. Command-line argument domain

2. Application domain

3. Global domain

4. Registration domain

You obtain a value from the user defaults by requesting it from the singleton NSUserDefaults object, obtained with [NSUserDefaults standardUserDefaults]. The generic method is -objectForKey:, but there are alternate messages that return the same value cast or converted to a more convenient type: -stringForKey:, -boolForKey:. -integerForKey:, -floatForKey:, -dataForKey:, -stringArrayForKey:, -arrayForKey:, and -dictionaryForKey:. User defaults will convert between common representations. For example, requesting a string with the value "YES" as a Boolean will return the numeric constant YES (true). The code in Listing 26-1 tests a user defaults setting to determine how a view should be drawn.

---

[3] Apple Inc., *Framework Programming Guide*, http://developer.apple.com/documentation/MacOSX/Conceptual/BPFrameworks/, 2006.

Listing 26-1. Reading User Defaults

```
if ([[NSUserDefaults standardUserDefaults] boolForKey:@"ShowTerrainInMap"]) {
    [terrainMap draw];
}
```

NSUserDefaults searches each domain, in order, for the key and returns the value from the first domain that contains it. Values set in a high level domain supersede the values set in lower domains.

The command-line argument domain is the highest domain and is populated with argument values included on the command line when the process was launched. Normally there are no command-line arguments, but you can include them during development by editing the launch parameters of the application's executable. The form for a command-line argument value is -key value. Launching an application with the arguments -ZombieNightVision NO will create the key/value pair ZombieNightVision="NO" in the arguments domain.

The application domain is used to store the user preferences for your application. This is a persistent domain. That is, values set here are automatically saved in a property list file on disk, and automatically reloaded the next time your application launches. The property list file is named using your application's identifier, in the directory ~/Library/Preferences. The TicTacToe application in Chapter 20 stores its user defaults in the file ~/Library/Preferences/com.apress.learnobjc.TicTacToe.plist.

■**Tip** You can create a user interface for a simple application preference by binding a view, like a check box or text field, to an arbitrary property of the singleton NSUserDefaultsController right in Interface Builder. This object is a bindable controller whose properties reflect the values of the user defaults. Changing a property of the controller sets that value in the application domain, which will be preserved. NSUserDefaultsController can also be used programmatically, if you prefer that to the syntax shown in Listing 26-1.

The global domain is another persistent domain, but one you don't normally change yourself. This domain contains the user defaults applicable to all applications launched by the user. These include the user's location, time zone, currency, time and number formatting, preferred font, and so on. They are usually defined by the operating system and set using System Preferences.

Finally, there's the registration domain. This domain is not persistent, and it is empty unless you populate it yourself during program initialization. It's intended as a domain of default user defaults. That is, it provides a value when none of the other domains contains a value for a key. The code in Listing 26-2 initializes the registration domain with some values. If none of the other domains contain a value for one of these keys, the value in the registration domain will be returned.

Listing 26-2. Creating a Registration Domain During Application Startup

```
[[NSUserDefaults standardUserDefaults] registerDefaults:
    [NSDictionary dictionaryWithObjectsAndKeys:
     [NSNumber numberWithInt:999],  @"MaximumZombies",
     [NSNumber numberWithBool:NO],  @"ZombiesCanWiggleEars",
     [NSNumber numberWithBool:YES], @"ShowTerrianInMap",
     @"Bob",                        @"GenericZombieName",
     nil]
];
```

A popular alternative to hard-coding the registration defaults is to save them as a property list in your application's bundle. During application startup, load a dictionary with the values in the property list and pass that to -registerDefaults:. This also allows the property list to be easily localized for different languages.

You can learn more about user defaults from the NSUserDefaults class documentation and the *User Defaults Programming Topics for Cocoa.*[4]

isa Swizzling

Some of Objective-C's "magic" is accomplished with a trick called *isa swizzling*. It gets its name from the fact that it stirs, or swizzles, the isa variable that defines the behavior of an object.

Normally, an object's isa variable is set during +alloc and never changes. Changing an object's isa variable effectively changes the class of the object, which defines its structure and all of the messages it responds to. Clearly you can see that arbitrarily changing it could have drastic consequences.

A couple of technologies, particularly Key-Value Observing, take advantage of the mutability of an object's class to surgically replace the behavior of specific methods. Here's what Key-Value Observing does when you request to observe a particular property:

1. Gets the class of the object.

2. Creates a new subclass of the object's class.

3. Overrides the -class method with one that returns the Class of the original object.

4. Overrides the desired setter methods in the original class.

5. Sets the isa variable of the object to the new subclass created in step 2.

An Objective-C class is created programmatically using objc_allocateClassPair() (although KVO probably uses a private function called objc_duplicateClass()). Once the empty class is defined, you can add or override methods in the class using class_addMethod(), make it conform to a protocol with class_addProtocol(), or define instance variables with class_addIvar(). In fact, you can do anything programmatically that you can define in the Objective-C language.

When finished, the object behaves exactly like it did before, except that messages overridden in step 4 invoke the methods defined by KVO instead of the original class. Because KVO also overrides the -class method, the object still appears to be its original class. You'd have to peak at the raw isa instance variable to see a difference in the object.

---

[4] Apple Inc., *User Defaults Programming Topics for Cocoa*,
http://developer.apple.com/documentation/Cocoa/Conceptual/UserDefaults/, 2007.

Isa swizzling is a powerful technique, but it's rather technical and not for the faint of heart. This section is designed to be informative, rather than encourage you to try it yourself. But if you do encounter a strong need for a solution that involves this kind of object mutation, it's not beyond your reach.

64-Bit Programming

If you've been around a while, you've seen the size of microprocessor registers grow from 4 to 32 bits over the decades. It's inevitable that we now find ourselves in a transition from 32- to 64-bit processors. Hopefully, the transition to 128-bit processors is some time off.

For both Java and Objective-C programmers, the change heralds new memory capacities and the promise of improved performance. Most object-oriented programmers will find little to do during the transition—beyond updating their project settings to produce a 64-bit version of their application. If you program exclusively using Objective-C classes, methods, and properties, you'll find very little difference between the two environments. The biggest change for Objective-C programmers is the size change of some integer variable types, as listed in Table 26-2.

Table 26-2. *32- and 64-Bit Variable Sizes*

Type	32-Bit Size	64-Bit Size
char	1 byte	1 byte
short	2 bytes	2 bytes
int	4 bytes	4 bytes
long	4 bytes	8 bytes
NSInteger	4 bytes	8 bytes
pointer	4 bytes	8 bytes
long long	8 bytes	8 bytes

Most integer sizes stay the same, with the exception of long int. A long int is 32-bits long in a 32-bit architecture, and 64-bits long when compiled for a 64-bit architecture. The more easily remembered NSInteger (and NSUInteger) typedefs are equivalent to long int. You will notice that most Objective-C collection classes use NSUInteger values to count and address elements, allowing collections in a 64-bit architecture to contain more than 4,294,967,296 elements—something that's impossible to accomplish in the address space of a 32-bit processor.

■**Tip** A common mistake is to use the wrong format string specifier to format int values. The statement [NSString stringWithFormat:@"%d",(NSInteger)x] will not work when compiled for 64 bits; the integer format specifer ("%d") expects a 32-bit integer. Always match the format specifier ("%ld") with the type (long int) it expects.

The change in pointer variable size usually isn't an issue for Objective-C programmers. All pointers (object pointers, C type pointers, structure pointers, CFTypeRefs, etc.) are always stored in pointer variables. The change in size is transparent, as are cast conversions between different pointer types.

In addition to the size change, 64-bit long int, long long int, and pointer variables all change from a 4-byte alignment to an 8-byte alignment. The alignment of a variable determines which addresses the variable prefers to be positioned at. An 8-byte alignment means that a variable's address should be evenly divisible by 8. This mostly impacts the organization of structures, like the one shown in Listing 26-3.

Listing 26-3. Variable Alignment in Structures

```
@interface Marker : NSObject {
    int            tag;
    long long int  position;
}

@end
```

In a 32-bit architecture, the relative address offsets of the tag and position variables in Listing 26-3 would be 0 and 4, respectively. When compiled for a 64-bit architecture, the relative offsets would be 0 and 8. The size of the variables didn't change, but the preferred address alignment for the position integer changed from 4 to 8. The compiler inserts 4 unused bytes between the two variables to align the second variable to an 8-byte address boundary. This means that the size of this object in memory is 4 bytes larger when compiled for 64-bits, even though the variables' sizes didn't change.

Here's a short checklist of best practices that will keep your code running smoothly in both 32- and 64-bit architectures:

- Never store or pass a pointer value in an integer variable, or vice versa.

- Store returned NSInteger values in NSInteger variables. Specifically, NSUInteger count = [collection count].

- When using NSInteger values, use the corresponding "integer" object message: -[NSCoder encodeInteger:forKey:] instead of -[NSCoder encodeInt:forKey:], -[NSString integerValue] instead of -[NSString intValue], and so on.

- Match format string specifiers with the correct variable type.

- Don't depend on, or make assumptions about, the size or organization of structures.

- In general, design using objects and properties rather than manipulating structures and pointers.

Those are the big ones, but there are hordes of smaller details. If you're considering compiling 64-bit Objective-C code, you should begin by reviewing the *64-Bit Transition Guide for Cocoa*.[5] Also read some of the many reasons you might *not* want to convert your application to 64-bits in the *64-Bit Transition Guide*.[6]

Summary

Unlike Java, which tries to abstract many of the details of the runtime environment, Objective-C applications run as native code and interact directly with the operating system APIs. You can use introspection to run applications on older versions of the operating system that might be missing newer APIs and features. Cocoa bundles and frameworks simplify the deployment of complex applications and libraries, while user defaults make it easy to manage configurable preferences and properties. With some attention to a few details, you can produce applications that run smoothly on the latest generation of 64-bit processors.

Epilogue

Congratulate yourself. You've learned a lot about Objective-C! And not just the basics—this book has explored some really advanced techniques. You've learned how similarly Objective-C and Java approach primitive types, control structures, class inheritance, protocols (interfaces), garbage collection, archiving (serialization), exceptions, threads, and collections. You've learned the subtle differences—syntactic, technical, and philosophical—in how Objective-C invokes methods. Most importantly, you've explored some genuinely new concepts like categories, Key-Value Observing, and class clusters. You have (hopefully!) embraced some new design patterns, like delegates, singletons, and using nil object pointers, to your advantage. You've also learned how Objective-C embraces design patterns like Model-View-Controller and lazy initialization, while taking unique approaches to the subscriber/provider and factory patterns.

There is, of course, much more to know about Objective-C, the class frameworks, and C than can ever be put into a single book. But I genuinely hope you found this book to be instructive and that it has accelerated your knowledge and skills toward your ultimate goal. Java and Objective-C are both great languages. Given their many similarities, there's no reason why you can't be proficient in both—expanding both your horizons and your opportunities.

---

[5] Apple Inc., *64-Bit Transition Guide for Cocoa*, http://developer.apple.com/documentation/Cocoa/ Conceptual/Cocoa64BitGuide/, 2009.
[6] Apple Inc., *64-Bit Transition Guide*, http://developer.apple.com/documentation/Darwin/Conceptual/ 64bitPorting/, 2009.

Index

■ ■ ■